D1202246

Problems of
World Modeling

Problems of World Modeling

Political and Social Implications

Edited by
Karl W. Deutsch
Bruno Fritsch
Helio Jaguaribe
Andrei S. Markovits

Ballinger Publishing Company ● Cambridge, Massachusetts
A Subsidiary of J.B. Lippincott Company

 This book is printed on recycled paper.

International Standard Book Number: 0-88410-656-X

Library of Congress Catalog Card Number: 77-953

Printed in the United States of America

Library of Congress Cataloging in Publication Data
Main entry under title:

Problems of world modeling.

"One of a series of continuing meetings of the Research Committee 7 on Quantitative and Mathematical Approaches to Politics, within the International Political Science Association."
1. International relations—Mathematical models. 2. International economic relations—Mathematical models. I. Deutsch, Karl Wolfgang, 1912- II. International Political Science Association. Research Committee 7 on Quantitative and Mathematical Approaches to Politics.
JX1291.P76   327'.01'51   77-953
ISBN 0-88410-656-X

Contents

List of Figures

List of Tables

Preface

This book is inevitably incomplete. It represents an early stage in a large research enterprise, not its completion. This enterprise is not being carried out by a single organized project but rather by the independent efforts of many scholars from different academic fields in numerous countries. Yet, these efforts already have become interdependent and complementary. They are beginning to constitute a whole that is more than the sum of its parts.

The common aim of our endeavor is to find out where the political, social and economic development of the world is going. This knowledge is needed for governments and citizens, for national and international organizations, for public planners and private enterpreneurs, because the large trends of world development set the framework, conditions and limits within which smaller actors must make their choices. Yet, this knowledge is not available at the present. Some experts know about likely trends in world population, others about the changing balance of scarce material and energy resources and needs. Certain scholars study trends in national incomes and international economics, while others are concerned with changing conditions for political reform or stagnation, integration or secession, war or peace. Nobody, however, has as yet succeeded to put these different prospects and kinds of knowledge into a coherent whole.

This is just what our present efforts are all about. Modern computers permit the processing of large amounts of factual information, provided that we develop the intellectual capacity to analyze and understand the implications. This capacity can be developed only by people, not by machines. Our early efforts may well be limited to putting together a few sectors of world development, such as projections for world food, energy and capital, with projections for expectable trends in conflicts within and among nations. Eventually, however, efforts will be made to put together information from more sectors, and in the end, some scholars in one country or another will try to get a more comprehensive picture of probable trends for the world as a whole.

The conference held at Harvard University in February 1976 was dedicated to this purpose as is the present volume which is a publication of the World University of the World Academy of Art and Science. The results will show their effects in many research projects in the United States, Western and Eastern Europe, as well as in Latin America and elsewhere in the developing world. We have learned from each other and we hope that our readers will learn from our insights and our mistakes.

May, 1977

Karl W. Deutsch
Bruno Fritsch
Helio Jaguaribe
Andrei S. Markovits

✱ *Introduction*

Background and Purpose of the Volume and the Conference

※ *Chapter 1*

The Context of the Conference

Hayward R. Alker, Jr.

This is one of a series of continuing meetings of Research Committee Seven on Quantitative and Mathematical Approaches to Politics, within the International Political Science Association. Karl Deutsch for years was chairman of that group and more recently has persuaded me to take on this role, which I prefer to call that of "convener" of the committee. The committee has had several meetings; the one that I remember most vividly was held in Mannheim in 1971. Specialists interested in this topic have also met at the regular IPSA World Congresses since 1964, and they will once again hold several sessions, one of them devoted exactly to the subject of this week's meeting, at Edinburgh. We also hope to have a future meeting of the Research Committee in Japan at some point. This committee has long been interested in quantitative international analysis along the lines exemplified by Karl's own work, although not exclusively in that direction. We have a somewhat split personality, which means conbining an interest in questions of more global types of quantitative political analyses with a more general interest in mathematically oriented work on any political research problems. The continued set of more general representative functions and a particular interest in quantitative, world-oriented studies have been continued. This conference is a specialists' meeting, focused on a particular topic, a topic that we have been particularly interested in for the last several years.

A second set of sponsoring relationships comes from the International Social Science Council (ISSC), which is headed now by Stein Rokkan who was the previous president of the International Political Science Association. He has, I think, through suggestions from Karl Deutsch and others, encouraged the International Social Science Council to sponsor a series of meetings on world modeling questions. These include those of a normative nature and, particularly, validity issues associated with world modeling. In that context, a series of meetings have been initiated which somewhat overlap with the work of this Research Committee. The first one was the meeting, at Rio de Janeiro in November 1975, to discuss the work of the Bariloche group. This is the second meeting in their series, and they are planning a third meeting, with various Institutes of the Academy of Sciences of the Soviet Union, to be held in June in Moscow. It represents another set of concerns that is truly interdisciplinary, beyond a political science focus, and something that is being given considerable priority within the International Social Science Council.

Some years ago, Karl Deutsch and I wrote a proposal for the discussion of world modeling to UNESCO, which has given valuable—though limited—support to many of the meetings of both the International Political Science Association and the International Social Science Council in the past. Just recently, the money became available with a very small lead time, through the good offices of the American delegation to UNESCO. Under the Country Participation Program, American funds to UNESCO can be used for projects such as this one.

The fourth intersecting circle of sponsorship that has supported another set of world-modeling-oriented work is associated principally with the World Order Models Project, in which Richard Falk, Saul Mendlovitz, Rajni Kothari, Johan Galtung, and teams in various parts of the world, including Latin America, Europe, and the United States, have participated. Deriving from such efforts, some of the people who are here have had a number of meetings on related topics before. There was a meeting in Africa last year, which Dieter Senghaas and Saul Mendlovitz attended, at which they talked about transnationalism and world militarism. These efforts have had a rather different concept of "world modeling" which adds some interesting ideas to the more statistically oriented studies. Karl and I wanted their views represented here.

The World University of the World Academy of Art and Science has had a deep and continuing interest in the subject of this conference. It has been good enough to provide support for the meeting and the publication of this volume, which will constitute one of its series of publications.

I think this completes the major list of supportive and sponsoring organizations. Karl Deutsch will give you a more substantially focused discussion of the kind of subjects we want to deal with on our agenda as it has evolved.

❋ *Chapter 2*

Toward Drift Models and Steering Models

Karl W. Deutsch

I should like to say something about the general thrust and intentions of the conference. The aim of this conference is to make a contribution to an ongoing chain of activities, to developing simulation models of major, general trends in world economics, world politics, and world ecology.

Such models are not a luxury. In order to make intelligent plans or policies, for a national government or for a regional group, one has to take into account world conditions. It is in this context that we hope to examine global characteristics at a sufficient level of disaggregation for them to be of use in studying regional development. The change in petroleum prices produced changes in the national plans of India; the change in Western petroleum consumption has recently been producing changes in the economic balance and the national planning of Iran. No country in the world today can completely disregard world conditions in making its national policies. A world model, therefore, which one might think of as the last priority of a busy national decision maker, turns out actually to be a serious precondition unless economic and political plans of nations are to become largely exercises in fantasy. The framework that a good world model can provide is not the same as giving exact predictions. Yet, there are major plans and trends which, if they can be identified and the degree of their interdependence and the expectable extent of their interactions be ascertained, allow one, through the use of modern technology, statistics, data files, and computers, to keep track of more detail than any particular decision maker could. The basic assumption for the whole enterprise is that there is a significant degree of interdependence. This may form a hierarchy, perhaps among nations constituting a geographical region or perhaps between countries such as Britain and Australia, which do not form a geographic region but do form a region of increased interdependence.

The second point is the interdependence within sectors and among them. The demographers have vividly reminded us that most other expectations—economic activities, demand for raw materials, among others—may depend, in part at least, on demographic changes. Demography, in turn, depends to some extent on the availability of food; food may depend in part on the availability of energy and of assorted resources such as fertilizers. We have, therefore, a demography sector interdependent with the sectors of food, energy, mineral, and biological resources. We have an ecology sector including pollution, environmental damage, availability of usable water and air. We have an economic sector involving world trade and, what perhaps has been less thoroughly studied, the amounts and types of investment that become available. People usually try to list investments or the control of investments primarily in order to make statements about what is loosely called dependence. Up to now, we rarely have had data on the extent of this dependence. Too often in social science a variable is first looked at as if it were an all-or-none property. We have an unconscious notion that below a certain threshold we forget about dependence and above a certain threshold we overestimate it. Thus we go from ignorance to overestimation. Instead of this, the actual amounts of latitude for decisions, the degrees of freedom, and the range of alternatives that continue to be available should be problems for social scientists to study.

Once this is accomplished, these aspects may be incorporated into a better model than we have had in the past. We have both a sector of activities of multinational corporations and a sector of what Samuel Pisar in France has called "transideological corporations," such as exemplified by the Fiat company when it built or collaborated in building the Togliatti works in the Soviet Union. This is a clear case of a transideological corporation; another might be a Hilton Hotel being built in Yugoslavia. In these cases, we go beyond the nation state, and even beyond the boundaries of ideological world subsystems.

There are also the questions arising from the sociological sector, such as changing class patterns, changing patterns of marginality, and changing patterns of migration, both within nation states and across boundaries. There are the concerns of the subsystem of politics, such as the blocs, the regional organizations, the international organizations, and the alliance systems. And there are the military subsystems, such as the strategic interdependence of countries, the balance of armaments and arms races, the formation of blocs, and even the question of military confrontations, the frequency of near-wars, civil wars, and what today are sometimes called "clandestine operations" and penetration. All these do have a significant effect on national planning.

Finally, we have the sector of communication systems—mass media, the mails, the transmission of scientific information and of lifestyles as well as culture, which range all the way from the diffusion of the knowledge of how to make penicillin through cultural and lifestyle matters, such as bluejeans, rock music, and more importantly equal rights for women.

Among all these sectors, we have the additional task of looking after interaction effects. What is the effect of all this upon the capability of governments to act? What does it do to the life expectancy of governments? There is also a general secular trend we must take into account. On the whole, populations increase, economic resources increase, the amount of horsepower, energy, production of metal, for example, are continually increasing. This means that although in the past it may have been sufficient to pay attention only to the primary and direct effects of human behavior; the bigger any kind of operation becomes, the more important become the secondary, remote, or indirect effects. If you throw a little mercury into water, the stream may still be usable. As your factory, paper mill, or other mercury-producing enterprise becomes bigger, the water becomes more poisoned. The same is true of the number of automobiles in Los Angeles, which makes the air to some extent not very suitable for breathing in that part of the world. There is the problem, let us say, of damming and channeling water with the problems of silt deposition and salination. It is the scale of enterprise that changes critically the circle of consequences that has to be taken into account. This again requires, therefore, taking into account a larger number of indirect interaction effects than ordinary unaided human memories can completely encompass. To some extent, the thinking, memory, and decision aids of computers change from being interested experiments or things that look like luxuries to becoming necessities. By that time, the techniques for doing these things right will either be available or lacking. We are trying now to work on the technique that will be needed then. The distance between now and then may be anywhere between five and fifteen years. Out of this, we get two sets of long-term aims—one, developing an early warning system in terms of sectors where critical developments may arise, and two, identifying the places and times of high risks. Where and when will the economic subsystems be most likely to get into trouble; where will the trade plans fail most spectacularly; where will the sociological damage be highest; where will the arms races, the confrontations, and the combination of economic burdens of armament and of the combination of action-reaction processes and internal national autistic arms processes be most pernicious?

This leads immediately to normative aspects of our work. Perhaps it might be useful to distinguish drift models and steering models. A drift model is a model that says, if mankind mostly moves with its existing momentum, then chances are that outcomes will be of a certain type. If we try to use foresight, or try to intervene, what are the possibilities, what are the options for interventions, and what are the limits of the expectable results of intervention? Perhaps it might be useful to think of this in terms of three time horizons.

A short time horizon is one in which the *momentum* of social development is probably overwhelming. It is said of a ship, the Queen Elizabeth, that if the engines are thrown into full reverse, the ship will still continue to move forward for one and a half miles. It is said of the standard Chevrolet that it cannot turn in less than a 42-foot turning radius and that, when it moves at 60 miles per hour on the highway, it cannot stop in less than 220 feet. What is the turning radius of a nation state? What is the turning radius of a trend in world development? We find, therefore, a relatively short-term future which is primarily determined by momentum and is extraordinarily resistant to any kind of steering effort.

There is a second time horizon, a time slice which comes after the first, where it is possible to foresee and possible to intervene. This would be comparable to the region beyond the 220 feet where you can stop or the 42 feet where you can turn the car.

And there is a third time slice which is so far in the future, and where we are so poorly supplied with information, that again we cannot steer because we do not have the needed information. In the very short term, steering is very ineffective, powerless. In the very long term, steering is blind because we cannot foresee. It is in the intermediate time slice that steering can be both powerful and tolerably well informed; and locating the crucial zone is, of course, one of the questions that interests us in modeling.

The drift model gives us the probabilistic distribution of outcomes without intervention; the steering model, then, will involve the differential accessiblity of process links—not all links in an interdependent process are equally accessible to steering. At our present stage, where we are using multivariate analysis, even for detailed problems in social science, we shall not go back again to the philosophy of Marx or of Hegel before him, which assumed that in every complex situation there was one, and preferably only one, master link that a philosopher of sufficient insight, like Hegel or Marx, or later Lenin, could identify. Stalin still kept writing about what he called the decisive links. His countrymen, looking with great concentration upon what he called the decisive link, for a long time overlooked his crimes. Even if undertaken with peaceful or good intentions, the single link approach is one of the most dangerous approaches.

In the modeling approaches we are using it will be asked: what is the smallest assemblage, the smallest subset of critical links, with which a process could be controlled or changed? We can be fairly safe in saying that this subset of critical links will be larger than one. The nineteenth-century concentration on the single master link will simply not be good enough, yet on the other hand, it is to be hoped that the subassembly of critical links will be small enough to permit some action.

But we may get an opposite outcome—namely, that it turns out that social science deals mainly with social developments that are produced by the concatenation of a large number of weak processes. It might then be the case that no single process accounts for more than two or three or four percent of the variance of the outcome. This would be awkward, but it could be true. While we do not know yet whether this is true, I hope that some people here have some information or judgments to contribute on these issues. Even if social development is produced by many weak processes, it is possible that the concatenation will add up to a statistical distribution that can be identified. It may then turn out that we can find out what can be done about shifting some parameters of that statistical distribution.

We need to know the steering capabilities not only of the nation state, but of the international organizations and of the world society and the political world system, and what contributions subnational groups, whether they be labor or management, can make to the steering performance at higher system levels. What are the relevant steering capabilities and requirements? How great will be the expectable *loads* upon the highly imperfect steering and control facilities of mankind? What will be the *lag* between critical needs and the moment that awareness arises and steering efforts are undertaken? What will be the *gain* or the power of these steering efforts and of the organizations that make them? How much of a difference can they make? And how much of *lead* and foresight can be developed? This is, again, where our models become important. Modeling activities could critically increase the lead of mankind's foresight. We know from cybernetic theory that lead is the critical variable by which both failure of steering and oversteering can be reduced or avoided. This then involves a review of our data sources and how they can be improved. What are our mathematical capabilities, in terms both of theory and mathematical techniques, and what computer capabilities and systems are available?

What we are aiming at, essentially, is not a single project, but a network of research activities, including both global and partial world models, sectoral models, and national and regional models. Professor Rastogi has now produced models for about five national political systems. Our task will be to make recommendations for the computer languages, for coding conventions and the setting up of data files, so as to find a tolerable compromise between the need to transfer and combine our knowledge from many centers and countries, and the exuberant imagination of researchers and computer specialists at each center which promptly produces special abbreviations and special languages making everything compatible. We will also try to explore the possibility of a double bookkeeping, whereby people will use fancy local computer languages and a translocal Fortran version that will run on different machines and thus be understood by scholars in different countries. If this is rejected, we will have to find other ways of keeping the different computing and data processing systems in touch with each other.

Our task is eventually to induce, wherever possible, practices through which all the centers and activities are both technically able—and from a policy point of view willing—to make data files, program decks, code books, and interpretations widely available, so that programs, whether of whole models or of subroutines, can be made to run in several places. Thus, it would be possible to achieve in this field what has long been commonplace in astronomy and in physics: to have experimental procedures so clearly described that experiments can be repeated from one end of the earth to the other. Astronomers' observational data are available to all astronomers at every major center of astronomy, so that the calculations can be checked in parallel. The same is true of meteorology. If this is possible in exchanging weather data, then I think eventually that we ought to do this in social meteorology, so that we can trace a little bit better the storm tracks of politics and society.

Hence, we have problems of the compatibility of concepts, data, existing models, programs, and computers. With all these, I think we should be able to have a fruitful conference. At the end, we may come out, not only with a better understanding, but with some concrete suggestions. And as we go on, we will see, for example at the Moscow conference, whether our colleagues in the Eastern countries will succeed eventually in persuading their governments that more is to be gained from exchanging models and information than from keeping it secret. The airforces of America and the Soviet Union might have good reasons to think that weather data have potential strategic and military importance and, therefore, actually might suggest that these data be treated as a national secret. On the other hand, since one cannot get a very good idea of the weather from within a nation's boundaries only, the United States and the Soviet Union are exchanging data about the weather. I do not know how many years it will take until they can exchange data about each other's social climate. But eventually, I think, it will happen. It remains one of the tasks that we have at this time and that we will have at the World Congress of Political Science at Edinburgh and at other international conferences.

Part 1

General Problems of World Modeling

 *Chapter 3*

Relevance for Policy: A Brief Exchange among Erwin Solomon, Karl W. Deutsch, and Hayward R. Alker, Jr.

1. ERWIN SOLOMON

I would like to see the meeting address itself to the practical problem of the use of these models. I think it is extremely interesting that a lot of the impetus for modeling has come from the United States, a country that does not engage in national planning. We talk about a tool for decision makers and policy makers as a way of giving modeling meaning. It should be directed toward such individuals within a context in which they can use these tools to take into account the variables being discussed in a meaningful way.

Member States of the United Nations are resistant to planning models with a big M, offered from without, namely, those which come complete with conclusions. Planning models, with a little m, I think have a much greater future, namely, those which offer a flexible framework. If models are in such a form that those who will suffer or benefit from them have a hand in their application, a problem which has, until now, lacked consideration in modeling research, then the result of this research can be put into practice, yielding results that go beyond analyses, books, and long-term projections about the world at large. I would like to see this work result in practical applications. I also would like to see the tactics discussed as to how this work can be put into a meaningful framework.

2. KARL W. DEUTSCH

I have one reminiscence from the history of science. In my hometown, Prague, around 1610 or 1612, a gentleman was working very hard on a model which nobody was using. His name was Johannes Kepler, and he calculated the laws of planetary motion. He was supported by his sponsor, Emperor Rudolph II of Habsburg who, like other sponsors since him, wanted scientific output on topics relevant to the decision maker—output that could be used. So Kepler, from time to time, had to take time off from calculating the laws of planetary motion and cast horoscopes for the Emperor.

In more recent times, one no longer speaks of horoscopes, but rather of "strategic studies." But the bifurcation of scientific effort is still there. It would be wonderful if people want to use our knowledge, but the decision makers either do not want to use such knowledge, or more often they are quite eager to use knowledge which does not yet exist. I am very much in favor of having knowledge applied, but first we must produce it. Some day we may at least get within a tolerable range of errors, over tolerable periods of time, so as to permit us to say, "Well, if things go on as they have, this is what we may expect within ten years."

We must necessarily leave it to the decision makers in different countries whether they choose to do anything about the way the affairs of their countries and of mankind are drifting. We might even be able to say what size of intervention would be needed in order to make any appreciable difference to the outcome. And there is a second question here concerning the expectable size of the intervention that is likely to be contributed. It is quite true that the governments of Western Europe, such as those of Britain, the German Federal Republic, or France, are more willing to intervene in developments they consider bad. But I am struck by one characteristic of the American people: we tend to neglect every problem until it has become almost desperately urgent. Then something usually gets done about it. The American political system has, at times in the past, shown an amazing capacity to learn and respond at the last moment. This makes the politics and economics of the United States something of a cliffhanger, but during the New Deal, at the time of World War II, and the Marshall Plan, responses eventually were made in the nick of time, but of sufficient size and with sufficient speed at the end so as to retrieve situations that might otherwise have deteriorated very seriously. I think we must say there are countries and subgroups in countries that have very different propensities to take predictions seriously and early, but even if they take them late, it makes a difference if there is knowledge available. I quite agree with Mr. Solomon, who has noted a very important point. We are still at the stage of the problem where we must design the product and produce it, even though with an eye to probable degree of initial acceptance. But the main problem of selling it will come later, and I hope we will get help from UNESCO [Editors' note: organization represented by Mr. Solomon at the Conference.] at that stage.

3. HAYWARD R. ALKER, JR.

I would like to follow up on Mr. Solomon's comments. I think the issue of practical utility is a very political issue. It seems to me, one of the good things that has happened in world modeling efforts is the development of clearly distinctive political epistemologies associated with these world modeling efforts. The Galtung world indicators project and the WOMP project (the World Order Models Project of Falk, Mendlovitz, and many other national teams) have developed orientations that should be described as political, normative, *and* scientific, providing some needed variability in this regard. The Bariloche model has a democratic, yet socialist orientation. In design, it has a normative focus and approach to modeling questions with implicit policy directions. I do not think that all advanced industrial countries want to get involved at the national level in such proposals.

In the U.N. context, much work at UNCTAD in Geneva has been along the lines of elaborating the significance and meaningfulness of strategies of self-reliance for the Third World within developing international political and economic orders. The extent to which a modeling approach can be seen as compatible with some redefined pattern of individual and collective self-reliance at, below, or above the national level of social activity is part of the political epistemology and orientational choice facing world modelers. It is deeply relevant to many scholars' attitudes toward modeling and toward the issues that modeling focuses upon. I do not think you are going to get meaningful cooperation in world modeling efforts without at least some convergence in orientations and compatibilities at the level of political epistemology.

This represents a deeper question. I would not want to hide the question, but on the other hand, I do not think there are now too many real possibilities for genuine North–South cooperation. Unless you have scientists with a relatively equal capability for doing scientific, critical, and constructive analysis, you introduce a number of power- and dependency-related issues into scientific development. Look at the distribution of computer science capabilities around the world! Why are there so few groups like Bariloche?

It seems to me that one could think of a number of convergences and concerns that do cut across some national boundaries. I am not sure I want to have live computer lines between the United States and the Soviet Union. That would be a new kind of hot line; now we have a cool line of direct scholarly communication. But on the other hand, if there is some criticism of this kind of activity, it seems to me there are many benefits associated with it. I think these are very deep and real issues.

※ *Chapter 4*

Some Issues Raised by Previous World Models*

Hayward R. Alker and
Ann Tickner

1. INTRODUCTION

This paper reviews some of the reactions of scholars of various
nationalities and intellectual disciplines to *World Dynamics* (Forrester, 1971)[1] and its more famous descendant, *The Limits of Growth* (Meadows et
al., 1972). It also discusses the initial responses of an international group of
researchers to the technical papers associated with a major follow-up study, *Mankind at the Turning Point* (ed. Mesarovic and Pestel, 1974). Thus our review
covers English language materials up to but not including the important work of
the Bariloche Foundation, *Catastrophe or New Society* (Herrera, Scolnik et al.,
1976). Unfortunately, the extent of genuine, interdisciplinary communication
about these studies has not been great and often evidences little attention to
issues already raised in a generally fragmented literature. Hence, on an issue of
direct relevance to popular concern with the quality of life, we here provide a
brief, but it is to be hoped inclusive, overview of the issues raised by critics of
the limits to growth arguments.[2] Because of the global nature of these issues,
this review also provides a case study of transnational relations, that is nongovernmental relations across national boundaries which increasingly affect

*An earlier version of this paper entitled, "Controversies Raised by The Limits to
Growth," appeared in *Systems Thinking and the Quality of Life*, Society for General
Systems Research, 1975. Our earlier thinking on the present subject was supported by a
grant from the Department of State to the Center for International Studies, M.I.T. with
which both authors were previously associated. Present revisions have been partially financed by Grant GS–2429 from the National Science Foundation to the Department of
Political Science, M.I.T. with which the first author is associated. All opinions expressed
or implied are those of the authors in their individual capacities.
1. Chapter 4 is entitled "Limits to Growth."

popular and governmental perceptions of national and international policy alternatives. All the above studies were stimulated by The Club of Rome, itself a nongovernmental, transnational organization.

2. AN OUTLINE OF THE WORLD
MODELS ANALYSES

Written in response to thoughts on "the predicament of mankind" by a founder of The Club of Rome (Peccei, 1969, 1970), *World Dynamics* (1971) is Forrester's most recent volume in an ongoing series of studies exploring the dynamic structure of social systems. In this book, he builds on his experience in solving similar analytical and prescriptive problems in the realm of industrial organization and urban political economy.

Methodologically, Forrester is especially concerned with the acceptance of his version of systems analysis, called "system dynamics," as the tool for understanding the behavior of all complex social systems that can be quantitatively modeled.[3] Such modeling is necessary because our inherited or "intuitive" cognitive capabilities are not well matched with the structure of complex social systems. In these systems, cause and effect are often not closely or linearly related, either in time or in space. Feedback relations may also violate intuitive notions of unidirectional cause-effect relationships. Because of such structural complexities, intuitive, incremental, short-term policy adjustments will be wrong most of the time: in the long run they often exacerbate rather than correct the symptoms they were intended to relieve.

Following from this methodological perspective, Forrester's key structural idea is to interpret the dynamic behavior of nonlinear social systems in terms of the varying, relative dominance of positive (action-magnifying) or negative (deviation-correcting) feedback loops. All actions are seen as possibly taking place within such loops. A key step in structural understanding, is therefore, the identification of such loops within the complex set of modeled relationships.[4] These loops connect usually goal-directed actions to their effects on surrounding contexts, which in turn make likely more or less of the same actions, i.e., positive and negative feedback. Within the feedback loops of Forrester's systems,

2. Some of our remarks apply as well to critical restatements of the Forrester–Meadows World Models by Nordhaus (1973), the Dutch Global Dynamics group (Rademaker and Cuypers, 1974), a Stanford revision (ed. Porat and Martin, 1974), and another interesting alternative (Boyd, 1972).

3. For a clear, careful and rigorous delineation of the class of models that can be specified within System Dynamics, see (Day, 1974).

4. In the case of linear systems, dynamic behavior can be rigorously derived from an expression dividing boundary transformations by internal (including feedback) transformations. For a rigorous treatment of social structural analysis in feedback terms, the reader is referred to Cortes, Przeworski, and Sprague (1974) or Willems (1971).

two kinds of variables are to be found, levels and rates. The levels, which may be basic states or derivative ones, result from processes of accumulation (technically, discrete summation approximations to continuous integration). Rates are flows (controlled by one or more systems level and by other rates) that cause the levels to change. Exponential growth is generated by the dominance of positive feedback loops over the equilibrating tendencies of negative feedback loops.

In the case of *World Dynamics*, these structural ideas have a straightforward application. The World Model has five basic, highly aggregated, causally interdependent system (state) levels: population (*P*), capital investment (*CI*), natural resources (*NR*), fraction of capital devoted to agriculture (*CIAF*), and pollution (*POL*). By assuming exponential growth processes (rates) affecting each of its five key variables, Forrester's World Model predicts an overdetermined collapse of the world system when any or all of these exponentially growing levels collide with a fixed environment, probably within the next 50 to 100 years. This collapse is indicated by a sudden decline in population levels and an earlier, more gradual decline in the quality of life ratio. Both the death rate and the quality of life ratio, two important derivative variables in the World Model, depend multiplicatively upon: 1. depletion of nonrenewable natural resources, 2. rise of pollution, 3. increase in crowding and, 4. decline in food supply.

The "standard" computer run of the World Model assumes no significant political or structural changes in the functioning of the system from that of the past hundred years. Based on these assumptions, the collapse stems from a depletion of natural resources due to the ever growing demands of/for industrial capital stock, and decline begins around 2010, placing an increasing stress on population during the normal time lag before it also begins to decline. In the standard run, the overall quality of life can be seen to have been declining continuously from about 1950, although the material standard component thereof reverses itself only just before 1990.

After describing the behavior of the standard run, Forrester goes on to change some of the assumptions that have gone into the construction of the model in order to show that its overall tendency toward collapse cannot be changed by standard policy reformulations, even if used in combination. First, to correct for resource depletion, Forrester assumes technological innovations reduce natural resource usage to 25 percent of its 1970 rate. In a new model run, population and capital investment continue to grow until pollution levels become critical, leading to a sharp decline in population and capital investment. Second, if the (nonrenewable) natural resource usage rate is set to zero and pollution drastically reduced because of some other technological breakthroughs, another run shows population will still rise sharply and fall suddenly because of the effects of crowding on the quality of life. Finally, if the psychological stresses of crowding can also be eliminated, through social adaptations, Forrester maintains that a severe food shortage will be a further limiting factor on population growth, a shortage inherent in capital investment and productivity limitations.

These then are the limits to growth, limits which, according to Forrester, we are rapidly approaching. As shown by the tendency toward collapse exhibited by the model under a limited variety of remedial assumptions, they defy solution according to certain "obvious" or conventional policy prescriptions. In particular, technological solutions tend to relieve pressures temporarily, only to allow population to grow again. The feedback loops of Forrester's world system always adjust population slightly to exceed existing food supply, in part because economic growth is not assumed to diminish birth rates. If conventional solutions are inadequate, then vast structural changes are indicated in a reevaluation that calls for basic trade-offs between present- and future-oriented actions. Forrester prescribes a world system where all growth is ended and a point of equilibrium is reached. Since Forrester does not believe that conventional population control methods can be successful (in fact, they seem to him to be self-defeating because resulting rises in the standard of living are seen as part of a positive feedback loop leading to more, longer-living children), equilibrium is attained through the somewhat drastic method of controlling all capital investment (including social capital and medical and educational facilities) and through the control of food supply.

Such measures can be achieved by conscious choices to restructure values toward a lower emphasis on growth, or failing this they will come from social forces such as coercion and war:

> As a background to the deliberation on how to choose a balance of pressures, we must be always aware that the world system will make a system-determined choice for us (i.e., collapse) if man is unable to negotiate a more favorable compromise." (Forrester, 1971:119)

The equilibrium standard of living will in any case, on the average, be lower than that presently existing in the United States.

While the basic thesis of *World Dynamics* remains unchanged in *The Limits to Growth* (Meadows et al., 1972), its policy implications have been made more palatable to conventional sensibilities; consequently it has received greater attention from policy makers. Written in a popular style, largely by Donella Meadows, *Limits to Growth* has generated a vast literature. It is based on a more complex and refined version of Forrester's World Model which has fifteen basic and derived level variables. Modelled mainly by Dennis Meadows, World III (as it is called), derives from research with a larger data base than its predecessors; but it too exhibits the same tendencies toward collapse, both in the standard run and during reruns allowing certain hopeful changes in the basic assumptions. Consequently, the Meadows arrive at essentially the same prescriptions as Forrester, although they elaborate in more detail the conditions envisaged at a state of equilibrium. Population would be stabilized by 1975 and industrial capital by 1990, with resource usage considerably reduced. Pollution would be reduced also, to one fourth its present level, and economic preferences of society would be shifted toward education and health facilities and more intensive food production. It is this emphasis on shifting capital toward social services that makes the Meadows' equilibrium state appear more palatable than Forrester's. While the authors of The *Limits to Growth* feel that their assumptions about the rapid stabilizing of population and capital are unrealistic, in apparent disagreement with Forrester they do believe that an effective policy of birth control and an effort not to increase industrial output per capita would go a long way towards avoiding global collapse in the quality of life.

Responding to widely read critiques of the earlier studies, e.g., *Models of Doom* (Cole et al., 1973), The Club of Rome encouraged Mihajlo Mesarovic and Eduard Pestel to construct and analyze a less deterministic, more disaggregated, multilevel world model.[5] Entitled *Mankind at the Turning Point*, this second report to The Club of Rome attempts a constructive critique of the Forrester-Meadows efforts (see Mesarovic and Pestel, 1974, and the technical papers in Mesarovic and Pestel, eds., 1974).[6] The Mesarovic-Pestel model has three major structural characteristics.

1. The world system is represented in terms of ten interdependent subsystems or regions, nations grouped in terms of similar traditions, proximity, and levels of development.
2. As illustrated in Figure 4-1, within each region, there is a multilevel (here meaning hierarchical, not just multivariate) structure of discipline-linked variable strata. Natural, group, and individual phenomena, as well as the realms of choice and causal determinism are carefully distinguished.
3. The model is structured more easily and explicitly to include human capabilities to elaborate, adapt, choose, and restructure governmental policies. Its interactive, man-machine format encourages analyses of alternative

5. Consistent with the highly transnational character of The Limits to Growth debate, funding again came for this next set of modeling activities from a private source in the industrialized Western societies, the Volkswagen Foundation. Mesarovic is a Yugoslav-American systems scientist, and Eduard Pestel is a West German academic, engineer and research administrator, also a member of the Executive Committee of The Club of Rome.

6. Forrester and Meadows, on the other hand, have become somewhat alienated from current Club of Rome activities, participating more actively in other transnational meetings and getting other sources of financial support. Since a controversial interview on the merits and limits of international *triage*, (involving the proposal by Lorenz, Hardin, and others to cut off assistance to states unable to avoid mass starvation, a concept Forrester did not explicitly endorse) Forrester has been working mainly on a socioeconomic model of the U.S. (see Forrester, 1974; Green, 1975).

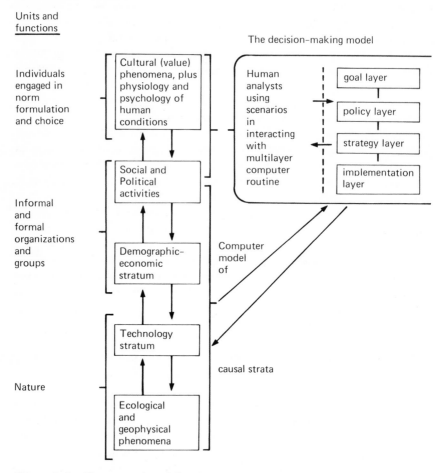

Level of strata (within each region)

Units and
functions

The decision-making model

Figure 4-1. The general multilevel organization of a Mesarovic-Pestel regional submodel, including an elaboration of its decision-making submodel. This figure represents our modification and condensation of Figures 4-3 and 4-4 of Mesarovic-Pestel, 1974, pp. 50, 51; see also Richardson, 1974, various figures.

plausible scenarios facing decision makers, as well as interactions among decision makers using computerized routines as planning aids. Figure 4-1 shows how aspects of the top two strata are respecifiable in a more elaborate hierarchy of increasingly specific measures of goal definition and implementation by decision makers. These are simulated by both human analysts and computer routines acting in concert vis-à-vis the lower level, deterministically modelled "causal strata."

Obviously, this framework is an attempt to disaggregate world models so that likely regional crises in the quality of life can be more adequately identified and responded to, in a way that does not overemphasize mechanistic causal determinisms ("dynamics"). It makes explicit individual and collective human differences, limits and capabilities for handling development problems. In the theoretical working papers of the Mesarovic-Pestel group, the quality of life is reconceptualized qualitatively in terms of Maslow's hierarchy of human needs: physical (survival, safety, security); social (belongingness, love and self-esteem); individual (self-actualization). But because important parts of social and individual needs are *implicitly* in the minds of human analysts involved in scenario exercises (simulation runs) with the Mesarovic-Pestel model, social and individual needs do not appear explicitly in their computer routines (Mesarovic and Pestel, eds., Volume 6, c.143-c.147). Mesarovic and Pestel start from a multilevel structural notion of world dynamics different from that of Meadows, arguing that the world system displays counterintuitive tendencies, not because of its complexity, but because it is in disorder. When a system is in crisis, its strata move together with a high degree of interdependence, corresponding, for example, to the impinging of political and ecological factors on economic relations. The response to the crisis that they suggest is a fundamental restructuring of the system, not toward equilibrium but toward an orderly kind of partly decoupled "organic growth." This restructuring should take place "horizontally," i.e., a change in relationships between regions, and "vertically" through change in value systems, individual attitudes, and certain social, economic, or technological strata in their regional models (as distinguished in Figure 4-1).

Given the fact that, for Mesarovic and Pestel, the key growth problem of the future is *not* environmental limits, but the widening gap between the developed and underdeveloped countries, their first series of analyses is built upon alternate "scenarios" aimed toward narrowing this gap. Their standard scenario run depicts how the gap would change if the historical pattern of development.were to prevail (it is assumed that fertility rates in all regions would reach equilibrium within 35 years). Under these conditions the gap (defined in terms of GNP per capita) continues to widen and in Southern Asia and Africa will remain above twenty to one. To attempt to reduce this gap, an alternative, continuous aid scenario (2) is devised. Aid would be given over 50 years, starting in 1975 and reaching an accumulated amount of $7200 billion. If aid is delayed until 2000 (scenario 3), total aid necessary by 2025 amounts to $10,700 billion, significantly higher than needed under scenario 2. Scenario 4 provides the increased aid in the next 25 years, and none after 2000, in order to reach the target of reducing the gap between developed and underdeveloped countries to five to one by 2025. Here total cost is less than $2500 billion, or a maximum annual figure of $250 billion, one-third the cost of scenario 2. The outcome of these computer runs demonstrates that costs are greatly increased by delayed action: the authors go on to apply the same kind of analysis to population policy, demonstrating that in this area too, delay is costly, a point made as well by the authors of *The Limits to Growth*.

A second major area of concern is the potential for conflict in the world system: Mesarovic and Pestel consider the increasing competition for scarce resources to have high conflict potential. (A similar view is found in Choucri, Laird, and Meadows, 1972). Growth, since it relies on a higher use of resources, can only create circumstances more conducive to potential for conflict. Mesarovic and Pestel consider the case of oil. Oil producers are assumed to be working toward goals of maximizing economic growth and wealth and increasing the life span of their reserves; consumers are assumed to want to ensure oil imports necessary for their continued economic growth. A series of scenarios are devised with these potentially conflicting goals in mind, based on the long-run pricing of oil over a 50-year period. The conclusion reached from alternate pricing structures is that a price rise of three percent per annum up to an "optimal" level (above 50 percent higher than the initial value) is beneficial to producers and consumers alike. The authors maintain that this conclusion applies to all finite resources—there is an optimal price which should be determined on a global rather than a unilateral basis: this they feel is important for reducing conflict attributable to resource constraints. They go on to analyze the oil market in terms of withholding of production and conclude once more that cooperation is more beneficial to both sides in the long run.

A further analysis has been conducted with regard to a third major issue, the food problem. Through the use of alternate scenarios, the conclusion is reached that a global approach, including a balanced economic development for all regions and an effective population policy, is necessary for a solution to the food crisis. At the cost of some economic growth, using capital transfers and population controls, "triage" need not lead India or the rest of non-Communist Asia into massive starvation (Richardson, 1974). The reader will also find these types of arguments, developed independently, in the work of the Bariloche Foundation group (Herrera, Skolnik et al., 1976).

As reviewed in Clark and Cole, with W.M. Curnow and Hopkins (1976), both the British and Japanese governments and the Japanese Club of Rome have also encouraged and funded follow-up studies to *The Limits to Growth*. Several of the more interesting features of the Japanese efforts have been the use of a national economic planning model in conjunction with a "rest of the world" version of Meadows' World three, a heavier focus on balance of payments problems, and the structural differentiation of growth mechanisms for developed, as opposed to developing, countries.

3. DIMENSIONS OF CONTROVERSY

Having summarized analyses of the world models sponsored by The Club of Rome, we shall now review the controversies engendered by them in the English-language scholarly literature we have read. To the extent that it is generally adequate, the reader should be able to fit any particular questions raised by the previous summary into the following outline. First, we review methodological issues, then debates about model realism, and finally we discuss underlying normative and/or political and/or ideological controversies.

Methodological Issues

1. Perhaps the most general methodological question is whether world modeling should be thought of as valid at all. Answers depend on whether it is defined as a literary, philosophical, legal, religious, ideological, or scientific analysis of the future. In other words, should the various modelers be thought of as legitimately preventing, constructing, exploring or merely mirroring certain futures? Thus the most comprehensive, interdisciplinary critique by Cole et al. (1973) question the nature of the basic enterprise. They resist Meadows' invitation to come up with better alternative models, at least in part because of the scientifically questionable nature of *any* model's general assumptions about social behavior. In spite of much scholarly skepticism, the Meadows' book has become a nonfalsifiable "bible" for many. On the other hand, Beres and Targ (1974) make an impressive case for the liberating effects of exploring future alternatives less formally, possibly in literary or religious terms. Jeremiah's prophecies were not without value, even if he was nonscientific; neither was George Orwell's *Animal Farm* nonprophetic.

2. Even when modeling is acceptable, there is a good deal of critical discussion whether a scientific, engineering, or policy perspective is most appropriate in analyzing world problems. In other words, should the analysis be primarily in a normative (optimal, planning), conceptual and methodological, or empirical mode? Like the Bariloche group but to a lesser extent, Mesarovic and Pestel are emphatically normative since they start with scenarios of a desirable future. Going beyond ad hoc lists of policy alternatives, Burns and Malone (1974) demonstrate how to find optimal policy mixes for Forrester's models. Typically, such an approach identifies instruments and targets and then uses some kind of optimal control methodology for the sequencing of instrumental actions within various constraints to achieve those targets. Forrester and the Meadows, on the other hand, emphasize the descriptive and methodological utility of their modeling. Of course good perspective studies should rely on provisionally adequate scientific knowledge, which many modelers feel is not yet available.

Underlying the issue of the appropriate scientific, engineering, or policy approach to world questions is the problem of contextual interests influencing the knowledge cumulation process. Habermas (1972) suggests there exists a specific connection between logical-methodological rules of inquiry and knowledge-constitutive interests. The empirical-analytic sciences incorporate a *technical* cognitive interest in feedback-monitoring prediction and control. The historical-hermeneutic sciences (including much legal analysis and the nineteenth-century field of missionary-oriented biblical translation) invoke *practical* interests in understanding and consensus development, not based on formalized, lawlike abstractions; classical social and political theories, as well as Freudian and Marxist critical science, have developed in the light of an explicit, emancipatory, cognitive interest. In terms of the world modeling debate, perhaps the most relevant methodological questions implied by these claims are the following: to what extent are the analytical methodologies participatory, advisory, or technocratic? Beres and Targ (1974) obviously lean toward a more participatory, mobilizing, qualitative conception of normative "model" construction; both Forrester and, perhaps even more, some of his technically advanced critics lean toward a more technocratic epistemology.

3. Depending on the preferred objectives and mode of model-based communication, there is the further question of the relevance of various types of deductive inference. We have already seen how Mesarovic and Pestel use computer simulations with human players. Nordhaus (1973) and Rademaker and Cuypers (1974) prefer to work with more mathematically tractible versions of the Forrester–Meadows models, ones with more linearized relationships and more orthodox production functions. An even larger review of alternative, deductive future-analytical approaches in international relations can be found in Choucri and Robinson, eds. (forthcoming).

4. Before exploring Day's (1974) question of appropriate model classes for futures studies, a philosophically prior question concerns the choice of formal and/or informal modeling languages. Mesarovic and Pestel found FORTRAN IV more adequate for their purposes than DYNAMO, used by Forrester and Meadows. Saunders (1974) and Alker (1973) raise the modeling language issue more generally: should not more powerful list processing languages or their metalanguages (LISP, IPL-V, PLANNER, GPS, ECL, for example) be used to model anticipatory problem solving, as well as social restructuring processes? The importance of linguistic communication in world decision processes raises further questions as to the adequacy of algebraic languages like FORTRAN *and* DYNAMO for representing such processes.

5. Most concretely, given a clear set of analytical purposes, a commitment to computer-linked modeling, and a formal analytical language, there is still the question of the best (perhaps mixed) modeling approach for futures studies. Bayesian approaches to decision making under uncertainty and non-Bayesian stochastic econometric treatments (as used in some Mesarovic–Pestel analyses) differ from the discretized, generally nonlinear, but calculus-oriented state-variable approach required of DYNAMO users. Shubik's scathing review (1971) contains a long list of distinguished, but uncited futures modelers who have not been methodologically preoccupied with "systems dynamics." As we have already seen in The Club of Rome studies, modelers clearly disagree on what model classes and associated structural notions are most valuable in analyzing the human predicament.

Part of the issue here is the wide variety of model-oriented approaches to, and philosophies of, systems analysis. Econometric approaches are frequently criticized by Systems Dynamics advocates, and vice versa. General systems theorists like Kenneth Boulding or Donald Campbell go beyond both such approaches. World-oriented computer modeling has also been the focus of a vigorous interdisciplinary tradition, originating in the work of Harold Guetzkow on the Inter-Nation Simulation (see Smoker's summary article in Alker, Deutsch, and Stoetzel, 1973). Choucri and North (1974) have found deep demographic-technological pressures toward conflict-laden expansion in the behavior of all the nineteenth century's great powers. The theoretical and validational traditions of these studies present alternative world modeling approaches perhaps observing more careful investigation by those unfamiliar with them. (See also Clark and Cole, [1976] and Bossel et al. [1976] for alternative world-oriented modelling approaches.)

a. Model Realism Issues. By definition, no model completely captures the reality it imitates. The complexity of environmental, technological, social, economic, and political processes ensures this will be true of all world-modeling efforts, which therefore must be thought of as strategically chosen, simplified representations for particular purposes, perhaps serving larger, unconscious functions as well. Validating the realism of such simplifications must therefore depend in part on their previously discussed methodological uses and their subsequent analytical and sociopolitical functions.

1. Perhaps the most general criticism of the realism of world models has been directed toward their fundamental misrepresentation of adaptation and generativity as features of socioenvironmental structures. The price system (and to a lesser extent its administrative equivalent in socialist societies) adapts almost continuously to scarcities by encouraging more efficient substitutions and diminishing some forms of consumption and growth; yet the earlier studies of limits subsumed (or ignored) such adaptive mechanisms. Technological adaptation and invention have regularly responded to, and frequently overcome, resource scarcities and pollution damage. Birth control preferences and practices have historically diminished population growth when equitable economic development has occurred (see Nordhaus, 1973; Roberts, 1974; Cole et al., 1973). It is highly significant, therefore, that many later world model analyses with such adaptive feedback mechanisms included (even the technical follow-up studies by Meadows et al., 1974) show plausible ways of postponing or eliminating global growth catastrophes beyond a 200-year time horizon, (e.g., Boyd, Mesarovic–Pestel, Rothkopf-de Vries). Thus the Malthusian confrontation of exponential growth in production and population with linear or single-shot adaptive responses may be fundamentally inaccurate. The post-hoc shift from a descriptive, policy-generating purpose to a "conceptually clarifying" rationale cannot be defended as a justifiable response to such arguments.

2. Methodological discussions of open and closed simulation modes (with

or without human players) and structure-modifying modeling language alternatives are derived from a related concern: the desire to redefine unrealistically deterministic, "outer" physical limits in terms of potentially changeable social, economic, and political "inner" limits to equitable, nonecologically destructive, reformed growth. Language grammars suggest a much richer, humanly relevant model of nondeterministic, but still limited structural generativity and problem solving (Newall and Simon, 1972; Alker, 1973). Even systematic searches for optimal policies in fixed structures ignore the humanistic and scientifically defensible idea of memory-based, planned structural transformations. (Laszlo, 1973). Calls for more accurate disaggregations of global relationships into more meaningful within-nation and within-region social categories reflect a concern with the unrealism of many globally defined mechanisms, not just an argument against scientific parsimony. (Galtung, 1973, [and several comments in the Mesarovic–Pestel, eds. 1974] moves in this direction, by recognizing different socioeconomic systems in different world regions, but projects none of the evident structural changes now occurring in Southeast Asia, movements toward a model of resource self-sufficiency, communal agricultural autonomy forced ideological homogenization, and equitable economic development.)

4. The sensitivity of nonlinear models to small changes in parameters and functional forms has frequently been recognized: it is even part of Forrester's argument about the frequently counterintuitive behavior of complex social systems. Concomitantly, however, there have been a large number of specific objections to the scanty data bases and casual estimation techniques used to justify particular equations in the original Limits of Growth volumes. Charges include the absence of Cobb–Douglas production functions, the omission of pollution generated by the service sector, the unrealism of population growth functions, unrealistic capital requirements for resource extraction, inaccurate resource consumption, and understated pollution absorption rates. Each has important consequences for model projections and derivative prescriptions. The ease with which radically different, plentiful, or horrendous futures can easily be generated from plausible (but often incorrect) alternate models is perhaps the most telling result of the critical studies. Without much more thorough interdisciplinary, conceptual, and empirical investigation, world model realism cannot be taken for granted, either putatively or prescriptively.

b. **Underlying Normative–Political–Ideological Conflicts.**   One can think of normative debates about the quality of human life, their limits and possibilities, as inherently political. This perspective has already been implied in the above discussion of whether growth limits should be defined as outer, physical limits, or inner, sociopolitical limits. Several commentators, especially Galtung (1973), have objected that Forrester's multiplicative quality-of-life index gives inordinate attention to the ideological concerns of affluent suburbanites, such as crowding and pollution effects, when the rest of the world is more concerned with malnutrition, equitable economic development, political oppression, and technocratic elitism. Beres and Targ (1974), for example, prefer characterizing the quality of collective human existence negatively, as an absence of human misery. They cite Barrington Moore's (1973) concept of human misery, which includes deaths from war and starvation, but also torture, illness, the extractions by ruthless authorities of the fruits of prolonged labor, and the denial of and prosecution for freedom of expression.

1. One major consequence of such reconceptualizations of the "inner limits" to growth has thus been the issue of equity in economic, social, and political development (ulHag, 1973). If all growth has to stop, the clear implication, assuming present power realities to be stable, is that it will do so in a way that keeps the Third World poor and dependent. The major political argument of those, like Mesarovic and Pestel, who project only modest resource price increases over the next 50 years is, in effect, that significant, growth-generating aid and technology transfers to the South are possible without destroying the prosperity and even further development of the industrialized West. The opposition to "triage" type policies or continued political dependencies is quite clear, and is derived from fundamental Western humanistic values.

2. A separable issue, of obvious political significance, concerns the modes of production best suited for achieving the desired growth and/or redistribution future. Here both radicals like Galtung (1973) and conservatives like Forrester converge in criticizing contemporary capitalism, while liberal economists like Nordhaus (1973) and Kaysen (1972) are particularly incensed by the slighting of the price system's adaptive and innovative "feedback" properties. Radicals and Conservatives also tend to admire the ecologically sensitive, participatory, decentralized, order-maintaining, population-limiting, autonomy-enhancing aspects of Chinese agrarian communism, when compared to the patterns and quality of growth in other Third World countries. As liberals, Mesarovic and Pestel tend to minimize the likelihood or desirability of such revolutionary changes in domestic and international political economy.

3. Boyd (1972) identifies an important ideological dimension of the more academic debates as one of "Malthusians" versus "technological optimists," a distinction Dennis Meadows accepts (in Cole et al., 1973), but modifies to include more Eastern, normative preferences for living contemplatively and less exploitively in harmony with one's environment. Many of the apparent "methodological" and "validity" concerns of the previous sections can be reinterpreted in these terms. Malthusian conservatives doubt that the market liberals' "hidden hand" will generate more "renewable resources" than Hobbes' "nasty world," because of unanticipated, usually negative, action consequences. Which feedback loops exist, with what nonlinearities or relative coefficient magnitudes, often reduces to a question of nonsubstantiated or even nonfalsifiable ideological beliefs about an unknown, perhaps unknowable, sociotechnological future. Formal languages, emphasizing restructuring generative possibilities, point potentially in the more technologically optimistic direction. Part of the hostility to Forrester and Meadows from those econometrically

trained may also reflect a muted form of technological optimism: the belief that ameliorative policies can be found within the nearly linear structural models that their statistical data and optimizing methods tend to assume and confirm.

4. Most generally, the political debate has involved differences in attitudes concerning the form and direction of a new international order responsive both to growth, redistribution, and problems of limits within and between nations. Malthusian conservatives, some nationalistic liberals, and most radicals distrust global international cooperation. On the other hand, Falk (in Laszlo, 1973) calls for a decrease in the power of the biggest national actors, plus a stronger reliance on transnational and regional intergovernmental actors as important steps toward a new global world order. Brzezinski (1973) sees himself somewhere between "global humanists" like Falk and nationally oriented "power realists." The Club of Rome is itself a transnational actor, visibly affecting some policy pronouncements, tending toward a Brzezinskian direction. A widespread transformation of commodity prices and international monetary arrangements of greater benefit to Third World governments *and* people (ulHag, 1973) is also being sought. There is growing awareness in the industrialized West of the related issues of redefining trade and monetary institutions created at the height of U.S. economic dominance in the late 1940s. New forms of transgovernmental cooperation in environmental monitoring and control are now also being called for (Strong, 1973).

4. CONCLUSION

The Limits of Growth became a bestseller in the United States, Western Europe, and Japan. Despite the tremendous disciplinary disparities of political scientists talking about freedom of expression, ecologists measuring irreversible pollution damage, economists talking about Cobb-Douglas production functions, and engineers talking about optimization methods, the arguments one hears and reads in different parts of the industrialized West (including Japan) are remarkably similar. Transnational social, economic, technological, and environmental interdependence increasingly brought about an interpenetration of national policy spaces—publically perceived and politically discussed sets of policy alternatives. Perhaps most significant in this regard has been the debate, reinforced by a larger North–South global cleavage, whether the limits-to-growth issue might be better reformulated as the need for a new, more equitable, and less destructive world economic–environmental order.

SELECTED REFERENCES

Alker, Jr., Hayward R. "Cybernetic Measures of Political Capabilities." Cambridge, Mass.: mimeo, 1973. Forthcoming in a book edited by Mircea Malitza.

Alker, Jr., H.R., K.W. Deutsch, and A. Stoetzel. *Mathematical Approaches to Politics*. New York: Elsevier, 1973.

Alker, Jr., Hayward R., Karl W. Deutsch, Andrei S. Markovits "Global opportunities and constraints for regional development: A review of interdisciplinary simulation research toward a world model as a framework of regional development." *Social Science Information,* 16(1):pp. 83–102, 1977.

Beres, Louis R. and Harry R. Targ. *Reordering the Planet: Constructing Alternative World Futures.* Boston: Allyn and Bacon, 1974.

Bossel, Hartmut, Salomon Klaczko, Norbert Müller (Eds.) *Systems Theory in the Social Sciences.* Basel: Birkhäuser Verlag, 1976.

Boyd, Robert. "World Dynamics: A Note." *Science,* 177 (August 11, 1972).

Bradley, Paul. "Increasing Scarcity: the Case of Energy Resources," and other articles. *American Economic Review,* 63 (May), 1973.

Brown, Lester R. "A Global Predicament." *Dialogue,* 6, 1973.

Brzezinski, Zbigniew. "U.S. Foreign Policy: The Search for Focus." *Foreign Affairs,* 51 (July): pp. 708–727, 1973.

Burns, James R. and David W. Malone. "Optimization Techniques Applied to the Forrester Model of the World." IEEE Transactions on Systems, *Man and Cybernetics* 4 (March 1974).

Choucri, Nazli, M. Laird, and D.L. Meadows. "Resource Scarcity and Foreign Policy: A Simulation Model of International Conflict." Cambridge, Mass.: Center for International Studies, (March 1972).

Choucri, Nazli and Tom Robinson, eds. *Forecasting in International Relations.* San Francisco: W.H. Freeman. forthcoming.

Choucri, Nazli and Robert North. *Nations in Conflict.* San Francisco: W.H. Freeman, 1974.

Clark and Cole, with Curnow and Hopkins. *Global Simulation Modeling.* New York: Wiley Interscience, 1976.

Cole, H.S.D., Christopher Freeman, Marie Jahoda, and K.L.R. Pavitt, eds. *Models of Doom.* New York: Universe Books, 1973.

Cole, Sam. "World Models, Their Progress and Applicability." *Futures* (June 1974).

Cortes, Fernando, Adam Przeworski, and John Sprague. *Systems Analysis for Social Scientists.* New York: Wiley, 1974.

"The No Growth Society." *Daedalus* (Fall 1973).

Forrester, Jay W. *World Dynamics.* Cambridge, Mass.: Wright-Allen Press, 1971.

Forrester, Jay W. "Understanding Social and Economic Change in the United States." Cambridge, Mass.: M.I.T. (Dec. 2), mimeo, 1974.

Galtung, Johan. "Limits to Growth and Class Politics." *Journal of Peace Research* 1–2, 1973.

Green, Wade. "Triage: Who Shall be Fed? Who shall Starve? *The New York Times Magazine.* (Jan. 5), pp. 9–11, 44–45, 51, 1975.

Herrera, A.O., H.D. Scolnik, et al. *Catastrophe or New Society? A Latin American World Model,* Ottawa: International Development Research Center, 1976.

Habermas, Jürgen. *Knowledge and Human Interests.* Boston: Beacon Press, 1972.

International Bank for Reconstruction and Development "Study by Special Staff Force on the Limits to Growth." Washington, D.C.: (September 1972).

Kaysen, Carl. "The Computer that Printed out W*O*L*F*." *Foreign Affairs* 5 (July); pp. 660–668, 1972.

Laszlo, Ervin, ed. *The World System: Models, Norms, Variations.* New York: George Braziller, 1973.

Meadows, Dennis L. et al. *The Dynamics of Growth in a Finite World.* Cambridge, Mass.: Wright-Allen Press, 1974.

Meadows, Donella H., Dennis L. Meadows, Jφrgen Randers, and William K. Behrens III. *The Limits to Growth.* New York: Universe Books, 1972.

Mesarovic, Mihajlo and Eduard Pestel. *Mankind at the Turning Point.* New York: E.P. Dutton, 1974.

Mesarovic, M., and E. Pestel, eds. "Multilevel Computer Model of World Development System." Laxenburg: International Institute for Applied Systems Analysis. Extract from the Proceedings of the Symposium held at IIASA, Laxenburg, 1–4 (April 29–May 3, 1974) and Summary of Proceedings.

Moore, Jr., Barrington. *Reflections on the Causes of Human Misery and Upon Certain Proposals to Eliminate Them.* Boston: Beacon Press, 1973.

Newell, Allen and Herbert A. Simon. *Human Problem Solving.* Englewood Cliffs, N.J.: Prentice Hall, 1972.

Nordhaus, William D. "World Dynamics: Measurement without Data." *Economic Journal* (December 1973).

Peccei, Aurelio. "The Predicament of Mankind." *Successo,* 12 (June): pp. 149–156, 1970.

Peccei, Aurelio. *The Chasm Ahead.* London: Macmillan, 1969.

Porat, Marc U. and Wesley Martin, eds. "World IV: A Policy Simulation Model of National and Regional Systems." *Stanford Journal of International Studies,* 9 (Spring, 1974).

Rademaker, O., and J.G.M. Cuypers. "Progress Reports No. 1 and 2." Eindhoven, Netherlands: Project Group Global Dynamics; reprinted with Summary of the Proceedings (Mesarovic and Pestel, eds.), 1974.

Ridker, Ronald G. "To Grow or not to Grow: That's not the Relevant Question." *Science,* 182 (December 28, 1973), pp. 1315–1318, 1973.

Richardson, John M. "Alternatives to Starvation: A Scenario Analysis of the World Food Problem, 1975–2020." Cleveland: Systems Research Center, Case Western Reserve University, mimeo., 1974.

Roberts, Marc J. "The Limits of the Limits to Growth," in Edward W. Erickson and Leonard Waverman, eds. *The Energy Question: An International Failure of Policy, Vol. 1.* Toronto: University of Toronto Press, 1974.

Rothkopf, M.H. and H. de Vries. "Modeling Future Energy Supply." Amsterdam: reprint., 1974.

Saunders, Robert S. "Criticism and the Growth of Knowledge: An Examination of the Controversy over *The Limits to Growth." Stanford Journal of International Studies,* 9 (Spring, 1974).

Shubik, Martin, Review of *World Dynamics. Science* (Dec. 3, 1971).

Strong, Maurice F. "One Year after Stockholm—An Ecological Approach to Management." *Foreign Affairs,* 51 (July 1973).

ulHag, Mahbub. "A View from the Developing Nations." *Dialogue* 6, (1973), pp. 21–30.

Willems, Jan C. *The Analysis of Feedback Systems.* Cambridge, Mass.: M.I.T. Press, 1971.

Chapter 5

The Bariloche Model

Carlos Mallmann

I wish to begin, by way of an introduction, by stating why we started work in this field and then go into the substantive part of my presentation. I will report on what we call the Latin American World Model, carried out at Bariloche, Argentina, in the Fundación Bariloche.

As to the history of the model developed at Bariloche, the group started in 1970, in Río de Janeiro, at a meeting convened by Cándido Méndes, to study and analyze the World III Model. The decision was taken initially to look at the World III Model in order to try to give another perspective, a Third-World point of view on global modeling. This was decided at Río de Janeiro, and a request was presented to Fundación Bariloche to carry it out. The first preliminary document was written by five consultants at the end of 1971. The actual group was formed and worked for approximately four years, completing its work at the end of 1975. The product of this work is going to appear in some ten technical reports and a book for the general public entitled *Catastrophe or New Socie-*

The authors of the Latin American World Model include Graciela Chichilnisky, who worked on the mathematical and economic aspects; Gilberto Gallopin, food and pollution; Jorge E. Hardoy, housing and urbanization; Amílcar O. Herrera, group coordinator and director of the pollution project and nonrenewable resources; Diana Mosovich, housing and urban problems; Enrique Oteiza and Gilda Romero Brest, education; Carlos Suárez, energy Hugo D. Scolnik, mathematics and demography; and Luis Talavera, mathematical, demographic, and computational aspects. Five part-time consultants also worked on the model.

The project has received support from many sources, including substantial aid from the Social Sciences Division of the International Development Research Centre, in Canada. Technical support was recieved from many U.N. agencies, such as the International Labor Office and FAO. Additional support for specific aspects of our work has been received from the Club of Rome, IIASA, Vienna, Austria; CELADE, Santiago, Chile; SPRU, University of Sussex, U.K.; CEUR, Instituto Di Tella, Argentina; and the United Nations Economic Group for Latin America. Technical assistance has been received from Honeywell Bull, Argentina, and Xerox, Argentina.

ty? I have with me the first English draft of the book, which is being sent out now to the publishers.

I would like to go a little bit further into what the consequences of carrying out this work represents to our present and future endeavors in this area and especially to the Bariloche Foundation. The world modeling effort we have completed is now part of a group project which will continue research on the satisfaction of human needs and development factors on a world, regional, national, and perhaps even local level. It is part of our institutional policy to continue this work in the future. The specific developments we are now contemplating include the further development of the World Model, which I am going to present today, and the construction of a regional model for Latin America. We are also involved in organizing courses and seminars to transmit our experience on this work.

Let me now present the Latin American World Model. This model was actually designed to answer the following question: what are the restraints to the satisfaction of survival needs for all present and future human beings? The answer that resulted from the work is that restraints are essentially of a sociopolitical nature, not of a material nature, because there are natural and human resource utilization strategies that can achieve the two main aims of the model. One is the stabilization of the world population without imposition of birth control, the second is satisfying every human being in terms of his basic material and educational needs.

In order to show what this means from the point of view of human needs, I would like to refer to some information from my paper "Quality of Life and Development Alternatives." It concerns an analysis of the different kinds of needs human beings have, analyzed from two perspectives. First, from the point of view of the categories of values to which they pertain, and second, the kind and category of satisfiers that satisfy them. From this second viewpoint, there are psychosomatic or intrahuman satisfiers. For example, rest and nutrition in survival needs; psychohabitational or extrahuman needs in the survival group; housing and natural predictability; and in the psychosocial or interhuman kind of satisfiers, things like employment, income, social predictability, from the viewpoint of survival.

As we move from this survival level, we confront protection needs, love needs, needs of education and understanding, self-government and government, recreation, creation, giving meaning to oneself, and synergy. I will not go into the analysis of this group of needs, which is based on many empirical and theoretical results of psychology and social psychology. I do, however, wish to point out that the aim we are trying to pursue at Fundación Bariloche is to move into a more detailed description of these needs. Our Latin American World Model is really a first step in trying to satisfy the essential needs of existence. This means survival, protection, and education, which are of first priority for two-thirds of the population of the world who live in misery with respect to these satisfactions.

This is essentially the world model we are going to present. It places its greatest emphasis on the satisfaction of the three survival needs by trying to find out whether it is possible for the present and future population of the world to meet them. This means, in terms of nutrition, 3000 calories per person per day, and 100 grams of protein per person per day; in housing, to have one dwelling unit per family, with approximately 10 square meters per person and all related required services.[1]

From the point of view of employment and income, our model assumes full employment. From the health perspective, which is really a proxy indicator for the existence variable, it requires a life expectancy at birth of the order of 70 years for the entire world population. In terms of education, it stipulates twelve years of formal education. This means education between the ages of six and eighteen.

The proxy indicator of life expectancy at birth is maximized in each year's optimization of the model. This is done because we think it is a good proxy indicator of the satisfaction of basic needs throughout life and society. We believe it to be a much better indicator, for example, than gross national product.

Let me proceed to the second point of the conceputal model (as opposed to the formalized mathematical model). This is the full participation of the people in the decisions that affect their lives. Hence, we are envisaging a society that is not predetermined, aside from the satisfaction of basic needs. This means that we are trying to maintain diverse cultural aims, above and beyond the satisfaction of survival needs.

A third main assumption is our goal of trying to build a society compatible with its own ecosystem. This means that it is nonconsumist. As a result, we are trying to design a very rapid material development until basic needs are satisfied and, after that, a different kind of aim which will go more in the direction of large, human, nonmaterial growth in order to maintain compatibility with the ecosystem.

The conceptual model is only partially formalized, because many of the concepts included in it cannot as yet be formalized. The part which is formalized is a normative model that sketches a way to attain a specific aim and calculates the time needed to carry it out. The main aim of the model is to solve the problems of both present and future misery and scarcity in which two-thirds of the world population lives. This is the main goal.

The model is constructed in such a way that the world has been divided into four regions: Developed Countries (i.e., Europe and scattered developed countries such as Japan and the U.S.), Latin America and the Caribbean, Africa, and Asia. I would like to point out that after this work was completed, we also worked with the fifteen Leontieff regions of the world, so our categorization is not the only possibility. The standard runs of the model, however, have been carried out using our four regions. Essentially, the formalized topics are population, health, food, housing, and education. Nonrenewable natural resources, energy, and pollution, were analyzed conceptually, but are not formalized with explicit variables in the model.

This is essentially the structure of the model. In addition, I would like to

---

1. Housing is assumed to be of an urban nature in our model, as concerns services.

point out that all the sectors that were formalized are mathematically linked in the model. Although from the mathematical point of view each of these sectors has been constructed in a modular way, so that it can be used separately, there are still strong links between the different variables.

The optimization process used is a rather novel tool which was presented at the UNESCO meeting in Poland last year. Dr. Scolnik and Dr. Talavera have published a paper on it. It makes possible the maximization of a function of many variables without using derivatives, which in turn are subjected to many constraints. These constraints are included in the model within a hierarchy that can be varied and changed at will.

In our case, the maximized variable is, as I said before, life expectancy at birth. The variables on which life expectancy at birth depend are, for example, food, housing, education, primary population, and the like. We have approximately 30 constraints for these variables in a hierarchy which can be changed, so that when one condition hinders the achievement of the objectives, it can be made weaker than the previous one, so as to find out what happens. Mathematically, the problem is solved as a discrete-time, optimal control problem, using new mathematical programming techniques.

I would now like to go into a bit more detail with regard to the different sectors of the model, starting with the economic model. The five sectors of the economy into which the model has been divided are food production, housing and urbanization, education, consumer goods and services (which are kept at their minimum level, 50 percent of the economy of the gross national product of the region), and the capital goods sector. Each of these sectors has a Cobb–Douglas production function, with the salaries paid, the capital of the sector, the alpha i specific for the sector, and a technological factor.

For the labor force, we have used for the period 1960 to 1970, the values published by the International Labor Office, so that they vary according to their tables. This is also done for the projections up to 1980. From 1980 on, the standard runs of the model are carried out with the labor force as a constant percentage of the future population. This assumption is discussed later on, in different runs, to see how it affects the model. Thus, the fact that in the standard runs this has been maintained as a constant does not mean that one has to do it. The reason for using constant values is the difficult predictability over time.

Capital stock was estimated for each sector, as was technological change. In the standard run, food used 1 percent, housing services 1 percent, education 0.5 percent, consumer goods and services 1 percent, and capital goods 1.5 percent. We have also run the model without technological factors. As a matter of fact, they were not included in our first presentation of the model in Vienna, in 1974.

The alpha is in the historic period from 1960 to 1970 are computed by an optimization process that adjusts the alpha is of 1960 and 1970 so that the whole model reproduces some fifteen main variables, including things like gross regional product, population, education, and life expectancy. I can show the results of that optimization process for the values of alpha i which have been used in the economic sectors and compare them with the values given by those adjusted alpha *is* for some of the variables. As an example, we have in regions one, two, and three, Developed Countries, Latin America, and Africa. The real values and the calculated values for population are 1056 million compared to 1032 million; 277 million compared to 271 million; and 330 million compared to 331 million, respectively. These are comparisons of the calculated values in 1970 achieved by starting the model working in 1960. One puts in the 1960 values, lets the model run without optimization, and sees how it reproduces the values for 1970. For example, in life expectancy, it is 70.4 years compared to 70.45; 61.83 years compared to 61.05; and 45.9 years compared to 46.2.

One element also added to the model last year was international trade. We used the UNCTAD data on international trade in order to calculate the trade for each region, and for the five sectors of the economy into which the model is divided. We used the values published for 1970; the total balance for each region and the percentage of the gross regional product were given. This, then, is the summed total of balanced interchanges. In future runs, it is assumed that from 1980 on, international exchange reaches a state of equilibrium in a period of 20 years. This means that in the year 2000, these values balance out. It is assumed that this happens in a linear way from 1980 to 2000. This certainly can be changed, but again, this is the assumption of the standard run. The time evolution of the model is such that each year the capital of the next year is calculated by adding to the existing capital, the product of the fifth sector—capital goods— and deductions reflecting depreciation rates.

The model runs from 1980 on, which is the year in which the optimization process starts, in order to obtain a maximum increase of life expectancy, year by year. We have the population of 1980, which comes from running the model in a projective way, and capital in the year 1980. We also have the population in the secondary sector, the calories and proteins per person, the urbanization and housing variables per family and per person, the enrollment in school between ages six and eighteen, and the population in the primary sector of the economy. All these variables influence, as I will show, the demographic model, the birth rate, and the life expectancy with which one can then calculate the labor force available the next year, and the capital and labor variables required for the optimization process.

The optimization process does the following: it looks for the distribution of the ten variables in order to achieve a maximum increase in life expectancy during 1981. Since life expectancy is a function of the variables of the different sectors of the economy, the optimization renders the labor and capital variables for the production functions of each of the sectors, in order to calculate the calories and proteins, houses, education variables, capital production, and consumer goods production of the next year. These are the five sectors of the economy. Once you have the values, you can calculate the new population in the secondary sector of the economy, the calories and proteins per person, the houses per family and, of course, the capital for the year 1982. The same process then starts again for the following year. Thus, essentially, every year there is an optimization routine that makes the choice of the distribution of the ten variables in order to get next year's input.

As mentioned previously, hierarchical restraints are applied, for example, to restrictions of the highest proportion of changes from one labor proportion in one sector to another, as well as to the speed of capital increase. Another restriction is that a solution should never reduce the calories and proteins per person in the next year. As I said, there are about 30 restrictions of this type.

The population formulas were calculated through the use of a data bank with the population data of 121 countries for the years 1950, 1960, and 1970. They were calculated carrying out nonlinear multivariate analysis, in order to find a formula in which birth rate and life expectancy depend on socioeconomic variables. It turned out that the main variables needed in order to achieve the correlation with the 121 countries' data were the calories and proteins per person, the houses per family, education, and the active population in the primary and secondary sectors of the economy.

Knowing the life expectancy of the previous year, the age structure by sex of the population, and the birth or fertility rate for the previous year, one can, using the mortality and fertility tables, calculate the new population and the age structure for the following year. The formulas are exponential, resulting from nonlinear multivariate analysis. The accordance between them and the data of the countries is very close.

Let me note briefly the qualitative impacts of the different parameters of the formula. They show how life expectancy is affected positively by enrollment; enrollment in turns affects the birth rate negatively. Comparing the results of this kind of population model with United Nations' predictions, our standard run for the year 2000 gives 6419 for the total population in thousands of millions of persons; 6515 is the UN median value. Thus, we are practically at the median value. For 2050, our standard run gives us 10,404 thousand million—7.34 percent lower than the value of the median calculation projection of the United Nations, namely, 11,228. The U.N. low value for the year 2000 is 5977; our difference from this value is 7.4 percent. Thus, our calculations are on the average below the median UN projection. They are lower, as time progresses, because in the model satisfaction of basic needs is producing a decrease in birth rate, which has been historically shown in all developed countries. These are, of course, just some of the results of our demographic model.

Let met now briefly mention a number of additional aspects of our work. Our analysis of the food sector, using the optimization process, is a three-year work which was presented at IIASA, at the last meeting on food and world problems. The educational scheme shows how the production functions and the variables are calculated, as well as our housing and urbanization scheme. Figure 5-1 shows the way in which ten variables move in the developed region as a function of time. Here we have the years 1960, 1970, 1980, continuing in ten-year intervals up to 2060. This part of the model, the runs from 1960 to 1980, are carried out in the projective mode. This means that the optimization process is not being applied. From 1980 on, it is assumed that optimization is implemented and that the whole model works in order to maximize life expectancy. One can see, for example, that the birth rate decreases into a constant value. In regard to population, the total population is growing and is stabilizing. Life expectancy goes from 69.2 years at the beginning to 71.4 at the end, and stabilizes. Houses per family grow rapidly from a value of approximately 0.71. This means that 30 percent of the population do not have houses of the kind the model proposes. This goes up to a value of 1.5 houses per family. The 1.5 indicates, not that each family uses one and a half houses, but that the quality of the houses can be improved, since quality is presented in terms of cost. The increase of population year by year is a curve showing stability after certain oscillations. In Latin America and the Caribbean, the birth rate, for example, decreases rapidly when the optimization process is implemented; life expectancy grows from 55.8 years to 71; the total calories go up to the value of 3000 calories per person; and the houses starting at the level of 0.51 per family, go up to the value 1.5. Essentially, one achieves the targets a little before the year 2000. (See Figure 5-2.)

The results for Africa (Figure 5-3) show that the targets are reached later on, perhaps in the year 2010 or 2015. In Asia (Figure 5-4), the situation is more difficult. The situation is such that one cannot achieve the satisfaction of basic human needs with the parameters assumed for the standard run. One finds out, for example, that the new land available for food production drops to zero close to the year 2000. There are other problems that we could examine in more detail. Just in order to see what happens if one assumes larger food production, runs were carried out assuming four and six tons per hectare of food production. If one goes to six (and as you know fourteen tons per hectare represents the greatest food production observed, in a country like Holland), the situation is somewhat improved, although still quite difficult. It is assumed here that the region runs by itself, without bringing food in from other countries, or without producing food in artificial ways, such as protein production from oil. We could analyze what these conclusions mean for Asia.

Finally, I would like to show what these results mean in terms of income distribution, which is a piece of work carried out with the International Labor Office. Instead of using four regions of the world, the group of Dr. Hopkins, from ILO, and Dr. Scolnik, from our group, used the fifteen Leontieff regions. In column one of Table 5-1 we present the shares of the twentieth percentile of the twenty poorest percent of the population of the total world economy. We also give in column two the gross national products that should be our aim for the year 2000, in order to satisfy basic needs, if one assumes a perfect distribution (an egalitarian distribution for the fulfillment of basic needs); furthermore, column three shows the gross national products if income distribution is maintained as it is today. Finally, column four represents a ratio between columns three and two demonstrating the existing regional differences in terms of

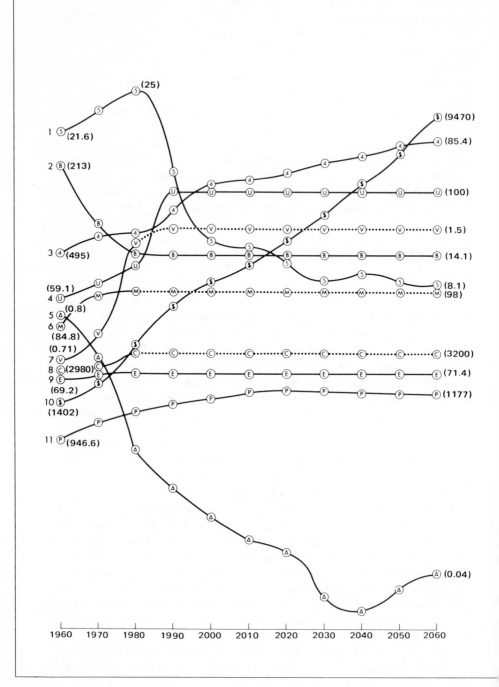

equality and the effort required to satisfy basic needs in egalitarian conditions. The average growth the economies of these regions had in the period 1960-1970 is shown in column one of Table 5-2; the yearly growth in the economy needed in order to achieve the GNPs maintaining the present distribution of income appears in column two. One can see then that growth in the less-developed South American countries should be 10.5 percent in order to achieve the satisfaction of basic needs, if one assumes that the distribution of income is maintained constant. The more-developed Latin American regions require 9.9 percent; the Far East and India, 10.5 percent. This is just to show that in order to carry out the program proposed by the model, one really has to carry out very deep structural and attitudinal changes. This is why we say that the main problem is a sociopolitical, not a material, resource kind of problem, in the sense that there are paths and strategies which can take us to the satisfaction of basic needs. But the main problem remains of a sociopolitical nature.

Finally, I would like to say two more things about the conclusions of our work. The first is the sociopolitical nature of the problem. The second is that we have now a tool which allows us to derive from value statements and proposals, plans for long-term action. This approach takes into account the fact that history is constructed by man. It is not a mere projection of the past. It also allows for the introduction of the quality of nonmaterial growth needs. What I want to point out is that, with the same methodology, one could bring in the other variables I spoke of earlier. We think that the model is realistic from the material point of view, in the sense that it expresses the aspirations of two-thirds of the world population. At the same time, it is certainly utopian in terms of the sociopolitical changes it assumes. The next step we have to carry out is to try to introduce the sociopolitical variables. Yet we thought it was essential to show that the limits are not material, that, in fact, the limits are sociopolitical. In this sense, we think that our conclusions are opposed to the ones which were contained in the Meadows' World III Model.

Finally, and most important, we have learned what we would like to work on

---

Figure 5-1. Time period and conditions required for developed countries to satisfy basic needs to given levels. (Source. Amílcar O. Herrera et al., *Catastrophe or New Society? A Latin American World Model* [Ottawa: International Development Research Centre, 1976], p. 84).

1. Percentage of gross national product allocated to sector 5 (5)
2. Birthrate (per 1000 inhabitants) (B)
3. Percentage of gross national product allocated to sector 4 (4)
4. Urbanization (percentage change of the population) (U)
5. Population growth rate ($\triangle$)
6. Enrollment (M)
7. Houses per family (V)
8. Total calories (C)
9. Life expectancy at birth (E)
10. Gross national product per capita in 1960 dollars ($)
11. Total population (P)

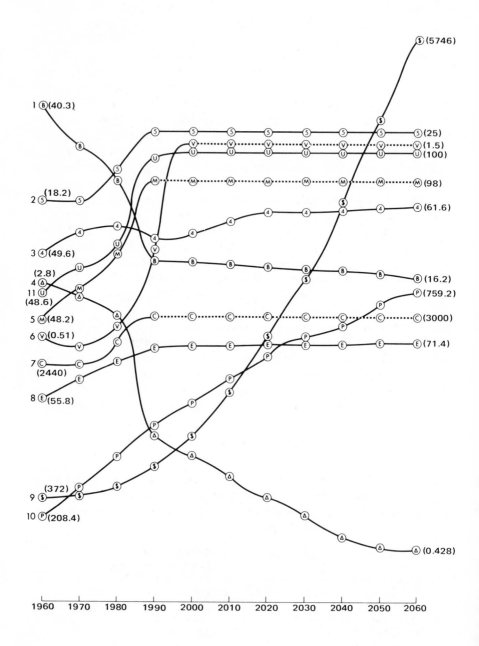

next. We have learned from the mistakes we made, although we think that we have a first, elementary tool in trying to analyze world problems. Essentially, we think that this is just one more learning tool that gives some of the necessary

Table 5-1. Results of runs of the model to establish the minimum GNP required to satisfy basic needs.

Regions[a]	*A* *Proportion of* *total income* *received by the* *poorest 20%* *(% of GNP)*	*B* *GNP per capita* *required to* *satisfy basic* *needs with* *egalitarian* *income* *distribution*	*C* *GNP per capita* *required to* *satisfy basic* *needs if the* *present income* *distribution is* *maintained*	$\dfrac{C}{B}$
North America	5.7	4407	15463	3.5
South America (more developed)	4.0	807	4035	5
South America (less developed)	4.1	740	3610	4.9
Western Europe (more developed)	4.6	2164	9409	4.3
Western Europe (less developed)	5.3	892	3366	3.8
USSR	10.4	1602	3081	1.9
Eastern Europe	10.4	1359	2613	1.9
Japan	7.7	2416	6275	2.6
Far East and India	7.3	428	1173	2.7
Middle East (oil-producing states)	5.6	540	1929	3.6
Africa (more developed)	5.5	451	1640	3.6
Africa (less developed)	4.8	505	2104	4.1
South Africa	1.9	1093	11505	10.1
Australia and New Zealand	7.0	2867	8191	2.8
People's Republic of China	No data	—	—	—

[a]Regions from model of the world economy of the United Nations.

Figure 5-2. Time period and condition required for Latin America to satisfy needs to given levels. (Source: Herrera et al., *Catastrophe or New Society?*, p. 89.)

1. Percentage of gross national product allocated to sector 5 (5)
2. Birthrate (per 1000 inhabitants) (B)
3. Percentage of gross national product allocated to sector 4 (4)
4. Urbanization (percentage change of the population) (U)
5. Population growth rate ($\triangle$)
6. Enrollment (M)
7. Houses per family (V)
8. Total calories (C)
9. Life expectancy at birth (E)
10. Gross national product per capita in 1960 dollars ($)
11. Total population (P)

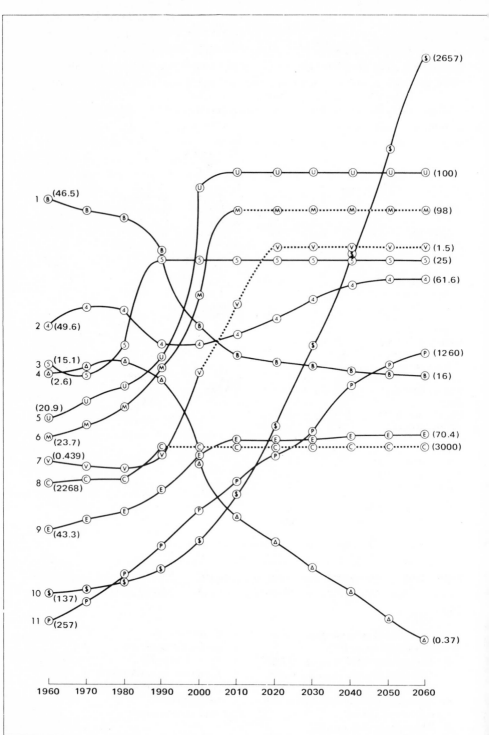

conditions to attain the objective, although it will never give all of them. They will never be sufficient, because a model will never, in the near future, represent reality. Therefore, we would like to stress the fact that models have this limitation; in addition, they are created within a subculture. This means that they are subculturally determined. Models must therefore be developed in many different parts of the world, so that we may have the benefit of learning the way in which different people from different cultures look at their problems and their future. We think this is the only way to try avoiding the subcultural determination of modeling efforts, although certainly we will not be able to avoid the fact that they are determined by the knowledge available in the world at any given time.

Table 5-2. Economic Growth Rates Necessary to Satisfy Basic Needs in the Year 2000, Maintaining the Current Income Distribution Structure.

	Growth rates in the period 1960-70	*Growth rates necessary to satisfy basic needs in the year 2000*
North America	4.5	5.3
South America (more developed)	5.3	9.9
South America (less developed)	5.2	10.5
Western Europe (more developed)	4.6	5.7
Western Europe (less developed)	6.7	7.9
USSR	7.0	4.1
Eastern Europe	5.7	3.4
Japan	10.6	5.9
Far East and India	5.3	10.5
Middle East (oil-producing states)	8.5	10.4
Africa (more developed)	4.1	11.5
Africa (less developed)	5.1	11.8
South Africa	6.0	12.8
Australia and New Zealand	4.9	5.6
People's Republic of China	4.4	No data

Figure 5-3. Time period and conditions required for Africa to satisfy basic needs to given levels. (Source: Herrera et al., *Catastrophe or New Society?*, p. 90.)

1. Percentage of gross national product allocated to sector 5 (5)
2. Birthrate (per 1000 inhabitants) (B)
3. Percentage of gross national product allocated to sector 4 (4)
4. Urbanization (percentage change of the population) (U)
5. Population growth rate ($\triangle$)
6. Enrollment (M)
7. Houses per family (V)
8. Total calories (C)
9. Life expectancy at birth (E)
10. Gross national product per capita in 1960 dollars ($)
11. Total population (P)

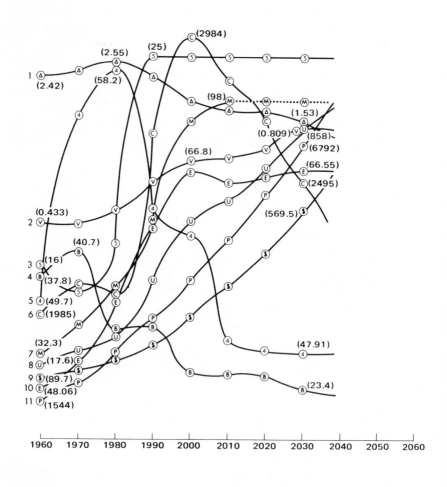

1 Population growth rate (△) 7 Enrollment (M)
2 Houses per family (V) 8 Urbanization (U)
3 Percentage of GNP allocated to sector 5 (5) 9 GNP per capita in 1960 dollars ($)
4 Birthrate (B) 10 Life expectancy (E)
5 Percentage of GNP allocated to sector 4 (4) 11 Total population (P)
6 Total calories (C)

Figure 5-4. Time period and conditions required for Asia to satisfy basic needs to given levels. (Source: Herrera et al., *Catastrophe or New Society?,* p. 92).

 *Chapter 6*

How Should We Model Policy Makers?

William D. Nordhaus

HOW SHOULD WE MODEL POLICIES?

The typical policy-oriented model contains physical constraints, behavior equations outside the control of policymakers, and policy variables. This is true of most economic models, and it can be seen in the present crop of global models. The treatment of policy variables is a problem that has not received much attention and is one I will discuss today.

Approaches to Modeling Policy

In all social systems there are policy variables which can be affected or determined to some degree by the responsible decision makers. These policy variables include the rate of investment, the allocation of capital, natural resources, labor between the different sectors, the level of taxation or subsidy of different sectors, the extent of family planning, and the like. What is the proper way of treating these variables? It is instructive to look at the treatment of policy variables in "global models" as an example of the various possibilities. Early models (such as *World Dynamics* and *The Limits to Growth*) treat policies in a very mechanical and deterministic manner; these works simply project trends rather than provide for adaptive response of the policy variables. Policy variables receive yet another treatment in the Mesarovic-Pestel model. In this treatment, the policy variables are left "open," in a reaction to the mechanistic treatment on the part of the Forrester-Meadows models. Other models, such as the Bariloche model, assume complete optimization of policy variables in response to changes in economic conditions.

Although both the mechanical and the adaptive or optimizing approaches have been criticized, neither has received much careful analysis. It is useful to start with the distinction between a normative view of policy and a behavioral view. The normative view has been quite common in the utilitarian tradition since Bentham. It relies on an abstract conception of the public goods, such as Bentham's, notion of the "greatest good for the greatest number", the social welfare function of Bergson and Samuelson, or the more recent maximin principle espoused by Rawls. These abstract principles may (or may not) represent commonly held views about the good or economic justice; in any case, it is possible to derive implications of these abstract principles for important social questions. In the normative tradition, then, optimization represents an attempt to draw normative inferences about policy by optimizing the abstract normative principle. Prominent examples in the economic literature in recent years are optimal economic growth and optimal income taxation, while Rawls has used his principle to investigate many aspects of just social policy.

A second approach to policy variables is positive or behavioral. A behavioral approach treats both private and public decision makers as actors with their own preference functions and constraints, and derives the corresponding behavioral relations. This treatment is in the spirit of modern behavioral economic and political thought in contrast to the older utilitarian tradition. Thus, one might try to determine the actions which are profit-maximizing on the part of firms, preference-maximizing on the part of consumers, vote-maximizing on the part of competing politicians, and work-minimizing or empire-maximizing on the part of entrenched bureaucrats. The first aspect of such an approach is that the agents in the public sector are treated as humans in the same way as in the private sector. The work of Joseph Schumpeter and a classic study by Anthony Downs provide important landmarks in this tradition. Economics has long been saddled with the paradigm of private decisionmakers who optimize their preference functions in a narrow fashion, and then proceed into government where they suddenly become Benthamite benevolent despots interested in maximizing the greatest good for the greatest number. One thing we have learned in recent years is that upon becoming Attorney General a bond dealer does not undergo a philosophical or behavioral sea change. The first aspect of a behavioral view, then, is to treat the public sector as a behavioral entity.

The second aspect concerns problems of estimation of the response functions of different agents. Two different ways of estimating response functions can be envisaged. The first—I will call "behavioral-descriptive"—would be a direct estimation of the behavioral rules or regularities and can be reliably estimated; the rules can be used to predict the response of agents to different environments. In economics this is the tradition of econometric modeling of supply and demand or of macroeconomic models; in modern "politicometrics," attempts have been made to estimate political responses to different conditions.

In many cases, however, the behavioral regularities may be extremely numerous and complex. If the behavioral regularities are difficult to estimate one can substitute the preference function of the agents into the problem and maximize the agents' objective function. This is the "behavioral-optimization" approach. In principle, the behavioral-optimization procedure yields the same answer as the econometric approach, but the informational requirements and the estimation procedures are very different. It is important to note that it uses the decision-maker's rather than a more general (say Benthamite) objective function. This makes the approach behavioral, by using optimization as a technique for understanding behavior.

A simple example from physics will make the two behavioral approaches clear. If one examines the behavior of flowing water, one can describe this process either by starting with a large number of possible differential equations—or by saying that water seeks the path of maximum descent. This second assumption provides a very accurate and fruitful approach to the description of the behavior of flowing water, but of course it is nonsense to assert that water molecules contain brains which direct such purposive behavior. Rather, the "as if" optimizing approach is a fruitful way of modeling the behavior of water.

Some Examples

I will briefly discuss three examples of the treatment of policy variables which throw light on the different approaches. The first relates to short-run macroeconomic modeling, the second to global modeling, the third to regional interaction.

POLICY VARIABLES IN
MACROECONOMIC MODELS

All current macroeconomic models contain a mixture of private sector behavior equations and exogenous policy variables. The latter generally include, for example, the money supply and government expenditure. In most models, policy variables are simply projected on the basis of judgmental forecasts as to the behavior of the Federal Reserve and Congress in the case of the United States. This procedure is somewhat unsystematic and unscientific.

Different approaches to the forecasting of important variables can be envisaged in light of the remarks above. The normative approach would lay out an explicit social welfare function and optimize this with respect to policy variables. Although this is a useful exercise, it is not clear that it has any empirical importance.

The behavioral approach is more interesting. It has been suggested that it would be useful to examine the political equations corresponding to the macroeconomy. In the work of Kramer and others, it has been shown that electoral behavior responds significantly to macroeconomic conditions; in particular the rate of growth of per capita output in the year before elections is associated with a bigger vote for the incumbents. This macropolitical equation can be added to the behavioral equations of the system.

To close the system we need to have an equation for the behavior of policy-makers, be they the Federal Reserve, Congress or the Administration. Work by Bruno Frey at the University of Konstanz has developed behavioral-descriptive models as to how governments in the FRG and the US behave with respect to both economic and political variables. In some preliminary work, Frey has shown that there is some predictability in economic policy, with the state of the economy, the ideology of the party in power, and the time before elections significant determinants of macroeconomic policy. Unfortunately for forecasters, the quality of the fit is quite poor, which is simply a reflection of the fact that the political forum is very noisy.

There have also been examples of applying the behavioral-optimization approach to this issue. In earlier works I showed how a macroeconomic system behaved when vote-maximizing politicians were steering the economy. The optimization by policy makers leads to a maximum condition which describes the laws of motion of the policy variables, which, in turn, describe a "political business cycle" with an internal periodicity equal to that of the electoral cycle. My colleague, Ray Fair, has performed more detailed calculations with his large macroeconomic models describing in detail how such a system would behave.

To summarize, there are several approaches to the inclusion of policy variables in macroeconomic models, all of which are in their infancy. Fundamental empirical difficulties may constrain the fruitfulness of such an enterprise, but at least it will help clarify some rather mystical notions about the functioning of macroeconomic policy and the nature of policy constraints in a democratically-run economy.

POLICY VARIABLES IN GLOBAL MODELS

The second example applies to the topic of this conference—the treatment of policy variables in global models. The first class of models (the Forrester-Meadows model) treated policy variables in a completely mechanical way; in the Forrester model, for example, there was no separation of policy variables from technological ones, and as a result the model had the appearance of assuming that societies were completely non-adaptive in their decisions. The second class of models (the Mesarovic-Pestel model) failed to consider policy variables by refusing to make predictions. Thus, the choice of policy variables was left to the bewildered user.

In the third model, the Bariloche model, a very interesting treatment of policy variables was taken. The paragraphs that follow report on the presentation of the Bariloche model made in Baden, Austria in October 1975. Perhaps the most original and interesting aspects of the Bariloche model are the details of the objective function and the optimization. The objective function is unique in two respects: first, it is designed so that its basic variables are quantifiable in natural units rather than in value units (or utilities). Second, it is an objective function which "satiaties" at relatively low levels of performance.

More specifically, the basic objective function is to maximize

$$(1 + \text{qlife}) \text{ le} \tag{1}$$

subject to numerous constraints, where

le = life expectancy at birth

and

qlife =
  - 0, when the "basic needs" *have not* been satisfied;
  - *share* of consumption (excluding "basic needs") in GNP (including "basic needs"), when the "basic needs" *have* been satisfied.

As far as the basic needs are concerned, there are four categories—food, education, housing, and health—and the targets for these are set in quantitative terms:

(i)   Calory intake per capita must exceed 3000 per day, and in addition have a reserve for "rainy" days.
(ii) At least 98% of the relevant population must be enrolled in school, from age six, for twelve years.
(iii) Each family must be provided with a "house" of minimum quality; this is basically fifty square meters plus certain sanitary and other equipment.
(iv) Health enters directly through the objective function.

The model then maximizes the value of the objective function subject to the constraints. The authors suggest that in principle they would like to define the optimal path as one which attains the required levels of the "basic needs" in minimum time and, presumably, succeeds in maintaining them. Neither the techniques nor the objective function seem designed to perform this task well. The actual procedure is to maximize the objective function every year; i.e., myopically, without taking into account the effect of current decisions upon future levels of the "basic needs."

It is not clear whether the authors believe that the procedure actually used is equivalent to the technique of minimizing the time to satisfy the basic needs and to maintain that level. A simple example will show that in general this is not the case. Consider a very simple economy in which there is a fixed pool of resource $R > T$, and where T is the lifetime of the society, life expectancy at birth is a concave function of consumption of the resource, and where the basic needs require one unit per period. A perfectly myopic policy, one which maximizes life expectancy at birth, will have a "potlatch policy." All R units will be consumed in the first period, after which society collapses. (It is interesting to note that this policy does not look dissimilar to the outcomes for Africa and Asia in the model runs without economic aid.) In this example, there are several policies for minimizing time to meet basic needs and to stay at that level since it can be done immediately; any sensible policy in this context would surely not look like the myopic policy just mentioned.

The surprise, at first blush, is that the outcomes of the model runs do not look ridiculous (as does the myopic policy just described). It is here that the constraints play a most important role. It appears that the authors have constructed the constraints so that it is impossible to have a potlatch policy. The most important variable controlling the distribution of consumption over time is the rate of investment. The runs, however, are constrained within the much too narrow band of 21% to 25% of GNP during the phase before the basic needs are satisfied. This constraint is puzzling, for it certainly has no serious ethical or economic rationale, until it is understood that the myopic policy would drive the investment rate in a myopic direction. Other constraints can be interpreted in a similar manner.

Consequently, it can be argued that the results of the optimization cannot at this point be taken seriously as prescriptions for development. It is imperative that the authors quickly tackle the problem of a more reasonable objective function. I suspect, however, that this will be a most difficult endeavor mainly because of the nature of the constraint set. First, if the researchers continue to use the objective function described in equation (1), they will have difficulties due to a kink at that point where the basic needs are satisfied. More significantly, I think that the underlying constraint set is not a convex set because of the way in which consumption has a restraining effect on population growth.

A second question which is raised by the model is the universality of the particular objective function used. The introduction of life expectancy as a primary variable is explained as follows:

> In the model, life expectancy at birth was selected as the key variable to be maximized, due to the fact that besides being affected by all the endogenous socioeconomic variables of the model, it is a much better indicator of the real conditions of life in a society, than a purely economic index such as the gross product. Moreover, it reflects quite clearly an unequal distribution in a country or region when compared with the GNP per capita.

There are two strands in this argument: first that life expectancy is affected by all the endogenous variables, and second that it is a superior indicator. The first reason is correct, but it is a very dangerous principle to use in an optimizing model. To illustrate the danger, suppose that the true objective function is U (le, qlife) = 4/5 log (le) + 1/5 log (qlife), where U is a preference function, and le and qlife are defined above. Further, let us assume that in societies where development proceeds more or less without control, the two variables (le and qlife) move very closely together. Assume that the model has correctly described the constrain set between them as $(le^2 + qlife^2)^{1/2} = k$, where k is a function of time, labor and capital. The constraints and objective function are shown in Figure 6-1, with the "optimal" solution; e.g., the preference maximizing solution given at (le*, qlife*).

Let us suppose that, within an optimizing framework, we follow the reasoning cited above and use life expectancy as a proxy variable for the true objective function. Clearly, we would end up at point B in Figure 1, with a long but miserable life. On the other hand, if we take the stereotype of the economic criterion function, maximizing the quality of life, we end up at point E with a short but affluent life. This problem is especially acute in optimizing models, where the optimization focuses with single-minded obsession on objectives with high payoffs and ignores completely those with low payoffs. (The problem is compounded if the feasible set is known only imperfectly. The optimal plan will be even more distorted if some of the behavior relations are measured with great error and no account of this is taken in the optimization).

In light of the cautions outlined above, the question arises whether the

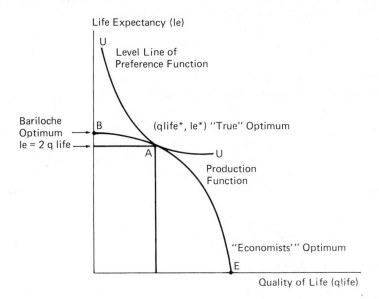

Figure 6-1. The figure shows the danger of using proxy variables in optimization. The true preference function is UU, while the constraint is BAE. A true optimum will lie at A, while "single-minded" or proxy optima will lie at B for the Bariloche optimum and at E for the "economists'" optimum.

Bariloche group has used a distorted objective function. This is obviously a matter of society's preferences, but for my taste they have overestimated the value of pure longevity and underestimated the value of the quality of that longevity. It is much more difficult to construct an objective function with all the aspects of a desirable life style; but if we are to avoid the distortion of looking at single indices (whether GNP or life expectancy) we must do it correctly. The use of GNP (or more properly, a generalized consumption measure) in optimizing programs is open to many objections, most significantly that the usual accounting system is too narrow, rather than it being too broad. If we are to correct for the deficiencies of the GNP, we must include many items which are left out such as leisure, culture, environmental goods, and the like. The Bariloche group has gone in the opposite direction, *leaving out* important variables which usually are believed to enter into economic welfare. For all its shortcomings, I think that some generalized consumption measure (including perhaps physical constraints of the kind used by the Bariloche group *and* correcting for the length of life) should be used instead of the simpler objective function of life expectancy.

A related problem lies in the use of the *share* of consumption in GNP as the index of the quality of life. I cannot imagine how this could occur. Perhaps it comes from the idea of a relative income notion, i.e., that once the basic needs are satisfied, further consumption leads in an addictive fashion to the craving for further goods. (Is this the definition of a consumer society?). Perhaps in some ultimate way, human beings get satiated at some level of consumption, maybe around that presently experienced in the United States or Western Europe; if this is the idea, then it should be introduced explicitly rather than through the share of consumption.

The substance of the Bariloche model represents then a very interesting and novel use of optimization to close the model; i.e., to drive the policy variables. I admit, however, that I am uncertain as to the exact motivation of the optimization. Is it normative-optimizing or behavioral-optimizing? Given the tone of the report, I suspect that it uses optimization as a way of implementing what the Bariloche group regards as a desirable set of objectives; that is, it is normative rather than behavioral in its content. If this is so, then its predictive content only extends to policymakers sharing the Bariloche group's objectives. My guess is that the objective functions of most politicians I know bear little resemblance to those embedded in the Bariloche model.

MULTI-REGION GLOBAL MODELS

A final complication which arises in the introduction of policies into global models is the manner of putting multiple decisionmakers into the same model. Thus in the Bariloche model, there are four regions, and each of the four regions has its own objective function. The decisions are thus completely independent, for there are no trade flows in the model, and each sector is a completely decomposable part of the system.

In other examples, there is true interaction. Thus in the theory of international trade, there are large numbers of producing and consuming agents. Each of these agents maximizes its own objective function, and the outcome is the equilibrium of such a system of equations, if, indeed, one exists.

A similar dichotomy exists in models of the energy sector. Some models (Project Independence and the work of Alan Manne or Wolf Häfele) assume that there is no international trade, thus alleviating the problem of coordination of decisions. Other models, such as Nordhaus', assume free trade, so that the outcome is that corresponding to a competitive allocation.

The recent events on the international energy market suggest the appropriate treatment of relations between regions is a global model. We have experienced nations and regions setting policy variables so as to maximize the preference function of the nations or regions involved. Other regions and nations in turn, adjust their policies to these policies. Thus in 1973 OPEC set the price of oil toward a monopoly price; i.e., the price maximizing OPEC's welfare. Since that time, OECD countries have been adjusting their energy policies to optimize their own regional welfare subject to the behavior—and potential retaliation—of OPEC. More generally, a behavioral hypothesis for policy variables regarding global models would be that each region sets its policy variables so as to maximize the welfare of the region's objective function (or the region's policymakers' objective function, to be more precise) subject to the region's constraints and subject to the hypothesized response functions of other regions. The equilibrium of this going maximization process could be considered a behavioral-optimization outcome.

Such a process is technically a non-cooperative equilibrium—with the Nash equilibrium being a particular case of such a solution. Although it seems a very plausible outcome for the process of multi-region global models, it should also be noted that it introduces very deep game-theoretical problems since the strategies of the different regions are not independent.

CONCLUSIONS

The theme of this paper has been that economic models in general, and global models in particular, must devote more attention to the inclusion of policy variables. Social scientists have in the past confused the normative aspects of policy with the descriptive side, and as a result the stock of equations that describe the behavior of policymakers is slim. Perhaps stable behavioral equations do not exist—and indeed there are good theoretical reasons to suppose that political behavior is more unstable than economic behavior. Nevertheless, if we are to make progress in building models where numerous policy decisions are made, and if we are not to opt out completely, then we must quickly build a stockpile of theoretical models and empirical regularities from which to draw components for the construction of world models.

 *Chapter 7*

Major Accounting Problems for a World Model

Richard Stone

1. INTRODUCTION

Accounting is usually associated with economics, whether it be the economics of a firm, an industry, a country, or the whole world. But other aspects of life on this planet are amenable to an accounting treatment. One is the impact of man's activities on the environment. Another is the growth of the population and its distribution over regions and, within regions, over different sociodemographic categories. In this paper I propose to discuss ways of accounting for these three fundamental aspects of life. In sections 2, 3, and 4 I show that accounting ideas have something to contribute to each of these aspects and sketch out the nature of these contributions. In section 5 I summarize their results and indicate which of them are advanced enough to be incorporated in a world model. Finally, in section 6 I indicate the decisions that the model builder will have to face when it comes to assembling and connecting such vast quantities of information from so many different fields. The paper ends with some general conclusions and a list of works cited.

2. ACCOUNTING FRAMEWORKS: ECONOMICS

Without question, accounting for economic stocks and flows in the regions of the world, as suggested in Leontief (1974), is a formidable task. The best way to see what it entails is to consider the national accounts and their disaggregation.

The Statistical Office of the United Nations has spent many years integrating a wide range of economic statistics into its System of National Accounts (SNA), the latest version of which is contained in UNSO (1968). All the tables I shall use to illustrate this section are taken from the SNA. Although such tables are fairly familiar to social scientists, I propose to set them out and describe their contents in some detail because they are the prototypes of the accounting framework I shall adopt, *mutatis mutandis,* throughout this paper.

a. **Economic Stocks and Flows: The National Accounts.** The main stocks and flows that take place within a national economy and between that economy and the rest of the world can be conveniently presented in terms of four national accounts relating to production (domestic product account), consumption (income and outlay account), accumulation (capital transactions account), and the rest of the world (balance of payments account), together with an account for revaluations and an opening and a closing balance sheet. A numerical example in matrix form, taken from UNSO (1968), is set out in Table 7-1. Here, accounts and balance sheets are represented by row-and-column pairs, with the convention that monetary incomings (in the case of balance sheets, net assets) are shown in the columns.

If we begin with the production account we find in row two the sources of revenue to the productive system: sales to private and public consumers, 210; domestic investment in fixed assets and stocks, 47; and exports, 52. In column two we find two figures: gross value added, composed of income payments to the factors of production *plus* depreciation *plus* indirect taxes *minus* subsidies, that is the gross domestic product, 255; and imports, 54.

In the consumption account we find: the net domestic product, 255 minus 19 (depreciation) equals 236; and factor income (net) received from abroad, 5. The total of this row is the national income *plus* indirect taxes (net) and the uses to which it is put are private and public consumers' expenditure, 210; saving, 27; and gifts, grants and other transfers to the rest of the world (net), 4.

The account for accumulation, together with the revaluations account, connects the opening and closing balance sheets. Thus, in row four, the opening net worth, 693, *plus* saving, 27, *plus* revaluations, 44, give closing net worth, 764.

Table 7-1.   The National Accounts, Including Balance Sheets, in Matrix Form

	1	2	3	4	5	6	7
1. Opening assets, net				693			
2. Production			210	47	52		
3. Consumption		255		-19	5		
4. Accumulation	693		27			44	764
5. The rest of the world		54	4	-1			
6. Revaluations				44			
7. Closing assets, net				764			

Note: In the columns net assets are balanced by net worth. (*Source:* UNSO, 1968.)

Correspondingly, in column four, opening net assets, 693, *plus* net domestic investment, 47 minus 19 equals 28, *plus* net lending abroad, minus 1, (that is, 1 unit was borrowed from abroad in the example), *plus* revaluations, 44 give closing net assets, 764.

The account for the rest of the world, being the last to be discussed, introduces no new entries but simply complements the domestic accounts to form a closed system.

I do not propose to elaborate further on the national accounts, since this is done in great detail in UNSO (1968) and in many national publications.

b. Interindustry Transactions. In Table 7-1 there is only a single production account and, moreover, it is consolidated: all purchases and sales between branches of production are cancelled out so that nothing is recorded at the intersection of row and column two. In fact, such purchases and sales are very large, and they can be brought to light if the single production account is disaggregated into a number of branches to form an input–output table. Many of the problems encountered in constructing such tables are discussed in UNSO (1968, Chapter III; 1973); here I shall summarise them as briefly as possible.

In setting up accounts for different branches of production, it is usual to define these branches by combining establishments into groups, called industries, according to the nature of the goods and services they produce. Each industry has its characteristic range of products, which are used, at least in the first instance, to define product groups, or commodities; but in addition it may produce, in the form of subsidiary products and by-products, commodities characteristic of other industries. With these definitions, the number of industries is equal to the number of commodities and the square submatrix, with industries in the rows and commodities in the columns, usually termed a make matrix, contains off-diagonal elements corresponding to subsidiary products and by-products. An example containing such a submatrix in its top left-hand corner is set out in Table 7-2.

In this example, there are thirteen domestic industries and an equal number of domestic commodities. Each of the thirteen rows at the top of the table shows the composition of the output of one of the industries; and each of the corresponding columns shows the sources (including competitive imports) of one commodity. Columns fourteen through eighteen relate to commodities that cannot be produced domestically and so are complementary to domestic output. The treatment of import duties and commodity taxes is designed to enable commodities to be valued in various ways. The lower part of Table 7-2 shows the destinations of commodity supplies; and the table as a whole is one way of presenting a complete set of commodity accounts.

Industry accounts, based on the same set of data as Table 7-2, are set out in Table 7-3. The upper part of the table shows the gross outputs of the thirteen industries, and the lower part shows the production costs of these industries.

Table 7-2. Sources and Destinations of Commodity Supplies

Columns 1–13 fall under the heading *Competitive commodities*; columns 14–18 fall under the heading *Complementary commodities*.

Sources of Supply	1 Agriculture, forestry, fishing	2 Mining	3 Food, beverages, tobacco	4 Textiles, wearing apparel, leather	5 Rubber, chemicals, petroleum products	6 Basic metal industries	7 Metal products, machinery, equipment	8 Manufacturing n.e.c.	9 Gas, electricity, water	10 Construction	11 Transport and communication	12 Distribution	13 Services	14 Agriculture, forestry, fishing	15 Mining	16 Food, beverages, tobacco	17 Basic metal industries	18 Manufacturing n.e.c.	Commodity taxes, net
1 Agriculture, forestry, fishing	1,695							16											-147
2 Mining		974	3					3	3	1									8
3 Food, beverages, tobacco			3,637				1	1	1										353
4 Textiles, wearing apparel, leather				2,907			2	5	1										105
5 Rubber, chemicals, petroleum products		1	69	8	2,917	1	9	20	61	1		7							63
6 Basic metal industries					12	2,639	58	6	54	1									7
7 Metal products, machinery, equipment						85	7,929	21	3	38									329
8 Manufacturing n.e.c.		4		3	7	1	18	2,983	8	17									85
9 Gas, electricity, water				6	109		3	13	1,187										37
10 Construction						1	6			3,151									3
11 Transport and communication											3,313								33
12 Distribution			27	28	29							3,818							77
13 Services						1	5				1		4,920						583
Producers of government services																			
Producers of private nonprofit services																			
Import duties	25	1	26	21	17	3	41	20											
Imports, c.i.f.	741	129	592	200	423	151	382	419			558		291	457	423	130	204	116	1,288
Total	2,461	1,109	4,354	3,173	3,519	2,882	8,454	3,507	1,318	3,209	3,872	3,825	5,211	457	423	130	204	116	2,824

Destinations of Supply

Intermediate consumption, industries	942	867	819	1,463	2,495	2,478	3,336	2,352	707	1,000	1,668	845	1,340	316	423		204	116	1,613
Intermediate consumption, producers of government services	15	20	26	20	137		534	112	66	197	81	41	385						72
Intermediate consumption, producers of private non-profit services																			
Final consumption in domestic market, households	1,434	192	3,266	1,257	333		796	621	459	312	981	2,800	2,862	141		130			1,159
Increase in inventories	28	-18	48	46	62	116	204	77	-1			29							
Gross fixed capital formation	42	19					1,865	88	86	1,698	110	11	169						59
Exports		29	195	387	492	288	1,719	257	1	2	1,032	99	455						-79
Total	2,461	1,109	4,354	3,173	3,519	2,882	8,454	3,507	1,318	3,209	3,872	3,825	5,211	457	423	130	204	116	2,824

(*Source:* UNSO, 1968.)

Table 7-3.   Industrial Outputs and Costs

			Industries		
		Agri-culture, forestry, fishing	*Mining*	*Food, bever-ages, to-bacco*	*Textiles, wearing apparel, leather*	*Rubber, chem-icals, petro-leum products*
		1	*2*	*3*	*4*	*5*
Gross output at basic values		1,711	984	3,661	2,927	3,087
Commodity taxes, net		-147	8	353	105	63
Gross output at producers' prices		1,564	992	4,014	3,032	3,150
Competitive intermediate inputs						
Agriculture, forestry, fishing	*1*	76		641	211	14
Mining	*2*	3	19	18	25	197
Food, beverages, tobacco	*3*	281		473	4	18
Textiles, wearing apparel, leather	*4*	8	6	12	1,116	64
Rubber, chemicals, petroleum products	*5*	175	33	143	213	784
Basic metal industries	*6*		28	7	2	24
Metal products, machinery, equipment	*7*	73	44	90	62	104
Manufacturing n.e.c.	*8*	12	30	126	40	90
Gas, electricity, water	*9*	12	21	26	28	88
Construction	*10*	51	46	11	18	16
Transport and communication	*11*	69	36	81	62	117
Distribution	*12*	54	20	53	57	57
Services	*13*	56	19	100	78	117
Complementary intermediate inputs						
Agriculture, forestry, fishing	*14*			149	73	94
Mining	*15*					333
Food, beverages, tobacco	*16*					
Basic metals	*17*					
Manufacturing n.e.c.	*18*					19
Commodity taxes, net		13	12	891	21	22
Primary inputs						
Compensation of employees		341	570	436	675	464
Operating surplus		367	50	343	172	370
Consumption of fixed capital		120	50	61	70	95
Indirect taxes, net		-147	8	353	105	63
Total costs		1,564	992	4,014	3,032	3,150

(*Source:* UNSO, 1968.)

				Industries			
Basic metal indus-tries	*Metal products, machinery, equip-ment*	*Manu-fac-turing n.e.c.*	*Gas, elec-tricity, water*	*Con-struction*	*Transport and commu-nication*	*Dis-tribution*	*Ser-vices*
6	7	8	9	10	11	12	12
2,770	8,087	3,044	1,296	3,171	3,317	3,873	4,926
7	329	85	37	3	33	77	583
2,777	8,416	3,129	1,333	3,174	3,350	3,950	5,509
120	24	102	271	34	41	7	6
		4			32	7	
4	59	69	1	8	16	84	16
164	290	174	93	95	133	121	75
812	1,353	17	14	202	15	3	1
101	2,091	111	57	165	217	78	143
30	253	747	17	466	33	203	305
119	98	59	85	7	7	84	71
15	35	16	3	553	58	114	63
117	159	98	47	79	670	98	36
120	120	100	23	54	55	89	43
109	303	155	27	122	76	121	57
73	17						
204							
		97					
10	38	24	41	27	116	142	256
475	2,493	895	295	1,061	1,353	1,616	2,073
232	592	305	105	256	151	984	1,369
65	162	71	217	42	344	122	412
7	329	85	37	3	33	77	583
2,777	8,416	3,129	1,333	3,174	3,350	3,950	5,509

These costs are made up of the cost of intermediate products (including the commodity taxes charged on them) and what in the table are called primary inputs, namely, payments to the factors of production, depreciation, and indirect taxes (net), though in fact the last item does not pay for any kind of input at all. I do not propose to go into the technicalities of the concept and treatment of commodity taxes, which are explained in UNSO (1968), but I ought, perhaps, to say that, despite appearances to the contrary, they are not in fact wrongly named either in this table or in the preceding one.

The first thirteen rows of the lower part of Table 7–3 constitute a form of input–output table that shows the inputs of commodities into industries. It is usually considered desirable to have a table that shows the inputs of commodities into commodities, though industry by industry tables are also sometimes used. In order to construct such tables we must combine this part of Table 7–3 with the make matrix in Table 7–2. This can be done in a number of ways, depending on the assumptions we make about technology, as explained in UNSO (1968, Chapter III). A commodity by commodity matrix of coefficients, derived from Tables 7–2 and 7–3 on what seem the best assumptions, is set out in Table 7–4. The assumptions used to construct Table 7–4 lead to evident, though not very important, absurdities: the negative numbers in row one. They are a small price to pay for the much less plausible values of certain coefficients when alternative assumptions are used.

c. **Changing Input Structures.** The coefficients in an input–output matrix such as Table 7–4, or for that matter in any conceivable input–output matrix, will inevitably represent average input structures; it is impossible to reach a degree of disaggregation that will avoid this. But if we had data for individual establishments, we should soon become aware that different establishments in the same industry usually had widely differing input structures. There are many reasons for this such as: (1) the industry may have a wide range of characteristic products, so that the product mix of different firms may be very different; (2) the age of plant may be different in different establishments, with the typical result that the establishment with new plant will need less labor per unit of output than the establishment with old plant, even though it uses the same amount of raw materials; (3) different processes may be used, for instance electricity can be produced from coal, oil, water power, or nuclear energy; and all these technologies may be found to coexist in a single country; and (4) in highly heterogeneous economies that contain a traditional sector and a modern sector all these factors may operate together to produce great divergencies.

More important in the context of model building, all these factors can change over time, thereby altering the average input structure in many industries. Technical change is likely to play an important role in bringing about these alterations, but so may other considerations such as exogenous changes in relative prices.

Table 7–4. Commodity × Commodity Input–Output Coefficient Matrix

(Basic values)

	Agriculture, forestry, fishing	Mining	Food, beverages, tobacco	Textiles, wearing apparel, leather	Rubber, chemicals, petroleum products	Basic metal industries	Metal products, machinery, equipment	Manufacturing n.e.c.	Gas, electricity, water	Construction	Transport and communication	Distribution	Services
	1	2	3	4	5	6	7	8	9	10	11	12	13
Agriculture, forestry, fishing	1	45	−1	175	73	2	44	2	33	198	11	12	−2	1
Mining	2	1	19	5	8	70			1			10	2	
Food, beverages, tobacco	3	166		129	1	4							1	
Textiles, wearing apparel, leather	4	4	6	3	384	19	1	7	22	1	2	5	19	3
Rubber, chemicals, petroleum products	5	103	34	40	73	254	59	35	57	77	30	40	31	15
Basic metal industries	6		28	2	1	7	299	167	4	21	64	4	1	
Metal products, machinery, equipment	7	43	45	25	21	34	31	263	35	43	52	65	20	29
Manufacturing n.e.c.	8	5	30	34	13	27	10	30	249	13	147	10	53	62
Gas, electricity, water	9	7	22	7	9	30	44	12	19	64	2	2	22	14
Construction	10	30	47	3	6	5	5	3	4	3	176	18	30	13
Transport and communication	11	40	36	22	21	38	43	19	32	37	25	202	25	7
Distribution	12	32	20	15	19	19	44	14	33	19	17	16	23	9
Services	13	33	19	27	27	37	39	37	51	22	39	23	31	12

Direct requirements per 1000 units of final demand calculated on the assumption that $A = B\,[C_1^{-1}(I - \widehat{D_2'\hat{\imath}}) + D_2]$ (Source: UNSO, 1968.)

With our present knowledge, it is virtually impossible to model this complex situation on a countrywide scale and so a number of different methods have to be combined, as outlined in Stone (1976), in an attempt to update and project input-output coefficients. The process can be divided into two stages, each of which can be carried out in several ways.

As regards the first stage, there is usually a considerable amount of current data about particular entries in the table to be updated, data which are more reliable than any estimates we could make. The entries in question should be removed from the table and subtracted from its marginal vectors before any mechanical adjustment method is applied; and they should be added back to the adjusted partial table only at the end. Another method, which can be used, if time series of past values of some of the coefficients are available, is to model the process of change as in CDAE (1968, Chapters II and III), where Wigley made use of a stock adjustment model to trace the substitution of oil for coal in a number of British industries. If a suitable explanatory model cannot be devised, it may be possible to make a trend analysis as in Almon et al. (1974), where a number of examples are given of logistic trends fitted to data for the United States. Finally, it is possible to appeal to industrial, commercial, and technical expertise rather than to statistics, as has been done at Battelle-Columbus and described in Fisher and Chilton (1972).

This brings us to the second stage. Whatever we manage to achieve at the first stage, we shall not be able to construct a completely balanced table of intermediate product flows. To obtain this we need either an adjustment procedure, such as the RAS technique described in Stone (1962) and Bacharach (1970), or some form of programming.

Another approach, which might give better results if it could be followed, would be to set up submodels for multiprocess industries and try to model the future contribution of the different processes to total supply. This modeling would not be of the simple input-output type but would be based, presumably, on some cost minimization technique subject to capacity constraints. The outcome would be a process mix that was in some sense optimal and would provide an average cost structure for the industry as a whole. The general idea is well illustrated by the work of Wigley in CDAE (1968, Chapter V).

d. The Distribution of Income and Wealth. While, as we have just seen, the SNA makes detailed provision for the disaggregation of the domestic product account, it does much less when it comes to the income and outlay account. It deals in some detail with institutional sectors but does not disaggregate the household sector. This limitation is to some extent repaired in UNSO (1972) which sets out proposals for a system of statistics of the distribution of income, consumption, and accumulation consistent with and complementary to the SNA.

Statistics compiled on these lines would provide distributions of income and wealth classified by various criteria: size, household composition, socioeconomic status, and so on. Time series of such statistics would enable us to see how the distributions change but not the detailed movements that result in such changes. For this purpose, we should have to connect successive distributions, that is, we should need information about individual movements from one year-end to the next. Thus, an income recipient initially in a given income group must, over a given year, either remain in that group or move to a different group or cease to exist; conversely, an income recipient finally in a given group must either have been in that group initially or have moved in from a different group or have come into being in the course of that year. This information could be arranged as in Table 7-6, in section 4 a. below; that table relates to sociodemographic categories, but these can easily be substituted with income groups.

Once the data are arranged in this way, it is possible to derive from them a matrix of coefficients, or transition proportions, and hence to make projections by treating the evolution of the distribution as a Markov process, provided a number of fairly restrictive assumptions are satisfied. However, even if such statistics were widely available, which they are not, contemporary efforts to bring about greater equality would, if they persisted, lead to changes in the transition proportions which would be difficult to deduce from any past experience. This is a theme to which we shall return below at several points.

e. Capital Transactions. Most econometric models concentrate on the "real" side of the economy. In the case of capital transactions, this means domestic investment in fixed assets and, while it is usual to model depreciation and saving behavior, little is said about transactions in financial claims and revaluations which, together with saving, connect the opening and closing liabilities of the institutional sectors. The SNA makes provision for all these elements, and the subject is treated in greater detail in UNSO (1974).

In CDAE (1971), Roe presents detailed capital transactions accounts, revaluation accounts and balance sheets for Britain over the years 1957–1966 on lines similar to those proposed in the SNA. Treating sectors and claims as analogous to industries and commodities, he experiments with one of the input–output models of financial transactions suggested in Stone (1966). The results, in the form of matrices of financial multipliers, bring out the considerable degree of financial interdependence in the British economy but are of little value in forecasting because the coefficients are too unstable. This is not very surprising, and in Roe (1972) a number of reasons for this instability are given, which could be investigated statistically.

f. The Balance of Payments Account. Apart from the fact that the balance of payments account may embody the disaggregations made in other accounts, for instance of commodities or financial claims, the type of disaggregation most obviously appropriate to this account is by foreign country or region. Unless the world economy is treated as a single entity, the question of connecting the regions into which it is divided is bound to be a major preoccupation for world model builders. However, this is something best considered when we have worked through the problems that arise in setting up accounting structures for individual countries and come to the question of putting all these structures together.

3. ACCOUNTING FRAMEWORKS: THE ENVIRONMENT

When the word *environment* is uttered nowadays, the echoing word is almost invariably *pollution.* Indeed, quite a number of solid quantitative studies have appeared recently on this subject. But pollution does not by any means exhaust environmental issues. Equally important, in the long run, are the changing uses of land and the changing balance between the demand for and the known reserves of natural resources. Much has been written, as for instance by Ehrlich and Ehrlich (1970), on these issues too, but as far as I am aware nobody has yet found out how to organize all environmental data within a single coherent framework. The Statistical Office of the United Nations has begun work on a system of environmental statistics, but this work is in its early stages and no documents have so far resulted from it. Consequently, in this section I shall not be able to draw on a unified formalisation such as that which underlies the national accounts.

a. **Pollution.** While pollutants, the evils as opposed to the goods produced by an economic system, are not recorded in the national accounts, the costs of abating these pollutants, in so far as they are abated, are recorded. However, they are not usually separated from the other costs incurred in business or government activities. This unsatisfactory state of affairs is beginning to improve, witness the new statistical series on pollution abatement and control recently introduced into the American national accounts by the Bureau of Economic Analysis of the U.S. Department of Commerce. In these tables, three types of pollution are distinguished: air pollution, water pollution, and solid waste; and the costs of abatement and control are in each case allocated to the sector of the economy that actually incurs them. The conceptual and statistical issues that arise in constructing these tables are described in Cremeans (1975) and Cremeans and Segel (1975).

The outcome of the Bureau's work is an explicit and fairly comprehensive recording of abatement costs. But this is not the end of the story. While it is useful to know the cost of any abatement that is taking place, it would also be interesting to know the cost of eliminating pollution altogether. This question is tackled in Leontief (1970), where an accounting framework is proposed for handling pollutants in terms of an extended input–output matrix, partitioned into four quadrants, with an equal number of additional rows and columns. Each new row shows the quantities of a particular pollutant emitted by the various branches of production, including the new branches designed to abate pollution; and each new column shows the input structure of one of these "antipollution" branches. On the assumption that each branch, whether traditional or new, is required to have all the pollutants for which it is directly responsible abated by the appropriate new branch, emissions can be regarded as a measure of the input of abatement services and so, naturally, appear in the input structure of all branches. An application of this scheme to the problem of air pollution is given in Leontief and Ford (1972).

This is a somewhat schematic account of Leontief's ideas, and I hope it is not misleading. If the matter were handled exactly as I have suggested, it would be necessary not only to measure the input structures of the new abatement services but also to remove from the input structures of the traditional industries any abatement costs incurred by them. I do not propose to discuss how this cost-accounting problem could best be solved in practice. Further, much pollution arises from consumption rather than production, but I do not think that this fact makes many difficulties for Leontief's conceptual scheme.

Since the abatement of pollution requires resources and since these are limited, it is reasonable to ask whether complete elimination is in the best interests of society. Leontief's scheme does not enable us to answer this question, but it is helpful in assessing the situation because it enables us to estimate the changes in production levels and in costs that would follow throughout the economy from any degree of abatement of any particular pollutant. A numerical illustration of how to calculate the optimal level of abatement is given in Stone (1972). An important change of emphasis is made in Meade (1972), where it is pointed out that the consumer is likely to think not so much of the abatement itself as of its product (cleaner air, cleaner water, and so on) and that this is a variable depending on the amounts of pollutants emitted.

Finally, I should like to mention the Strategic Environmental Assessment System (SEAS), which has been developed since 1972 by the Washington Environmental Research Center for the U.S. Environmental Protection Agency. It is intended for use in forecasting the state of the environment and consists of a set of coordinated modules, or submodels, that can be constructed separately on a common plan and then assembled. Thus the national interindustry economic forecasting model is the one described in Almon and others (1974), and other modules handle the generation of production residuals, the regionalisation of national emissions, abatement cost calculations, and so on. A general outline of the system is given in USEPA (1974) and the use of input–output in it is described in Ayres, Noble, and Stern (1974).

b. Land Use. Although I do not think it is usual to do so, the changing patterns of land use, like the changing patterns of income distribution, could be recorded and analyzed in terms of the standard matrix illustrated in Table 7-6, in section 4 a. below. In this case, units of area would take the place of human beings, and types of land use would take the place of sociodemographic categories. The analogue of births and deaths (the outside world in Table 7-6) would not normally be important, although land too may appear and disappear; for example, coastlines are continually modified by the encroachment and recession of the sea. By recording flows from one type of use to another, this data system would enable us to see not only the net changes in land use (calculable as the differences between successive stock vectors) but also, more specifically, which type of use was gaining land from which.

It is evident that the same method could be applied to many other entities: buildings, for instance. In this case, births and deaths would be represented by constructions and demolitions; and the other flows would take the form either of conversions (from apartment to office, say) or of structural and other improvements and disimprovements.

c. Natural Resources. There are many natural resources, like metals and fossil fuels, that some people think are in danger of exhaustion in a matter of decades, though others consider these fears greatly exaggerated if not wholly groundless. However this may be, the subject ought to be taken into account in a world model, since any large shift in the balance of supply and demand is likely to affect both availabilities and prices.

Table 7-5 contains a highly simplified accounting framework for the product of one of the extraction industries, say a metal. We start with an opening stock of 1000 units, which includes both visible stocks and known reserves. Of this, 10 units are mined, leaving 990 units to form a component of the closing stock. Of the 10 units mined, 9 are transferred to the metal industry for fabrication and 1 unit is added to the stocks of the mining industry. Of the 9 units fabricated, 6 are transferred to consumers, intermediate and final, 1 unit is transferred to reclaimers in the form of scrap, 1 unit is "extinguished," that is cannot be reclaimed or recycled in any form, and 1 unit is added to the metal

Table 7-5. Accounting Framework for the Product of an Extraction Industry

	Extraction	Fabrication	Consumption	Reclamation	Extinction	Closing stock	Totals
	1	2	3	4	5	6	
1. Extraction		9				1	10
2. Fabrication			6	1	1	1	9
3. Consumption			3	4		−1	6
4. Reclamation					1	3	4
5. Discovery						13	13
6. Opening stock	10					990	1000
Totals	10	9	6	4	6	1007	

industry's stocks. The 6 units consumed are matched by 3 units transferred to reclaimers, possibly from products replaced by the new purchases, 4 units extinguished and a reduction of 1 unit in consumers' stocks. Of the 4 units reclaimed, 1 is extinguished and 3 are added to stock. Apart from these transformations, 13 units of new reserves are discovered during the year. The increase in stocks is equal to discoveries minus extinctions, that is 7 units, as can be seen by adding up the components in column six and comparing this total with the opening stock.

Table 7-5 is only a first, rough attempt to bring together in an accounting form the main elements in the determination of changes in visible stocks and known reserves of natural resources. Here I do not go beyond accounting, though it seems to me that with a little more thought and a study of the existing literature, the scheme I have outlined could be adapted to the purposes of analysis and forecasting. In so doing, however, we should have to bear in mind that there are several important exogenous variables: the pace of new discoveries and their cost; and the extent of reclamation, which can vary enormously depending on public attitudes toward what I have called extinctions.

4. ACCOUNTING FRAMEWORKS: SOCIAL DEMOGRAPHY

By social demography I mean the study of the size, composition, and growth of a population when the individuals in it are classified not only by the demographic categories of sex and age but also by social categories reflecting characteristics drawn from such fields as education, employment, or health. This subject has been studied in recent years by a group convened by the Statistical Office of the United Nations to formulate a System of Social and Demographic Statistics (SSDS), and a report was published last year as UNSO (1975). Subsection a below describes the standard matrix of this system in a particular field of application.

Although the SSDS has a fairly wide coverage, there are certain areas, one of them being politics, which the group did not think were ripe for systematization for official statistical purposes. Despite earlier work and, in particular, the very interesting studies published in Alker, Deutsch, and Stoetzel (1973) it was felt "that this complex subject cannot easily be laid out in terms of statistics and quantitative analysis," although "it seems reasonable to suppose that the next two decades will see considerable advances in the application of quantitative methods to political problems." In this section, I make two excursions into this domain: one, in subsection b, relates to the recording of changes in social and political attitudes; and the other, in subsection c, to individual perceptions of the connectedness of world problems.

a. **Human Stocks and Flows: The Standard Matrix.** If we take the individual human being rather than the dollar or the pound as our unit of account, we can relate human stocks and flows within an accounting framework similar, though not identical, to that used for the national accounts. This framework has already been mentioned twice in this paper, first, in connection with the distribution of income and second, in our discussion of the changing patterns of land use. A simple numerical example, taken from UNSO (1975), is set out in Table 7-6.

In Table 7-6, the population is divided into nine categories, or states, which represent stages in a sequence from infancy, through various states of education and employment, to retirement. The numbers in each state at the beginning of the year appear in the final row of the table in columns one to nine and the corresponding numbers at the end of the year appear in the final column, rows one to nine. Thus from column one we see that there were 2033.2 small children who had not yet gone to school at the beginning of the year; of these, 1603.2 remained in their initial state, that is at home, throughout the year, 411.8 went to nursery and primary schools, 8.3 went to secondary or special schools and the remainder, 10.9, left our country through death. From row one, we see that by the end of the year the corresponding total was 2037.8 composed of the 1603.2 who remained throughout the year in their initial state and 435.6 new entrants, through birth and net immigration. The remaining columns and rows can be given a similar interpretation.

If we ignore the final row and column of Table 7-6, which contain respectively the opening and closing stocks of the population classified by state, the remainder of the table forms a partitioned matrix in which the population is divided into four groups. First, those in the scalar submatrix at the intersection of row and column 0 (zero in this example) arrived in our country after the year had begun and left it before the year had ended and so are not recorded in either the opening or the closing stock. Granted that the table does not attempt to record visitors (as opposed to migrants), the zero is clearly a mistake, since a large proportion of infant deaths take place in the first few months of life; in fact, about 8.3 of the deaths shown in row 0, column one, and an equal number of the births and net immigrants shown in row one, column 0, should be transferred to the scalar submatrix. Second, those in the submatrix at the intersection of row 0 and columns one to nine were present in our country at the beginning of the year but not at the end of the year and so are recorded in the opening but not in the closing stock. Third, those in the submatrix at the intersection of rows one to nine and column 0 were present in our country at the end of the year but not at the beginning, and so are recorded in the closing but not in the opening stock. Finally, those in the large square submatrix at the intersection of rows and columns one to nine were present at both dates and so are recorded in both stocks. These statements presuppose that migrations are recorded gross; we have seen, however, that in Table 7-6 they are in fact recorded as net immigrants, and this implies that all the numbers in row and column 0, and, of course, in the final row and column as well, should be increased by the number of emigrants in the relevant category.

Table 7-6. The Standard Sociodemographic Matrix, Illustrated by the Sequence of Learning, Earning, and Inactivity

Final state	Initial state										Numbers in final states
	0	1	2	3	4	5	6	7	8	9	
				(Thousands)							
0 Outside world		10.9	1.1	0.5	0.1		0.1	1.2	89.8	178.6	282.3
1 Preschool	435.6	1603.2									2037.8
2 Nursery and primary schools	-4.0	411.8	2055.9								2463.7
3 Secondary and special schools	-1.5	8.3	325.4	1327.9							1660.1
4 Further education	0.2			24.7	43.7		0.9		43.6		113.1
5 Teacher training colleges				4.4	0.7	13.5	0.2	1.4	5.5		25.7
6 Universities	1.5			23.8	2.2		75.8		12.3		115.6
7 Teachers					0.3	7.6	4.1	192.9	0.6		205.5
8 Other employment	18.2			274.8	56.7	1.2	23.5	0.6	14414.5		14789.5
9 Home and retirement				0.1				2.1	162.4	2191.9	2356.5
Numbers in initial states	450.0	2033.2	2382.4	1656.2	103.7	22.3	104.6	198.2	14728.7	2370.5	24049.8

(Source: UNSO, 1975.)

If we treat column 0, rows one to nine, as an exogenous vector and form a matrix of transition proportions by dividing the elements in the columns of the matrix of survivors by the corresponding elements in the opening stock, it is not difficult to see that we can form a set of linear equations connecting the closing stock vector with the opening stock vector and the exogenous vector of new entrants. If the population were in stationary equilibrium, the closing stock vector would be equal to the opening stock vector, and the equations would take the form of an open Leontief model: the population stock vector would be a matrix transform of the vector of new entrants. The price equation corresponding to this quantity equation would enable us to connect the sociodemographic accounts to the economic accounts at many points. These simple models are developed and illustrated in Stone (1973b) and UNSO (1975).

Many difficulties are encountered in applying these models, and one in particular is shared with economic input–output analysis, namely, the systematic variation over time of some of the coefficients. An attempt to handle this problem by means of logistic trend analysis is given in Stone (1973a). Although I should not now use the method of trend fitting adopted there, the basic difficulty described would almost certainly arise were a more efficient method to be used.

b. Social and Political Attitudes. It seems fairly certain that, whatever takes place over the next generation, it will not be played out against a fixed background of social and political attitudes. In discussing these attitudes, it is perhaps useful to distinguish between the "activists," thirsting after various kinds of change, and the "silent majority" who stand by traditional values, whatever form these values may take in different countries. If the silent majority maintain their opinions, the activists are not very likely to get anywhere, because they will not be able to assemble a critical mass of opinion in favor of their views; they will remain a disaffected but impotent minority. But if, for whatever reason, the traditional values of the silent majority can be systematically eroded, then the chances of the activists building up a critical mass of sympathetic opinion are greatly strengthened and what is possible and impossible in the social and economic spheres is radically changed.

Accordingly, in building a world model, or for that matter a national model, for long-term projections, consideration ought to be given not only to economic, environmental, and sociodemographic changes, but also to changes in social and political attitudes. Economic models, however ambitious, are not very explicit on this question, but implicitly they seem to assume either that attitudes do not change or that, if they do, these changes can be ignored.

How then are we to measure changes in attitudes? Public opinion polls provide information on the attitudes of samples of respondents to various issues of social and political interest. Thus respondents might be asked to place their opinions on a scale varying from "highly favourable" to "highly unfavourable." A time series of such surveys shows whether, on some issue, public opinion is shifting, fluctuating, or stable. By incorporating a retrospective question about the respondents' attitudes at the time of the preceding survey, we could link successive surveys together and so apply the kind of analysis indicated in the preceding subsection. An attitude transition matrix might be approximately diagonal, indicating that existing divergences of attitude would tend to persist; or it might be upper or lower triangular, indicating that in the end everyone would come to take a highly favourable or a highly unfavourable attitude; or it might be more general, with nonzero entries on either side of the diagonal, in which case the implicit tendencies to change would not be obvious but would have to be worked out by calculating the dominant characteristic vector of the matrix. Of course, the transition matrix might not even be stable, in which case tendencies to change would themselves change. By dividing the sample up into groups, we could learn something about the segments of society that were contributing most to any change of attitude.

c. **Perceptions of World Problems.** A point of departure in the study of world problems is to identify and define issues generally considered problematical, at least in certain societies. A second stage is to see if any patterns emerge in respondents' perceptions of the influence that the elements of a given set of such problems exert on one another. The main objective at this stage is to find out how far problems are seen to be connected and how far they can be put in a hierarchy, those lower down being thought to result from the failure to solve those higher up.

This subject has been investigated at Battelle–Geneva and the analytical tools used are described in Fontela and Gabus (1974). Respondents are given a set of problems and asked to indicate the direct influence that they believe each problem exerts on each of the others, measured on a scale running by integers from zero to four. The answers can be arranged in a matrix, of the same order as the number of problems, in which the element in row j and column k measures the strength of the influence of problem j on problem k. If this matrix is normalized by multiplying all its elements by the reciprocal of the largest row sum, it is possible to form a Leontief inverse from it. If the normalized matrix is taken as a measure of the direct effects, this matrix, postmultiplied by its Leontief inverse, measures the direct and indirect effects.

The row and column sums of this matrix product enable the problems to be arranged in hierarchies according to (1) the degree of influence the respondent believes them to exert, directly or indirectly, on other problems and (2) the degree of influence the respondent believes them to undergo, directly or indirectly, from other problems.

Many methods, which I shall not describe, can be applied to information organized in this way in attempts to detect similarities and dissimilarities in the perception of world problems.

5. CHOOSING THE PIECES

I have taken a very broad view of what can be considered accounting problems and have tried to show that an orderly presentation of incomings and outgoings, inward and outward flows, influences exerted and undergone, and an explicit treatment of the relationships between flows and stocks have something to contribute in almost all the main areas discussed in connection with world model building.

In saying this, it is no part of my message to suggest that all the areas I have mentioned ought to be tackled by the meticulous and heavily data-demanding methods I have outlined. Indeed, for the time being it would manifestly be impossible, with some exceptions, to use these methods, either because the data do not exist at all or because, even where they do exist, we have almost no practical experience of using them in the ways suggested above. In such cases we must fall back on less demanding methods.

Economics is clearly the field from which the most can be expected from accounting methods in the short run, particularly with regard to sections 2 a and b above. The *Yearbook of National Accounts Statistics* UNSO (1957-) contains national accounting data in as far as possible a standard form; and UNSO (1973) shows the range of countries for which comprehensive input–output tables have been compiled. As regards section 2 c, many developed countries update and project their input–output tables, but standard practices have not been formulated in this area. Much less can be expected with regard to sections 2 d, e, and f.

As regards section 3 a, I should have expected that few systematic data were available, though Leontief (1974) suggests that this expectation may be unduly pessimistic. As regards sections 3 b and c, a great deal of information is undoubtedly available, but how complete it is and how far it is suited to the analytical needs of a world model, I cannot say.

As regards section 4 a, a great deal of demographic data exist, though, as in the case of economic data, they vary greatly in comprehensiveness and reliability. In the main social areas, such as education, employment, and health, there is a considerable amount of information on stocks but very little on flows. I know almost nothing of the position as regards sections 4 b and c. Although I am aware that public opinion polls have been conducted in some countries for many years, I do not know of any substantial body of data which indicates trends and shifts of opinion in different parts of the world on topics relevant to a world model. However, this is not my field, and I am looking forward to learning how political scientists propose to handle these issues.

My conclusion on the topics discussed in sections 2, 3, and 4 is that in a number of important areas, in particular 2 a, 2 b, 3 a, and 4 a, the accounting problems are reasonably well understood and in some of them the data currently available would probably be sufficient to support a world model; but in other areas, simpler methods would have to be adopted in the short run. These remarks refer to the problems of assembling the pieces (national accounts, input–output tables, and the like for individual countries, not to the problems of connecting them within countries or of connecting countries together to form regions. I shall discuss these subjects in the next section.

Before I do this, however, there are a few general points to be made about the relatively satisfactory pieces like the national accounts.

In the first place, as I have said, even where data are widely available, they are almost never available for all countries. If the missing countries are small Pacific islands, it probably does not matter very much; but if one of them is mainland China, with about one-fifth of the world's population, the position is rather different. So here we have a choice between defining the world as made up of the countries for which we have "adequate" data or "guestimating" the missing bits.

In the second place, in discussing the national accounts I have referred repeatedly to the SNA. This system is widely used but not in the communist countries, which organize their national accounts, as described in UNSO (1971), according to the principles of the system of balances of the national economy or material products system, usually abbreviated to MPS. In Stone (1968), it is shown that the SNA can be transformed into the MPS and vice versa; but this requires the isolation of specific items, and so would be difficult to carry out without the cooperation of the countries concerned. So here we have a choice between making the transformations or devising two variants of the model, each capable of contributing to a common outcome.

In the third place, the national accounts, and the same could be said of most other coordinated bodies of statistics, are based on incomplete, inconsistent, and in some degree unreliable sources. The usual response to this problem is to recognize the inconsistencies and then sweep them under the carpet or, to be more precise, decide to alter one estimate to agree with another although it is perfectly well known that both are subject to error. I have been campaigning on and off for over thirty years for applying to this problem a well-known statistical adjustment procedure based on subjective estimates of error; my latest contribution to this monologue is in Stone (1975). So here we have a choice between carrying out the adjustments or sweeping the problem under the carpet. I expect the latter procedure to prevail; and perhaps it should, in the context of a world model, since if the model builders undertook the task for all the countries of the world, they would probably do it badly, and in any case would be able to do nothing else for many years.

This brings us to the subject of putting the pieces together.

6. PUTTING THE PIECES TOGETHER

This subject can be divided into two quite separate questions: (a) connecting the pieces within a single country; and (b) connecting the countries to form regions and expressing the data for regions in comparable units.

a. Connections within Countries. The SSDS, UNSO (1975), has a good deal to say not only about the connections between different branches of social demography, such as education and health, but also about the connections between sociodemographic categories and the economic accounts. Here the emphasis is on common classifications which, for instance, would enable student numbers in different parts of an educational system to be matched with the corresponding costs or would enable expenditures on social benefits to be matched with the number of recipients in different social groups.

A constructed example of the combination of demographic and economic accounts is given in Stone (1970a). People are assumed to have job preferences which respond to relative wage rates, and consumption preferences which respond to incomes and relative prices. In the very simple case given, it is not difficult to work out the wage rates, prices, and income distribution which will balance supply and demand in both factor and goods markets. This problem of integrating the two sets of accounts is discussed independently and in a much more developed form in Schinnar (1974) and in Cooper and Schinnar (1975).

b. Connections between Countries. Models which involve the aggregation of economic data from different countries raise the question of how to convert the information expressed in local currency units to a common unit of account. On the assumption that what we are mainly trying to combine are constant-price series, the simplest answer is to convert them all to a common currency, say dollars, by using the exchange rates of the base year. This is probably adequate for aggregation purposes, since exchange rates are being used to weight the component series and index numbers are not usually very sensitive to small variations in the weights.

However, as is well known, exchange rates are an unreliable guide to the relative purchasing power of currencies, and it is desirable therefore to take into account, as far as possible, the work that has been done on international comparisons by means of the construction of index numbers between countries. The latest large-scale research effort in this area, reported in Kravis et al. (1975), is Phase One of the United Nations International Comparison Project. The main results relate to ten countries in 1970; and further volumes are in preparation.

Thus, while we may expect eventually a wide country coverage from this project, the method involves many technical difficulties and is extremely demanding of data. Accordingly, attention should also be given to the regression methods proposed in Beckerman (1966) and Beckerman and Bacon (1966) for extending the results of the index number method of comparison to countries where it proves impossible to apply this method directly.

Quite apart from the difficulties of reconciling currency units, there is an even more pervasive practical problem which I shall do no more than mention here. This is the problem caused by differences in institutional arrangements: it is not a simple matter to combine the educational statistics of England and Wales with those of Scotland, or those of the French-speaking and German-speaking cantons of Switzerland. As I see it, there are two ways of coping with this problem. One is to rest content with highly aggregated variables. The other is to devise a classification system, such as the International Standard Classification of Education, UNESCO (1974), which does not rely on institutional criteria of classification but into which the institutions of different countries can be fitted approximately. I shall not pursue this subject any further, since it would require another paper at least as long as this one.

7. CONCLUSIONS

In my view, accounting problems are of three types. There is the intellectual (much as I dislike this word, it is the correct one in this case) type of problem, which bears on the formulation of the concepts, definitions, and classifications needed in assembling large masses of data into a coherent whole. There is the practical type of problem, which concerns the collection, selection and harmonization of these data. And there is the emotional type of problem, which arises from likes and dislikes for certain categories of data, and taxes the model builder's ingenuity with biased and incomplete information.

If this view is correct, then I think that our main headache in constructing and filling in the accounting framework for a world model will not come from the intellectual side: without wishing to exaggerate achievements in social accounting, I do not think it can be said that we do not know how to set up economic or sociodemographic accounts adequate to the needs of large-scale models, or that we do not know how to disaggregate these accounts so as to accommodate all the detail that might be required. Our troubles will come much more from the practical and the emotional sides.

On the practical side, as I have already said, we shall have to deal with a large number of countries at very different stages of statistical development. Although no country produces all the information we should like in a consistent and reliable form, a few do approximate this ideal, at least in some area; but the majority are still far removed from it. This being the case, how can we compensate for the uneven development of statistical systems in different parts of the world? If we exclude from our model the badly documented countries, we shall have to leave out a large proportion of the world's population. But if we try to repair the gaps and inconsistencies ourselves, I fear we shall find either that the task is beyond our strength or that the results of our work are disappointing because its statistical base is too shaky.

It might be argued that if the model were limited to the economic and strictly demographic aspects of the world, the results might not be too disappointing, since economic and demographic statistics are already fairly well developed, so that the gaps could be filled in without too much inaccuracy. Perhaps this is true if all we want is an economic and demographic representation of the world as it is now. But if we are interested in projections, then, as an economist who has been convinced for many years that social influences should play a bigger role in "economic" models, I should like to question whether we have yet got the balance of our variables right.

Let me take an example among many. In times when predominant opinions are comparatively stable, it is reasonable enough to think of the economy as driven by its own mechanism against a barely changing backcloth of social attitudes. Thus, not so long ago it was generally believed that the purpose of production was to produce goods and services and incidentally provide people with employment and incomes, and economic projections were based on this belief. But if it comes to be believed that the purpose of production is to provide people with employment and incomes and incidentally produce goods and services, we can be pretty sure that economic systems will cease to work in the way we are accustomed to. A model that did not reflect such possible changes in attitudes might be positively misleading.

I shall go further. Let us suppose that we have enough information on current opinions all over the world to introduce them as one of the determining variables in our model, thereby getting some idea of possible future changes. But will these changes in fact occur? And if they do, how widespread and how long lasting will they be? Which countries will accept them, which reject them, and which ignore them? Revolutions come and go, national characteristics seem to persist and, when subjected to revolutionary ideas, to have a remarkable capacity for transforming these ideas in their own image. I need go no further than mention the national transformations of Christianity. It should not be impossible to devise a quantitative presentation of the permanent and the impermanent elements in the attitudes of different peoples through history.

These are all practical problems. They are serious but not, in principle, insoluble. Insofar as the gaps are due to the uneven development of statistical systems in different parts of the world, they could be repaired by a proper infusion of training and money. Insofar as they are due to the uneven development of the relevant subject areas, all that is needed is for the interest and energies of social scientists and historians to be channelled towards a quantitative approach to their subject: once these scientists had set up the appropriate framework, the data would flow in like pins towards a magnet, as has happened with national accounts statistics in the last thirty years. These developments would take patience and time, but they are not inconceivable.

On the emotional side, the problems are more intractable and can never be completely surmounted. There will always be countries that refuse to publish statistics on certain social phenomena, such as illiteracy, unemployment, or crime, because they consider them damaging to national prestige; politicians who veto the introduction of certain questions, such as race, religion, marital status, and what have you, in the census; businessmen who withhold information for reasons of commercial rivalry. Indeed, fears of "planning" on the part of the business community have on many occasions prevented improvements in the censuses of production and distribution; in the United States in the early 1950s, such fears succeeded in bringing official work on the compilation of input–output statistics to a halt for several years. Many other examples could be given of prides and prejudices that result in our knowledge of the world being less complete and less objective than it might be.

These considerations make me somewhat sceptical of the reliability of the results we might obtain from a world model at the present time. But this does not lead me to the conclusion that work on such models ought to be discouraged; quite the reverse. There is something rather foolish in the view that ideas should be developed only if we can see our way to their immediate application. Most ideas take time to develop, and if we do not make a start, we put off the moment when we can expect to reap a reward. And, during the development period, the work we are able to accomplish helps to extend and systematize some of the partial data and analyses on which, in the first instance, the formulation of policies will in any case have to rely.

8. A LIST OF WORKS CITED

Alker, Hayward R., Karl W. Deutsch, and Antoine H. Stoetzel (1973). *Mathematical Approaches to Politics*. Amsterdam: Elsevier, 1973.

Almon, Clopper, Jr. et al. (1974). *1985: Interindustry Forecasts of the American Economy*. Lexington, Mass.: D.C. Heath and Co. Lexington Books, 1974.

Ayres, R.U., S.B. Noble, and M.O. Stern (1974). "Input–Output in Environmental Protection Agency's Strategic Environmental Assessment System (SEAS)." Vienna: Paper presented at the Sixth International Conference on Input–Output Techniques, Mimeo. 1974.

Bacharach, Michael (1970). *Biproportional Matrices and Input–Output Change*. Cambridge: At the University Press, 1970.

Beckerman, Wilfred (1966). *International Comparisons of Real Incomes*. Paris: Development Centre, OECD, 1966.

Beckerman, Wilfred, and Robert Bacon (1966). "International Comparisons of Income Levels: A Suggested New Measure." *The Economic Journal,* 76: 303 (1966), pp. 519–36.

Cambridge, Department of Applied Economics (1968). *The Demand for Fuel, 1948-1975*. No. 8 in *A Programme for Growth*. London: Chapman and Hall, 1968.

Cambridge, Department of Applied Economics (1971). *The Financial Inter-*

dependence of the Economy, 1957–1966. No. 11 in *A Programme for Growth.* London: Chapman and Hall, 1971.

Cooper, W.W., and Arie Schinnar (1975). *A Model for Demographic Mobility Analysis under Patterns of Efficient Employment.* Pittsburgh: Carnegie-Mellon University, Institute of Physical Planning, Report No. 60, mimeo., 1975.

Cremeans, John E. (1975). "Conceptual and Statistical Issues in Developing Environmental Measures—Recent U.S. Experience." Aulanko: Paper prepared for the IARIW conference, 1975.

Cremeans, John E., and Frank W. Segel (1975). "National Expenditures for Pollution Abatement and Control, 1972." *Survey of Current Business,* 55:2 (1975), pp. 8–11, 35.

Ehrlich, Paul R. and Anne H. (1970). *Population, Resources, Environment.* San Francisco: W.H. Freeman, 1970.

Fisher, W. Halder, and Cecil H. Chilton (1972). "Developing Ex Ante Input–Output Flow and Capital Coefficients." *Input–Output Techniques* (ed. A. Brody and A.P. Carter), Amsterdam: North Holland, 1972.

Fontela, Emilio and André Gabus (1974). *Structural Analysis of the World Problematique.* Geneva: Battelle, Geneva Research Centre, 1974.

Kravis, Irving B. et al. (1975). *A System of International Comparisons of Gross Product and Purchasing Power.* United Nations International Comparison Project: Phase One. Baltimore: Johns Hopkins University Press, 1975.

Leontief, Wassily W. (1970). "Environmental Repercussions and the Economic Structure: An Input–Output Approach." *A Challenge to Social Scientists* (ed. Shigeto Tsuru), Tokyo: Asahi, 1970. Reprinted in *The Review of Economics and Statistics,* 52:3, (1970), pp. 262–71.

Leontief, Wassily W. (1974). "Structure of the World Economy: Outline of a Simple Input–Output Formulation." *American Economic Review,* 64:6 (1974), pp. 823–34.

Leontief, Wassily W., and Daniel Ford (1972). "Air Pollution and the Economic Structure: Empirical Results of Input–Output Computations." *Input–Output Techniques* (ed. A. Brody and A.P. Carter), Amsterdam: North Holland, 1972.

Meade, J.E. (1972). "Citizens' Demands for a Clean Environment." *L'industria,* no.3/4, 1972, pp. 145–52.

Roe, Alan R. (1972). "Enforcement of the Balance-Sheet Identity in Financial Analysis." *Input–Output Techniques* (ed. A Brody and A.P. Carter), Amsterdam: North Holland, 1972.

Schinnar, Arie (1974). *A Multi-Dimensional Accounting Model for Demographic and Economic Planning Interactions.* Pittsburgh: Carnegie-Mellon University, Institute of Physical Planning, Report no. 52, mimeo., 1974.

Stone, Richard (1962). "Multiple Classifications in Social Accounting." *Bulletin of the International Statistical Institute,* 39:3 (1962), pp. 215–33.

Stone, Richard (1966). "The Social Accounts from a Consumer's Point of View." *The Review of Income and Wealth,* 12:1 (1966), pp. 1–33.

Stone, Richard (1968). "A Comparison of the SNA and the MPS." Warsaw: Paper presented at the Symposium on National Accounts and Balances, 1968. In Stone (1970b).

Stone, Richard (1970a). "Economic and Demographic Accounts and the Distribution of Income." Novosibirsk: Paper presented at the Symposium on National Economic Modelling, 1970. Russian translation: *Economical and Mathematical Methods*, 7:5 (1971), pp. 658–66. English version: *Acta Oeconomica*, 11:2–3 (1973), pp. 165–76.

Stone, Richard (1970b). *Mathematical Models of the Economy and Other Essays.* London: Chapman and Hall, 1970.

Stone, Richard (1972). "The Evaluation of Pollution: Balancing Gains and Losses." *Minerva*, 10:3 (1972), pp. 412–25.

Stone, Richard (1973a). "A System of Social Matrices." *The Review of Income and Wealth*, 19:2 (1973), pp. 143–66.

Stone, Richard (1973b). "Transition and Admission Models in Social Demography." *Social Science Research*, 2:2 (1973), pp. 185–230; also in *Social Indicator Models* (ed. K.C. Land and S. Spilerman), New York: Russell Sage Foundation, 1975.

Stone, Richard (1975). Direct and Indirect Constraints in the Adjustment of Observations. *Nasjonalregnskap, Modeller og Analyse* (essays in honour of Odd Aukrust), Oslo: Statistisk Sentralbyrå, 1975.

Stone, Richard (1976). "The Expanding Frontiers of Input–Output Analysis." *Bulletin of the International Statistical Institute*, vol. XLVI, bk. 1, 1976.

United Nations, Statistical Office (1957-). *Yearbook of National Accounts Statistics.* New York: United Nations, annually.

United Nations, Statistical Office (1968). *A System of National Accounts.* Studies in Methods, Series F, No. 2, Revision 3. New York: United Nations, 1968.

United Nations, Statistical Office (1971). *Basic Principles of the System of Balances of the National Economy.* Studies in methods, Series F, No. 17. New York: United Nations, 1971.

United Nations, Statistical Office (1972). *A Draft System of Statistics of the Distribution of Income, Consumption and Accumulation.* E/CN.3/425, February 3, 1972. New York: United Nations, mimeo.

United Nations, Statistical Office (1973). *Input–Output Tables and Analysis.* Studies in Methods, Series F, No. 14, Revision 1. New York: United Nations. 1973.

United Nations, Statistical Office (1974). "Draft International Guidelines on the National and Sector Balance-Sheets and Reconciliation Accounts of the SNA." E/CN.3/460, New York: United Nations, July 24, 1974. mimeo.

United Nations, Statistical Office (1975). *Towards a System of Social and Demographic Statistics.* Studies in Methods, Series F, No. 18. New York: United Nations, 1975.

UNESCO (1974). *International Standard Classification of Education (ISCED). Three Stage Classification System: 1974.* Com. 74/ISCED/3. Paris: UNESCO, 1974.

United States Environmental Protection Agency (1974). *Strategic Environmental Assessment System (SEAS).* Washington, D.C.: United States Environmental Protection Agency, 1974.

 *Chapter 8*

Discussion on Accounting Approaches
among Walter Isard, Anatol Rapoport,
Otto Eckstein, and Hayward R. Alker, Jr.

1. WALTER ISARD

I find myself in full agreement with Professor Stone's approaches.

However, I think I can add a few points, and hope to indicate a major direction for fruitful research.

A first minor point concerns the environmental data base that Professor Stone talks about, which I think is much more extensive than he has led us to believe. There is a tremendous amount of data compiled here in the United States with a potential for widespread application, for example, to power plants in Poland, to the iron and steel industry in India, and to many industrial sectors in regions all over the world. This comprehensive data base can easily be extended over the next two or three years. I think the same is true for obtaining data that would permit the breakdown of the household sector, by labor force and occupation, for example. However, I do not want to talk about these little things.

One point does seem worthy of major note. I have the impression that Professor Stone perhaps is seeking more precision and accuracy than is warranted in terms of the big assumptions that must go into our world order models. Therefore, it might be justifiable to use some other approaches that utilize less precise data but can embody larger chunks of the real world. For example, I am thinking of the balanced regional input–output approach that Leontief and I have used in the United Sates where, in spite of the fact that each region has different production coefficients and a substantial variance in industry structure, it is appropriate to use the national input–output coefficients for all the regions. This assumes, of course, that regions are somehow or other little replicas of the nation, a partial truth only. But on this basis we can make a great deal of progress in considering policy alternatives. I would suspect that a similar crude approach to the world and its regions would greatly extend the kinds and range of policy alternatives that could be considered.

The part which I like most about Professor Stone's paper is the last, that with which perhaps he is least satisfied. Specifically, I refer to his comments on attitude transition matrices, matrices that suggest or indicate perceptions of influence. Alternatively, one could construct different kinds of matrices, such as matrices reflecting the interdependence of decisions, and the influence of one decision upon another. Now I say this because I think these kinds of matrices, no matter how infirm they may be, would still help us to move in the direction of defining elements such as trade-off functions among policies, or crude welfare functions, which inevitably creep into all our modeling no matter what we do. For example, the Mallmann–Bariloche model does not escape setting up and using trade-off functions. They are implicit in the model all the time. I think we also saw this in the discussion when we talked about introducing the multiregion framework to recognize different regional objective functions. This was evident even when Professor Mallmann gave a strong argument for using life expectancy as the single dimension for an objective function. He had many constraints in his model, and each one inescapably involves trade-offs.

I like to be guided by transition matrices when I am involved in practical work. Here, I disagree with Professor Stone. I do think some of us ought to be around, trying to be helpful to the policy makers. Now when I think of practical research, I often see it in a sort of recursive, programming framework. Things like attitude transition matrices, however infirm they are, can be extremely helpful in identifying some relevant, though crude information for consideration in the give-and-take among policy makers. This is certainly clear when you start getting different regional groups together trying to define environmental policy. This, then, is the direction that I very much like about Professor Stone's paper. I hope that some of the nonaccounting type of social scientists, or those who have not previously adopted this kind of accounting approach, might try to do so in terms of some such variables as attitudes and influence. It might be worthwhile to see to what extent these variables can be introduced into the world order models.

2. ANATOL RAPOPORT

I find myself very interested in what Professor Stone had to say and cannot really offer any adverse comments, since he has disarmed the audience by pointing out all the limitations of the models that he has spoken on. I would like, however, to stress some of their aspects, all of which have been brought out by Professor Stone. Before doing so, I would like to join Mr. Isard in registering one point of disagreement; namely, that I categorically reject the picture of a scientist being solely concerned with understanding phenomena. I do believe that the scientist has a responsibility, especially in those instances where the results of taking various courses of action may be very different and may have a tremendous impact on the lives of all of us, indeed, on the life of the human race. Therefore, I do not agree with the position of abandoned responsibility in this respect. Neither do I agree entirely with Mr. Isard's position, that the way to be practical is to be helpful to decision makers. In some cases, one should be helpful to decision makers, and in other cases one should act to the contrary; and indeed, inhibit rather than facilitate their actions, be destructive rather than constructive. If you grant that there are such cases as that, then we agree.

With respect to those points that have already been brought out, I would like to emphasize even more strongly the changes of goals. I very much liked Professor Stone's point about the small change that might take place in the economic system by shifting from a universal assumption that work is done in order to produce goods and services to one that enterprises exist in order to give employment and, more incidentally, to produce goods and services.

Let us for the moment think about the change in the conception of the military establishment. With respect to economic enterprises, the change is rather frank. As a matter of fact, people will admit and even approve of the attitude that says the primary purpose of the economic establishment is to provide gainful employment. Now supposing we say that the primary purpose of the military establishment is to provide careers for its personnel and enable it to rule tremendous financial empires and, only incidentally, pay lip service to the avowed purpose of protecting a country from invasion. This may be factually true, but it is not admitted to be the case. This point is very significant, and can be magnified many million fold in importance when it comes to such organizations as the military establishment.

With regard to the issue of secrecy, data are needed. Nevertheless, the political complexes of certain countries make it impossible to gather these data. In other words, it is openly acknowledged that in order to have some sort of information about the world, we need certain data, and yet there remain obstacles to getting them. This state of affairs in itself becomes a problem. Scientists must address themselves quite emphatically to this problem and not simply say, "Well, these data are unavailable and therefore, I cannot go on with my research." Here is another case where the scientist must become an activist if he wants to continue his role as a scientist.

My next point concerns the disaggregation of the household. This, to me, is a very important point. I do not consider it a mere detail, because I think it makes a great deal of difference as to what the household spends its money on. The same is true of the detailed disaggregation of data about the goods produced. All types of things are produced, from supersonic planes to automobile tires to cinnamon flavored toothpicks. To the economist, all of these things are simply commodities. He is interested in volume. He is also interested in the exchange value of these commodities, but not at all in what they contribute to human existence. I submit that there is a great deal of difference between these various kinds of goods. Thus, I feel strongly that all these points, which have made clear the inadequacies of the model, become instigators for the kind of research that I believe to be very important.

Let me now consider two final points. The first is the seduction of numbers. It has been said that some things, such as demographic and economic data, are easy to quantify, while other factors are not so easy. Therefore, one searches for indices. Thus, those things that are easy to quantify tend to become central in any program of research, simply because they are easy to quantify, thereby allowing one to get on with model building and mathematical deductions. Therein lies a grave danger. For example, in the cost–benefit analysis which is applied to all kinds of situations, one speaks of trade-offs, as if trade-offs are always the rational type of procedure. How much of this are you willing to give up? I can give you any number of instances where such trade-offs are completely unthinkable, as with certain matters of safety. If you have reduced the chance of an accident to, let us say, one chance in a billion; but then say. "Well, we can save a tremendous amount of money by raising the possibility of accident from one in a billion to one in a million," you propose a thousand-fold increase of risk. Quite aside from the fact that both risks are infinitesimal from all practical points of view, the reaction to this as a trade-off might be an extremely dramatic one.

Who is to say that this type of reaction is not to be considered? Any number of incidences come to mind, such as the case, a few years ago, when the polio vaccine was first introduced and five children died in California as a result of vaccination. What was the price of this trade-off? Suppose a vaccine was developed that prevents leukemia 100 percent of the time but introduced a certain risk of death of its own. In other words, the drug has a mortality rate of its own. Let us suppose that the mortality of the drug is only one-tenth the mortality risk of the incidence of leukemia. Now, even though the risk of death is only one-tenth as great, I venture to say that nobody would buy it, or that very few people would buy it. While this does not on the surface seem rational, as risk is risk, it nevertheless, is risk under different circumstances. In one case, the child dies by the will of God, in the mind of most people, and in the other case, the child dies at the hand of the nurse—these are two entirely different things. Now who is to say that this is not a rational point of view? It is simply putting different values on the scales. What is needed is openness, and explicit statements of what these values are; not simply taking for granted that in taking a risk one calculates its cost–benefit relations.

I recall another instance, a real case in the South Pacific during World War II. The mortality rate of the bomber pilots on certain missions was so great that only one-quarter of them would complete their mission assignments, a 25 percent survival rate. Somebody seriously proposed filling the planes half full of gas and sending them on one-way missions so that only half as many planes would be used. The idea was that each pilot would draw a white or a black ball. If he drew a white ball, he would go back to the United States, and if a black ball, he would go on a one-way mission. Total risk among the pilots thereby would be reduced in a real manner from a 75 percent mortality rate to 50 percent. Nobody bought it. Can you wonder? Would you buy it? And if I don't buy it, would you say I am not rational?

This is very old—going back to the eighteenth century—only the Saint Petersburg paradox proved that it is not rational to bet on the basis of expected amount of utility. Then, the whole utility function came into existence, with much more sophisticated ways of gauging things. We need these kinds of investigations and an avoidance of naive uses of cost–benefit analysis. Indeed, we must reject naive types of economic thinking, which simply assume that certain values can readily be quantified and that decisions can be made on these quantitative bases.

Let me add one final point concerning pollution, another case where trade-offs under certain circumstances are probably irrelevant. Think of all the cases of mercury and fish, the cases of carcinogenic foods. I do not think that you could really specify what the maximal risk should be in probabilistic terms. Once such products are publicized, there is a clamor to get them off the market. Who is to say that this sort of an absolutist attitude is not rational?

In addition to the pollution of the atmosphere and the hydrosphere, there is also such a thing as semantic pollution, one of my pet subjects and one on which I often speak. We live in an ocean of ideas, words, and beliefs. All of our actions, including the action that we are engaged in here, secrete into the semantic atmosphere. There, ideas interact with each other, some being destroyed in the process, others being linked together, and still others resulting in the emergence of new ideas. This activity is real, it is not a fantasy. We can have no clear analysis of what goes on there, but I am absolutely convinced that it is part of reality, that we live in this semantic atmosphere, and that this semantic atmosphere does become polluted. It gets polluted with ideas that have outlived their natural span, becoming corpses and rotting. There is nothing to remove them from the semantic environment. I am speaking of precisely those outmoded ideas that nowadays govern the decision makers of the most powerful states. What are we going to do about that pollution? This is the last question I would like to pose. I should think, coming back to the responsibility of the scientist, that it is really his prime task to contribute to the cleaning up of the semantic environment.

3. OTTO ECKSTEIN

Professor Stone has given us a rich presentation. I will try to select a few items for comment from the point of view of a working model builder. Let me begin by pointing out some relationships between the development of accounting systems of the type that Professor Stone has pioneered in economics, and modeling itself. My feeling is that unless the accounting system leads to a model, it probably never should have been created. If you view the accounting system simply as information, you probably would not force it into the consistency framework, the adding up of properties and the conceptual uniformity that accounting systems require. That is because accounting systems require you to take real information and combine it with highly estimated information. They are a blend of high-quality and low-quality information. If the purpose, for example, of an economic information system was only to do business-cycle analysis by informal methods, you would probably not have national income accounts at all. They are only justified if they become models.

Once they become models, it is my belief, the distinction between the accounting system and the model becomes synthetic; in fact the two blend together. There is no clear separation between data creation and data use. The primary data, the basic business reports and basic population reports, all data that are gathered in raw forms, are really separate. But once the statisticians get hold of these data and convert them into accounts, the fact of the matter is that they are really building a model. If ancient data are used, the model is historical; but if its data are reasonably contemporary, the model represents a mixture of forecasting and historical estimation. The time separation is synthetic. For example, consider the national income accounts released by the U.S. government on January 20, 1976. Probably half that information was a forecast of what the government thinks the numbers will ultimately be, and half of it was the actual analysis of the data on hand. An apparently fundamental relationship everywhere is that, on the one hand, there are data-originating agencies and, on the other hand, there are analysts, scholars, and model builders who use these data. This is illusory because, in fact, data production is itself a modeling and forecasting effort.

In econometric modeling, we are forced to blend many kinds of sources. We are unable to adopt only one kind of accounting system, such as national income accounts. This creates difficulties. There are inconsistencies, certainly in the American data, and probably in every other. I am suspicious of countries where the data are consistent, because it suggests to me that there is hardly anyone involved in producing them. They are able to maintain internal consistency by having everyone in one office. The bigger the effort, the less consistent it is likely to be—the more problems it will pose.

Now let me raise the question of the world model. I believe in a world model. I am sure—as an enthusiast of my kind of modeling—that it can be done. I think it can be very useful. A world model could make major scientific contributions. But is it a realistic scientific undertaking at this time? I think that is a close decision. One cannot build a model until there is a basic framework to analyze. We do have the United Nations System of Accounts in economics. In the noneconomic areas, we are operating mainly with fragments of other systems. I am not sure that outside of economics we are ready to do world modeling. I am simply not familiar with all the data bases that exist.

Second, you must have some understanding of the process you are going to model. I do not believe that you discover much by the model per se. The model consists of a series of hypotheses. If they are well founded in a large body of scientific literature, the model may be valid. If the model is simply constructed by making it up from whole cloth, it is not likely to produce anything much better than what went into it.

Third, you need a group of people with the will and the intellectual resources to model. I think probably the group here at this conference demonstrates that there is a will and that a group exists that would do the work. Finally, you need a problem, or several problems, to which the model would ultimately pertain. I do not think that models are ever constructed in the abstract, without the goals of solving some problems. Although the link between the model and the ultimate solution of a problem may be remote, I think all modeling is motivated by a desire to solve some perceived problem. Here again, I think there are a lot of problems that unite the world, problems that we confront together, which justify a modeling effort.

In my modeling work, it has been my experience that the answer did not lie in one model. There is a limit to the complexity of a model because, in the end, a model does have to be understood by somebody. It cannot exceed either the ability of human beings to grasp the information that goes into it or the relationships that it encompasses.

I am very suspicious of counterintuitive models. A counterintuitive model tells you something that flies against your common sense. You must understand why it is counterintuitive, and as it gets bigger and bigger, you spend all of your time explaining why the model produced the counterintuitive results it produced. Therefore, the world model would have to be on a rather narrow subject, if any human being is to understand it.

Now, what would I propose if I were building the world model? What should the world model represent? I would begin with a model of food, because it is the most fundamental problem that the world confronts. A large fraction of the world population has inadequate food. We found out a few years ago that the entire world can suffer acutely and millions can starve if the world food economy goes astray. The agencies responsible for analysis, such as the Food and Agricultural Organization or the U.S. Department of Agriculture, did not have serious world modeling work in existence at the time. If they had ever had it in the past, they had let it die. The world would have been dramatically better off if there had been a world food model, even if it had been relatively simple. Thus, I would begin with food, and perhaps particularly with fisheries, because fisheries are a kind of food supply that has innumerable externalities. Therefore, the world and the United Nations as an organization have a special interest in maintaining some rationality that conceivably could be reflected in world models for fisheries.

Second, after food and fisheries, I would model the world GNP. I stress this because it is, after all, the primary determinant of the standard of living of the world population. To know how well people live on the average you have to know the world GNP. To know that, you have to know the individual countries' GNPs. This is also an area we understand and one on which a lot of work has been done, such as Project Link at the Wharton School, which has collaborators around the world. My own organization, Data Resources, does modeling of various countries. It is an area where there is a state of knowledge. Although the knowledge is primitive, you do not have to invent the whole subject from scratch for the purpose of the present project. You have someplace to begin.

Third, I would model population, because it represents another problem that unites the world. If you think of the overall progress of the world, at least in economic terms, and perhaps ultimately in environmental terms, you must have some understanding of population. Therefore, I would focus on this aspect of world modeling.

Finally, if I still had some energy and resources left over, I would turn to capital and international financial flows. Here again there are externalities. There are interrelationships that are practical, affecting the lives of people each year. If you look at the impact of the energy crisis, it sets loose capital flows decisive to the economic well-being of many countries. There are many areas of modeling that I do not understand. If I knew more about political modeling, I might decide that modeling war and peace was more important than any of the above. But I must leave that subject to other members of the conference.

4. HAYWARD R. ALKER, JR.

First, let me speak to the question of how to make this work more useful and how to include political variables. From my point of view, there is a lot to be said for doing modeling and analytical indicator-type research that does not commit one to levels of world models that require 50 man-years or the Messarovic and Pestel magnitude of effort. Some of the secondary, complementary analyses that one can do in the input–output framework do not necessarily require 50 man-years to accomplish some interesting and relevant results. This, in my opinion, is a strength of that tradition. But it also seems to me that one must reformulate it in various ways to make it more politically suggestive and useful. I think some of Mr. Rapoport's comments were relevant to these issues, for instance the question of categories, such as military budgets or coercion costs, that might be added by private scientists. These are not usually separate rows in input–output matrices, but for political and analytical purposes it might be interesting to treat them this way. Leontief often added a row for labor-force reproduction costs. It seems to me that there are ways of making the models more interesting and relevant in the indicator accounting framework without having a deep, wide-reaching valid structural model.

A second point relating to the open Leontief model is the existence of a strong and powerful set of papers with which I have severe disagreements. This work is by James Coleman, a mathematical sociologist, and Gudmund Hernes, an excellent political scientist in Norway. They have a model of collective decisions and power in collective decisions that exhibits a one-to-one mathematical isomorphism with the Leontief input–output open systems model. Thus, in terms of this kind of power analysis, there are a whole series of very interesting models that are mathematically isomorphical with Leontief input–output analysis. (I feel that political "deep structures" are often slighted in such an approach, however.)

This leads me to my third point. It has been mentioned that one can translate between Soviet and Western type data sources, and between Eastern European and Western type data sources. You can go a little bit further, if you read the kind of work done by Brody, Maarek, Morishima, and Sraffa. One finds a Marxian version of input–output analysis in the literature, which I am sure you are aware of, but which was not emphasized in your talks. It gives the labor theory of value a formal type of representation. These authors go beyond the obvious limitations technically associated with that method of valuation. Evaluation in this approach is, however, different from that given by exchange value. This fact leads to very interesting discussions of North–South exploitation relationships, such as Emmanuel's book, *Unequal Exchange*.

I would like to mention several sources which, as extensions of input–output analysis, are intellectually and politically rather important and, perhaps, practically relevant as well. The next type of modeling application is the sociodemographic table that Professor Stone presented for us in his paper. It is almost exactly the basis for Boudon's interesting simulation models in his book, *Education, Opportunity, and Social Inequality*. There are a number of global types of analysis that one could do in the same way. We have simple but interesting findings from Nathan Keyfitz' paper. It is its simple, illustrative manner that I think is so suggestive. One might do some kind of global class analysis, sociodemographic type analysis, out of these aggregate statistics, to the extent that they are available. On this basis, one might explore the reproduction of stratification systems, social hierarchies, and inequalities in class distributions or educational systems in the way that Boudon has done. It seems that these types of table data can be obtained from national account statistics. There is a modeling tradition, as Eckstein has noted, that goes with that kind of data. It is very interesting and could be applied in developing contexts. Scolnik's work for the Bariloche group suggests a number of arguments compatible with that kind of modeling. While they are not complicated, I think such approaches interesting and revealing about social structure. In conclusion, let me note that I thought the learning-earning-retiring life cycle model was marvelous. I would add yearning, to complete the feedback aspect of the system.

Part 2

Politics and Classes

 *Chapter 9*

World Resources and the World Middle Class

Nathan Keyfitz

How much economic development is possible? Surely the planet and its materials are finite and not even all its present four billion people can live like Americans, let alone the six or eight billion that on present trends will be alive when a stationary world population is established. Indeed, there is doubt whether the 250 million people expected to populate the U.S. in the year 2000 will be able to live as Americans do today. How far, then, can industrial society spread through the preindustrial world before it reaches a ceiling imposed by space, raw materials and waste disposal?

That is the wrong question to ask, if human knowledge and capacity for substitution and the resilience of economic systems are unbounded, as they may well be. In that case the right question—and certainly a more tractable and pragmatic question—is how *fast* can development progress, whether toward an ultimate limit or not? What rate of technical innovation can be attained, oriented to allow a corresponding rate of expansion of industry, and how many of the world's people will that expansion enable to enter the middle class each year?

Attainment of the middle-class style of life is what constitutes development in countries as widely separated geographically and ideologically as Brazil and the U.S.S.R. In the process peasants gain education, move to cities and adopt urban occupations and urban patterns of expenditure. Changes are involved in people themselves, in where they live, in their kind of work and in the nature of the goods they consume. These changes can be visualized in terms of a definable line, comparable to the poverty line officially drawn in the U.S., across which people aspire to move. The pertinent questions then become: How many people are moving across the line each year, what is their effect on resources, at what

Reprinted from *Scientific American,* vol. 235, no. 1 (July 1976). Used with permission.

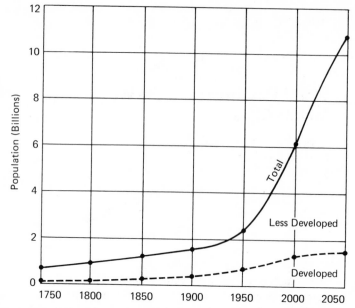

Figure 9-1. The "population explosion" curve is the result of more-than-exponential growth; the annual rate of increase has itself been rising, most sharply in the past century, largely because of the decline in infant and childhood mortality. In this layer chart the total population (projected to the year 2050 according to the United Nations medium estimate) is given for countries currently classified by the U.N. as "developed" (broken line) and "less developed (solid line).

rate can resources be expanded by new techniques and therefore what is the size of the window through which the world's poor will climb into the middle class during the remainder of this century and beyond it?

A main issue of development for many of the people of Asia, Africa and Latin America is how to enlarge that window into the middle class. Since, according to a generally accepted view, it is middle-class people who limit their families, the rate of movement into that class helps to determine the level at which the world population can be stabilized, and that level in turn will determine the degree of well-being that can be supported by world resources. And if shortage of resources makes the opening into the middle class as it is presently constituted so narrow that the majority will never be able to pass through it, then the sooner we know this the better. The Chinese rather than the Brazilian-Russian pattern of development may be what people will have to settle for.

The questions I have raised are difficult for many reasons, including the lack of statistical information, uncertainty about the capacity of productive systems to substitute common materials for scarce ones and uncertainty about the directions in which technology will advance. Some data and some pointers are available, however.

Let us begin with population. The world population, according to the United Nations estimates I shall be following, passed the four-billion mark in 1975. It had passed the three-billion mark in 1960. Whereas the last billion was added in fifteen years, the first billion had taken from the beginning (one or two million years ago) until 1825. The growth has been far faster than exponential growth at a fixed rate of increase (as with compound interest); instead the rate rose from something like an average of .001 percent per year through the millenniums of prehistory to 1.9 percent through the decade and a half from 1960 to 1975.

Apparently the rate of increase will not rise further. The same 1.9 percent, according to the UN medium variant, will hold until 1990, and by the end of the century the increase will be down to 1.6 percent per year. (see Figure 9-2). Other estimates place the peak earlier and make the decline in rate of increase faster. Insofar as the increasing rate of increase constituted a population "explosion," we can draw relief from the fact that we are now down to "only" exponential growth. (This peaking was inevitable because of what mainly caused the rise to begin with: the decline in mortality during infancy and childhood. Mortality improvement after the reproductive ages does not affect increase much and in the long run does not affect it at all. Once the chance that a newborn infant will survive to reproduce itself gets up to about .90, the scope for further rise is limited, and whatever rise takes place will be offset by even a small decline in the birthrate.)

Those who worry about the population explosion can take some comfort in this peaking of the rate of increase, but not very much. Dropping to exponential growth still leaves the world population increasing (on the UN medium variant) by about 75 million per year now, with the annual increment rising to 100 million by the end of the century. And the absolute increase, rather than the rate, seems to be what matters. To feed the present yearly increment requires nearly 20 million tons of additional grain each year, which is more than the Canadian wheat crop and about the same as the crops of Argentina, Australia and Romania taken together. To look after the annual increment of population on even a minimum basis is going to be difficult enough; the real issue, however, is not how many people can live but how many can live well.

Production of most things consumed by the world's people has been increasing at a higher rate than the 1.9 percent per year of population. During the period from 1960 to 1973 meat output increased at 2.8 percent a year, newsprint at 3.7 percent, motor vehicles at 6.8 percent and energy consumption at 4.9 percent, and the rise was similar for many other commodities. These numbers can be taken to mean that on the average mankind is year by year eating better and reading more, becoming more mobile and substituting machine

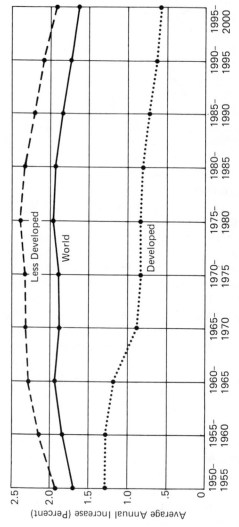

Figure 9-2. The rate of increase of population is apparently reaching a peak during the present half decade. The average rate of increase per year is plotted for five-year intervals for the developed (dotted) and less developed (broken) countries and for the world as a whole (solid). The rate of increase turned down several decades ago for the developed countries and is expected to do the same thing soon in the less developed countries. The "explosion" is ending, in the sense that the growth of the world population will be less than exponential.

power for the power of human muscles. Such a conclusion would seem to be confirmed by worldwide figures on productive activity or income. For example, adding up the gross domestic products of all countries for 1970 yields a gross world product of $3,219 billion, an average of $881 per head. The total has been going up at nearly 5 percent per year in real terms, that is, after price increases. Even allowing for the 1.9 percent increase in population, we seem to be getting better off individually at about 3 percent per year. Projecting on this basis, real goods per head would double every 23 years; each generation would be twice as well off as the preceding one. To dispose of twice as much wealth as one's parents, four times as much as one's grandparents, surely cannot be regarded as unsatisfactory; the world, such figures seem to show, is moving toward affluence. That conclusion requires substantial qualification.

The division of a total number of dollars by a number of individuals to obtain an average per head has a long tradition; dividing one number by another is an innocent operation and without any necessary implication that everyone obtains the average, and yet it puts thoughts into people's minds. The first thought might be that things are not bad with $881 per head for the entire global population—a conservative conclusion. The second thought might be that things would indeed not be bad if the total was actually divided up—a radical viewpoint that has been voiced often in recent years. Income is an aspect of a way of life, however, and only a trifling part of a way of life is directly transferable.

The fallacy of redivision is encouraged by putting income into terms of money and performing arithmetical division. To say we should divide income so that everyone in the world can have his $881 is to solve a real problem with a verbal or arithmetical trick, because behind the numbers is the fact that Americans live one way and Indians another way. If, starting tomorrow, Americans were all to live like Indians, then their higher incomes would simply disappear. There would be nothing to transfer.

How much is transferable depends on the extent to which Americans could consume like Indians while continuing to produce like Americans. Simon Kuznets and others have pointed out that as soon as one tries to plan a transfer the tight bond between production and consumption frustrates the attempt. For example, the cost of travel to work is called consumption, but if people stopped traveling to work, production would fall to zero. What about the cost of holidays and entertainment, which are elements of consumption but which refresh people for further work? What about nutrition, education and health services? And what about the enjoyment of consumer goods that is the incentive to work and earn? All of these and many other parts of consumption feed back into production. Moreover, to discuss massive transfers of capital would be futile for political reasons even if it were economically practical: the declining U.S. foreign-aid budget shows how unappealing to the major donor this path to world development is.

Because the world population is heterogeneous, no style of life is in fact associated with the world average of $881. Following that average through time leads to the mistaken impression that things are getting better every year and will do so indefinitely. Even a two-way breakdown of the average is a major step toward realism.

Of the total world population of four billion estimated for 1975, 1.13 billion, or nearly 30 percent, live in developed countries. The fraction of the annual increment of population accounted for by those countries is much less, however: only 10 million out of 75 million, or 13 percent. The annual increment in the less developed countries is more than 65 million, and it will rise to 90 million by the end of the century (again on the UN medium estimates). This division of the world into two kinds of countries, rich and poor, or more developed and less developed, has become familiar since World War II. That world 1970 product (or income) of $881 per head is in fact an average of the developed countries' $2,701 and the less developed countries' $208.

Recent fluctuations obscure the long-term rates of increase, but suppose income for the rich and poor countries alike increases at 5 percent per year in the long term. On the population side, suppose the future increase is .5 percent per year among the developed countries and 2.5 percent per year among the less developed. Allowing for these population numbers brings the 5 percent annual gain in total product that was assumed for both down to about 4.5 percent for the developed countries and only 2.5 percent for the less developed ones.

The result is a widening gap between the two groups of countries, an exercise in the mathematics of geometric increase. (See Figure 9-3.) Think of the developed countries starting at $2,701 per capita and increasing at 4.5 percent per year in real terms; after 25 years they have risen three-fold, to a per capita income of more than $8,000 in 1995. By that time the income per head in the less developed countries has not even doubled: their $208 has risen to only $386. By the year 2020 the grandchildren of the present generation will have, in the one set of countries, more than $24,000 per head and in the other countries the still very modest $715—one thirty-fourth as much as the rich, and not yet as much as the 1970 world average!

The calculation shows how a heterogeneous population is bound to develop a widening gap between rich and poor if per capita rates of increase are frozen. I have assumed that all national incomes increase at 5 percent per year. Overall national-income growth is not conspicuously different, on the average, for the poor and the rich countries, and so it is the differences in population growth that are decisive.

To speak of developed and less developed countries is an improvement on treating the world as being homogeneous, but it has been overtaken by the events of the past three years. Where two categories of countries once sufficed, we now find we cannot do with fewer than four.

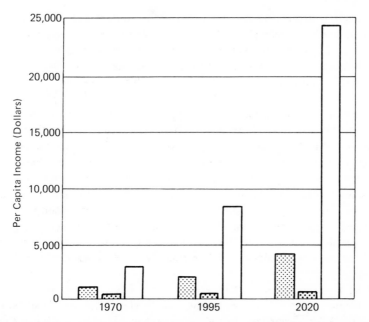

Figure 9-3. The widening gap between per capita incomes in the developed and in the less developed countries is caused by the more rapid growth of population in poor countries. UN figures for the developed (*white*) and less developed (*dark color*) countries and for the world as a whole (*gray*) were projected on the assumption that total income will continue to increase at five percent per year in both sets of countries but that the population of the developed countries increases at only .5 percent per year while that of less developed countries increases at 2.5 percent.

   The shifts in raw-material prices have created resource-rich countries such as Abu Dhabi and Venezuela, whose wealth is comparable to that of the developed countries, which by way of contrast can be called capital-rich. Some countries that were poor have actually been developing, including Singapore, Korea, Taiwan and Hong Kong. Finally there are the many countries that are truly poor, lacking (in relation to their population) both capital and resources. We have, then, the resource-rich countries, the capital-rich countries, the developing countries and the poor countries. Specifically identifying and classifying all cases to provide numbers for population in these groups is not easy. (Indonesia has resources but not enough so that any likely rise in prices would make its 135 million people rich.) The new categories of resource-rich and developing countries might be defined in such a way that they total 200 million people each; the fact remains that most of the world's people are in countries that have no leverage through either control of capital or control of resources.

   No country is homogeneous, however; the poorest countries contain some rich people and the richest contain some poor. Nations and their governments dominate our age so completely that individuals too easily drop out of political as well as statistical view, yet the welfare of governments is not a worthy ultimate objective; it is the people of the poor countries who deserve our concern. And so what follows will deal as directly as possible with people.

The typical poor person and the typical middle-class person are easy to visualize; the first is a peasant in Java, Nigeria, the Brazilian Northeast or elsewhere in Asia, Africa and the Americas; the second is a city dweller in San Francisco, Frankfurt, Leningrad or Tokyo with an office job that puts him well above the poverty line. There are less obvious representatives. Along with the peasant group one should count as poor the wage laborer of Calcutta or the urban unemployed of the U.S. And the middle-class group includes the unionized construction worker, the bus driver, the keypunch operator and the successful farmer in the U.S., Europe, the U.S.S.R. or Japan; that some of these are considered blue-collar is secondary to their earning a middle-class income.

In survey after survey most Americans, when they are asked where they think they belong, place themselves in the middle class. The self-classification by which most Americans tend to call themselves middle-class and Indians tend to call themselves poor accords with the distinction I have made. Most of those called middle-class in the world live in the cities of the rich countries, but some of them live in poor countries and some live in the countryside. The crucial part of the distinction is that middle-class people are in a position to make effective claim to a share of the world's resources that accords with modern living.

With an income measure of welfare, people fall on a continuum and the location of the poverty line is arbitrary. As a country grows richer its standards rise, so that the same fraction of its population may be defined as "poor" even as everyone in the country is becoming better off. In the case of the U.S., however, it has been possible to reach broad agreement on a Social Security Administration definition of poverty based on relatively objective criteria. An average urban family of four, including two children, is said to require $3,700 a year (at 1974 prices) to pay rent, buy clothing and meet basic nutritional needs, and similar levels are set for other types of household.

"Middle class" describes a style of life and can cover not only physical necessities but also such conventional needs as power lawn mowers and winter vacations in Florida. It needs to be specified separately for each culture before one can see how many people enjoy it and what the energy and resource consequences of the enjoyment are. Pending such a study I propose to call middle-class those who are above the equivalent of the U.S. poverty line, wherever they may live. Cultural differences make poverty in one country intrinsically noncomparable with poverty in another country, but they make average money incomes just as noncomparable. The effort to quantify important notions must not be prevented by some degree of qualitative difference; the fraction under the level of consumption represented by the U.S. poverty line is not the definitive way of measuring the world's poor, but it will serve for the moment. In the U.S. that fraction was 11.6 percent in 1974, an increase from 11.1 in 1973 but a decrease from 22.4 in 1959. Of the U.S. population of 210 million in 1973, some 23 million were poor; call the remaining 187 million middle-class. Let us try to find indexes that will provide a corresponding number for other countries.

Passenger cars in use might be taken as roughly proportional to the middle-class, or above-poverty, population. In the U.S. in 1973 the number of passenger cars was 101 million and in the world as a whole it was 233 million, a ratio of 2.3. Insofar as the 233 million passenger cars in the world are being driven and ridden in by a world middle class, we can multiply the U.S. middle class of 187 million by 2.3 and derive a world total of 430 million middle-class people. This number is too low, because automobiles are less a part of daily life even in other affluent countries; we know that trains continue to be used in Eurpoe for much travel that is done in the U.S. by automobile.

Let us try telephones as the indicator. The world total in 1973 was 336 million telephones and the U.S. total was 138 million. On this index the world middle class was 187 million times 336/138, or 455 million. With electric energy as the indicator a similar calculation gives a world middle class of 580 million. Each one of these indicators is surely defective. One can nonetheless hope that their defects are more or less constant over the 20 years or so that I propose to apply them to establish a trend.

A slightly different way of doing the calculation is to take it that modern living requires about four metric tons of crude oil a year for heating, air conditioning and motoring, so that the world output in 1973, 2,774 million tons, could cover the needs of 700 million people. (The calculation is approximate because some poor people do use a little oil and large supplies go to military and other government uses.)

Averaging the several approaches gives a world middle class of 500 million for 1970. What is important is that the corresponding average number—indexed on automobiles, telephones, electric energy, oil and other items—was something like 200 million for 1950. That indicates an average increase of 4.7 percent per year in the world middle class: the workers, and their families, who are integrated into industrial society, utilize its materials as the basis of their jobs and apply their incomes to consume its product. In doing so they have an impact on resources and on the environment. Just how great is the impact of change in status from poor to middle class, particularly compared with the effect of population change?

Raw materials are used by people, and so, if all else is fixed, the drain on resources must be proportional to the number of people. If each year the world population is 1.9 percent larger than it was the year before and nothing else changes, then each year resources are claimed by 1.9 percent more people, and in the course of 37 years we shall be on the average twice as dense on the land and shall be consuming twice as much iron and other metals and twice as much crude oil. This statement is not true of pollution, where more-than-proportional effects enter. It is true of resources insofar as technology for production and patterns of consumption both remain constant.

Actually they do not remain constant; they exert effects in opposite directions. Technology has been stretching the use of materials. We know how to put the tin on the can more thinly; we can make rubber and fabrics out of coal; we recycle aluminum. The movement, guided by price changes, is always toward less scarce materials. As income goes up, however, per capita consumption increases: more cans are used, albeit each with a thinner layer of tin. Worse still, new materials are invented—detergents, plastics, insecticides—that take a long time to reenter the cycles of nature once we are through with them. It is the net effect of these tendencies that we need to estimate.

One way to get at the net effect of increased consumption per head and of technological improvements is to determine the residual change after population increase is allowed for. Let us try this for energy consumption in the U.S. in 1947 and 1973. The 1947 consumption was 1.21 billion tons of coal equivalent and the 1973 consumption was 2.55 billion. Meanwhile the population rose from 144 million to 210 million. If the larger population of 1973 had held to the same volume and patterns of consumption and production as the smaller population of 1947, it would have required 1.77 billion tons of coal equivalent. Hence of the total increase of 1.34 billion only .56 billion was due to population growth; the remainder of the increase, .78 billion, was due to affluence. Affluence was more important than population. (See Figure 9-4.) Similar calculations can be made for metals and other materials, for pollution, for the primary caloric content of food, indeed for any kind of impact that can be measured.

As an alternative way of analyzing the consumption of materials, consider that from 1950 to 1970 the part of the world population that was affluent went from 200 million to 500 million: while total population increases at 1.9 percent per year, middle-class high consumers increase at 4.0 percent. Each high consumer requires the equivalent of three-quarters of a ton of grain, whereas the poor get by on a quarter of a ton. (The consequent ratio of land use is less than three to one, because agriculture is more efficient in rich countries.) The middle-class person requires from fifteen to 30 barrels of oil, whereas the poor person makes do with one barrel at most in the form of kerosene, bus fuel and fertilizer. The land and energy content of clothing may be in a rich-to-poor ratio intermediate between those for food and for transport. As a kind of average of these several ratios, suppose the middle-class person has five times as much impact on the

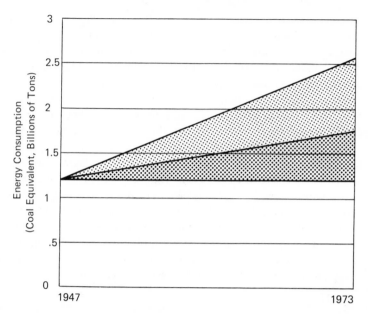

Figure 9-4. U.S. energy consumption would have increased from 1.21 billion tons of coal equivalent in 1947 to 1.77 billion tons in 1973 if it had merely kept pace with the rise in population. In fact, however, energy consumption rose to 2.55 billion tons in 1973. The increment (*light color*) due to a rise in per capita consumption stemming from affluence was larger than the increment (*dark color*) attributable to population growth. The same is true of many other materials.

material base as the poor person. Then the average person on the high side of the poverty line must be taken as being equivalent to five people on the low side in fuel and metals consumed. In considering impact we therefore calculate as though in 1975 the planet had not four billion people aboard but 6.4 billion. Of these, 3.4 billion were poor and three billion represented the fivefold impact of a world middle class that probably numbered 600 million.

This would make the average total impact of the small middle class on resources somewhat less than that of the large number of the poor. The middle class has been increasing at 4.7 percent per year, however, and the poor less than half as fast. At the growing edge the increase of affluence has much more effect than the increase of population; the movement of people into the middle class has more effect on materials and the environment than the increase in the number of poor people.

Indeed, it has so much effect that if the population explosion is now ending (in the sense that the world rate of increase is peaking at 1.9 percent per year and starting to decline), we now face another explosion. It arises from the arithmetic of combining two exponentials, which is to say two progressions (population growth and middle-class growth) each of which has a fixed ratio.

The effect can be expressed in stylized form by supposing the 1975 population of four billion projected forward in the ratio 1.6 every 25 years (equal to the fixed rate of 1.9 percent per year). Suppose at the same time that the middle class triples every 25 years (equivalent to a fixed 4.5 percent per year), as it did from 1950 to 1975. The poor population is the difference between the resulting numbers. If the people above the poverty line average five times the impact of those below it, then we must add five times the middle class to the number of poor for the total impact. The result is a steadily increasing rate of increase of the impact, from 2.7 percent per year in 1950-1975 to 3.1 percent and then to 3.5 percent. (See Figure 9-5). This is based on continuance of 1950-1970 rates of economic development and of population growth. Population growth will slow down, but that will not greatly reduce the impact, which in this illustration would be increasingly due to affluence. Our difficulties in maintaining the population and affluence levels of 1976 suggest that this model will not work. We cannot hope to keep tripling the middle class every 25 years. The main reason is shortage of resources.

Natural resources account for only about five percent of the value of goods and services produced in the U.S. and other developed countries. Resources are hence curiously two-sided: extracting them accounts for only a small part of the cost, yet they are the sine qua non of existence, to say nothing of progress. And particular materials do run out. England's Industrial Revolution was in part a response to a firewood crisis: cheap coal was substituted for wood, which had become scarce and very dear. In America, on the other hand, wood was cheap and labor was dear, so that houses were built of wood rather than stone, which is more labor-intensive. Now timber is dear here also, and masonry and aluminum are substituted in some products. Plastics take the place of paper in packaging. Cultivated southern pine is used for newsprint instead of the limited pine and spruce of the northern forests.

Thus history shows the resilience of the productive system, its ability to substitute commoner materials for scarce ones. Nevertheless, the extrapolation of this capacity must take account of time. Invention, innovation and capital replacement can proceed only at a certain pace. It is this pace of innovation that needs to be studied, since it sets the rate at which industrial society can spread in the face of environmental and resource limitations.

Limits to the spread of industrial society under present technology are suggested by the record of trade in raw materials over the past quarter-century. To take one example in 1950 the production and consumption of energy were in virtual balance for the developed countries as a whole. Their deficit amounted to less than 4 percent of consumption. By 1973 production in the developed countries had nearly doubled but consumption had far outrun it and the deficit had swollen to a third of consumption.

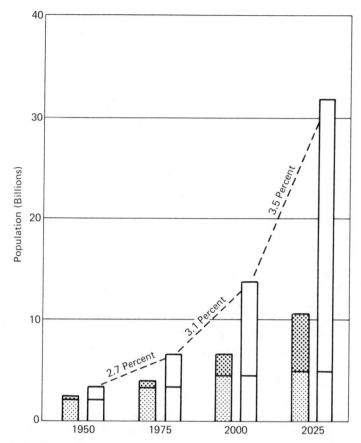

Figure 9-5. The future impact on world resources is affected by the growth of the middle class, whose members are assumed to consume five times as much as poor people. In population alone the middle class (*dark gray*), increasing at 4.5 percent per year, would eventually be larger than the poor population (*light gray*). When the middle class is multiplied by five, the resulting "consumption population" (*white*) is seen to grow at an annual rate that increases from 2.7 to 3.1 and then to 3.5 percent. World resources are already strained by the 1975 "consumption population."

The story for metals and other resources is not very different. No country, developed or not, has been provided by nature with a greater quantity and variety of mineral and other resources than the U.S. Yet even the U.S. had become a net importer of minerals by the 1920s, and it now imports all its platinum, mica and chromium, 96 percent of its aluminum, 85 percent of its asbestos, 77 percent of its tin and 28 percent of its iron—to select from a long list. Of course, the shortages of some of these minerals are not absolute but are a matter of price. The U.S. could produce all the aluminum it needs for domestic clay, but bauxite from Jamaica is cheaper. Having virtually exhausted the iron ore of the Mesabi Range, the U.S. resorts to lower-grade domestic taconite and to imports, in a proportion determined by prices.

The increase of more than four percent per year in the number of middle-class people who have come on the scene is too rapid in that these high consumers have to comb the world for resources, but on the other hand it is much too slow to satisfy the billions of people who are waiting in the wings. Whereas Europe, Japan and the U.S.S.R. have made great gains during the UN Development Decades, most of Asia and Africa are dissatisfied with their progress. Moreover, a realistic calculation would probably show a larger gap between the impact on resources of those who have raised themselves from poverty and that of those who are still poor. The weight of a middle-class person is in many respects more than five times that of a peasant. It is to keep the argument conservative that I suppose the ratio is five times and that the world middle class triples every 25 years.

The combination of these two modest assumptions produces, as we have seen, a surprisingly high measure of impact for the end of the century, by which time the middle class, which was at 600 million in 1975, would increase to 1.8 billion and have the effect of five times that number, or nine billion. The total impact projected to the year 2000 is, then, that of nine billion plus 4.6 billion poor, or 13.6 billion people. This compares with an impact of 6.4 billion for 1975, calculated in the same way. If strains are already apparent in materials and energy, what will happen with a doubling of the rate of consumption?

The accelerating impact that appears from recognition of two categories of people rather than one category is offset in some degree by the decline in the impact per dollar of income once income rises beyond a certain level. People take very high incomes in services rather than in more and more automobiles. Moreover, the relation of impact to income varies from one culture to another, as an anthropologist would point out; an economist would add that the relation can be counted on to change as raw materials, and hence the goods made from them, become scarce and costly compared with less material-intensive forms of consumption. Although the impact on materials may taper off with increased wealth, the impact on air and water may be greater than proportional. There may be thresholds: the air may hold just so much carbon monoxide, a lake just so much fertilizer run-off, without undue effect, but beyond a certain critical point the effect may quickly rise to disaster levels. Such critical points clearly exist in renewable resources. Fishing or cutting timber up to a certain intensity does no damage at all, but continued over-fishing or overcutting can destroy the fish or tree population.

The rate and direction of development of the period 1950–1970, unsatisfactory though it may be in that the absolute number of the poor would continue to increase until well into the 21st century, is still faster than can be sustained on present strategies. The resilience of the economic system, and technical innovation in particular, can be counted on to respond to needs, but only at a certain rate of speed. One can imagine sources of energy, the capacity to dispose of wastes and substitutes for metals all doubling in the century to come, but it is not easy to conceive of such a doubling in the fifteen years that would keep the middle class growing at 4.7 percent per year.

To say that civilization will collapse when oil supplies are exhausted, or that we will pollute ourselves out of existence, is to deny all responsiveness and resilience to the productive system. The geologist or resource expert tends to focus on the material and technical process he knows and may be less than imaginative with regard to how a substitute might be found to deal with a shortage. On the other hand, the economist may be too imaginative; he may too readily suppose substitutes can be found for anything as soon as it becomes scarce. The ensuing debate between pessimistic raw-material experts and optimistic economists has generated whatever knowledge we have on the subject. The middle ground to which both sides are tending is that every barrier that industrial expansion is now meeting can be surmounted by technological advance, but not in an instant. It is not a ceiling on total population and income that we have to deal with but that window. How large can the window be made?

One conclusion to be drawn from the arithmetic I did above is that a projection in terms of ratios is probably wrong in principle; in the face of natural and human limitations the pace of advance may be determined in absolute numbers rather than ratios. If, for example, pollution effects are proportional to fuel burned, then successive absolute increments in fuel consumption have the same bad effects on the fixed volume of the atmosphere. We should think not of the percent expansion of the middle class but of its absolute increase.

The calculation made in this way starts with the annual growth in world population of 75 million at the present time, gradually increasing to 100 million by the end of the century, and compares that increment with the number annually emerging into the middle class. If the latter went in a straight line from 200 million in 1950 to 500 million in 1970, then the average annual increase was fifteen million. My stylized model, wherein industrial society expands through the emergence of people from the peasantry into city jobs as capital expands (while those not yet called remain at their old peasant incomes), goes back ultimately to Adam Smith. This simple application of the Smith model suggests that currently fifteen million people join the middle class each year and 60 million join the poor. Even if the middle-class increment could rise to 20 million per year, the poor would still be increasing by 80 million per year at the end of the century. This at least is one reasonable extrapolation of the process of development in the post-war period. Other population estimates are lower than the UN's, but accepting them would lead to the same result: the large majority of the new generation will be poor. Therein lies the harm of rapid population growth.

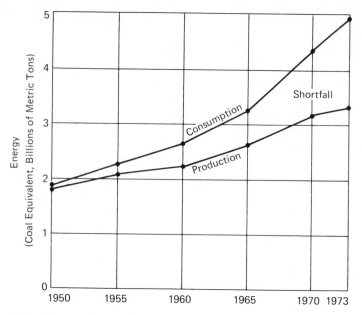

Figure 9-6. Consumption and production of energy were about balanced in 1950 in the developed countries: they produced the coal, oil, gas and hydropower whose energy they consumed, except for a small shortfall made up by imports from less developed countries. By 1973 rising production had been outstripped by consumption; shortfall amounted to a third of consumption.

The natural increase of the affluent population will create difficulties in the years ahead even though birthrates are low. Suppose the window is wide enough for 20 million to pass through it each year. Who will they be? The way the world is made, the children of the currently affluent of America, Europe and Japan will have first claim. The U.S.S.R. has found no way of preventing its elite from placing their children in the elite, and neither has the U.S. On the basis of 600 million for the middle class in 1975, a net natural-increase rate of .5 percent means three million children per year in excess of deaths. Apart from children who simply replace their parents or grandparents, of the 20 million net admissions each year three million would be further children of those who have already entered the middle class and seventeen million would be new entrants. And these seventeen million new entrants would be divided among the poor of the developed countries and those of the less developed countries, with the former having the better chance. Poor people in the poor countries sense that the odds against them and against their children are great.

All of this, it should be noted, can be seen as a critique not of development but of one particular model of development. The distinction between poor and middle-class represents the Brazilian and the Russian direction but not the

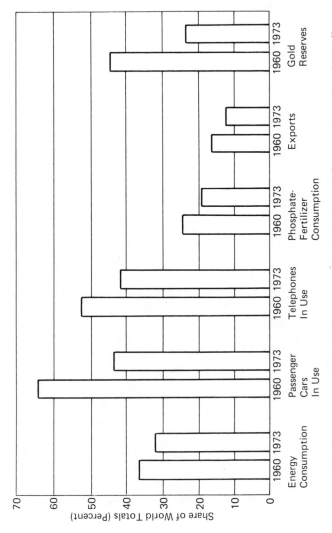

Figure 9-7. The increase in affluence outside the U.S., particularly in Japan and Europe, has reduced the disproportionate U.S. share of energy consumption, durable goods and other indicators of wealth. Movement of more people across the poverty line would extend this effect.

Chinese. Whether because of China's special culture or the personality of Mao Tse-tung, both the specialization that equips people for middle-class jobs and the durable structures of industry and administration in which those jobs have their place have been insistently denied there. It is asserted that everyone can do everything, that people ought to take turns working as peasants, driving trucks and being scholars; people need only so much to eat, to wear and to live in, and consumerism beyond that austere minimum is vice, not virtue. Whether this view can spread among other cultures and without a regime of the same type is not clear. There is little present sign of its spreading even to India, let alone to Japan, Europe or America.

Thomas Malthus gave us a land theory of value, Karl Marx a labor theory and development economists since World War II a capital theory. Land, labor and capital are plainly all needed (and to assign priority to any one may be as much an ideological choice as a practical one), but a dynamic factor superimposed on all of them is new scientific and technical knowledge. At many points we need to know more in order even to discover the problems we face: only recently have we found out that insecticides can be dangerous poisons to organisms other than insects, and that the current world-wide rise in skin cancer may be related to depletion of the ozone layer of the upper atmosphere. Knowledge is needed even to see where the window restricting passage into the middle class is located, and only knowledge can open it wider.

Other ways of widening the window have been suggested. One is to raise the price of the raw materials on whose export some less developed countries depend for foreign exchange. Price increases such as those of the Organization of Petroleum Exporting Countries (OPEC) can have little overall effect, however, on the number of middle-class people in the world (although they have some effect on whether the newly middle-class will speak Spanish or Arabic or English). Who ultimately bears the burden of such price raises is not clear. Some of the burden is carried by poor countries that are not endowed with raw materials; when the repercussions have worked themselves out, India may find it has contributed a higher proportion of its income to Saudi Arabian opulence than the U.S. has. Certainly some U.S. fertilizer that would have gone to India before 1973 now goes to the Middle East; German chemical-plant investments are similarly diverted. The offsetting of oil price rises by French arms sales to Iran has everything to do with national power and little to do with the total distribution of poverty or even the national distribution. The main point is that only a small fraction of the world population is in resource-rich areas.

A second way to help more people escape from poverty might be for those who have already entered the middle class to moderate their consumption. In principle, if one meat eater cuts his consumption, then five grain eaters can increase theirs. If American automobiles were smaller, more metals and fuels would be available for automobiles in Zaïre and Bangla Desh as well as—more immediately—fertilizer plants in those countries. If urban Americans were to live like the equally affluent Swedes, U.S. energy consumption might be halved. The trouble is that goods, as well as jobs that require materials, fit into other social activities in an interlocking scheme that is hard to change; social configurations are as solid a reality as raw materials. After two years of talking conservation, the U.S. consumes as much fossil fuel as ever. Faced with a world shortage of raw materials, every person of goodwill wants to see wasteful practices reduced, but the intrinsic limits on transfers I mentioned at the outset and the enormous inertia stored in producing and spending patterns make reduced consumption an unlikely way for the U.S. to help the poor countries.

Foreign aid and investment along conventional lines are a third possibility, but they have been disappointing. They have aided in the development of some countries (Canada is a striking example), but for various reasons the volume is inadequate to the magnitude of the problem for most of the world's population. Even where investment is solidly based in economics some intellectuals argue that it creates dependency, and the politicians of poor countries often respond by expropriation. Ironically the very mention of expropriation is expensive for the poor country because it makes investors demand a higher return.

One can say that better prices for raw materials, reduction of consumption by the rich countries and conventional foreign aid and foreign investment all ought to be pursued, but the experience of the 1950s and 1960s shows that they will not make a decisive difference in the size of the window through which escape from poverty is sought.

What will make a decisive difference is knowledge: of how to produce amenities with less material, how to substitute materials that are common for those that are scarce, how to get desired results with less energy and how to obtain that energy from renewable sources rather than from fossil fuels. We have seen some results in the past decade. With the advent of integrated circuits, a calculator that cost $1,000 and weighed 40 pounds is now replaced by one that costs ten dollars and weighs a few ounces. Artificial earth satellites have lowered the cost of communication; they provide television in Indian villages and may ultimately make telephone calls around the world as cheap as local calls. Synthetic polymers have replaced cotton and wool and thus released land. The list of what is still needed is too long to itemize: efficient solar collectors, compact storage batteries to run automobiles on centrally generated power, stronger and cheaper plastics (for automobile bodies, for instance) and so on.

If the time dimension in the implementation of these inventions is crucial, then everything that is done to hasten invention will pay off for the world movement past the poverty line. There are many stages, from pure scientific investigation to the translation of science into technology, to the engineering that makes a production model out of a working prototype and finally on to parts contracting and the assembly line, and each stage takes time. The U.S., once foremost in the speed with which it could convert knowledge into the production of goods, is said to be losing this preeminence; a slowing down would have bad consequences not only for the American competitive position among industrial nations but also for the world escape from poverty. The need is not confined to scientific and engineering knowledge; prompt solutions are also required of many problems in biology and medicine, climatology and geophysics. The technical and social knowledge for birth control is of special importance; whatever the size of the window through which the poor escape into the middle class, the lowering of births will at least bring closer the day when world poverty ceases to increase in absolute amount.

Some part of American research has been directed specifically to labor-intensive devices suited to poor countries, and that line of investigation ought to be encouraged. Even after the Green Revolution, for example, poor countries still have special agricultural problems. Apart from such specific research, the U.S. helps all countries when it develops knowledge that makes its own industry more efficient.

A particular preoccupation of the less developed countries is dependency; even commercial indebtedness is seen as neocolonialism. The technical evolution of the poor countries along lines suited to their own needs will be aided by American expansion of knowledge in that it will widen the choice of techniques available to them. In order that any such American contribution not create commercial indebtedness, it would be advisable to place the new knowledge and inventions in the public domain as the common possession of mankind rather than in patents on which royalties could be drawn.

Both production constraints and environmental constraints limit the growth of the world middle class. The way the U.S. can help to open the window is not through schemes for division of the existing product but by contributing knowledge that will expand the product. Solving production and environmental problems starts at home, but any genuine contribution will have value worldwide. Incentives can be devised to direct technology in environment-saving rather than environment-damaging directions. No one can forecast how much time it will take to solve any one technical problem, let alone the complex of problems, but that time—whatever it may be—will be shortened by a larger and more immediate mobilization of scientific and engineering talent.

Chapter 10

The New Interimperial System

Helio Jaguaribe

1. INTRODUCTORY REMARKS

The first consideration we must bring to this work on the new international system and emerging configurations is a recognition of the decisive influence exerted by World War II. The fact that the scholarly community has taken a long time to understand and acknowledge this influence is in great part due to the ideological conflicts that followed the war and continued into the Cold War period. The extent to which most scholars have been affected by the idea dominant in the West within this period—namely, that world domination by Soviet Russia had either to be contained, according to the Truman Doctrine, or to be pushed back, according to Eisenhower and Dulles—is truly amazing. The fog of the Cold War, however, is finally dissipating after this extended period of time, and it is becoming possible—as several fine attempts already show—to understand the new international system emerging from that conflict.

Today most people acknowledge that a first effect of the events in the post-Cold War world has been the overcoming of the balance-of-power system. Such a system had prevailed since the Congress of Vienna, which settled world affairs after the Napoleonic Wars, and continued to prevail to a greater or lesser degree after World War I. Between World Wars I and II, we had a balance of power based on a European-centered system with increasing U.S. influence. The latter became adjustable to the European system, indeed gradually became a part of it. Only after World War II did the balance-of-power system, either European- or American-centered, become noticeably no longer a convenient explanation for the actual behavior of the United States. Following the Cold War disputes focused on the aggressor's existence and identity, an increasing consciousness developed that a new imperial system was emerging in the world.

2. THE NEW SYSTEM

Like some other writers, George Liska (whom for simplicity's sake I have singled out) in his work, *Imperial America,* which is perhaps the most significant effort exemplifying this quality, acknowledges for the first time that there was an American empire. The originality of Liska's thinking in acknowledging those indications that suggest the existence of an American empire rests in the fact that, until that point, such an acknowledgment had always been connected with various accusatory positions. Liska introduced the notion of an American empire as an historical fact—neither bad nor good—just an historical fact, like the Roman Empire. This empire must be studied, perhaps also fought, but certainly understood. The recognition of its existence is compatible with analytical understanding. Basically, I accept Liska's view along with those of other scholars who take this position. Taking it as a basis, I think we can presently observe the consequences of new international forces following the long historical process that passes through the two world wars and accounts for the present state of the world. The world has been affected by a profound change. The balance of power and the alliances between nations have been superseded by new arrangements in which the two superpowers, whatever their arguments, their interests, and their rationalizations for their behavior, have objectively become imperial systems.

Today we are confronted with what could be called an interimperial system, in which the two superpowers exercise the function of imperial centers and establish in the world a double line of relationships. This consists of a relationship between the two empires—which could be called an interimperial relationship—and the perhaps even more important aspect of the relationship existing within the area of influence of each empire, i.e. between its center and its periphery. The latter aspect I would call an intraimperial relationship. These center-periphery relationships are characterized by a basic domination-dependency pattern, while the interimperial relationship, which was shaped initially in the form of sheer conflict, became a conflict-cooperation relationship. This situation started with each imperial center believing itself to be the representative of major human aspirations. Correspondingly, each imperial power felt that the other represented an extremely negative power that should be neutralized for the sake of mankind. This relationship has evolved into coexistence wherein we find both conflict and cooperation. Thus, we have a conflict-cooperation interimperial relationship and a center-periphery, domination-dependency intraimperial relationship.

It is interesting to look briefly at the two emerging empires. I think we can discern in them elements of similarity, as well as of difference. The most important elements of similarity are, first, the fact that each is a center and in that sense is characterized by a center-periphery relationship. I suggest that the center-periphery relationship is more important than the conflict-cooperation relationship. This is true because the U.S. and the U.S.S.R., like other empires in history, actually devote most of their activity to the domination of their own periphery in the name of causes that are decreasingly supported by the dominated peripheries. Thus, the fact that these empires were constructed as instrumentalities of a cause—the diffusion of socialism and the elimination of exploitation from the Soviet side; or, from the American side, the containment of totalitarianism and the defense of the market—does not alter center-periphery relations. This is the most important similar aspect of the two empires. Of course, they are also characterized by a need to participate repeatedly in a conflict-cooperation relationship. Finally, they are both characterized by a propensity to exercise a preemptive occupation of any vacuum of power in the world. For both empires, this means preventing the growth of the other's empire, thereby affecting their own dynamics of expansion.

3. THE AMERICAN EMPIRE

I suggest that the U.S. as a center of an empire is characterized, first of all, by an all-pervasive, loosely coordinated influence throughout the world, "pulled" by local elites rather than imposed on them. One of the interesting characteristics of the American empire is that as imperialism it is much less "pushed" than "pulled" imperialism. This in part represents the demand of local elites who depend on imperial support to maintain their own power. The connection between imperial expansion and imperial demands by the local elites produces a special pattern not reproduced in the Soviet empire.

Another important feature of the American empire is its objective nature. In this sense, the extent to which the American empire is without an imperialistic design or an imperialistic plan is often acknowledged even by its critics. There is not so much American imperialism as there is an American empire. It is not necessary to be an imperialist to have an empire, although in the long run empires probably become increasingly difficult to manage when they are not inhabited by an imperial plan.

A final aspect which I think is important to observe concerning the American empire is of an objectively negative character: the fact that the American empire, for reasons of immanent interest to the total development of the American capitalistic process, has become essentially, insofar as the economic aspect is concerned, a corporate form of capitalism which is inherently spoliative vis-à-vis its periphery. The corporative form of capitalism is a spoliatory form of appropriation. Because of its inherent spoliative aspects, it tends to induce the allied local elites to display a dysfunctional national behavior. Thus, the elites of nations allied with the American empire tend to behave dysfunctionally, from the point of view of their own societies. In this sense, they are spoliative elites both because they are connected with a system that is inherently spoliative and because of the particular characteristics of corporate capitalism.

4. THE SOVIET EMPIRE

Now, if we turn to the Soviet empire, I think we will find a different picture. While the U.S. exercises an all-pervasive influence that is loosely coordinated, the influence of the Soviets on their empire has an opposite nature: it is monolinear. Areas dominated by Russia are not subject to multivarious types of Russian influence. Instead, there is a complete connection of the controlling apparatus of the political system with little influence on other aspects. This means that Russian influence is not all-pervasive, but rather exerts a tightened, monolinear political control, following the hierarchy of the parties. As distinct from the American empire, there is a Russsian purpose of empire, the old, traditional czarist propensity to Great Russian imperialism. In this sense, Russia has changed much less than Russian authors would like us to believe. There is old Great Russian imperialism, which maintains itself for essentially social anthropological reasons. This empire demonstrates little compatibility, if not almost total incompatibility, with local autonomy; the American empire on the other hand—because it is a "pulled", not a "pushed", empire—is precisely incomparable with that of the U.S.S.R. insofar as the local elites maintain their internal dependency vis-à-vis the empire.

Finally, as opposed to the American empire, where the economic relationship —because of the features of corporate capitalism—is inherently of a spoliative character, the center–periphery economic relationships of Russia are not inherently spoliative, although they may be so for political reasons. For instance, it is absolutely clear that during certain times the Soviet Union imposed a heavy price on its satellites for recovery from war damages. This, however, was a political decision. It was not something inherent to the economic relationship between them. After that period, the Soviet Union, to its own disadvantage, has paid a great price in importing expensive East German equipment in exchange for cheap Russian raw materials. Paradoxically, the Russians have benefitted from the Middle East crisis because their oil has become dearer. And so it is redressing a disadvantageous balance of trade between Russia and her satellites.

5. THE NEW STRATIFICATION

The consequence of the new interimperial system that emerged with World War II has been a reorganization, a reshaping of international stratification. As can be seen in Figure 10-1, expressing conditions of the 1950s, the world is divided into four levels of stratification corresponding to (one) general primacy, (two) regional primacy, (three) autonomy, and (four) dependence.

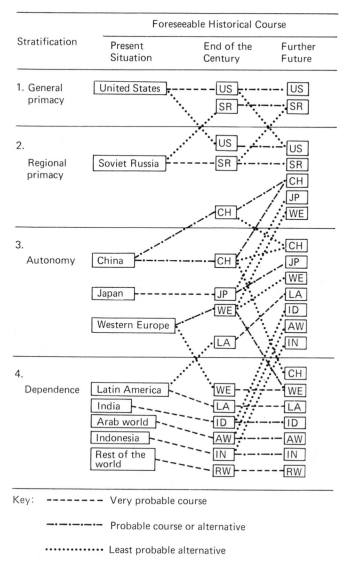

<table>
<tr><td colspan="4" align="center">Foreseeable Historical Course</td></tr>
<tr><td>Stratification</td><td>Present
Situation</td><td>End of the
Century</td><td>Further
Future</td></tr>
</table>

Figure 10-1. The emerging interimperial system.

(Source: Helio Jaguaribe, *Political Development* [New York: Harper and Row, 1973], p. 374).

General primacy is characterized by the inexpugnability of the core territory of the concerned nation and of its system, which maintains a broad regional paramountcy in addition to its general world predominance in areas or sectors not specifically protected. This was obviously the case of the United States, as it emerged from World War II as a system empowered with general primacy. The category of regional primacy is characterized by the inexpugnability of the core territory in terms of a narrow regional paramountcy and a large degree of world influence, but smaller than that associated with general primacy. This was the case of the Soviet Union. Autonomy is a level characterized by a capability for imposing high costs on potential agressors, but neither empowered by inexpugnability nor capable of enjoying a large independent world role. This has been the typical case of the European countries, Japan, and to an extent, Canada. Finally, dependency is a condition of the countries that do not have the sufficient capability for reaching any of the former levels. This is the condition of the rest of the world.

In Figure 10-1, there are some speculations about the probability of change as the situation could be defined in the 1950s, with the probabilities of some countries, such as China, becoming empowered with regional primacy by the end of the century.

6. EMPIRE AND IMPERIALISM

What has occurred to this new interimperial system which shaped the world as a consequence of processes that reached their maximal effect with World War II? I think that in the course of the 1960s, the nature of this system, which had previously been fixed, started to present some propensities for change which have reached a visible acceleration in the 1970s. I will try briefly to describe the changes affecting, first of all, the top of the system.

In the case of the U.S., with the aggravation of contradictions caused by the Vietnam War there is an intensification of the incongruence between its imperial condition and the lack of an imperial design. The United States is an empire, whether it likes it or not, acknowledges it or not. This is because the imperial condition, which involves the fact that there is a center–periphery relationship having both a large amount of stability and its own patterns, is the essential characteristic of the existence of an imperial system. This center–periphery relationship is not managed as such, with the consciousness of its condition, because the United States sees itself, for a number of reasons, as a nation among others, albeit a greater nation.

Of course there are already, in academic circles, scholars like Liska and the people at Johns Hopkins University, among others, who have developed a more clear understanding of these aspects. Scholars in the United States and elsewhere are starting to understand this relationship, but as of now, ît is neither a widely understood aspect of American society nor a guideline for policy. The Vietnam war, for example, was fought as if it was not an imperial frontier war but a national war, which, of course, it was not. This misunderstanding resulted in a total lack of support for the war. Its supposed national character was demystified first by students and then by the public in general. The United States was simply not able to exercise the totality of its power to win a war or to annihilate a rebellious society, as the Romans, for instance, had done when it was necessary to act independently of their humanistic internal values.

7. NEW SOVIET PRIMACY

A second point I think important to acknowledge is that the Soviet Union is reaching general primacy sooner than was expected, despite the fact that the Soviet Union has not been able to solve some very important problems of its own internal economy—among them, as is well known, technological problems that have created increasing demands for borrowed technology. Perhaps, however, a more important problem in the Soviet Union is its own legitimacy which maintains, 50 years after the revolution, a dictatorship in the name of a proletariat that supposedly has been in power for 50 years. It is in total contradiction with its own theoretical assumptions. The dictatorship of the proletariat has turned out to be a necessary precondition for bureaucratic domination which involves a complete lack of capability for building a workable legitimacy. All those aspects notwithstanding, which would, and of course do, negatively affect Soviet strength, the great Soviet concentration on heavy equipment and military development has permitted the U.S.S.R. to achieve a power parity with the United States at an earlier date than expected.

The SALT I agreements and the Vladivostok understanding of October 1974 raised, as is well known, the acceptance of an upper limit on both sides' weapons; 2400 ICBMs with 1320 MIRVs. This involves basic equality and parity. On the other hand, the Soviets have developed a new tactical capability through an extremely fast improvement and increase of their navy, which allows them now to displace important local units and to assume pre-emptive occupation of specific areas. One of the reasons why Angola was possible is that today the Soviet Navy is as powerful as the American. This navy arrived in Angola first, as the United States Navy had in Lebanon some years ago. The Soviets are now able to accomplish by themselves the same operations that the United States did earlier. The most important difference between the present period and the 1958 situation is that whereas the Soviets had only ICBMs during the earlier situation, now they also have conventional ships.

8. CHINA

Another change has occurred within the international system: the acceleration of the ascent of China to regional primacy. The Chinese do not yet have the technological–military conditions for inexpugnability, in the strict sense of the word, because inexpugnability comes from the capability to inflict a second strike whatever the extent of the damage suffered through aggression. Although the Chinese certainly do not have a second strike capability, in exchange for this they have such tremendous manpower facility that the possibility of inflicting heavy damage on Russia by conventional invasions is enough to deter any pre-emptive Russian action vis-à-vis the Chinese. This role of the Chinese necessitates that the West accept them, whether they like it or not, as indispensible allies in the contest with the Soviets. These two conditions have accelerated the ascent of the Chinese to regional primacy.

9. NEW AUTONOMY

A second type of change observable in the international system affects it at another level. It is directed at the level of intraimperial relationships. Not only the interimperial relationships have been affected by the emergence of the Soviets to the level of general primacy and the ascent of the Chinese to the level of regional primacy, but also in both empires the center–periphery relationships have been submitted, in recent years, to important changes. I think that we can observe this in two respects. The first is the general softening of intraimperial sanctions in both empires, attributable, on the one hand, to the greater capability for self-sufficiency of the periphery and, on the other, to the substantial decline in the legitimacy of the centers for interference. The centers have lost the right to interfere because the myth of their cause, which until very recently served the function of justifying building up their own power, has been demystified. No one, from the average U.S. citizen to a sufficiently well informed Angolan in Luanda, believes that the West exists to defend democracy and international liberty. The demystification of this apparent commitment of U.S. military power to a high cause has substantially reduced U.S. capability for interference, as these actions increasingly become possible only in the name of the naked exercise of power in the service of self-interest. This also has happened to the Soviet Union. Nobody, from the Soviets themselves to people throughout the world, believes that the Soviets are defending socialism and therefore building up ICBMs to suppress the exploitation of man by man. Thus, the interference of the Soviets in areas like Czechoslovakia and Hungary is increasingly understood as the sheer exercise of naked power. Because of this decline in their legitimacy, the centers substantially have lost not the actual capability to interfere but some of the elements that are important for implementing possible interference.

On the other hand, there is a diversification of the possibilities for autonomy. In the 1950s and through the early 1960s, autonomy was essentially a capability for playing a general independent role. I think that we are now witnessing a subdivision of the extent and grades of autonomy. We therefore should speak of general autonomy, regional autonomy, and sectoral autonomy. General autonomy remains what it was in the 1950s—a capability of playing an independent role. France and Japan are good examples of this type of autonomy. Today, however, we have developed another aspect of autonomy, regional autonomy. The emergence of regional autonomy can be ascribed to the decline of the centers' capability of manipulating their peripheries. Regional autonomy connotes a capability of playing an independent regional role. Egypt is a good example of this type of role—a regionally autonomous country, although not generally autonomous. Brazil is also becoming an obvious case of regional autonomy, as is South Africa. Finally, the last oil crisis and a number of other connected events have led to the appearance of a third level of autonomy, which I call sectoral or specific autonomy. The capability of playing this role depends specifically on the respective sectoral role, as the OPEC countries have shown.

10. THREE THIRD WORLDS

I would also like to comment on a third important change in the international picture which is not so much a new change as it is the aggravation of a tendency. This is the increase in economic differentiation. For example, at one time the world was practically divided into two blocs: the "free countries," as they were self-labeled, and the so-called "socialist countries." Other countries were supposed to incorporate themselves sooner or later into either the socialist or the free camp. As a matter of fact, the world has developed a different tendency: agglomerating the interests, characteristics, and values first of a group of countries that have developed and maintained a sort of basic market system of economy, constituting what is usually called the First World; second of a group of developed countries with centrally planned economies, constituting the Second World; and finally of a group of developing or underdeveloped countries, constituting the Third World. The Third World is a group of countries that are becoming increasingly conscious of their own condition, even though communication among them is still extremely poor and, as an empirical fact, relatively rare. There is, nevertheless, an increasing understanding in these countries that they share some important common patterns and conditions that involve an objective common interest for them all.

A more recent development has been a further subdivision of the Third World into a Fourth World, and sometimes even a Fifth World. To give an example of this sort of thing, a relatively recent edition of *Time* magazine summarized the current opinion about these several worlds and presented a picture of the world divided into five parts. The Third World was identified with 620 million people of still poor but developing countries, like most of Latin America and the OPEC countries. A Fourth World, with 930 million people, was credited with some potential for development, but remained dependent on significant foreign aid. Finally, a Fifth World of 175 million was identified, consisting of destitute and practically helpless countries.

Rather than the fivefold subdivision of the world, I prefer to suggest a division of the Third World into *A, B,* and *C* areas. The *A* Third World would represent countries with self-developing, diversified economies, typically recognized as the case in regard to Brazil, Argentina, and Mexico. The *B* Third World countries would be those capable of self-development based on particularly rich natural resources. This case is clearly different from that of the *A* World, but it is also one where the capability of self-development is apparent as is true of the OPEC countries and a few other countries particularly rich in some raw materials. Finally, the *C* Third World countries are those unable to achieve development without massive and long-term foreign aid, places such as Mali, Chad, Ethiopia, or Bangladesh. These countries are really in the condition that the world modeling experiments have confirmed. Even if they were organized with the same values as the Bariloche model, they would present an incapacity for development without external aid.

Let me bring my presentation to a close with some conclusions concerning the results of these changes in the new international system. Today we have to recognize two parameters of stratification in the international system. One is the level of capability for international independent roles. This represents a remnant of the interimperial system which I have discussed. The second parameter is determined by the level of development, a consequence of this diversification of the interimperial system into the general five-world picture. As a result, we have the new international system presenting a stratification according to levels of international capability. Within the framework of this general stratification, there is also a new subdivision of the five sectors of the world as functions of the allegiances developing among the two developed worlds and the three factions of the underdeveloped world. As shown in Figure 10-2, there is an observable propensity for the *A* Third World to establish relationships oriented to the First World, demonstrating a conflict–cooperation aspect but nonetheless predominantly First-World oriented. On the other hand, the very poor Third World countries are oriented toward the Second World, although they also maintain conflict–cooperation relationships. Finally, the OPEC countries and the countries I have classified in the *B* Third World are playing off the First and Second Worlds but are manifesting a clear intention not to be absorbed by either.

11. DESTABILIZING FACTORS

My final comments concern the destabilizing factors observable in the present system. I stress three main points concerning the United States, the Soviet Union, and the problem of world authority.

In regard to the United States, I think it is clear that the world in general and the U.S. in particular are confronted with problems resulting from the fact that the U.S. exemplifies an empire without imperial design and planning. It is becoming increasingly difficult for that empire to manage its affairs without an imperial design supported by domestic and international public opinion. The American empire is a liberal empire, and a liberal empire cannot work without support of domestic and international public opinion. So the American empire apparently is confronted with a dilemma. It can retrogress to regional primacy, giving up U.S. interests, or most U.S. interests, in Asia and Africa and the U.S.

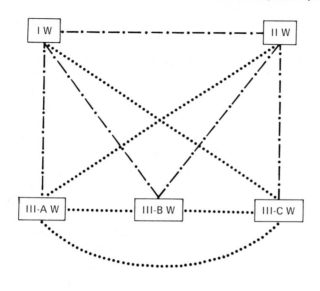

Key —·—·—·— Close cooperation–conflict

················· Loose cooperation and remote conflict

New Autonomy

1. General   China—regional primacy
                 Western Europe—Japan—Canada—Brazil (?)

2. Regional   Brazil—Mexico—Argentina—Australia—Egypt—Iran—India—Indonesia

3. Sectoral   OPEC countries

Figure 10-2. The Five-World system.

role as the Western arbiter of the Third World. Implicit within the idea of "fortress America" is the belief that the U.S. is strong enough to defend itself and the inexpugnability of its own core territory. This is exactly the definition of a regional primacy, no longer a general primacy. Conversely, the United States could maintain its interests in managing its empire while adjusting its own institutions, values, and ideas to its objective situation. The latter choice is what I call the adoption of an imperial design and strategy, supported by domestic and international public opinion, equipped with the necessary institutional and material means. Now this course of action, obviously, is open to tremendous discussion.

My second conclusion concerns the Soviet Union. The problem of the Soviet Union is the problem of empire without legitimacy or popular support. Thus, it becomes increasingly difficult for the Soviet leaders to maintain the Socialist-Communist myth, the justification of their legitimacy for everything. They are overly dependent on a legitimation that is no longer legitimate. The demystification of the Soviet Union is rapidly increasing, through the dissidence of the Soviet intellectuals, the de-Sovietization of the Western Communist parties, and finally, the Chinese rebellion. Thus the Soviets, like the U.S., are confronted with a dilemma. The Soviet dilemma apparently consists in whether they accept change or pursue the consolidation of an authoritarian, technocratic rule in a totalitarian state capitalism, relying increasingly on its internal repressiveness and its external military capability. Either they will become a sort of new Ottoman Empire or they will have to reestablish the Socialist idea, with its profound domestic and international view based on humanistic practice and democratic rule, a view absolutely incompatible with the despotic technocracy ruling the Soviet Union.

12. WORLD AUTHORITY

The final point I should like briefly to discuss is the problem of the need for a world authority. It has become in our time an indispensible requirement for the general international stability of the world. There are many ways this can be done, but whatever they are some minimal functional requirements can be discerned and identified. World authority is indispensible for the stable preservation of peace and the peaceful arbitration of world conflict. It is obvious that the ad hoc continuous agreements of the United States and the Soviet Union to settle areas of conflict do not present a stability and predictability compatible with any assurance of a long-term peace. They are renewed each time without any assurance that they will work finally to prevent the expansion of conflicts that can become unmanageable once they reach certain proportions. Such a situation is extremely risky, and it is obvious that it will not last long.

World authority is indispensible for the preservation of the world ecosystem, whether we emphasize the perspective of the Bariloche model, in the sense of stressing that what is most important is the redistribution of wealth, or take the Mesarovic–Pestel view that what is important is the good management of resources. It is obvious that the world's ecosystem cannot be abandoned to its automatic, self-redressing capability, which is becoming increasingly insufficient. Thus, the preservation of a world equilibrium of the ecosystem is increasingly dependent on internationally coordinated action, involving the existence of international authority.

Finally, it is equally obvious, as a correlate of the same question, that we need an international management of world resources, dependent upon an international authority. The present international system does not provide conditions for a world authority because of the impracticability of asserting a stable U.S.-U.S.S.R. cooperation for the joint management of the world. Neither the United States nor the Soviet Union alone is able to do so, by virtue either of a lack of means or increasingly a lack of legitimacy.

Establishing a stable international system involves three main requirements. The first concerns a new international economic order, generalizing the conditions needed for a world consensus. As Celso Lafer's contribution to this conference will note, the only way to reduce differences is to accept the differential pace of growth of the poor countries relative to the rich, including massive transfers to encourage this process. These things are extremely easy to put in a mathematical model but extremely difficult to implement.

The second requirement is a profound adjustment of the American empire to its world role. This requires making U.S. interests and values reciprocally compatible, leading to a real international economy in the framework of an international democratic system. I suggest that the United States, given its culture and institutions, is confronted with a choice of either retreating to the idea of Fortress America, giving up an important area of world interference, or legitimizing its role in the field by internationalizing its internal democratic process. What makes this particularly difficult is that the U.S. has managed, in the name of democracy, an imperial, authoritarian empire, commanded by the spoliative economic expansion of corporate capitalism. This empire is simply not compatible with U.S. internal values, and it creates a conflict that is very difficult to solve.

A final complex requirement is a profound adjustment of the Soviet empire to its world role, with the reestablishment of humanistic values and practices and democratic forms of socialism. This looks to be at least as difficult as the taming of domestic corporate capitalism.

13. CONCLUDING REMARKS

I cannot help but conclude these comments with a profoundly pessimistic view. I believe that an analysis of the world system today indicates a high improbability for the timely achievement of the minimal conditions for stability. As a consequence, there is a high probability for further deterioration of the present world imbalances to the point of disruption, which is likely to happen in a couple of decades. Short of an apocalyptic nuclear outcome, this involves the disruption of the international economy, which is already quite visible. A provisional balance might be achieved, but if it is not treated in a structural way, it will again bring about new disruptions. The process of disruption, including the disruption of the ecological balances, will go on, with unpredictable catastrophic consequences on the biosphere. Finally, those two disruptions, economic and ecological, are very likely, in addition to other factors, to produce naval conflicts, which will create a third catastrophe on the seas.

✳ *Chapter 11*

More Self-Reliance as an Alternative Policy

Dieter Senghaas

During our discussion it has been stated that many development plans and scenarios can be modeled but that the development issue involves inherently political problems. Let me concentrate in my short presentation on something that is not merely a plan or blueprint but a reality—a reality in terms of some development alternative which has, I think, some implications for world modeling. If we look not at the Meadows–Forrester model (because it takes the world as a whole) but at the Messarovic-Pestel model and some further models developed later, there is one striking characteristic with respect to the latter ones. In all of them there are particular problem areas emerging from the most acute problems like hunger, illiteracy, insufficient health and housing facilities, and lack of social welfare devices. But there are also countries and regions in these disaggregated models that no longer show these problems but nevertheless belong to the Third World according to prevailing statistical criteria and indicators. Which are these countries and regions? First China, second North Korea, third Albania, fourth Cuba, and if you go back in time, fifth Southeastern Europe. Some decades ago all these countries were underdeveloped according to prevailing definitions of underdevelopment; and all were peripheries to one degree or another—according to the prevailing definition of a periphery within the theory of periphery capitalism. Cuba was terribly peripherized, so was Korea by the Japanese for 60 years; the same holds for Albania which was penetrated by the Italians like a colony. China was peripherized to a certain degree but not so deeply as the others. What is interesting is that none of these countries continue to have those very problems we are debating here. In general, there is no hunger and no illiteracy, although habitat may still pose something of a problem. Furthermore, in all of these countries an exemplary health system has been developed (exemplary in the context of the still very low mobilization of the productive forces). What is the background to this success story? (I would like to label the development of these countries a success story, especially if one compares their development with that of the rest of the Third World and if one defines development, as is presently fashionable, as a process leading to the satisfaction of basic human needs.) The background to this achievement is threefold. I am referring to these cases because they represent a *development alternative* that has to be viewed *apart* from their official ideologies, of which we may approve or disapprove.

First, all of these countries have been dropouts. They have severed themselves from the prevailing world economic structure, e.g., the capitalist world market with its intrinsically unequal distribution of income and its unequal international division of labor with respect to the metropolitan–peripheral relationship. All of these countries have concentrated their efforts on their own development. In so doing they have been pursuing strategies of self-reliance, or what the North Koreans call *Juch* which is a pragmatic philosophy of self-reliance.

Second, all these countries have substantially restructured themselves internally. Some 20 years ago they were all peripheries. To be sure, the concept of periphery denotes something very specific within the capitalist world market. It means integration into an unequal international division of labor whose outcome results in a very specific society and economy. What are their determinants? If, e.g., one thinks in terms of an input–output matrix, a periphery economy shows the absence of linkages and feedbacks among those economic sectors that are the most dynamic in any viable society, namely, agriculture, the industrial production of mass consumption goods, and the local production of producer goods and technology. I have analyzed this peculiar structure in a paper distributed to the participants of this conference.[1]

Periphery economies have specific deficiencies that manifest themselves in incoherent economic circuits. Part of their reproduction dynamics is located in the metropolitan economies, a phenomenon easily shown with the help of input–output matrices. All the cases to which I referred above were, to some degree, peripheries of that type. None of them can any longer be labeled a periphery economy. All have been successful in substantially increasing their agricultural productivity, in systematically building up an industrial sector—not for the production of luxury consumer goods (as is the case, for example, in Brazil, with the help of multinational corporations) but for the production of simple and essential consumption goods made available to most of the population. In addition, all of them have succeeded in developing some kind of basic goods and capital goods sector. Moreover, all of them created some kind of indigenous

---

1. Dieter Senghaas. "Multinational Corporations and the Third World: On the Problem of the Further Integration of Peripheries into the Given Structure of the International Economic System," pp. 257–276 in Dieter Senghass (ed.) "Overcoming Underdevelopment" (special issue), *Journal of Peace Research* 12(4), 1975.

technology. The final result has been a convergence of the structure of production with the internal structure of demand. Most important, the total population has been productively integrated into such a restructured economy.

As you all know, according to some of the current frameworks of analysis, some of these processes should not have happened. For example, prevailing theory tells us that one needs a certain size of internal market to develop all these sectors, particularly concerning the capital goods sector. Without a certain size of internal market, according to this theory, it becomes uneconomical to pursue such an autocentered development strategy. The prevailing theory maintains that some 100 countries of the 130 countries of the Third World are inherently unfit for the development of an indigenous producer goods sector. But Albania, with a bit more than two million inhabitants, is accomplishing precisely this type of development, and North Korea has succeeded in building up a coherent economy by deliberately disregarding the prevailing doctrine of comparative advantage. And it behaved like all successful development cases of the past 100 years, i.e., contrary to the liberal, free-trade doctrine and its cosmopolitan assumptions.

This brings me to my third point, which is the buildup of some kind of equal division of labor among Third World economies. Without such a restructuring of the regions and subregions of Latin America, Africa, and Asia, there is no chance that the present periphery economies of the Third World will ever escape their dependent position within the present metropolitan–peripheral relations.

The philosophy I have briefly presented here is very old. It was developed more than 100 years ago by Friedrich List in his book on the political system of the national economy published in 1841. His basic question was whether and how development is possible within a highly stratified international economy, the stratification being defined by different levels of productivity. At that time, England was on the top; the United States, France, Germany, and some other countries on the second level; and List put into a third category all other countries. List's argument was very simple: if one pursues a strategy of development within such a highly stratified international economy without protecting oneself against the more productive economies, one has to become a periphery. List put his basic ideas into a theory of the production of productive forces (which is much more than the often mentioned infant industry argument). What does production of productive forces mean? According to List, one mobilizes the productivity of agriculture, one creates an industrial sector for the production of mass-consumption goods, and one produces one's own machinery and technology within such a framework. It is particularly important to create systematic linkages among these various activities. This scenario and development theory is not only a paradigm, or whatever else the label might be, it is not only a blueprint, rather it is part of reality. It has been, implicitly or explicitly, the basic strategy for the successful development of the capitalist metropoles, of

Japan (which had all the prerequisites for becoming a periphery in the middle of the nineteenth century), of the Soviet Union after 1917, of China after 1949, and of the other cases to which I have already referred.

What are the implications of these experiences and of this notion of development for world modeling? I would like to state them in terms of imperatives. The first imperative would be *dissociation*; the second would be restructuring in terms of building up coherent economic circuits (to put it very economistically, although there are obvious sociological and cultural implications, of course); and the third imperative would be the gradual buildup of *new schemes of an equal division of labor* within a regional or subregional context as a means to promote the development of self-reliant and coherent societies and economies on the spot. The general implication of this perspective is not how to further integrate the problem areas of the present world into the capitalist world market but how to decentralize the tremendously hierarchical structure of the present world economy. Normatively put, these restructuring processes between the metropoles and the peripheries, within the peripheries and among the peripheries, are the very object of modeling activities if these purport to be of any use to development policies.

(Editors' note: After comments and criticisms from members of the conference, Professor Senghaas proceeded to reply. We have excerpted some salient passages which help illustrate and accentuate some of the major points of the previous presentation.)

I would like to respond to Bruno Fritsch, Bruce Russett, and Jorge Dominguez. First, I would like to comment on the criticism concerning the alleged romanticization of my cited examples. I personally thought that I was very unromantic in my presentation. I simply took what I considered to be a certain consensus within this room, i.e., the basic need satisfaction as the first criterion for a development strategy. My label "success story" was precisely related to this aspect. If you take other indicators of the Bariloche project which we have debated here, such as, e.g., life expectancy, then again the cases to which I was referring are success stories. In all these success stories, there might be certain characteristics we do not admire. Let me take the case to which I referred only briefly, namely, Japan after the Meiji restoration in the nineteenth century. Japan's development has been a success story with respect to some fundamentals, although this success story was linked to militarism and imperialism from very early on and although even today housing is not very well developed in this country. Still, we would consider Japan as conforming to certain achievement criteria we believe essential to a developmental success story. I used the smaller cases for the purpose of illustration; I could have used China, the Soviet Union, or the Southeastern European countries. I used the smaller cases because some basic tenets of the prevailing economic theories are particularly related to these smaller cases, in that they stipulated that certain things cannot be done and cannot happen in cases with a small internal market. Thus, the basic message of all success stories is the following: disregard the doctrine of comparative advantage and build up your own productive forces in a self-reliant manner.

My second remark is directed at Jorge Dominguez. Dissociation does not mean autarchy. Autarchy is but one extreme case within a spectrum of dissociation. I am quite aware, of course, that Cuba is to a large extent integrated into some kind of world market with its sugar economy, but the basic question is whether, despite this integration, a diversification of the Cuban economy takes place or whether Cuba is still a monoculture and enclave-type economy. The data which I know from Cuba is that, despite the still prevailing role of sugar production, the contemporary Cuban economy is far less a monoculture than it was before 1959. Cuba cannot be compared with North Korea, where a tremendously diversified economy in all areas has gradually been built up. By the way, North Korea refused not only to integrate itself into the capitalist world market but also into an unequal socialist division of labor totally dominated by the Soviet Union at the end of the 1950s, when the Soviet Union tried to persuade North Korea to become a raw material supplying country within the COMECON. The leadership at that time, particularly Kim il Sung, said no. Then the Soviets implemented an embargo that made the North Koreans quite imaginative with respect to developing their own forces and initiating a strategy of self-reliance. After more than fifteen years the North Koreans are gradually opening up to their wider environment (as are the Chinese), *selectively* cooperating also with capitalist countries. Cuba is different from North Korea, but has also ceased to be a periphery economy.

Chapter 12

Challenge to Models: How Can Patterns of International Dependence and Participation be Qualified and Simulated?

Fernando Henrique Cardoso

The title of my commentary was, as suggested here, "Challenge to Models: How Can Patterns of International Dependence and Participation Be Quantified and Simulated?" I am not going to speak to these issues directly, but I think it might be useful to add some considerations which take into account a particular set of preoccupations, the attempts made primarily by Latin Americans. These have sought to emphasize the importance of political processes, but more than that, the importance of some special shapes of this political process, to which we could refer as the perspective of dependency.

I was stimulated by the presentations here, and while Professor Deutsch was speaking I tried to clarify in my mind how someone preoccupied with problems of Latin American politics could make some additional remarks to his illuminating reflections. Perhaps what was absent from Professor Deutsch's exposition was the kind of linkage that exists in an historical situation between politics and the economy. In methodological terms, these interrelationships may be summarized by one word: "structure." Whenever a Latin American political scientist tries to reflect about power, economy, society, relations among classes, and relations among nations, the approach is a *structural* one. We try to see how the different interests fit into one particular pattern of a structured set of relationships. In other intellectual traditions, the idea of information flow, flow of expectations and of process, is emphasized more than in the structural approach. If we want to make progress, the main question is how can we deal with these *processes* and still employ a *structural* approach? How can we try to solve the problem of structural change? Perhaps some types of differential topologies would be more powerful in terms of explanation and more useful to represent the type of analysis that we have in mind.

In the analysis of underdeveloped countries, the main question is not how to measure the flow of information or how to measure the problems of formation of consensus for this simple reason: in vast parts of the world, mechanisms of consensus and degrees of information are not that important in political terms. The problem of "how can a society form a kind of consensus" is not necessarily an important political problem, because the decision process is oriented and constrained by other kinds of decision-making processes. Decisions do not depend on the amount of information possessed by people; they do not adjust to the expectations of people. Expectations and information are, however, particularly important at the elite level.

Let me give an example: the problem of child mortality. First of all, this was a *permanent* phenomenon in Brazil, Asia, and Africa. Politically, the important question is not just the level of change in the rate of mortality. What is important is the fact that some groups willingly try to use this as an argument to criticize other groups in the elite. Thus, the basic instrument for a political stake, in some types of political structure, is not based on knowledge about the flow of information and mass behavior. Yet to some extent, political behavior is based fundamentally on the allocation of values. In underdeveloped societies, the values are, to some degree, stable. To produce changes at that level requires "structural changes," not just changes in terms of *degree* in a given pattern.

This may explain why social scientists in Latin America always look at societies structurally and at changes in societies as a kind of revolution—a dramatic change in structure. Of course, I am exaggerating; nevertheless, this kind of intellectual perception—even if too rigid—is more in conformity with what really happens in these societies. This may also be the reason why some kinds of theoretical models—including computerized ones—are so poor, from our perspective. Most of these models are unable to explain patterns of political change and the interrelatedness between politics and the economy, considering the structures of these societies and the breakdown in these structures. I am not criticizing the usefulness of these types of models for *some* kinds of political processes. They cannot, however, be used to understand the problems emphasized by the tenor of our own discussions. If we want to understand what happens in underdeveloped societies in terms of dependency, it is necessary to try to construct some kind of indicator that expresses processes of change implying deep structural change. While we may be discussing this at two different levels, it seems to me that it is, nonetheless, a problem which should concern world modeling.

If political variables are to be included in a world model, we should try to put them in such a way that at least the basic process of change would be primarily referred to as a relationship between structural changes in each society and the new international economic order. On the other hand, political independence of some people, or the creation of new states, as well as the reorganization of internal patterns of income distribution, have to be represented in the model, taking into account that those processes are disruptive within societies. Perhaps through the third type of model there is a possibility for the technical representation of those processes. Apparently, the problem is how we can represent change at the level of the parameters. How can we represent a type of process that is not shock absorbing? This is very important: is it possible in technical terms? This is not my problem but a problem for modeling experts. If it will be possible, in technical terms, to represent disruptive and non-shock-absorbing processes, this will be, it seems to me, an important step forward in reaching more comprehensive types of analysis using models.

In the case of dependency, the main idea—a simple one—is that we will have to take into consideration the fact that some structures lie behind the distribution of resources. This pattern encompasses all types of resources—economic, natural, and political. There are fixed patterns that foster recurrent types of behavior, not just within societies but between them. I am not going to discuss why this is the case, but the fact is that some nations are haves and others are have nots. Second, the idea refers to the fact that not only are some recurrent patterns of appropriateness of resources occurring at the international level, but also internally in each country the resources are not equally distributed. These are, of course, truisms. But the fact is that we do not necessarilly take into consideration such basic things as the unequal distribution of resources among nation states and, internally, among different peoples and classes. The perspective of dependency emphasizes that because of this differentiation, some nations and some groups within each set of nations have different opportunities to realize themselves, to perform in political and economic terms. This is a simple statement, but it contains the nucleus of the whole idea of dependence. It seems to me that it is not impossible to represent structural differences in some kind of particular model.

There are some additional problems that are not problems of representation but problems concerning the very nature of the explanation in the model approach. It is possible to think in terms of a simple model, such as the first models that were constructed by some mathematicians. Let us look at a dichotomized model: we have two main groups of nations or classes; the developed nations and the underdeveloped nations; the rich and the poor. Such a model, however, will constitute a poor kind of representation. The fact is that we have different patterns of development, different types of relationships among nations and between classes in the developed countries, as well as within the underdeveloped countries. So it will be necessary to construct complex models. It is not easy to take into account every kind of differentiation in a model. On the other hand, to use the perspective of dependency in a model will require some theoretical elaboration. So far as I know, the dependency literature is not yet rich enough in this sense. It is not yet feasible to have a more concrete representation of the various types of interlinkages possible within this general frame of analysis that emphasize domination as a basic question in national and international society.

I am referring to this problem because the other area of dissatisfaction that derives from the use of models is that the aggregate form of utilization of data in available models remains at a very general level of analysis. Even the fifteen regions presented by Leontief are not detailed enough to permit real political analysis. Yet even the idea of region cannot be useful in political terms. Take India or Brazil—how can we, with some degree of realism, speak in terms of the average income distribution in these countries? How can we speak about the patterns of political behavior in these countries, even if we restrict ourselves to the entrepreneurial classes? The various types of links among classes and links between the local and international ruling class are extremely diverse within these countries. Of course, we can make an assumption that, as far as we are using the state as a kind of summary of what occurs in these countries, it is possible to speak in terms of a nation state, but that assumption is not enough to allow good political analysis.

Let me take an example to emphasize the necessity for more precision and the urgency for analysis to depart from the aggregate level of information. In Africa and Asia some theorists are emphasizing that because of dependence, the pattern of dominance and of economic exploitation of these regions produced homogeneous characteristics valid for the regions as a whole. From these alleged common features, the concept of the Third World was created. The United Naions literature reinforces the idea that the Third World is, in fact, a concept because it refers to one political reality. Nevertheless, other theorists do not agree with this. I, for instance, do not agree with so vague an image as Third World, a term employed as if it referred to a scientific concept. The effects of imperialism and some common features of dependency are not enough to homogenize the whole Third World. It is quite clear that the internal reaction in countries like Mexico, South Africa, or Pakistan is not the same as a reaction in Ecuador, Bolivia, or Uganda. The internal processes, the general class differentiations, and the economic processes that occur in these countries are not the same. We have different types of economic links and different types of social structures. Some countries do have real economic accumulation, capitalist accumulation. In my own country, Brazil, in spite of imperialism and perhaps *through* foreign and multinational penetration, capital is increasing, new classes are appearing, and the class conflict now has taken on a different flavor. Therefore, it is necessary to go much more into the details of the situation, especially of its structure.

Another fascinating problem suggested in our discussion is that economists are finally discovering that economy is politics. We are rediscovering political economy. How can we really understand what is occurring in societies if we do not have a vivid idea about the relationships between the political and the economic aspects? More than that: the question is not just the interrelationship between two dimensions. Some participants in our seminar have referred to this problem in terms of a kind of internal mutation. Some economic variables become political variables. Thus, it is not enough to consider that an economic structure produces a political system, or, on the contrary, that some values at the political level influence the shape of the economic structure. In the historical development of structures, they assume different facets, sometimes appearing as purely economic structures, at other times appearing as political structures. This is a challenging problem to be expressed by mathematicians and represented in models.

Behind this process lie the very problems of the nature of social change and the nature of history. We are, in fact, discussing dialectics: how one thing can be transformed into another. In this pursuit, we are putting aside the positivist assumption. We are considering that at some moments economic process is transformed into political process. But these processes are transformed by the interior, and not transformed because of the addition of another dimension or quality. Thus, we are really handling sophisticated, complex problems which have to be viewed through a sophisticated technological instrument.

KARL W. DEUTSCH'S QUESTIONS

I would like to put three questions to Professor Cardoso. The first concerns the concept of structure. Would he elaborate on it? It is often treated as if a structure was something fixed and given that can be changed only with great effort or at great cost. There is much truth in this. Yet, structuralist theorists such as Lévi-Strauss or Piaget make the explicit point that the structure includes the entire transformation group of the elements concerned. I wish he would explain to us the notion of structure from that perspective.

My second question relates to the notion of dependence and its treatment as an all-or-none relationship. Countries are viewed as either dependent or independent. Would it be possible to discuss dependency, at least to some extent, as a matter of degree, even though there may be thresholds in the relationship? How much of a range of discretion do dependent classes, groups, or countries still retain? What can they do to increase or decrease their amount of dependence? This leads then to the overall dependency structure in the world. It is often described as something almost tangible. The matter of the writings and discussions are then concerned with unmasking it. Yet one then has the feeling that emancipation is discussed as something that will come about only sometime in the future, after a great rise in consciousness. This trend of analysis often seems to dominate discussion, instead of a discussion focusing on emancipation and the reduction of dependent structures as an ongoing process in which the world is already moving.

This leads to the last point: I had a feeling that Professor Cardoso is right in identifying my stress on flows and changes. In many ways, what we call structures are processes that maintain a certain state of affairs. There is usually, I think, behind, beneath, or inside every structure a collection of self-maintaining or state-maintaining processes. Nontheless, I do think it is easier to describe structures in terms of processes than to describe processes in terms of structure. The two really belong together. In many ways, I think, our concerns are very similar. Professor Cardoso's approach and my own have much in common.

FERNANDO HENRIQUE CARDOSO'S REPLY

Let me try to elaborate a bit more on what I had in mind when I referred to structure. First of all, what I said referred not to my own thought but to the mood in the Latin American approach to the problem. To my mind, the problem of structure cannot be analyzed as a kind of rigid, fixed, and nonmoving social phenomenon. Structure, for me, is *not* the residual of some flows. Thus, my approach to the problem is similar to your own, although we may be moving in different directions. Our approach is similar in the sense that I also believe that it is impossible to represent any status—any state of affairs of a social process—as a fixed point. Some changing processes are always occurring. Some persons are trying to enforce a situation; some other persons, groups, or classes are trying to transform this situation. So the structure is a result of these different processes and has a dynamic character. This dynamic process, from my point of view, should be represented as an internal dynamic process. That is what I referred to at the very end of my commentary. That is the difficult problem in terms of models: whether it is possible to represent a process of change as an *internal* process strong enough to change the shape of the structure. That is my approach to this problem.

The second question concerning dependency is closely related to the first one. Dependency is a pattern, a structure that has been reproduced or transformed by groups. Thus dependencies also are general patterns of relationships that are submitted to these forces. These forces enforce dependence as well as oppose it. It is necessary to recognize that, in spite of the fact that most of the analyses of change in dependence situations refer to the complete rupture in a pattern of dominance, this is only one type of change. As was mentioned previously in this conference, the French Revolution, after all, occurred only in France, but capitalist transformations occurred all over the world. The same is true vis-à-vis the problem of dependence. The oil crisis has allowed several different countries which are oil producers to be more autonomous, to some extent, even without a break with the capitalist system.

I am not saying that all kinds of change are possible at all moments. This is not the case—there are constraints, some of which are persistent. Processes of change in dependent countries are moved not only by local forces but also by international politics. Let me give a direct example. The way the multinationals are now operating all around the world is new. If we compare the behavior of multinationals today with what occurred until World War II, we will find two different patterns of dependency relations linking developed and underdeveloped economies. In the first case, until World War II, but not necessarily because of it, the bulk of the external investors in the Third World were mainly interested in the control of raw materials such as oil or copper which were used abroad in the First World. The situation becomes quite different when, for instance, General Motors or Volkswagen start to produce cars in Mexico or in Brazil. As far as those cars are produced to be consumed internally, there necessarily occurs some degree of internal differentiation in these societies, including some income distribution to permit local markets to absorb industrial production. This is quite clear. Thus, even with the same amount of foreign investment, we can have two different types of behavior in the economic system. I am not saying that after the industrialization of the periphery, dependency disappears. I am saying that we have another type of dependency, and other social classes sustain this new type of dependency.

Let me give you another simple example. Generally, in order to assess what is new in the Third World when it starts to become developed, emphasis is put on the huge amount of foreign capital invested in these countries. This trend is important, but it is crucial to go further in the analysis. When General Motors or any other car producer starts to produce in the periphery, other types of industrial production are required, because the automobile plants of multinationals put together different parts of the car. However, not necessarily all producers of parts are foreign. Sometimes they are local. Are these local entrepreneurs the same "national entrepreneurs" as before? No, they are not. Before the multinational penetration, the local entrepreneurs had no ties, no relations with foreign groups or foreign capital. They were not economically connected with international enterprises or markets. Now, it may be true that some of them, perhaps a majority, are local in the sense that they were born in the country and even that they control national capital. But through their links with the multinationals that buy their products, they also become integrated into the world productive system.

So we have a different class of local producers—different because it is related to another class (international capitalists) in a different way. Therefore, if you really want to understand something, it is not enough to say, "This is a dependent country." It is necessary to ask "What type of dependence?" What are the degrees of alternatives for these countries? The degrees are not the same when you compare different kinds of countries. In some cases, when we have typical enclave production, as in Bolivia or as in Venezuela in the past, the lack of a local bourgeoisie is an important feature. There were foreign entrepreneurs and the state. The state collected taxes from the foreigners and distributed them to the local politically dominant classes; but the local politically dominant classes were not necessarily the entrepreneurial classes. They were not necessarily a "bourgeousie" in the purest sense of the word. Thus we find a specific situation in enclave economies. In some cases, the working classes are a much more "modernized class" than the local entrepreneurs because in enclave situations the workers work directly with the international economic system, whereas local dominant groups do not.

Thus, what I mean by dependency implies different types of relationships between the local groups and the foreign groups. There are different configurations of this process. Different policies are at the disposal of groups and classes in different situations of dependency. The dynamic of each society will depend on the status of these groups, on the interest of these groups, and on the values of these groups. Values are necessary to shape the economic situation, the structural situation. Thus it seems to me that to understand a dependent situation it is necessary to put these different processes together. In any case, the structure is the result of efforts to maintain one situation of domination by some groups and to change such a situation by others. Some small changes or marginal changes are always occurring. But to understand basic trends in the dynamic of societies, it is necessary to characterize the main oppositions and the structural shape of every significant type of linkage.

The last question was, it seems to me, explained to some extent by my comments in response to the two previous questions. I understand Professor Deutsch's point of view. He also thinks in terms of structure; but what I said is that, in general, persons who are more interested in Third World political questions try to *emphasize* structure, and frequently persons oriented toward another, more complex political process in the First World try to emphasize flows. It is a matter of emphasis. It is also a matter of real differentiation in terms of situation and perspective.

✳ *Chapter 13*

The New International Economic Order: Social Implications and Political Requirements

Celso Lafer

1. MODELS AFTER WORLD WAR II

One of the basic issues of the international order viewed from the perspective of underdeveloped countries is the sharing of the costs and benefits of the international transfer of resources. For this reason, I would like to start by discussing some models that have been institutionalized in post–World War II organizations, in order to examine whether these models, in their institutionalized forms, are or are not responsible for the persistence of certain patterns of distribution that explain present world stratification.

As is known, the model-building trends after World War II should be viewed in the context of overcoming the difficulties that prevailed in the 1930s, which had led to both protectionism and autarky. New institutional models of economic cooperation were first suggested and then created by the international system under the basic influence of the United States. Of these, the two more important ones, for our purposes, were GATT and the International Monetary Fund. If one looks at GATT, one can say that its basic mechanism is the bargaining process among leading producers and consumers of items that are negotiated in this arena. The major products of underdeveloped countries are not traded within GATT, and this situation has led to their lack of appropriate bargaining positions in this arena. In fact, underdeveloped countries were not and are not main producers or consumers of the items that are the substance of the bargaining process in GATT. As far as the IMF is concerned, it can be said that fixed parities did not increase the liquidity of underdeveloped countries and thus did not help their continuous problems of balance of payments. The conclusion is simple: these two basic models that dealt with trade and money are not geared to the specificity of underdeveloped countries. For this reason, alternative models of international cooperation were also suggested to adjust the model building trends to this specificity. Such models include: (one) substituting market mechanisms for planning of some sort in the trade of commodities; (two) fostering the industrialization of underdeveloped countries when the lack of success of commodities agreements led to a new search for opportunities for underdeveloped countries; and finally (three) granting preferential access for the manufactured goods of underdeveloped countries to the markets of developed countries. These models had a limited impact. Hence the conclusion that models of economic cooperation created and institutionalized after World War II were successful in overcoming protectionism and autarky in North–North relationships and—with détente—in East–West relationships. However, as far as North–South relationships are concerned, not only were the basic models (GATT and IMF) unsuited to deal with them but also, in the perspective of underdeveloped countries, the alternative models had scant impact in changing the unfavorable sharing of costs and benefits in the international transfer of resources. In other words, model building with relevant legal and political impact in terms of the institutionalized interplay of facts, values, and norms, did not contribute in any significant way to change one of the issues of international order, namely, the growing inequality of the international system, which is essential to the position of the underdeveloped world.

2. THE LEGITIMACY CRISIS

The situation described above led to alternative views. In the 1960s, UNCTAD (United Nations Conference on Trade and Development) provides an interesting example of search and change, basically produced by analysis that induced a legitimacy crisis of the international economic order. In other words, although UNCTAD had no relevant impact on the effective bargaining power of states, debates within its context created an awareness that the values that prevailed in the post-World War II models of economic cooperation were not as perfect as they seemed. This legitimacy crisis was intensified through the international redistribution of power that came about in the late 1960s, with the growing importance of Japan and the European Economic Community, and in the early 1970s, when OPEC in a sense altered for the first time certain types of patterns of conduct in North–South relationships. I will not go into greater detail about these aspects, since Professor Jaguaribe has discussed them in his paper. However, I would like to emphasize that one of the main traits of this process is the occurrence of a disjunction between order and power in the international system. The positive power of great states, that is, their capability to determine the basic values and issues defined by the international system, has declined. As a result, the power differential among states has diminished and what I would call, following Organski, the negative power of all states, that is, their capability of preventing others from taking undesirable action, has increased.

The possibilities arising from this situation, I suggest, are of two types: either a trend toward paralysis of decision and consequently an ungovernability, as Professor Deutsch would say, of the international system, or alternatively, new models. To sketch some eventual characteristics of these new models is the aim of this paper.

3. COLLABORATION, CONSENSUS, AND RECIPROCITY

The increase in the bargaining power of most states requires collaboration. *Collaboration* comes from *collaborare*, to work together, which is the key for the setting-up of an order that requires stronger consensus, since the possibility of imperative imposition tends to decline with the general increase in bargaining power of the actors of the international system. Consensus begs for reciprocity, which derives etymologically from *re* and *pro*, that is backward and forward. This idea of movement contained in the origins of the word conveys intuitively the reasons why reciprocity can be used as a permanent formula for research, a *topos* in the Aristotelian sense, that confers a pragmatic dimension to the discourse. This is why social theory, from Marcel Mauss's *"Éssai sur le don"* to Lévi-Strauss *"Les Structures élementaires de la Parenté,"* has considered reciprocity as a basic dimension of social interaction that leads from hostility to alliance, from anguish to trust, from fear to friendship.

In the international sphere, the process of reciprocity can have two aspects. It can be a reciprocity based on identical behavior, which is, so to speak, relatively easy to establish, since in this case the problem is to set up the same type of rights and obligations. In fact, because they are of the same type, they can be measured, legally established, and controlled. Diplomatic immunities, or the formal validity of treaties, illustrate this assertion. However, in associations for exchange, equal return, as Aristotle said, does not hold men together, and what is required is reciprocity in accordance with a proportion that establishes equivalent behavior. The big problem for the new models that are going to have to deal with the international order, is to discover mechanisms through which equivalent behavior can be measured and accepted through consensus. This is a question related both to values and to the fact that time can modify the equivalence of behavior.

With respect to the problem of values, it can be said that efficiency, growth, full employment, income distribution, price stability, quality of life, and economic security are common criteria through which models of economic cooperation can be judged. These criteria are not all mutually compatible and are, of course, value laden. That is why model building and model choosing require a hierarchy of values. Since the hierarchy of values is subject to change over time, the economic trade-offs, the cost-benefit analyses—a problem also raised by Professor Rapoport in his comments—in the choice of models become extremely complex when there are doubts regarding the importance of values associated with these criteria. May I be permitted to venture a hypothesis to illustrate my point. In a certain sense, the models created after World War II by the basic economic values then prevailing do have a certain relationship to utilitarianism. Utilitarianism is probably an ethic developed in and by a society that starts to have surplus and abundance. In what sense are values determined by utilitarianism, and hence applicable to developed societies, compatible with an international economic order that faces the problem of scarcity? How can an ethic based upon abundance and affluence be blended with an ethic of scarcity to permit, through consensus and collaboration, a hierarchy of values that can establish criteria through which trade-offs can be bargained and negotiated?

With respect to change modifying, in time, the equivalence of behavior independent of the change in values, models for the international order will require both the planning of performance and risk planning. The planning of performance implies techniques that reduce future uncertainty regarding equivalent behavior by assuring outcomes. From a legal and political point of view, the European Economic Community provides an interesting example of a process through which outcomes—that is the planning of performance—have been negotiated in an institutionalized model. However, this type of planning raises significant accounting problems of the type mentioned by Professor Stone in his paper. In fact, outcomes must be measured and have a unit of account, and this is no easy matter in an uncertain international system of which the monetary order is part and parcel. To give an example: In the negotiation of the new coffee agreement, one of the basic issues that separated producer-underdeveloped countries and consumer-developed countries was the unit of account through which the comparative prices of coffee from 1962 to 1975 and their fluctuations could be judged. More than one criterion was available, and thus consensus regarding what was reciprocity based on equivalent behavior became a dilemma. That is why new models also require risk planning. Risk planning, I would say, is an attempt to insert, into institutionalized models, safeguards to avoid the pitfalls of change by avoiding the indefinite continuation of models through obligatory renegotiation. Legal clauses of the type of nullification and impairment that exist, for instance, in GATT and in other mechanisms of economic cooperation are examples of risk planning.

Both risk planning and performance planning are related to the learning capacity of the international system. The learning capacity of large political systems, as Professor Deutsch has mentioned, is in a certain sense related to recommittable resources in terms of liquidity preference, optimum redundance in terms of communication, and so forth. These have been reduced, as this conference has shown, either in terms of the several Club of Rome models, which have projected images of long-term stagnation, poverty, and exhaustion of resources, or in terms of the Bariloche model, that has brought to our attention that even if there are no physical limits to growth, provided the world wants to achieve certain outcomes, the political aspects of redistribution must be faced. Be this as it may, exhaustion of resources or redistribution of resources, both mean the lack of a great amount of recommittable resources, and hence conflict.

In what sense is this foreseeable conflict an asset or a liability to the learning process of the international system? The answer to this question, I submit, is crucial for the alternatives to the present international system. If this conflict is an asset, new models are to be expected. If the conflict is a liability, ungovernability is the outlook for the future. This question, by the way, is also valid in terms of political development within states. Can an economic and political crisis that implies a diminution of recommittable resources lead to the opening up of a political system?

4. CONCLUSIONS

I tried briefly to examine in the first part of my presentation what could be considered one aspect of dependency theory, namely, how do international organizations created after World War II, that are so to speak institutionalized models of international cooperation, work? How do they operate, and how do they reach or fail to reach the interests of the underdeveloped countries? The last query was basically directed to the issue of the distribution of costs and benefits in the international transfer of resources. My conclusion is that both the global models and the more specific models that were attuned to the needs of the underdeveloped countries did not bring any substantial change in the patterns of inequality; on the contrary, they increased them. I then proceeded to point out, in the second part of my presentation, the disjunction between order and power that is a product of the present trends of the international system. This disjunction, I suggest, increased the bargaining positions of most countries and reduced the capacity of the center of the system (the developed world) to impose and maintain a certain type of order that does not take into account the interests of the periphery (the underdeveloped world). This led to the alternatives of either an ungovernable international system or new models. If we are to have new models, I ventured to say in the third part of my presentation, these new models require the emergence of consensus and collaboration. Consensus and collaboration require reciprocity that can be considered as a formula for research, a backward and forward movement in accordance with the etymological origins of both words. Reciprocity founded on equivalent behavior—a prerequisite of association for exchange—is difficult to establish, both because of the redefinition, across time, of values and because of the change, across time, of the equivalence of behavior. Thus the dilemmas of trade-offs in the negotiation of new models require, in view of uncertainty, risk planning and performance planning. The viability of risk planning and performance planning is closely related to the learning capacity of the international system. When the recommittable resources of the international system are dwindling in accordance with the perspectives of both the Club of Rome models and the Bariloche model, increasing conflict is a likely trend. In a sense, this trend may be either an asset or a liability to the learning process, thereby either providing an opportunity for the creation of new steering models, that can overcome the probability of results or even dragging us into a global and drifting ungovernability.

Part 3

The Data Question

Chapter 14

Data Priorities for Modeling Global Dependence

Bruce Russett

My discussion will focus on the priorities for data analysis, but since the conference is drawing to a close, there must be a much broader attempt to establish priorities than would be right for me in any way to do. I will not establish priorities, but I will suggest some of the things I hear and see as they fit my own interests. Fred Kochen, in his excellent paper, suggests a wide variety of kinds of information and possible data that we ought to have readily available if we are going to do any serious global modeling. Out of his broad list, for the sake of manageability I will limit myself to measures of variables of interest to us, or of functional relationships between the variables.

In the process of listening to this conference, I heard a wide variety of ideas about the sort of things we ought to be measuring. First of all, I heard a good bit about the values of decision makers, what their objective functions look like. I also heard some calls for information on decision-making processes. Much of what we have talked about is so-called objective information on characteristics of various units in the system, that is, national or subnational units. But I think we should not pass over the concern with values and decision-making processes. I have not yet heard a consensus in this conference as to whether this information is interesting, valuable, or necessary to the enterprise that might come out of this. Because these are going to be very difficult data to get, we ought to be sure that they are not only interesting but very important before we give them a high priority, even though I am inclined to give them one.

Second, and I am encouraged to think in this direction by our friends from Bariloche, I hear calls requiring information on the quality of life. Now this, fortunately, is an area where we have a good deal of experience in measurement problems. That is not to say that everything is perfectly reliable or perfectly valid, but relative to some other things this is a fairly good area for us. The exception to this observation is that we have much better information for averages or aggregates than we do for distributions of quality of life measures within subsystems. One of the messages I am going to close with is that, even though I am formally a student of international politics, I think one of our most pressing needs is for information of various sorts about what goes on within national or perhaps other large aggregate subsystems, quality of life being a key one.

Third, we obviously need measures of conflict and cooperation. This again is, relatively speaking, a good area, especially on the conflict measures as in the Michigan Correlates of War Project. There are various others. Richard Merritt has reminded us that there are interesting potentials in mail-flow data. Values of decision makers constitute a hard area; quality of life and conflict and cooperation are, I submit, *relatively* easy. Others may disagree.

Fourth, we need a variety of economic data, especially interaction data, such as the kind that might go into an input–output matrix. If not Leontief input–output matrix data, then there are various functional equivalents that I shall try to mention in a moment. Again, it strikes me that we may be in better shape here on the international level than we are on the intranation level, especially once we get out of the developed Western countries.

Finally, there is the old problem of how to measure the political variables. This is, again, partly a matter of values, which goes back to my first point, but there are also other kinds of political conditions. It is, once again, within the system that these values become difficult to quantify. Let me briefly try to explain what I mean by comments on the questions variously identified as dependence, dominance, imperialism, or neocolonialism. Some of what I have been trying to do is spelled out in a very preliminary form in an article entitled "Some Proposals to Guide Empirical Research on Contemporary Imperialism" written with Raymond Duvall and appearing in *The Jerusalem Journal of International Affairs*, II:1 (Autumn 1976).

I think we have now come a little bit farther than that, with the aid of some very sharp and interesting students, and hope to present some preliminary results at the Edinburgh conference.[1] We have begun to do a little formal modeling and begun to get a better sense of what are the important variables we have to measure and what some of the functional relationships might look like, or at least as they are hypothesized in the literature. For example, we built a very crude model based on Johan Galtung's structural theory of imperialism. You might be surprised how hard it was for us to achieve even that crude model. It is not always easy to see what are the variables and the functional relationships. To do a Galtung model as one of the elements of a global model we would need various

1. See Raymond Duvall, Steven Jackson, Bruce Russett, Duncan Snidal, and David Sylvan, "A Formal Model of 'Dependencia': Structure, Measurement, and Some Preliminary Results," paper presented to the World Congress of the IPSA., Edinburgh, Scotland, August 16–21, 1976.

measures of dependence and most certainly, for example, internal distributions of quality of life. We also would need some political variables.

Another model is a type of generalized dependency model. We hope that it is in the spirit of Latin American dependencia theorists, partly as passed through Samir Amin and various other thinkers, especially from the Third World. We cannot pin this model on any single author, but we think it fairly well reflects the general approach of this school. It is very simple, and what I give you today will necessarily be an even more simplified version. I think, however, it illustrates some of the points where we are going to have the greatest difficulty in getting appropriate measures. But it will also illustrate some high priority items. I personally believe that while this is by no means the only thing we want to be modeling; any respectable global model has to have a major component that takes into account the structural relationships between center and periphery. I will draw an almost ridiculously simple picture for you. We will have a set of equations, operational definitions, and preliminary empirical results at Edinburgh.

Let me note also that I am very agnostic about this model. While I find the dependency literature highly stimulating and in a number of respects plausible, I want to treat it as a set of hypotheses rather than, in any sense, revealed truth. But if we try to put its perspective into a form of rigorous hypotheses, we can test them and, if they prove supported in an interesting degree, begin to express the model in rigorous terms, estimate the functional relationships, and make some forecasts based on different assumptions about how those functional relationships might remain or change. Here is the present crude diagram of some hypothesized relationships of dependence.

First we have various dimensions of external penetration and dependence— financial and technological, political and cultural. For the former we focus upon manifestations like debt and investment capital, and import of capital goods, patents, and licensing arrangements. On the political and cultural side, aspects of dependence could be measured by military ties (arms imports and military training programs) and educational exchange or news and mass media dependence (e.g., where television programs come from). According to the dependence

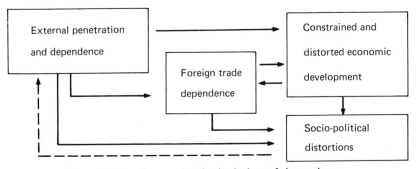

Figure 14-1. A very simple depiction of dependence.

literature, these lead to and maintain trade dependence, in the form of developing an export enclave in the dependent economy. Here we would use measures focused on concentration of trade (especially export) recipients and concentration of export commodities, and the share of foreign trade in total GNP (all as aspects of weak market power in the world economy).

Proceeding with this very crude presentation, dependence theorists then assert that all these forms of dependence lead to and are reinforced by major economic distortions within the dependent economy. Some writers emphasize low economic growth rates as the consequence, but for most that is not the relevant issue. Rather, they are concerned with the distribution of income and welfare within countries. Thus a dependent and therefore distorted economy might show rapid growth of GNP, but would also be characterized by gross and probably increasing inequalities in income and welfare. Many Latin American countries at the moment, especially Brazil, for example, show such high internal inequalities. Now whether this is attributable to dependence is a question to be investigated, but certainly Brazil's income distribution is both highly unequal and increasingly unequal over the past ten or twelve years. As I read the empirical data, there has been virtually no improvement (and perhaps a decline) in conditions for the poorest 60 percent of the population.

Some points made by Bruno Fritsch and Dieter Senghaas are relevant to another aspect of economic distortion. Not only inequality is at issue, but dualism as well, the kind of heterogeneity and lack of integration within the national economy that stems from an export-oriented enclave. Such an unintegrated economy may even have a large manufacturing sector devoted to import substitution in consumer goods for the upper classes, but one little oriented to capital goods needed in the primary—agricultural and extractive—sectors. I want to hear more from Dieter and others on this, but it does seem that a reasonable measure of such lack of integration as identified by the Latin American dependencia theorists might well be derived from national input–output tables. However, there is serious question as to whether there are adequate input–output tables for such economies, especially of the quality and comparability necessary to study a variety of countries and to watch changes in countries over time. I suspect such data may not exist, though I am not enough of an economist to be sure. Perhaps Professor Stone will comment.

If it is true that input–output data are not sufficiently available, then we are forced into some creative and, perhaps overly imaginative, surrogate indicators. One way to do this might be to look at the transportation network in a country. Here are simple diagrams representative of three different countries.

Country A is the simplest possible—it just does not have a national transportation network at all, being very underdeveloped. Country B has quite an elaborate transportation network which has access to most of the territory, however all roads lead to the port and there are few connections otherwise. Country C has a different kind of transportation network. The total road mileage or railroad track-

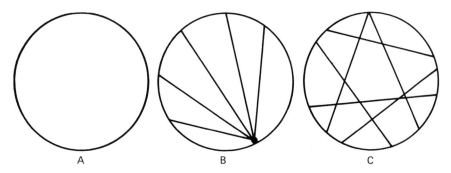

Figure 14-2. Transportation networks in three economies.

age may not be much more than in country B, but the pattern is different, and all points in the country are more or less directly connected. I think country B is an example of the kind of economy postulated in dependency models—"developed" in one sense, but geographically and economically unintegrated. Perhaps spatial data of this sort, derived from transportation grids, could substitute for unavailable input-output data while being faithful to the basic theory.

Other causal arrows in Figure 14-1 result from the assertion that as dependence leads to a heterogenous, nonintegrated, and highly unequal national economy, these economic distortions lead to certain kinds of political distortions. As a result of inequalities and unsatisfied aspirations in large sectors of the society, the regime may be faced with a tradeoff between participation and stability. If a wide variety of individuals, groups, and classes participate actively in the political system (as is implied by democracy), their conflicting demands will threaten the regime's stability and produce frequent regime changes. This can be pictured simply with yet another diagram.

The curve near the origin represents the choice facing elites in our hypothetical dependent country. You may have high participation and little stability, or very limited participation and substantial stability—but it is a choice to be made. For a nondependent country, a metropole for example, the choices are much less hard. With less inequality and a more integrated economy, the trade-offs are much less severe. Widespread political participation will not generate nearly so much threat to stability. Indeed, the true relationship in the metropole might better be characterized by a convex rather than a concave curve—greater participation may at some points produce greater stability.

When we talk about measuring these concepts, however, we again face problems. Stability is not too hard to measure. We have experience with various measures of protest, violence, and frequency of government change. But finding measures of participation is difficult. It is hard enough to talk about participation in parliamentary systems or other polyarchies, where you can get attitude measures from surveys or look at voting or other electoral participation or derive something from data on behavior in parliaments. I think we are increasingly

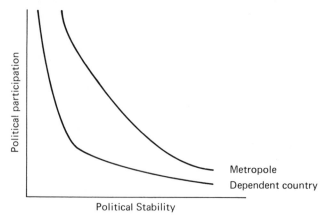

Figure 14-3.   Trade-offs between stability and participation.

aware of the limitations of this kind of measurement, even in polyarchies. Yet it is enormously more satisfactory there than are most of the alternatives for measuring participation in nonpolyarchies. And since most of the allegedly dependent systems are not polyarchies—and decreasingly so it seems—it becomes a serious challenge to devise satisfactory measures. Possibly we can do something adequate with the other side of the coin. That is if we cannot measure participation, we may be able to measure efforts to restrict participation—governmental acts of coercion through censorship, arrest, torture, and the like. But the need for adequate data is very great if we are to be able to talk scientifically about the problems identified in the dependency literature. We must measure participation by individuals, groups, and classes and devise aggregate measures of the extent of participation in entire political systems.

Finally, of course, there are causal arrows in Figure 14-1 that go back from economic and political distortions to dependence. Still greater dependence is produced by these distortions. I again apologize for the crudeness of this model, but I cannot do much more at this stage in our work and given the time constraints on this presentation. I think you can grasp a general sense of the problem and will agree that it incorporates a set of major issues for global modeling. While this is hardly the only problem of concern to global modelers, a serious evaluation of the causes and effects of dependency must be part of such a model. Once we have equations and data and begin to specify sone functional relationships, we can discuss the issues more precisely. Also, at that stage we may well find that we can work with fewer variables, or at least indicators, than may seem required at this stage—which would reduce what now appear to be formidable data-gathering requirements. I know a good bit of this work can be done in the context of simulation, but there is also need for application of some efforts other than simulation at the same time. Sharper theory, and nearer consensus on what kinds of problems are important, will help considerably in setting data-gathering priorities.

Let me close with two brief points, as we return to my assignment to identify priorities for data gathering. First, throughout this conference we have said very little about transnational actors. Some implications about such actors are imbedded in the dependence literature, and Hayward Alker has made some points about transnational actors, but mostly they have been neglected here. I suspect that this is a serious mistake. Second, I would like to conclude with reference to another of Fred Kochen's perceptive exhortations. We must start with disaggregated data capable of telling us what is going on within a variety of national subsystems. If we wish, we can always later aggregate such data into national, regional, or global units. But there are powerful theoretical reasons for going slowly, and in any case, it will be much easier to aggregate later where we wish than to proceed the other way if we have started only with the aggregated information.

Chapter 15

Further Analyses on Global Dependence: An Exchange with Bruce Russett

Dieter Senghaas

I shall try to be specific with respect to Bruce Russett's paper, but at the same time I should like to make some general remarks about the issues he raised. My first point is related to what I would like to call the logical status of dependency indicators. This is strongly related to what we have been debating here, and to remain brief I shall refer to just one or two examples used in the presentation of the dominance-dependency paradigm by Bruce Russett.

The first example he used was partner concentration. This certainly is an indicator for dependency, and it has been introduced into the literature by Johan Galtung and others. But dependency is measured by partner concentration only in a particular historical period, the time when colonial economies, which we call periphery economies today, have been integrated into the capitalist world market and related systematically (as exclave economies) to the economies of the metropoles. Partner concentration is a specific device in the takeoff period of colonialism. Let me give you one example. If you look at the export data of Ghana, you will observe that the exports of that country were still very much concentrated on Britain when Ghana became independent in 1957. Approximately 60 percent of the exports went to Britain. Today this ratio has decreased to something like twenty percent. Thus, partner concentration has been drastically reduced. Some of the exports now go to the United States, West Germany, France, and so forth. My argument is that loosening up partner concentration and diversifying exports to various metropoles instead of one major metropole are *under present conditions* no indicator of reduced dependency. I would like to explain this in some further detail later on.

Let me give you a second example, to which Bruce Russett also referred: commodity concentration. It is true that most countries of the Third World have some kind of monocultural economy. One, two, or three commodities constitute the bulk of their exports. Again, if you look at the data, particularly of the last ten years, there is undoubtedly a reduction in commodity concentration, a diversification away from only raw material and agricultural products to some sort of manufactured goods with a low degree of processing and a high degree of labor and raw material inputs. My argument again is that for a long period of time, maybe something like 50 to 200 years, commodity concentration has been an adequate indicator (among others) in measuring dependency. The reduction of commodity concentration is no longer a sign that dependency is reduced.

These countries are far more dependent today on importing machinery and technology to be able to produce precisely those goods they ship to the world market than they were before. Some simple indicators to measure this highly salient dependency are the ratio of imported capital goods to locally produced capital goods or the ratio of payments for imported capital goods to the total value of the export. These indicators have been going up drastically, and we observe something like a displacement effect within the total dependency context.

A third indicator could have been used by Bruce Russett in the Prebisch tradition: the development of the terms of trade. Declining terms of trade are often interpreted as an indicator of dependence, but this again is problematic. When the terms of trade have been, historically speaking, to the advantage of Third World countries, as was the case during the nineteenth century in the relations between British and Latin American economies, this leads precisely to the restructuring of local economies into periphery economies (enclave-type economies). Profitable terms of trade, therefore, did not prevent the peripherization of the Third World. Without positive terms of trade, these countries would never have become peripheries, since only positive terms of trade could motivate the local elites to integrate themselves into an international division of labor as it emerged between metropoles and peripheries in the nineteenth century.

The question then is, "What is dependency?" The first answer is that there is no one indicator or no five indicators measuring dependency with the same validity over time. I do think that dependency is reflected in a particular socio-economic configuration, and to understand dependency, one has to pursue a *deep structure analysis (Tiefenstrukturanalyse)* of this particular configuration. As I have done elsewhere, such a deep structure analysis would show specific deficiencies of periphery economies that result from their structural dependency or metropolitan economies. The most fundamental deficiency is the lack of interlinkages between agriculture (most of which is chronically stagnant), an industrial sector for the production of mass consumption goods (which cannot be bought because of the chronic lack of purchasing power), and a producer goods sector (which on the average is not built up since it is considered to be uneconomical to do so). The lack of these interlinkages strikingly contrasts with the hyperdevelopment of an export or enclave-type sector and an import sector importing the manufactured goods produced in the metropoles (at least within the division-of-labor scheme of the nineteenth century). These structural defects and distortions do show up in the input–output analyses of periphery economies. Accumulation processes in periphery economies are very different from the ones to be observed in metropolitan economies, both capitalist and socialist.

Dependency indicators have thus to be related to a deep structure analysis. And it might be that an indicator measuring dependency appropriately in a particular period of time (like partner and commodity concentration to which I referred earlier) will become fairly inappropriate for the analysis of dependency at a later stage in the process of dependent development, and new indicators will have to be introduced (like capital goods import, technology import, and so forth) that would not have made too much sense at an earlier period. But the use of such indicators has to be coupled with a deep structure analysis which, in my understanding, is a theory of the accumulation process and the reproduction dynamics of periphery economies within the capitalist world market.

Let me suggest a further illustration of what I referred to earlier. If you define dependency by partner concentration, this is a valid indicator for a time period of perhaps 100 years. You might observe that within these 100 years the amount of exports of a periphery to a particular metropole went down, but what you mostly experience at the same time are some displacement effects. New dimensions of dependency emerge within the overall context of dependent reproduction (which is a specific accumulation process to which I referred earlier). All indicators are highly contextuated, and their use therefore has to be specific. In addition, indicators of dependency measure dependency only insofar as the latter is analytically elaborated in a theory of dependent reproduction.

RUSSETT: *We cannot use the same indicator over time—can we use the same indicators in cross-sectional analyses?*

The same indicator can be used neither indiscriminately over time nor for cross-sectional analyses. In doing the latter, you would put together countries like Brazil with countries like Haiti or Senegal. To make a cross-sectional analysis, you have to disaggregate the total population of Third World countries into sets of countries with similar profiles. There are still some countries that show the typical nineteenth-century monoculture and enclave-type economy (you would have to put all the Gabons into one box). Then, you would have to put all the countries with a quite differentiated internal structure, such as Brazil, into another box. And third, you would have to place all countries located somewhere in between (like Nigeria). A further type of country would be the city state like Hongkong and its export-oriented industrialization. Another type would include countries like South Korea with potentialy large internal markets but a highly export-oriented structure (where most investments of the so-called runaway industries are located). I think that a systematic typology of periphery economies is feasible and that on this basis a cross-sectional analysis should be performed. If you do not base such an analysis on types of periphery economies, you are maneuvering your research directly into what Alker labeled "ecological fallacies" some ten years ago.

Finally, why does it make sense to talk about periphery economies in general, despite the actual existence of some five to ten particular profiles of periphery economies to be specified in a typology? It makes some sense, because the deep structure (*Tiefenstruktur*) of these various particular profiles is still the same. Despite the existence of the various profiles, these countries are still different from metropolitan economies since they lack key interlinkages that are the objective basis for the development of their own internal market. These linkages between an increasingly productive agriculture, an industrial sector producing mass consumption goods, and a sector producing producer goods and technology, are still missing even in a differentiated and diversified case such as Brazil. If you take simpler cases like Pakistan, Egypt, or even Senegal and the most simple cases, like Gabon and Haiti, you will find the same underlying structural configuration that is precisely the basis for collectively labelling these economies "periphery economics." Without such an underlying pattern, this label would be purely formal and analytically arbitrary. As long as this underlying pattern or deep structure exists, the general notion of periphery economy and dependent reproduction is of theoretical and operational value despite the existence of different profiles, which are the result of the different levels of mobilization of productive forces within Third World countries.

✳ *Chapter 16*

Problems of Data Availability and Quality

Charles Lewis Taylor

My first contact with world models occurred in the summer of 1970 in a seminar jointly sponsored by an organization normally engaged in physical research and an institute devoted to public policy studies. In that meeting, the natural scientists and engineers proposed to the political scientists a common project to model the world and its processes. The response of the political scientists was one of incredulity: who could possibly put together a model of the entire world? That same summer, Professor Jay Forrester presented the first version of his model to a meeting of the Club of Rome in Cambridge.

How could distinguished political scientists in a prestigious university be so unaware of the possibilities? There are probably a number of explanations for their disbelief, but one was grounded in political scientists' inclination to rely upon large amounts of empirical data. The behavioral revolution of the late 1950s and the 1960s gave us a bias toward the use of data that has led us to use greater and greater amounts of them. Nevertheless, data to cover the entire world and its working relationships gathered together in one place and at one time to validate one model seemed well beyond the capacity of any relatively small group of scholars.

The world modelers, as it turned out, did not really have that many data in mind. In fact, the early modelers employed only bits, scraps, and pieces of data, and many of these were used essentially in analogies. There have been few attempts toward thorough empirical testing using a comprehensive collection of relevant data thus far. Presumably, however, the minimum data model represents only a beginning in global modeling. If the models are to become more realistic, they will need greater empirical reference and relevance. The setting of a topic such as this one among papers such as these implies the intention of introducing more data into world models.

Now the original fears of the political scientists come back to haunt us. It is easier to say that models ought to be informed by data and to define strategies by which to use the data than to identify and to collect the appropriate data. There are, to be sure, many difficulties related to the specification of models and to making them run, but in a significant sort of way, the scholar remains in control of the process. The collection of data is another matter. Here the scholar is at the mercy of all sorts of other people, not all of whom place his kind of priority on the searching out of truth. Even those who do sometimes lack the proper resources with which to function appropriately. There is a story that one country's population jumped by fifteen million when the distribution of funds was changed to a population basis. There are also stories of harried district officers with statistical questionnaires to fill out. Their rough guesses may be the best estimates to be had, but they still carry a large margin of error.

Moreoever, the difficulties are not limited to the "soft" areas. Publications in the "hard" sciences can say such things as, "49 percent of World recoverable energy reserves are located in North America. . . . Total World energy consumption in 1972 represented one percent of World energy reserves."[1] But we can ask in all seriousness, how on earth is this known? Estimations based on submissions to the World Energy Conference with a good degree of guesswork assume some sort of credibility when they are aggregated to the global level, but problems remain.

In Oklahoma, geologically one of the most thoroughly explored regions on earth, one of the major oil companies drilled in what promised, on the basis of expensive information, to be a productive field. After a significant amount of drilling, the company gave up deciding an oil strike was no longer likely. It sold the equipment in the ground and further rights to drill at the same site to a smaller, high risk company at a discount. The latter decided to exercise the drill rights and made a rich strike of oil. Another hidden data problem became evident during the recent oil shortage when proprietary information on stocks was not made public.

These details, of course, are of limited interest to the man with the chart that looks like a computer circuit. Some division of labor is absolutely necessary. There are the specialists in national accounts, demography, social indicators, geology, and political indicators. As models use more empirical data, however, another speciality must begin to develop. This is the speciality of gathering the data from several sources and putting them into form that is usable by the modelers.

The *World Handbooks of Political and Social Indicators* represent one set of

---

1. United States Department of the Interior, *Energy Perspectives: A Presentation of Major Energy and Energy-related Data* (Washington: Government Printing Office, 1975), p. 2.

efforts in this speciality.[2] The updating of these handbooks would be very useful in providing political and social information on a cross-national basis for continuing research. But updating is only a small part of what is needed. Explicit in the two earlier handbooks is the belief that countries are important for analysis; only data for country units were collected. Yet other units—regions, groups, individuals—play roles in world politics. These data are not so neat in their collection or presentation, but the reality to which they refer is important nevertheless.

As important as additional units of analysis are new series required by ever new theoretical needs. This requires, in a world of limited resources, some careful thinking about what kinds of data are important for global models. It then requires careful conceptualization of these data so that measurements are defined. Finally, effort must be made to get national and other appropriate bodies to measure the items needed. These tasks are especially important for the political variables. Perhaps the major reason why policy tends to be left open or remain mechanistic in the models is that insufficient thought has been given to its operationalization and measurement by political scientists. If policy makers are to be taken seriously as decision makers with their own preference functions, then we need to know something about these preferences.

World models, in my opinion, need to be more fully informed by data if they are to avoid being nothing more than expensive toys. Equally important, careful thought must be given to what these data will be, since whatever is quantified becomes central to the model.

2. Bruce M. Russett, *et al., World Handbook of Political and Social Indicators* (New Haven: Yale University Press, 1964); and Charles Lewis Taylor and Michael C. Hudson, *World Handbook of Political and Social Indicators*; Second edition (New Haven: Yale University Press, 1972).

Chapter 17

An Example of Data Use: Mail Flows in the European Balance of Power, 1890-1920

Richard L. Merritt and Caleb M. Clark

The relationship between the public and national policy has intrigued many writers. Some approach it normatively, asking what role the public *should* play in the policy process. Others have examined the public's image of leaders and policies or, alternatively, the leaders' perceptions of the extent to which the masses actually have a role to play in the formulation and implementation of public policies. The analytic problem becomes even more complex when we turn from a country's domestic policy to the one it pursues in the international arena. This paper examines some hypotheses about the nexus of public behavior and foreign policy in the troubled if exciting years that led up to World War I. Specifically, it focuses upon the international flow of mail as an indicator of informal patterns of communication, and relates such information to the structure of international alliances as it evolved during the three decades from 1890 to 1920.

PUBLIC PERSPECTIVES AND INTERNATIONAL ALLIANCES

International politics in earlier centuries was by and large an impersonal matter. Kings allied with or battled against one another as best suited their needs at the moment, with little regard for enduring relationships. Indeed, a cardinal principle of European balance-of-power politics was that rulers avoid permanent alliances or enmities. They had to be prepared at any time to shift their weight in the international setting so as to take advantage of a momentary opportunity or prevent another from gaining power that would destabilize the overall pattern of the European political system. Nor were the wishes of their populations accorded much regard. The masses were seen as objects—a source of manpower and taxes, commodities to be traded to offset political or military losses, or, as the German writer Grimmelshausen described in such graphic detail, fair game for marauding soldiers.

The rise of nationalism in the nineteenth century changed dramatically the nature of international politics in Europe. Increasingly the masses were permitted and, when it suited the needs of leading groups, encouraged to participate in political life. Ever larger numbers obtained the right to vote, territories called the "motherland" were endowed with well-nigh sacred attributes, and the notion of "national" armies, drawn from and supported by the surging masses, caught a firm grip on the popular mind. A concomitant development was increasing social mobilization. The emergence of large-scale industries, people flocking from the countryside to the industrializing cities, and the development of such social services as providing a basic education for all children produced literate and politically alert populations assembled in urban areas within each country. Finally, technological progress, including rotary presses, cheap newsprint, international news agencies, and easy transportation, enabled the masses to be kept abreast of what was happening in their own country and the world.

One consequence was a reconceptualization of the idea of public opinion. Whereas in earlier times it had meant the putatively informed and well-rounded political views of the privileged few, by the closing decades of the nineteenth century it was increasingly used to refer to the perspectives and predispositions of the masses. The availability of large aggregates of socially mobilized citizens gave political leaders an opportunity to enlist the masses in the pursuit of goals ever more often identified as the national interest. Propaganda became a dominant form of communication, both to one's own population and, beginning especially during World War I, foreign peoples. The willful encouragement of national hatreds was one more step away from the elaborate niceties of balance-of-power politics, a step that pushed the world back toward an earlier conception of total war for total ends.

Writers and statesmen in the first third of our century attributed to public opinion almost magical qualities. They argued that it was public opinion that required the state to pursue certain policies, or that world public opinion, if given an opportunity to develop, would put an end to war. With few exceptions, however, those who attempted to spell out exactly what this public opinion was and how it brought its influence to bear upon national political behavior fell into either vague generalities or else a hardboiled cynicism about the manipulability of the popular mind. There was no adequate way to take a full measure of the concept, to permit the analyst to go beyond a necessarily personal view of what dimensions public opinion actually assumed.

Those who emphasized the overriding importance of public opinion argued that it was a major factor determining the behavior of states. In the interaction between elites and masses, according to this view, it was the latter who prescribed to their leaders what policies they should pursue on such weighty matters as alliances and participation in wars. A leader pursuing unpopular policies in the international arena, it was felt, could not long maintain his policymaking role. The masses would unseat this leader in the next election, bring pressure to bear upon parliamentarians to force a change, or, if necessary, revolt. At the very least, goes the most general form of this proposition, public opinion sets "limiting conditions" to the behavior of elites, a framework within which leaders have substantial freedom of action but beyond which they may not go without jeopardizing their popular basis of support.

The alternative proposition is that the policies pursued by leaders set the tone of public opinion. The most generally accepted version of this argument sees a two-step or multistep flow of communication, from the elites through various layers of intermediaries (the press, local opinion leaders) to the masses. Accordingly, if political leaders opt for a particular alliance pattern or even for war, then the masses will readily concur or can soon be persuaded to do so. A variant of this position is that it is the business elites who, by manipulating the economic basis of politics, dictate what policies the formal political leaders will adopt. In either event, public perspectives and predispositions are consequences, not causes.

The outcomes predicted by either proposition are not restricted to the domestic political sphere. They also include popular images of foreign states and peoples, preferences in terms of such transactions as trade and tourism, and interpersonal relations across national boundaries. If popular perspectives and behaviors condition policies, then we might expect that alliances are more probable among states enjoying high levels of interaction, and that communication discontinuities between a pair of states make war between them more likely. Alternatively, if policies determine public perspectives and behaviors, then we might anticipate that the signature of an alliance between two states presages a rise in their communication transactions. (Emphasis on the instrumental role of business elites might predict increased communication transactions following upon growth in trade and investment between any two states.) The outbreak of war, in this second view, should enhance communication ties among allied states, while those between enemies will decline even after the war is over. Concomitantly, merely having a common enemy should bind peoples closer together in a broad network of interactions.

This paper explores some of the propositions outlined above, using as an indicator of a public's perspectives its propensity to send mail to and receive it from correspondents in foreign lands. The findings reported here are part of a more substantial project dealing with worldwide mail flows during the years from 1890 to 1961; later reports will extend the analysis of the European political scene into the years leading up to and following World War II, compare mail flows with other indicators of the structure of the international communications system, and treat methodological issues in greater detail (Clark & Merritt, forthcoming). Before looking at what data from 1890 to 1920 have to say about the

interaction of popular perspectives and national policies, however, a brief discussion of the data and analytic techniques used in this report is in order.

MAIL FLOWS AND THE STRUCTURE OF
INTERNATIONAL COMMUNICATIONS

Assessing the relationship between popular perspectives and behaviors on the
one hand and, on the other, policies pursued by national leaders, requires data
that are systematically developed, objective in the sense of being impersonal
(and hence, in principle at least, capable of being replicated by an independent
observer), and quantified. An obvious candidate for such an indicator would
stem from sample surveys of national populations. Occasional studies since the
end of World War II have provided such data (e.g., Buchanan & Cantril, 1953;
Merritt & Puchala, 1968), but comparable data for earlier times are simply not
available.

Another approach would rely upon the systematic analysis of the content of
communications across international boundaries or those which, although
domestic in origin and target, express perspectives relevant to international politics. In a pioneering project, Ithiel de Sola Pool, Harold D. Lasswell, Daniel
Lerner and others (cf. Pool, 1970) content analyzed the "prestige press" in
England, France, Germany, Russia, and the United States over the period from
1890 to 1949 in terms of symbols of democracy and internationalism. One useful indicator was the valence over time of international images, that is, the extent to which the newspapers expressed positive or negative attitudes toward
other countries. Analyzing editorial views has both its strong and weak points.
Prestigious newspapers presumably reflect and help to shape the views of policy-
making elites in a country, although, it must be added, we have no clearcut data
demonstrating a one-to-one relationship and numerous findings showing a surprising lack of congruence (reports in *The New York Times* on the recent conflict in Vietnam, for instance). Moreover, such newspapers are hardly indicative
of the mass mood (Namenwirth, 1973). As one among other sets of indicators,
however, trends in editorial content can give us valuable clues about a nation's
international perspectives.

Another potentially useful analytic approach would examine popular voting.
Legislative candidates espousing particular viewpoints on international affairs,
the argument goes, are likely to be elected to the extent that their views coincide
with those of the electorate. Research on isolationism in the United States
(Rieselbach, 1966) nonetheless suggests that this argument is fraught with problems of both conceptualization and measurement. For one thing, voters both as
individuals and as aggregates make their choice on the basis of a wide range of
factors, including but not limited to political issues and their perceptions of how
candidates stand on these issues. Some voters will cast their ballots for their
party's candidate regardless of what his or her views are. We cannot automatically

assume that the election of a pro-French or isolationist candidate reflects the voters' views either on France or isolationism without detailed knowledge, derived from survey research, on what the views of the voters actually are. For another thing, research on voters in the United States (Miller & Stokes, 1963) suggests that voters are most likely to misperceive the positions of congressional candidates on foreign affairs. The individual in Congress, too, has a clearcut notion of what his or her constituents think about foreign affairs—but more often than not is dead wrong! Such research in the era of sample surveys makes it risky at best to place much emphasis upon voting patterns as indicators of international perspectives, particularly for years before the development of surveying tools. Such voting patterns may nonetheless be suggestive of perspectives, and may prove to be useful in conjunction with other kinds of data.

Still a fourth type of indicator would derive from international trade patterns. Here we must look at both the aggregate flows of trade among countries as well as the actual amount of trade between each pair relative to what we might expect based upon each country's propensity to export and import commodities (Deutsch & Chadwick, forthcoming). Again, the problem of relating trade flows to popular images rears its head. We need either an empirically derived theory showing why such a relationship should exist, or data that can demonstrate that the two in fact covary. Research currently under way may well provide both.

Flow of International Mail. Doubtless since humans first learned to write, they have sent messages to each other via third persons. They have instructed servants and agents, reported news, inquired about wills and other legal matters, avowed eternal love, offered to buy or sell merchandise or services, threatened, and fired off a host of other messages. With time, governments emerged to regulate this flow of communications, put the postal service under their own wings, and taxed communicators for this service by requiring them to affix to their letters postage stamps that could be purchased only at government offices. By 1875 correspondence across international boundaries had increased to such an extent that the world's leading countries met to draft a Universal Postal Convention to facilitate its flow. The agency created by the convention, the Universal Postal Union (UPU) located in Bern, Switzerland, seeks among other things to regulate procedures for the international exchange of mail, encourage uniform rates, provide a system for clearing accounts, and keep statistical records on national postal systems and international flows of mail.

The mail-flow data collected by the UPU from 1890, and reported in its *Relevé des tableaux statistiques du service postal international,* can serve as a solid basis for analyzing changes in international communication. These yearly and later triennial statements encompass statistics on the foreign mail of individual countries, ordered according to place of destination. The categories of foreign mail analyzed here comprise what the UPU terms "ordinary and registered mail": regular letters, postcards, printed matter, business papers, small merchandise samples, small packets, and phonopost packets. Excluded, therefore, are such categories as letters and packages with declared value, COD deliveries, postal money orders, postal transfers, and newspapers. In making these distinctions, we follow the practice of other systematic studies of mail flows (e.g., Puchala, 1966).

Since the UPU has had to rely primarily upon reports by national postal agencies, its data understandably have their shortcomings. There were years in which some countries did not file reports, for instance, and other cases in which reporting procedures were not followed identically in all countries. Even so, the service performed by the UPU in gathering, collating, and publishing these data—a service that was regrettably discontinued in the early 1960s—is of great potential value to students of international communication.

Such data speak most directly to quantitative aspects of communication systems: the load in the communication channels, particularly its amount, direction, and change over time. To some degree quantitative data about international mail flows are also instructive about qualitative facets as well. Mail across international boundaries implies the existence of interpersonal relationships. It is not "France" that sends letters, postcards, and other items to "Germany," but rather Frenchmen who send them to Germans. They may do so because they are related by blood or marriage, because they are members of pen-pal, stamp-collecting, or other international clubs, or because they want to buy or sell goods and services. Still another part of the mail flowing from France to Germany comprises letters and postcards written by German tourists in France to their friends back home. Without additional information, we cannot expect aggregated data to distinguish among such diverse motives for sending mail. They can only point to the fact that such interpersonal relationships existed and describe their overall patterns.[a] Mail flows are thus similar to other interaction variables that make up the sum total of decisions by individuals, including foreign trade (which rests upon a plethora of individual decisions about purchasing or selling machine parts, hams, automobiles, and other commodities) and international tourism.

Even if mail-flow data can tell us little about the type of messages, and still less about the social and psychological characteristics of the communicators, they can tell us something about levels of gratification produced by the postal exchanges. There is to be sure no wholly satisfactory algorithm showing the actual relationship between interpersonal and intercountry behavior. In such an essentially voluntaristic activity as communicating by mail, it nonetheless seems reasonable to assume that continuing communication implies mutual satisfaction with the content of the messages. If people do not feel rewarded by their letter-writing activities, they can presumably stop corresponding. And, if enough people in a country feel the same way, aggregate levels of mail flows will fall.

[a]In some instances we can make better assessments of the type of message, such as mail flowing between the French colonies and the mother country at the beginning of the present century.

That they do not fall at some times between some pairs of countries indicates a degree of mutual reward that the citizens of the two countries derive from communicating.

International Power Relationships. Common sense and extensive research in social psychology (Gibb, 1969) both tell us that communication is basic to leadership. Without it, the potential or actual leader in a group cannot find out what its members consider feasible and desirable, suggest decisions to or impose them upon the members, coordinate their behavior, secure feedback about their responsiveness to commands, or perform any of the other leadership functions. Without communication, the group itself is likely to disintegrate, with each member going his or her separate way. The existence of facilities for and habits of communication does not, of course, guarantee coordinated behavior or the emergence of effective leadership. It simply makes them possible.

Communication patterns in a system are generally indicative of power relationships. Whatever the structure of the group, its leaders tend to be in the heart of the communications network, that is, where the load of messages is thickest. By the same token, their more ready access to communication facilities enables leaders more effectively to exert control. Research on family arguments among various ethnic groups in the American Southwest has revealed that, although the groups varied on several dimensions, one constant finding was that the spouse who talked more was far more apt to win the argument (Strodtbeck, 1954). It is not for nothing that revolutionaries place radio stations and other communication facilities very high on their list of targets to seize, or that shaky governments put mimeograph machines under lock and key.

Many writers have argued that communication and power structures are congruent in international politics as well. Mercantilists, for example, asserted that inhibiting communication among colonies would enhance their reliance upon the mother country, and hence the latter's ability to control them. Similarly, some political and economic leaders in the United States behave in the international arena as though control over such technologies as communication satellite systems will facilitate dominance of political ideology and commerce as well (Schiller, 1969). Studies of nineteenth-century Europe also emphasize the desire of major powers to avoid permanent communication and other linkages as a means of facilitating the maintenance of a balance among them.

What all this suggests—and what this paper will investigate—is that delineating the structure of a political system's communication network can serve at least as a first approximation of that system's power structure. There may be, of course, considerable slippage. Small groups (Whyte, 1955) or executive decisionmaking units (George, 1972) may permit and even encourage extensive interchange among lieutenants before a more limited range of options is presented to the leader for final decision. In like manner a half dozen letters containing orders for heavy machinery may be more important for the national economy than a hundred letters discussing the weather. Such observations reveal the need for a procedure to examine dimensions of the content of messages as a prelude to weighting them according to their relative importance for some specified purpose. The initial step nonetheless remains assessing the gross flow of such transactions.

Analyzing Mail Flows. The question of what statistical measures are most appropriate for analyzing international transactions, such as the flow of mail across international borders, is hotly contested. The simplest approach looks at the absolute number of items going from one country to another. The impact of such transactions on a country is then estimated by calculating their relative importance in terms of other variables. Examples include foreign trade as a percentage of gross national product or foreign letters per capita (Deutsch, 1956). Another approach examines the proportion of transactions going from one country to another as an indicator of the relative preference that the former accords the latter. Still another indicator would focus on relative preferences, but using a procedure to take account of variations in each country's share of the total sum of commodities (such as mail) being exchanged in the world. The usefulness of each approach depends upon the analytic goals of the researcher. Since this paper studies the salience of European countries for each other, the most appropriate mode of analysis would have to consider relative preferences, controlled for the size of each country's total mail flows.

The analytic model used for studying European mail flows derives from the "null model" developed by I. Richard Savage and Karl W. Deutsch (1960) to examine the relative acceptance of trade. It assumes that, all things being equal, the transactions between two countries will be a function solely of their propensities to export and import commodities. A country's propensity to export is the actual level of its exports expressed as a percentage of total world exports; its propensity to import is the actual level of its imports expressed as a percentage of total world imports (and, of course, total world exports equal total world imports). The product of country A's propensity to export goods and country B's propensity to import them (adjusting these figures to take account of the fact that the model does not permit a country to export something to itself) is the *expected* amount of exports from A to B. To the extent that the countries' *actual* trade levels exceeded what would be expected according to the null model, we may say that a special trade relationship exists between them. Such deviations might reflect factors of geographic distance, historical and cultural ties, or political and business linkages—any of which would deserve additional attention.

Although similar in conception, the procedure used here differs slightly from the null model developed by Savage and Deutsch and its later refinements (Chadwick & Deutsch, 1973). The original model relies on *both* the sending state's proportion of world exports and the receiving state's proportion of world imports to determine the share of world trade that would be expected to go from the first to the second country. In the case of mail flows, expected frequencies of transactions are derived from a *one-way* calculation based solely upon the receiver's proportion of world imports. The main reason for this variation, besides its greater computational simplicity, is that only about half the mail exporters reported data to the UPU. To exclude nonreporting states entirely from the analysis would render it too fragmentary to be of value. Even so, as will be seen later, missing data occasionally make interpretation difficult, and create practical problems such as the fact that transaction matrices with a much larger number of rows (representing importing countries) than columns (representing exporting countries) preclude the use of some advanced computer programs.

Phrased more formally, the transactions of any state *s* with any external state *r* should equal "by chance" *r*'s proportion of world transactions *W*. (Since *s* cannot transact with itself, *r*'s proportion of [*W* – *s*] is used for *r*'s percentage of world transactions. Thus the emphasis is on indices of *relative sending* (*RS*) rather than, as in the model developed by Savage and Deutsch, relative acceptance (*RA*). Once the expected volume of transactions between two countries is computed, both approaches measure the deviations from expectations predicated by the null model. This difference, divided by the expected volume of transactions so as to normalize the absolute difference between the actual volume and the expected volume, pinpoints positive or negative transaction linkages. The mathematical formula for the relative sending index uses here is:

$$RS_{sr} = \frac{(a_{sr} - A_{sr})}{A_{sr}} \tag{1}$$

where: RS_{sr} is the "relative" amount of mail sent from *s* to *r*;
a_{sr} is the actual proportion of mail sent from *s* to *r*; and
A_{sr} is the expected proportion of mail sent from *s* to *r*,

and

$$A_{sr} = \frac{R_i}{(W - S_i)} \tag{2}$$

where: R_i is *r*'s number of mail imports;
S_i is *s*'s number of mail imports; and
W is the total number of international mail items.

A quick calculation reveals that *RS* equals zero when the actual proportion of mail sent from *s* to *r* equals the expected proportion of mail sent from *s* to *r*

($a_{sr} = A_{sr}$). Accordingly, transaction linkages greater than the average (or expected) amount are denoted by positive values of the index, while negative values signify levels of interaction below the average (or expected) amount.

The magnitude of the coefficients may be viewed as a measure, expressed in percentages, of the degree to which actual transactions depart from expected values. For example, RS = +1.0 indicates that the actual transactions are twice as great as (or 100 percent greater than) expected. Similarly, RS = -0.5 shows that the actual transactions are half of "normal" expectations. The lower limit of the index, RS = -1.0, occurs when there are no transactions between the states in question. On the positive side, the index ranges upward to a varying maximum determined by the transactors' shares of world mail flows. From Equation (1) it can be seen that the RS score is computed from different expected proportions of r's share of world imports in the denominator of the statistic: the smaller this percentage base is, the larger will be the potential value of the index (Clark, 1973). Hence the magnitudes of RS scores among a set of large-scale transactors, such as the states comprising the European Economic Coummunity, may not be strictly comparable to those among a set of small ones, such as the Scandinavian states.[b]

This procedure was used to examine world flows of mail for four years: 1890, 1900, 1913, and 1920. Although the present paper reports data only from Europe, and principally only among the more politically active countries, the data are derived from *worldwide* matrices of RS scores for each year (cf. Chadwick & Deutsch, 1973). The full set of European RS scores may be found in Tables A-1 to A-4 in the appendix. In discussing the scores, it will be helpful to develop measures to summarize portions of each matrix. The technique used here simply finds the mean score for the set of individual RS scores being summarized. The existence of the "variable maximum" nonetheless poses a problem. The average of three scores such as -1.00, -0.80, and +43.80 is +14.00—a score that clearly misrepresents the actual distribution of scores in the set. Accordingly, in averaging RS scores, we shall adopt the convention that the range is from -1.00 to +1.00 (with any higher score counted only as +1.00), rather than from -1.00 to +∞. To do otherwise would be to make summary scores noncomparable in any meaningful sense.

FROM FORMAL TO INFORMAL
COMMUNICATION PATTERNS?

One idea, discussed earlier, about the interaction of public preferences and policy decisions hypothesizes that informal communication ties, including

[b]The magnitude of this varying maximum for RS should be smaller than for the RA model developed by Savage and Deutsch, since the denominator in Equation (1) for the RA is the product of two countries' proportions of world transactions and thus can attain much more minuscule values.

mutual images, trade relations, and mail flows, are a product of the policies pursued by national leaders. If policies are dominant, then the formation of alliances should enhance communication ties among the alliance partners and decrease communication ties with states outside the alliance. The occurrence of a major event tightening the alliance, such as a war, should merely exacerbate these trends.

This hypothesis about the dominance of policies can be stated more formally in a set of propositions. First of all,

1.1. Formal alliances increase interactions among alliance partners.

That is, the relative level of transactions in normal or peaceful times will be greater after the alliance has been operating for a while than before or just after its initiation $(t_{2,p} > t_{1,p})$. Moreover, regardless of what the level might have been during the earlier period, we would expect transactions at the later period to have risen above what might be anticipated by the operation of chance factors alone:

1.2. The level of interactions among alliance partners will rise above what chance factors alone would predict.

As noted earlier, a country's *RS* score equals zero when the actual proportion of mail sent from *s* to *r* equals the expected proportion of mail sent from *s* to *r* $(a_{sr} = A_{sr})$. The above proposition asserts that, after an alliance has been in operation for some time, the *RS* scores among its members will be higher than zero $(t_{2,p} \geqslant +0.00)$.

International crises, this line of thinking continues, should significantly alter the quantity and quality of communication transactions among alliance partners. The outbreak of war will make the partners cognizant of their reliance on each other and the discontinuities separating them from the rest of the world. Accordingly,

2.1. War increases interactions among alliance partners at a rate greater than that expected from the effects of the peacetime alliance alone.

A legitimate question at this point is by how much the outbreak of war will enhance intrabloc communication over the level that might normally be expected. As a matter of convenience we shall use 0.10 points on the relative sending scale as the expected increment due to war alone. (It would be possible to modify this proposition by operationalizing the expected differential in some other manner.) Hence, for this proposition to find support, the wartime level of interaction within a bloc would have to be $\overline{RS} = +0.15$ if the peacetime level had been $\overline{RS} = +0.05$ $(t_{2,w} > t_{1,p} + 0.10)$. It follows, then, that

2.2 The level of interactions among alliance partners in time of war will rise significantly above what chance factors alone would predict.

Again, we may interpret the term "significantly" as meaning a differential of at least 0.10 points on the *RS* scale ($t_{2,w} \geqslant +0.10$).

Each state, of course, is limited in the number of transactions it can undertake. If joining an alliance means that the state devotes more of its attention to its partners, then it is likely to reduce the amount of attention paid to others. In more formal terms:

> *3.1 The level of interactions between members of an alliance will diminish vis-à-vis members of another, potentially hostile alliance.*

There will be less trade between members of opposing alliances, fewer letters sent back and forth, and even decreasingly positive popular images ($t_{2,p} < t_{1,p}$). One consequence will be a dip in transaction levels below what might be expected if they were solely a function of the countries' propensities to send and receive mail:

> *3.2. The level of interactions between members of opposing alliances will drop below what chance factors alone would predict.*

After the alliances have been in operation for some time, regardless of what the interbloc *RS* scores had been in an earlier period, the scores for interactions between members of opposing blocs will drop below zero ($t_{2,p} \leqslant -0.00$).

Just as war, in this point of view, exaggerates the tendency to increased interactions among bloc partners, so, too, it pushes members of opposing blocs ever further apart in terms of communications. Thus,

> *4.1. War decreases interactions between members of opposing alliances at a rate greater than that expected from the effects of peacetime alliances alone.*

> *4.2. The level of interactions between members of opposing alliances in time of war will drop significantly below what chance factors alone would predict.*

Again, we may use a 0.10-point differential on the *RS* scale as an operational indicator of the significance of changes produced by war alone ($t_{2,w} < t_{1,p} - 0.10$, and $t_{2,w} \leqslant -0.10$).

Mail-flow data from 1890 to 1920 provide several opportunities to test these eight propositions. Looking at changes from 1890 to 1900, from 1900 to 1913, and from 1913 to 1920 will tell us what effects continuities and shifts in patterns of European alliances had upon communication patterns. The last of these periods, encompassing World War I, will give us an idea of the impact of war upon patterns of communication within and between alliances.[c]

Apparent Stability, 1890-1900. On their surface, the 1890s were stable years in terms of the structure of intra-European alliances. Those existing or created in the early years of the decade continued to function until well into the new century (Figure 17-1). On the one hand was the Triple Alliance among Germany, Austria (and, within the framework of the Dual Monarchy, Hungary), and Italy. Signed originally in 1882, it was reaffirmed in 1887, 1891, and then again in 1897. Meanwhile, Russia, rebuffed by the young German emperor, William II, who in 1890 refused to renew the "reinsurance treaty" signed three years earlier by his grandfather, moved ever closer to France. A consultative convention signed in August 1891 together with a military convention, initialled a year later but not formally adopted until January 1894, yielded a Dual Alliance that counterpoised France and Russia against the Triple Alliance in the arena of European politics.

Beneath the apparent stability of the 1890s, however, were rumblings of dissatisfaction and gaps in the alliance structure that made it volatile indeed. Early in the decade Russian leaders were quite outspoken in their preferences for an alliance with Germany rather than France. And Italy flirted with France. French efforts to wean Italy away from the Triple Alliance met with German concessions in 1891 that promised support for Italian claims in Africa. This support ultimately meant little as far as realizing Italian goals was concerned. Increasingly aware of its need for *rapprochement* with the French, the Italian government agreed in November 1898 to a commercial treaty with France that many saw as the beginning of the end of the Triple Alliance. Great Britain, by choice and necessity, remained at least temporarily aloof. Conflict with Germany over the Ottoman Empire and South Africa, with Russia over China, and with France at Fashoda in the Sudan had made it seem unlikely that England could secure any firm allies in the event of a serious crisis. Serbia was nominally independent but actually a protectorate of Austria. Then, too, the great powers were scrambling for pieces of the crumbling Ottoman Empire and vying for influence over the rest—a struggle in which the Germans gained ascendancy before the decade was over.

Given the world of the 1890s, and given the general hypothesis of policy dominance discussed earlier, we would expect certain changes to have occurred in intra-European communications. First of all, transactions between France and Russia should have increased markedly, particularly relative to their ties with

---

[c]A topic left undiscussed here is whether or not quantitatively enhanced ties of communication among a set of states leads to interdependence or even political integration. The stress here is on changes in mutual relevance.

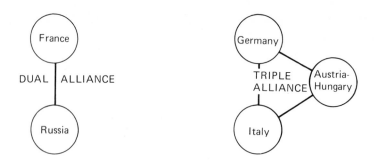

Figure 17-1.   Structure of the European Alliance System, 1890–1900.

states adhering to the Triple Alliance. Second, transactions should have grown stronger among Germany, Austria-Hungary, and Italy, again particularly so in relationship to transactions between these states and members of the Dual Alliance. Third, by the end of the decade, intrabloc relations in the two alliances should have been well above the levels that might have been predicted on the basis of chance alone.

Data on mail flows for 1890 and 1900 (Tables 17-1 and 17-2) provide consistent support, marginal at best, for only the second of these three expectations. France's strongest ties, it turns out, were with Italy, not Russia. Missing data make it difficult to state this with any degree of certainty (although data from 1913 would support the point), but Russia, in turn, had close communication relations with Germany. Ties between Austria and Hungary were extremely although expectedly strong. Within the Triple Alliance, Italy enjoyed a positive relationship only in the amount of mail it sent to Austria in 1890.

Summary measures of intrabloc and interbloc relationships bear out these conclusions. Among the ten intrabloc relationships reported in 1890, four (40 percent) were positive, while five of eleven (45 percent) interbloc relationships were positive. The average intrabloc relative sending score was $\overline{RS}_n$ = +0.04 (for the Dual Alliance, $\overline{RS}_n$ = -0.18; for the Triple Alliance, $\overline{RS}_n$ = +0.07). The average interbloc score was $\overline{RS}_x$ = -0.08. Ten years later, four in thirteen (31 percent) intrabloc relationships were positive, as were four in twelve (33 percent) interbloc relationships. The average intrabloc relative sending score dipped to $\overline{RS}_n$ = -0.02 (for the Dual Alliance, $\overline{RS}_n$ = -0.14; for the Triple Alliance, $\overline{RS}_n$ = -0.01), but the interbloc average dropped still more to $\overline{RS}_x$ = -0.16. The data and summary measures indicate:

1. Interaction within the Dual Alliance increased slightly from 1890 to 1900, but remained considerably below what would be expected if levels of transactions rested solely upon propensities to send and receive mail. (Note here, however, missing data for half of the Franco-Russian dyad.)

2. Interaction within the Triple Alliance in 1890 was only slightly above the ex-

Table 17-1. Relative Sending Scores for Major Committed Countries, 1890

Receiving Country	Sending Country				
	FRAN	*ITAL*	*GERM*	*AUST*	*HUNG*
FRAN	–	+.94	+.09	-.74	-.90
RUSS	-.18	-.65	+.75	+.73	-.89
ITAL	+.88	–	-.41	+.30	-.83
GERM	-.24	-.29	–	+1.78	-.59
AUST	-.86	-.08	+.52	–	+3.21

Note: Scores greater than +.15 are underlined.

Table 17-2. Relative Sending Scores for Major Committed Countries, 1900

Receiving Country	Sending Country				
	FRAN	*ITAL*	*GERM*	*AUST*	*HUNG*
FRAN	–	+1.11	-.15	-.52	-.82
RUSS	-.14	-.49	+.81	+.00	-.76
ITAL	+1.34	–	-.32	-.30	-.73
GERM	-.25	-.57	–	+.61	-.39
AUST	-.76	-.19	+1.02	–	+3.94
HUNG	-1.00	-.64	-.58	+1.86	–

Note: Scores greater than +.15 are underlined.

pected level and, contrary to the earlier prediction, dropped by 1900 to a level slightly below average.

3. Levels of interaction between the blocs declined, as predicted, from 1890 to 1900.

All in all, at least as far as intra-European exchanges of mail are concerned, the patterns of the 1890s do not provide strong or even consistent support for the hypothesis that formal alliances prefigure informal communications.

International Intrigue, 1900–1913.   The ensuing dozen years saw the apparent continuation of earlier alliance patterns. In June 1902, July 1907, and again in December 1912, the Triple Alliance was renewed for terms of six years, even though Italy was a more reluctant partner than before. The Dual Alliance also continued and was even strengthened in July 1912 by a naval convention. Turkey moved closer to Germany. Work on the railway line from Berlin to Baghdad, begun in the 1890s but slowed down by engineering as well as diplomatic diffi-culties, since the French, British, and Russian governments all saw it as a threat to their vital interests, resumed in 1911.

Meanwhile, however, serious cracks began to appear in the alliance of which Germany was the centerpiece. In November 1902, less than six months after the renewal of the Triple Alliance, but faced with irredentist activity that strained its relations with Austria, Italy agreed formally to remain neutral should France become involved in war. Italy also initiated military action to annex Turkish territory, including both Tripoli (1911)—after having received assurances from Russia (Racconigi agreement, October 1909) that the latter would not step in—and Rhodes (1912). Serbia, too, waged war to conquer Turkish lands. Serbian relations with Austria also deteriorated. Austria's annexation in October 1908 of Bosnia and Hercegovina prompted Serbia to begin working toward an alliance on the southern flank aimed directly at Austria. Five years later the Austrians forced Serbia to relinquish Albanian territory it had taken over as a consequence of the Treaty of London that had ended the first Balkan war.

The most significant change from the alliance patterns of the 1890s nonethe-less occurred elsewhere. After years of watching Germany enhance its political position in both Europe and the colonial world, Britain decided to stop sitting on the diplomatic fence, allied with none and distrusted by all. Agreements with France in April 1904 and Russia in August 1907 created the Triple Entente, an informal alliance that endured for a decade, until Lenin concluded a separate peace with the Central Powers in World War I. There were differences among the Entente partners, to be sure, such as British distress over Russia's ultimate acqui-escence in the matter of the Baghdad railway, no less than Franco-German dis-cussions on Morocco that excluded the British. Occasional efforts on both sides to improve Anglo-German relations came to naught.

As far as the formal structure of European politics was concerned, then, the three states of the Triple Entente (Britain, France, and Russia) were pitted against the longstanding Triple Alliance of Germany, Austria-Hungary, and Italy (Figure 17-2). If it is true that communication patterns are a consequence of alliances and other formal policies, then we should expect several changes to have occurred between 1900 and 1913 in European mail flows. Interaction should have been increasingly strong within the Triple Entente, grow stronger or at least remain stable within the Triple Alliance, and decline between the mem-bers of the two blocs.

The data are more supportive of the general hypothesis in 1900-1913 than during the previous decade (see Tables 17-3 and 17-4). Again we see strong linkages on the part of Austria with both Germany and Hungary and an asymmet-rical but moderately strong tie between France and Britain. Strong Italo-French and Russo-German relationships nonetheless suggest a far more complicated picture. It is also noteworthy that all these positive linkages grew stronger dur-ing the course of the thirteen years.

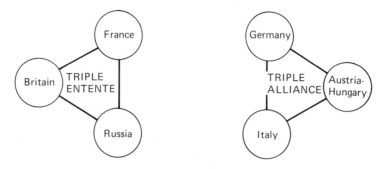

Figure 17-2. Structure of the European Alliance System, 1907-1913.

Summary measures show these trends even more clearly. Of the fourteen intrabloc scores reported in Table 17-3, five (36 percent) are positive, and somewhat fewer (four of sixteen, or 25 percent) interbloc relations are positive. In 1913 the same number of positive intrabloc scores existed, whereas the number of positive interbloc scores dropped to four of twenty (20 percent). Average relative sending scores among bloc partners grew slightly from $\overline{RS}_n$ = +0.03 in 1900 ($\overline{RS}_n$ = +0.26 for the Triple Entente, $\overline{RS}_n$ = -0.01 for the Triple Alliance) to $\overline{RS}_n$ = +0.07 in 1913 ($\overline{RS}_n$ = +0.03 for the Triple Entente, $\overline{RS}_n$ = +0.09 for the Triple Alliance). Average interbloc scores declined from $\overline{RS}_x$ = -0.23 in 1900 to $\overline{RS}_x$ = -0.31 in 1913. *In fine* we can see that:

1. Levels of interaction within the Triple Entente were greater than expected solely on the basis of propensities to transact, but they declined sharply during the course of the thirteen years.
2. Levels of interaction within the Triple Alliance grew, but only slightly, and even then the average was only a shade more than might have been expected by chance alone.
3. Levels of interaction between members of opposing blocs, low at the onset of the period, dropped even further by 1913.

As in the case of the 1890s, the predicted consequences of hostility were more in evidence than those anticipated to be produced by formal alliance.

Wartime Allies and Common Enemies, 1913-1920. The most clearcut test of the hypothesis that formal relationships breed informal ones comes with an examination of what World War I did to patterns of mail flow. With one exception, the principal alliances of the period before 1913 held tight after war broke out in mid-1914. The exception, of course, was Italy. Claiming that Austrian intervention into Serbia had nullified its obligations under the terms of the Triple Alliance, Italy declared its neutrality and sought territorial concessions from its

Table 17-3.   Relative Sending Scores for Major Committed Countries (Including Britain), 1900

| Receiving | Sending Country | | | | |
Country	FRAN	ITAL	GERM	AUST	HUNG
BRIT	+.66	-.00	-.03	-.74	-.93
FRAN	–	+1.11	-.15	-.52	-.82
RUSS	-.14	-.49	+.81	+.00	-.76
ITAL	+1.34	–	-.32	-.30	-.73
GERM	-.25	-.57	–	+.61	-.39
AUST	-.76	-.19	+1.02	–	+3.94
HUNG	-1.00	-.64	-.58	+1.86	–

Note: Scores greater than +.15 are underlined.

Table 17-4.   Relative Sending Scores for Major Committed Countries, 1913

| Receiving | Sending Country | | | | | |
Country	BRIT	FRAN	ITAL	GERM	AUST	HUNG
BRIT	–	+.72	+.01	-.05	-.78	-.62
FRAN	+.00	–	+.88	-.13	-.79	-.71
RUSS	-.40	-.21	-.57	+1.27	-.10	-.74
ITAL	-.45	+1.12	–	-.06	-.26	-.58
GERM	-.49	-.02	-.41	–	+1.36	-.35
AUST	-.84	-.73	-.12	+1.21	–	+4.98
HUNG	-1.00	-1.00	-.78	-.41	+3.75	–

Note: Scores greater than +.15 are underlined.

allies as the price for retaining membership in the alliance. Meanwhile, Italy also undertook talks with members of the Triple Entente. Before Germany and Austria could agree to the Italian terms, the country signed the secret Treaty of London (April 1915), denounced the Triple Alliance, and in late May declared war against Austria.

World War I itself, which began as a test of Austria against Serbia, soon engulfed most of Europe as well as many countries in the Western hemisphere, including the United States. One alignment, the Central Powers, included Germany, Austria and Hungary, Bulgaria, and Turkey (Figure 17-3). The most important Allied States were Britain, France, and Russia, plus Italy, Belgium, Serbia, Portugal, Greece, Rumania, and the United States. (Montenegro, San

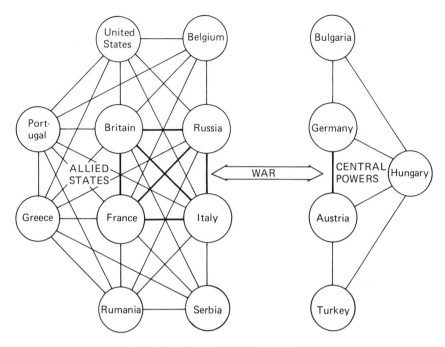

Figure 17-3.   Alliances in World War I.

Marino, Japan, Panama, and other countries will not be considered here.) Russia, however, withdrew after the Bolsheviks seized power in late 1917.

Presumably, according to the hypothesis of policy dominance, the experience of war would bind together members of each bloc—in terms of both increased ties with one another and hostility to members of the opposing bloc. As it turned out, this was not wholly the case. Tables 17-5 and 17-6 show rather that some traditional patterns of communication persisted despite the war. Especially noticeable are links of France with Italy, the prewar Serbia and postwar Yugoslavia with its neighbors, Austria with Hungary, and Rumania with Germany and Hungary. Some positive ties emerged across the lines of hostility, such as between Germany on the one hand and, on the other, Italy, Serbia/Yugoslavia, and Belgium. Meanwhile, Anglo-French ties deteriorated, and the Soviet Union substantially overthrew the lines of communication formerly enjoyed by Tsarist Russia.

Nor do summary measures show a clearcut pattern. Ignoring the postwar position of the Soviet Union (and including it would merely strengthen the trends reported here), the number of positive intrabloc linkages increased slightly from 46 percent of the total possible in 1913 to 50 percent seven years later. The percentage of positive interbloc ties, however, grew from 25 percent before the war to 42 percent afterwards. The average intrabloc relative sending

Table 17-5.   Relative Sending Scores for Major World War I Belligerents, 1913

Receiving Country	Sending Country									
	BRIT	FRAN	ITAL	PORT	RUMA	GERM	AUST	HUNG	BULG	TURK
USA	+.92	-.46	+.44	+.12	-1.00	-.05	-.58	-.03	-.48	+.01
BRIT	—	+.72	+.01	+.32	-.50	-.05	-.78	-.62	-.68	-.16
FRAN	+.00	—	+.88	+.78	+.59	-.13	-.79	-.71	-.05	+.34
BELG	-.24	+1.75	-.57	-.35	-.12	+.11	-.86	-.86	-.04	-.55
ITAL	-.45	+1.12	—	-.65	-.21	-.06	-.26	-.58	-.46	-.05
PORT	+.12	+2.54	-.49	—	-.76	-.34	-.86	-.96	-.93	-.36
SERB	-1.00	-.77	-.07	-.93	+4.41	-.28	+1.56	+3.28	+28.67	-.84
GRCE	-.45	+.58	+1.87	-.85	+7.90	-.46	-.04	-.75	+7.20	-.41
RUMA	-1.00	+.30	-.19	-.97	—	+.02	+.86	+1.41	+23.85	+17.34
RUSS	-.40	-.21	-.57	-.93	-.26	+1.27	-.10	-.74	+.69	-.33
GERM	-.49	-.02	-.41	-.51	-.06	—	+1.36	-.35	-.20	-.53
AUST	-.84	-.73	-.12	-.89	+.68	+1.21	—	+4.98	+.13	-.32
HUNG	-1.00	-1.00	-.78	-.99	+.55	-.41	+3.75	—	-.31	-1.00
BULG	-.22	-.53	-.47	-.95	+17.59	+.02	+1.03	+.28	—	+.24
TURK	-.15	-.79	+.71	-.86	+4.61	-.08	+.38	-.66	+6.75	—

Note: Scores greater than +.15 are underlined.

Table 17-6. Relative Sending Scores for Major World War I Belligerents, 1920

Receiving Country	Sending Country							
	BRIT	*BELG*	*ITAL*	*YUGO*	*GRCE*	*GERM*	*HUNG*	*BULG*
USA	+.31	-.45	-.13	-.45	+1.98	-.42	+.64	+.02
BRIT	–	+.58	+.47	-.92	-.15	+.15	-.77	-.45
FRAN	-.40	+1.51	+.47	+.33	-.29	-.37	-.92	-.61
BELG	+.27	–	-.85	-.92	-.34	+.82	-.92	-.69
ITAL	-.21	-.03	–	+1.04	+.89	+.24	-.08	+.97
PORT	+.42	-.21	-.36	-.97	-.54	+.51	-.94	-.74
YUGO	-.73	-.70	-.16	–	+4.16	+.70	+44.91	+19.70
GRCE	+.09	-.56	+1.59	-.36	–	-.21	-.89	+14.98
RUMA	-1.00	-.32	-.58	+1.43	+6.40	+.94	+8.89	+27.83
USSR	-.99	-1.00	-1.00	+.52	-.82	-.02	+.51	-1.00
GERM	-.72	+.39	-.67	+.57	-.33	–	+.91	+.53
AUST	-.88	-.91	-.53	+5.41	-.57	+1.19	+9.60	+2.04
HUNG	-.90	-.92	-.44	+16.50	-.69	+.81	–	+2.19
BULG	-.78	-.67	-.86	+13.86	+11.88	+.62	+.64	–
TURK	+.65	-.72	-.40	-.46	+12.21	-.41	-.85	+8.23

Note: Scores greater than +.15 are underlined.

score was $\overline{RS}_n$ = +0.01 in 1913 (for the Allied States, $\overline{RS}_n$ = -0.06; for the Central Powers, $\overline{RS}_n$ = +0.16) and in 1920 $\overline{RS}_n$ = +0.12 (for the Allied States, $\overline{RS}_n$ = -0.02; for the Central Powers, $\overline{RS}_n$ = +0.60)—a net gain of 0.11 scale points. The average interbloc score increased 0.13 scale points, from $\overline{RS}_x$ = -0.19 in 1913 to $\overline{RS}_x$ = -0.06 seven years later.

Putting these findings together suggests the following conclusions about the effects of World War I on communication patterns:

1. Mail-flow linkages among the Allied States grew moderately, but still remained at levels lower than might have been predicted solely on the basis of propensities to send and receive mail. Indeed, if we include the Soviet Union in our calculations for the postwar period, then the average relative sending score dropped from $\overline{RS}_n$ = -0.06 in 1913 to $\overline{RS}_n$ = -0.09 in 1920.
2. Levels of interaction among the Central Powers, already above average before the outbreak of war, became very strongly positive during the first year after the Versailles Treaty was signed.
3. Levels of interaction between belligerents grew more positive, although remaining below the level that would have been predicted by chance alone.

World War I was simply not the catalyst to changed communication patterns predicted by the general hypothesis that formal shifts in political alliances lead to commensurate informal shifts. The intensified interaction among the losers is nonetheless interesting. Whether it was merely a case of "misery loving company" or something else is a point to which we shall return later.

The Hypothesis Reviewed. Table 17-7 summarizes findings from the three case studies on the eight propositions outlined earlier. It suggests strong support for only one, that is, proposition 3.2: that interaction patterns between members of potentially or actually hostile alliances are less than might be expected if chance factors alone operated. Several others received mixed support. The anticipated magnification caused by warfare of negative patterns across hostile lines did not occur to any marked degree in World War I. To the contrary, the average level of interbloc interaction grew somewhat more than did that for intrabloc interaction. As far as the expected positive consequences of membership in blocs are concerned, the findings show stronger support at the aggregated level (that is, combining the scores for each pair of blocs at any given time) than at the level of the individual blocs. Most generally, the alliances centering on Germany and Austria were the ones most likely to behave as expected.

All in all, the findings from the period between 1890 and 1920 do not provide overwhelming support for the general hypothesis that communication patterns follow formal interstate patterns. It would appear that reality is more complicated than the hypothesis envisages. But what happens if we hypothesize the opposite—that communication patterns prefigure alliance patterns?

FROM INFORMAL TO FORMAL COMMUNICATION PATTERNS?

The second set of ideas outlined at the outset of this paper posits a dominant role for public perspectives in determining a country's foreign policies. Stated in a general form:

> 5. *Changes in communication patterns among a set of states precede commensurate shifts in formal alliance patterns.*

What this means is simply that strong positive ties between two populations—whether in the form of concrete interactions such as migration or trade, a common cultural heritage, or else mutually positive popular images—will make leaders in either think very seriously before undertaking hostile acts against the other. Leaders are unlikely to force alliances with states with which their own populations enjoy severe discontinuities in communication. Once communication among states rises to a level significantly above what might be expected by chance, however, then the probability of alliances among them becomes increasingly strong.

Table 17-7. Three Empirical Tests of the Policy Dominance Hypothesis: A Summary

Proposition	Prediction	Bloc[a]	Prediction Supported?		
			1890–1900	1900–1913	1913–1920
1.1. Formal alliances increase interactions among alliance partners.	$t_{2,p} > t_{1,p}$	A	YES	NO	YES
		B	NO	YES	YES
		(A + B)	(NO)	(YES)	(YES)
1.2. The level of interactions among alliance partners will rise above what chance factors alone would predict.	$t_{2,p} \geqslant +0.00$	A	NO	YES	NO
		B	NO	YES	YES
		(A + B)	(NO)	(YES)	(YES)
2.1. War increases interactions among alliance partners at a rate greater than that expected from the effects of the peacetime alliance alone.	$t_{2,w} > t_{1,p} + 0.10$	A	—	—	NO
		B	—	—	YES
		(A + B)	—	—	(YES)
2.2. The level of interactions among alliance partners in time of war will rise significantly above what chance factors alone would predict.	$t_{2,w} \geqslant +0.10$	A	—	—	NO
		B	—	—	YES
		(A + B)	—	—	(YES)
3.1. The level of interactions between members of an alliance will diminish vis-à-vis members of another, potentially hostile alliance.	$t_{2,p} < t_{1,p}$	A ↔ B	YES	YES	NO
3.2. The level of interactions between members of opposing alliances will drop below what chance factors alone would predict.	$t_{2,p} \leqslant -0.00$	A ↔ B	YES	YES	YES
4.1. War decreases interactions between members of opposing alliances at a rate greater than that expected from the effects of peacetime alliances alone.	$t_{2,w} < t_{1,p} - 0.10$	A ↔ B	—	—	NO
4.2. The level of interactions between members of opposing alliances in time of war will drop significantly below what chance factors alone would predict.	$t_{2,w} \leqslant -0.10$	A ↔ B	—	—	NO

[a] Bloc A = Dual Alliance (1890–1900), Triple Entente (1900–1910), Allied States (1913–1920).
Bloc B = Triple Alliance (1890–1900 and 1900–1913), Central Powers (1913–1920).

One way to proceed in testing this proposition is inductive, to determine what was the structure of the international communication system (based on average relative sending scores for each pair of countries) at a given point in time. Consider, for example, the case of the 1890s (reported in Tables 17-1 and 17-2). Of the three cases analyzed earlier, it will be recalled, actual communication patterns matched political alignments least well during this decade. A closer look at the mail-flow data reveals that it was Italy that was most out of tune with these formal alignments. This fact will hardly surprise anyone knowledgeable about the intra-European politics of the decade, for Italy was by no means the most enthusiastic member of the Triple Alliance.

Suppose, then, that we make a slight adjustment in the formal structure: "transferring" Italy out of the Triple Alliance into the Dual Alliance. Such a move would markedly improve the congruence of formal and informal communication patterns. The average intrabloc relative sending score rises to $\overline{RS}_n$ = +0.37 in 1890 (up from +0.04, based on formal alliances) and $\overline{RS}_n$ = +0.40 a decade later (up from -0.02, based on formal alliances). The average interbloc scores drop to $\overline{RS}_x$ = -0.26 in 1890 and $\overline{RS}_x$ = -0.41 in 1900 (down from -0.08 and -0.16, respectively, based on formal alliances). The number of positive intrabloc RS scores rises to 63 percent in 1890 and 60 percent in 1900, the number of positive interbloc RS scores drops to 31 and 13 percent, respectively.

Transferring Russia from the Dual Alliance to the Triple Alliance gives us an even sharper differentiation along communication lines. Again we recall the lack of a good fit between Russia's actual and expected transaction levels, given its formal participation in the Dual Alliance, and again we recall the efforts of Russian leaders to keep alive in the 1890s the reinsurance treaty of June 1887. Making this shift (and "keeping" Italy in the Dual Alliance) yields average intrabloc relative sending scores of $\overline{RS}_n$ = +0.48 in 1890 and $\overline{RS}_n$ = +0.43 in 1900, and depresses still further the average interbloc scores, to $\overline{RS}_x$ = -0.40 in 1890 and $\overline{RS}_x$ = -0.49 a decade later.

Going one step further, we may abandon all reliance on formal alliance patterns and look rather at the structure of the entire set of interactions during the 1890s of the major belligerents in World War I. To obviate some consequences of missing data, however, and to moderate the effect of exceptional fluctuations occurring in any single year, let us collapse the data for the years that began and ended the decade into a single set of RS scores for each pair of countries. The resulting pattern describes the overall structure of the intra-European communication system (as indicated by mail flows) for the 1890s (see Figure 17-4).

This procedure reinforces numerous earlier observations by making visible the various degrees of linkage among states. Italy is indeed closer to France in terms of mail flows than to any member of the Triple Alliance. Particularly striking is the strong Russian tie to Germany and moderately strong tie to Austria, no less than the fact that Russia's link to France was below the level expected by chance alone. Figure 17-4 also emphasizes high levels of interaction between

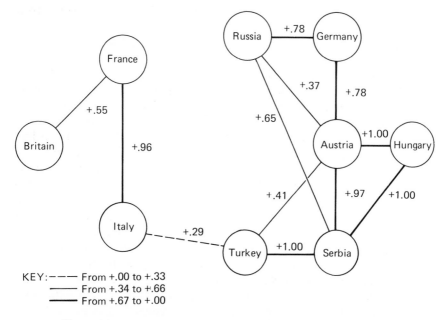

Figure 17-4. Intra-European Mail-Flow Linkages, 1890–1900.

Germany and Austria, and among Austria, Hungary, and Serbia. Britain, not totally out of the picture, has a moderately strong relationship only with France.

The critical question that the hypothesis of dominant perspectives asks is whether or not the communication pattern of the 1890s predicts subsequent shifts in international alliances. It does show, to be sure, the incipient British tie to France, realized in the Anglo-French entente of 1904. It also suggests that, in the event of an international crisis, Italy would be more comfortably aligned with France than its nominal partners and Turkey would be more likely to follow the lead of Austria than Britain—both developments that actually took place in World War I. But the place of Serbia and Russia in the "central European" network would not lead us to expect them to be arrayed against Germany and Austria when war broke out.

No better results emerge when we look at the events of the late 1910s in the light of the overall communications structure characterizing the period from 1900 to 1913 (Figure 17-5). The "western European" network remained much as it was during the previous decade, with France linked very strongly to Italy and moderately strongly to Britain, but in the absence of ties greater than chance would lead us to expect between the latter two countries. Germany's links with both Austria and Russia grew even stronger, and those among Austria, Hungary, and Serbia remained very high indeed. The major changes in the early 1900s vis-à-vis the 1890s were the severing of Russia's greater-than-expected interaction with Austria and Serbia, the dramatic decline in Turkish relations with Serbia, and the somewhat greater Italian interaction with Serbia and Turkey. Among the states in the central European network, the number of linkages at levels above that of chance alone declined from nine in the 1890s to six in the 1900s.

Indications of turmoil in the international politics of southeastern Europe notwithstanding, the basic finding revealed in Figure 17-5 is one of stability. The patterns of the 1900s are no better for predicting the shape of alignments in World War I than were those of the 1890s. In one regard, the later patterns are even more misleading, since they indicate an increasingly strong Turkish link with Italy—at a time when Italy was seizing Turkish territories and just before the two entered World War I on opposite sides of the fence! A closer look at the data for 1900 and 1913 nonetheless reveals that this finding is an artifact of collapsing the two sets of data. In fact, the Turkish-Italian *RS* score dropped from +1.36 in 1900 (based on Italian exports to Turkey only) to an average score in 1913 of +0.33—still substantially above average, it may be added.

The general proposition of dominant perspectives receives somewhat more support from the communication structure of European politics in the late 1910s, that is, during World War I (Figure 17-6). By now, of course, as a consequence of the Treaty of London of 1915, Soviet Russia's temporary withdrawal from an active role in the European arena, and the Versailles Treaty of 1919, the western European communications network has become an alliance of sorts. The qualification is important for, as the data suggest and events during the 1920s were to bear out, this alliance was none to strong.[d] Then, too, interaction among the defeated Central Powers and Serbia/Yugoslavia is exceptionally strong—stronger than it had been during either of the earlier two decades. These same states, along with Mussolini's Italy, would later form the core of the Fascist threat to Europe (although Yugoslav nationalists would eventually upset Hitler's timetable by rejecting the docile submission of their regent, Prince Paul, to German demands). Turkey, it may be seen, disengaged itself still further from any firm communications link with the central European states.

Russia, meanwhile, was disentangling itself from its relationship with Germany. The *RS* scores for German shipments of mail to Russia rose from +0.75 in 1890 to +0.81 a decade later, before reaching a peak of +1.27 in 1913; after the revolution and the Treaty of Brest-Litovsk, this score dropped to -0.02. This decline, of course, is symptomatic of Soviet Russia's withdrawal from European politics after 1917. Only its neighbors (excepting Finland and Bulgaria) exported greater-than-expected amounts of mail to the Soviet Union in 1920.[e] Before we

---

[d] In fact, the average *RS* score for the triad comprising Britain, France, and Italy, after rising from +0.41 in 1890 to +0.67 in 1900, dropped to +0.36 before World War I began and still further to +0.08 in 1920.

[e] As Table A-4 shows, mail exports to the Soviet Union were greater than expected for Norway, Denmark, Sweden, Poland, Hungary, and Yugoslavia; data are unavailable for the Baltic states, Czechoslovakia, and Rumania.

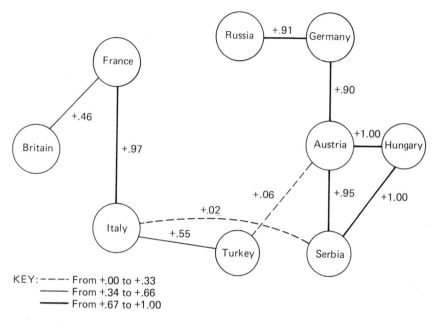

Figure 17-5. Intra-European Mail-Flow Linkages, 1900–1913.

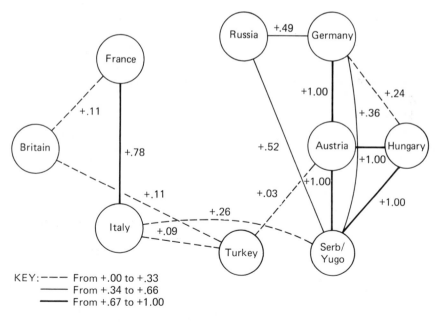

Figure 17-6. Intra-European Mail-Flow Linkages, 1913–1920.

stress this Soviet isolation too much, however, we should recall that in neither 1890, 1900, nor 1913 did Russia have positive *RS* scores with states in the western European communications network, including those with whom the country was allied at the time, and that Germany, with whom Russia enjoyed closest transactional ties during this period, shared a common border with Russia until the end of World War I.

The findings of the three case studies on the hypothesis of dominant perspectives are, then, rather mixed. In many regards the communications structures were better indicators or predictors of formal alliance patterns than were the latter of communications structures. In other regards there were distinct discrepancies. Throughout the 30-year period, however, the persistence of the basic patterns of interstate communication stands as a central fact. Movement there was, to be sure, but it disturbed only slightly the dominant trends. Indeed, a composite diagram averaging *RS* scores for each pair of countries for all four years analyzed (Figure 17-7) is not a bad fit for any of the individual years. And the pattern for any given decade is a better predictor of what the next decade would look like than is the entire set of "high political" shifts occurring in the intervening years. For practical purposes, the structure of the communications network shown in Figure 17-7 adequately characterizes the entire era from the end of Bismarckian diplomacy to the end of World War I. But what does this pattern of prevailing relationships tell us?

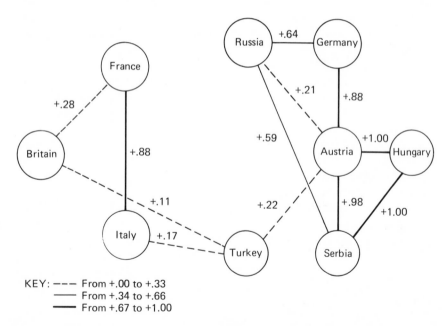

KEY: --- From +.00 to +.33
  — From +.34 to +.66
  ▬ From +.67 to +1.00

Figure 17-7. Intra-European Mail-Flow Linkages, 1890–1920.

IMPLICATIONS FOR FUTURE RESEARCH

The structure of mail flows in Europe from 1890 to 1920 proves to have been glacial rather than responsive to or responsible for every twist and turn in the highly competitive political arena of that era. Even the disastrous conflict of 1914–1918 had but a small impact on its basic dimensions. Changes during the next four decades—years encompassing the National Socialist episode in Germany, a worldwide conflagration that left great portions of Europe in smoldering ruins, and the postwar division of Europe into more rigid political blocs than it had known since the religious wars of the sixteenth and seventeenth centuries —remain to be investigated in detail, but preliminary analysis suggests that the communications structure remained essentially unchanged through at least the 1930s.

This observation raises a fundamental question: Are patterns of mail flow actually related to politically relevant phenomena? More research is needed, of course, before we can establish the validity, for later periods, of conclusions reached about the years from 1890 to 1920. It may turn out that the international communications structure is less intractable than it appears. But what if additional analysis of mail flows supports what is reported here?

A case can be made for the mutual independence of mail flows and political considerations. Correspondence is a form of human interaction entailing a fairly high level of personal commitment on the part of participants. Whatever the reason for writing, be it personal or related to business, it is a salient activity for those who undertake it. Letter-writing thus differs from merely holding images of foreign peoples—images a person may develop after reading a magazine article and reverse just as quickly. It also differs from trade, which is by and large an impersonal matter of using criteria of quality and cost to determine what items to purchase.[f] Perspectives and behaviors that are highly salient to individuals are usually able to withstand considerable political buffeting. If the correspondents in question are relatives or businessmen who profit from their overseas connections, then shifts in political winds are unlikely to affect their primary interest in keeping communication alive. Even if a war temporarily interrupts the opportunity to communicate, they will resume their former ways as soon afterwards as possible.

Such an interpretation is not, however, wholly satisfactory, if for no other reason than that it does not go far in accounting for the ebb and flow of communications across international boundaries. How then do we explain the deterioration in Anglo-French ties from 1890 to 1913 while those between France

[f]To the extent that traders are able to make their own business commitments seem important to the consuming masses, trading patterns may assume greater importance in the policies favored by these masses; some American businessmen are thus not averse to using current popular distress over Japanese whaling practices as a pretext for a boycott of *all* Japanese products, including those competing with their own products.

and Italy were improving? How do we explain the fall and then rise in Austro-Turkish *RS* scores? Before we discount the political relevance of mail flows on the grounds that they represent highly salient but idiosyncratic activities pursued by individuals for personal reasons, it would be well to examine other communication patterns to determine the extent to which they covary with shifts in mail flows. What the research reported here indicates (subject to further analysis of later time periods) is that such flows do not covary directly with shifts in alliances. Other variables that deserve attention include distance among sets of countries, cultural congruence, trade and investment patterns, and movements of individuals.

A second diagnosis suggesting the political irrelevance of mail flows sees them as a function solely of geographic distance. The general hypothesis is that levels of interaction between two social groups vary inversely with the distance separating them.[g] Substantial research (Tinbergen, 1962; Linnemann, 1966; Hughes, 1972) has shown aspects of international interaction that seem to follow this principle. It is also true, as Figure 17-7 (and more particularly Table A-4 in the appendix) shows, that distance is certainly not unrelated to levels of interaction as indicated by *RS* scores. But, if the proposition were completely valid, then we would expect only positive *RS* scores between neighboring states, and declining (and increasingly negative) scores the farther removed from each other any pair of states was. A closer look at the data presented in this paper reveals that this kind of relationship was by no means invariably the case: in the four years studied, 29 of the 152 pairs (19 percent) of contiguous states for which mail-flow data exist had negative *RS* scores.

The incongruence of the mail-flow data and the hypothesis tying interaction to distance forces us once more to look elsewhere for explanations. It will be particularly important to pay attention to those cases that do not fit the prediction derived from the hypothesis. It is interesting to note, for instance, that five of the eight dyads that ran counter to the hypothesis in 1913 included Russia as one of the pair (vis-à-vis Norway, Austria, Hungary, Rumania, and Turkey) or that three focused on Austria (vis-à-vis Italy, Switzerland, and Russia). Ignoring dyads containing states that remained neutral in World War I, we find that the two members of five of the six dyads (83 percent) with negative *RS* scores ended up fighting on opposite sides in that conflict, as did ten of eighteen (56 percent) with positive *RS* scores. On the other side of the coin, Norway and Sweden exported relatively more mail to far-away America than to neighboring Russia.

---

[g]An early formal statement of this proposition was the "gravitational model" of George Kingsley Zipf (1949), which saw interaction between two groups varying directly with the product of their population size and inversely with distance. Later analysts (e.g., Isard et al., 1960; Deutsch & Isard, 1961; Merritt, 1974) have stressed the need to add modifying variables or constants to account for political, social, technological, and other factors in the two groups' relations.

It is reasonable to believe that such deviations from expected patterns (on the assumption that the distance-interaction hypothesis has some validity) have political implications. The absence of positive relationships between neighboring countries, as indicated by *RS* scores, points to communications aversion and perhaps even hostility. It is not by accident that of approximately 50 pairs of contiguous countries in Europe from 1890 to 1961 there are two pairs that have had consistently neutral or negative mail linkages—France and Germany, and Belgium and Germany. By the same token, persistently strong mutual relationships among the Scandinavian states or some of the Balkan states or among Britain, Canada, and the United States suggest something more far-reaching than random fluctuations. Then, too, as Table A-4 shows, in 1920 (and later data indicate that this pattern persisted through at least the 1930s) Germany had an extraordinary high number of positive *RS* scores.

Several interpretations suggest themselves for such findings. One could argue the importance of linguistic and cultural areas in determining patterns of mail flows. Cultural areas identified with Romance, Germanic, Slavic, and Scandinavian languages stand out in the matrices of mail-flow data, albeit not without exception, and so do low interaction levels across cultural-linguistic boundaries. Clusters of countries with consistently high levels of interaction may well be on their way toward some degree of political integration, however unstructured it may be. Or we might see Germany after World War I as the central node of the European communications and political network, as the single country most in the position to determine the shape of future international alignments.

What any of the interpretations discussed in the last few paragraphs requires, however, is additional data against which patterns of mail flows can be matched. This paper has looked primarily at their interaction with formal alliance patterns within a restricted span of time. Future research will have to expand this temporal framework to include the events leading up to and the consequences of World War II. It will also be important to put such data together with other data on trade, migration, investments, cross-national images, accorded status, shared memberships in international organizations, and still other variables. Only then will we be able to state with confidence what mail flows mean and do not mean for political analysis.

APPENDIX

Tables A-1 through A-4 are presented on the following pages.

Table A-1. European Mail Flows, 1890

Receiving Country	Sending Country															
	NORW	DENM	SWED	GERM	NETH	LUXM	FRAN	ITAL	PORT	SWTZ	AUST	GRCE	SERB	BULG	RUMA	HUNG
USA	-.03	.32	3.54	.63	-.66	-1.00	-.35	-.26	-.92	-.64	-.49	-.80	-1.00	-.76	-.77	-.81
CANA	3.14	.18	1.11	-.21	-.69	-1.00	.84	-1.00	-.68	-.38	-.44	-.50	-1.00	-1.00	-1.00	-.94
BRIT	.53	-.07	-.38	-.18	-.04	-.91	.43	-.60	.40	-.38	-.73	-.20	-.94	-.78	.10	-.96
NORW	—	4.52	14.28	.39	-.17	-.91	-.55	-1.00	-.38	-.84	-.69	-.89	-.87	-1.00	-.72	-.97
DENM	.86	—	17.28	.44	-.73	-.89	-.79	-1.00	-.84	-.87	-.76	-.80	-.97	-1.00	-.90	-.99
SWED	20.31	2.96	—	-.63	-.91	-.99	-.88	-1.00	-.93	-.95	-.92	-.98	-.99	-.98	-.96	-.99
GERM	-.69	.96	-.23	—	.70	.98	-.24	-.29	-.67	.26	1.78	-.65	-.56	-.70	-.40	-.59
NETH	-.80	-.34	-.57	1.80	—	-.25	-.26	-1.00	-.76	-.40	-.66	-.85	-.94	-1.00	-.84	-.94
BELG	-.91	-.79	-.82	-.14	2.69	3.18	1.63	-.55	-.63	-.59	-.76	-.67	-.86	-.67	-.52	-.96
LUXM	-.98	-.91	-.97	.89	-.62	—	-.14	3.88	-.90	-.85	-.78	-.78	-.91	-1.00	-.21	-.99
FRAN	-.88	-.57	-.70	.09	.00	.71	—	.94	1.83	1.82	-.74	.72	-.63	-.46	.82	-.90
ITAL	-.97	-.91	-.89	-.41	-.85	-.80	.88	—	-.70	1.07	.30	1.01	-.57	-.45	-.50	-.83
SPAN	-.83	-.87	-.82	-.67	-.82	-.91	1.97	-.22	4.77	-.74	-.86	-.87	-.90	-.91	-.75	-.98
PORT	-.76	-.65	-.73	-.48	-.67	-.87	2.57	.27	—	-.72	-.68	-.92	-.70	-1.00	-.42	-.96
SWTZ	-.97	-.82	-.89	.37	-.62	-.82	.90	1.47	-.88	—	-.32	-.74	-.88	-.64	-.64	-.90
AUST-HUNG	-.98	-.91	-.95	.52	-.90	-.92	-.86	-.08	-.96	-.71	—	-.51	2.38	.67	.17	3.21
GRCE	-.97	-.90	-.91	-.65	-.87	-.86	.05	.52	-.94	-.78	1.23	—	-.27	4.61	6.72	-.84
TURK	-.99	-.98	-.97	-.48	-.93	-.93	-.80	-.42	-.97	-.83	.70	21.08	2.63	26.77	5.70	-.83
SERB	-1.00	-.92	-.95	-.51	-.97	-1.00	-.88	-.86	-.91	-.91	2.34	.09	—	23.03	5.23	1.92
MONT	-1.00	-1.00	-1.00	-.73	-.69	-1.00	-.85	-1.00	-1.00	-.79	3.82	.50	25.41	2.16	-1.00	-.63
BULG	-1.00	-.90	-.94	-.18	-.97	-.75	-.56	-.98	-.90	-.73	1.46	5.29	9.61	—	11.44	-.13
RUMA	-.98	-.96	-.99	-.03	-.87	-.94	-.46	-.64	-.98	-.72	1.43	1.83	2.93	13.51	—	1.43
RUSS	-.88	-.23	-.08	.75	-.68	-.95	-.18	-.65	-.88	-.54	.73	.26	.65	1.33	.03	-.89

Scores greater than +.15 are underlined.

Table A-2. European Mail Flows, 1900

Receiving Country	Sending Country															
	NORW	DENM	SWED	GERM	NETH	BELG	LUXM	FRAN	ITAL	PORT	SWTZ	AUST	BS-H	BULG	RUMA	HUNG
USA	2.93	.16	3.35	.26	-.44	-.33	-1.00	-.21	.49	-.37	-.54	-.63	-.96	-.73	-1.00	-.52
CANA	2.47	-.17	.70	-.02	-.55	-.80	-1.00	.78	-.01	-.64	-.23	-.73	-1.00	-1.00	-1.00	-.87
BRIT	.87	.36	.15	-.03	.51	.11	-.85	.66	-.00	.38	-.14	-.74	-.98	-.77	-.44	-.93
NORW	–	14.03	22.14	.73	.26	-.27	-.79	-.49	-.86	-.57	-.72	-.75	-.96	-.89	-.79	-.96
DENM	10.07	–	13.51	1.38	-.21	-.55	-.75	-.56	-.85	-.64	-.64	-.68	-.98	-.92	-.83	-.93
SWED	17.23	21.21	–	.80	-.06	-.56	-.94	-.35	-.83	-.63	-.68	-.76	-.98	-.86	-.75	-.92
GERM	-.25	.39	-.13	–	.75	-.19	.96	-.25	-.57	-.71	.59	.61	-.88	-.62	-.42	-.39
NETH	-.47	-.57	-.63	1.04	–	3.56	-.61	-.25	-.85	-.78	-.49	-.79	-.98	-.93	-.67	-.94
BELG	-.57	-.76	-.77	.04	2.74	–	4.14	2.01	-.55	-.59	-.44	-.72	-.98	-.26	-.12	-.87
LUXM	-.96	-.95	-.94	1.10	-.74	3.58	–	.10	-.59	-.96	-.66	-.80	-.95	-.84	-.66	-.98
FRAN	-.56	-.62	-.53	-.15	-.24	2.71	.74	–	1.11	.03	1.42	-.52	-.96	-.08	.38	-.82
ITAL	-.80	-.87	-.80	-.32	-.73	-.63	.27	1.34	–	-.45	1.30	-.30	-.85	-.43	.32	-.73
SPAN	-.44	-.79	-.74	-.63	-.71	-.27	-.90	2.62	-.24	7.05	-.59	-.83	-.99	-.92	-.85	-.97
PORT	-.32	-.74	-.80	-.41	-.62	-.26	-.83	3.25	.06	–	-.73	-.69	-.95	-.86	-.51	-.98
SWTZ	-.85	-.80	-.77	.68	-.41	-.59	-.73	.88	1.15	-.80	–	-.54	-.96	-.39	-.43	-.82
AUST	-.91	-.90	-.91	1.02	-.84	-.82	-.86	-.76	-.19	-.96	-.52	–	2.56	.35	1.01	3.94
GRCE	-.95	-.76	-.97	-.61	-.59	-.57	-.70	.61	3.09	-.86	-.75	.21	-.81	4.33	5.63	-.91
TURK	-.89	-.85	-.83	.00	-.60	-.37	-.73	-.74	1.36	-.92	-.53	.11	1.46	34.81	2.91	-.71
SERB	-.94	-.96	-.96	-.37	-.79	-.68	-.90	-.79	.11	-.94	-.81	.90	2.01	14.21	8.29	2.08
BS-H	-.98	-.98	-.98	-.90	-.99	-.97	-1.00	-1.00	-.51	-1.00	-.99	2.06	–	-.67	-1.00	1.90
MONT	-1.00	-1.00	-1.00	-.60	-.81	-.62	-1.00	-.86	1.44	-.59	-.80	1.48	5.82	5.77	1.28	-.17
BULG	-.94	-.96	-.96	-.11	-.75	-.26	-.82	-.55	-.06	-.94	-.69	.63	-.22	–	11.82	-.10
RUMA	-.97	-.95	-.96	-.12	-.82	-.68	-.92	.10	-.13	-.95	-.65	.42	-.79	12.56	–	1.34
HUNG	-.99	-1.00	-.98	-.58	-1.00	-.97	-.98	-1.00	-.64	-.99	-.91	1.86	2.82	-1.00	-1.00	–
RUSS	-.57	.22	.92	.81	-.53	-.32	-.91	-.14	-.49	-.85	-.45	.00	-.93	.16	1.03	-.76

Scores greater than +.15 are underlined.

Table A-3.   European Mail Flows, 1913

Receiving Country						Sending Country										
	BRIT	NORW	DENM	SWED	GERM	NETH	LUXM	FRAN	ITAL	PORT	SWTZ	AUST-BS-H	TURK	BULG	RUMA	HUNG
USA	.92	2.43	.05	1.91	-.05	-.51	-.87	-.46	.44	.12	-.64	-.58	.01	-.48	-1.00	-.03
CANA	4.28	-.21	-.80	-.86	-.92	-.78	-.95	-.92	-.80	-.97	-.62	-.92	-.66	-.72	-1.00	-.95
BRIT	–	.86	.20	.42	-.05	.75	-.87	.72	.01	.32	.59	-.78	-.16	-.68	-.50	-.62
NORW	.16	–	16.49	12.43	.80	-.33	-.93	-.60	-.88	-.57	-.80	-.87	-.55	-.92	-.80	-.95
DENM	-.22	12.24	–	14.12	1.41	-.60	-.82	-.61	-.85	-.75	-.67	-.71	-.19	-.87	-.63	-.93
SWED	-.21	11.21	24.48	–	.71	-.21	-.87	-.42	-.86	-.77	-.74	-.83	-.53	-.70	-.75	-.93
GERM	-.49	.11	.51	.33	–	1.10	1.75	-.02	-.41	-.51	.83	1.36	-.53	-.20	-.06	-.35
NETH	-.03	-.28	-.47	-.30	1.51	–	-.63	-.11	-.69	-.54	-.45	-.81	-.71	-.84	-.38	-.91
BELG	-.24	-.64	-.76	-.70	.11	3.38	2.52	1.75	-.57	-.35	-.53	-.86	-.55	-.04	-.12	-.86
LUXM	-1.00	-.98	-.97	-.97	2.83	-.73	–	.02	-.39	-.94	-.79	-.93	-.34	-.96	-.82	-.99
FRAN	.00	-.56	-.68	-.55	-.13	-.02	1.55	–	.88	.78	1.61	-.79	.34	-.05	.59	-.71
ITAL	-.45	-.83	-.84	-.83	-.06	-.84	.43	1.12	–	-.65	1.70	-.26	-.05	-.46	-.21	-.58
SPAN	-.40	-.62	-.85	-.80	-.02	-.67	-.89	1.65	-.37	5.05	-.52	-.92	-.34	-.94	-.84	-.97
PORT	.12	-.65	-.83	-.87	-.34	-.58	-.90	2.54	-.49	–	-.61	-.86	-.36	-.93	-.76	-.96
SWTZ	-.36	-.85	-.82	-.78	.90	-.36	-.67	.85	.79	-.62	–	-.57	-.74	-.26	-.39	-.78
AUST-BS-H	-.84	-.92	-.85	-.89	1.21	-.86	-.90	-.73	-.12	-.89	-.53	–	-.32	.13	.68	4.98
GRCE	-.45	-.90	-.85	-.78	-.46	-.41	-.79	.58	1.87	-.85	-.26	-.04	-.41	7.20	7.90	-.75
TURK	-.15	-.86	-.85	-.78	-.08	-.64	-.65	-.79	.71	-.86	-.65	.38	–	6.75	4.61	-.66
SERB-MONT	-1.00	-.94	-.92	-.88	-.28	-.70	-.80	-.77	-.07	-.93	-.52	1.56	-.84	28.67	4.41	3.28
BULG	-.22	-.87	-.91	-.81	.02	-.70	-.84	-.53	-.47	-.95	-.09	1.03	.24	–	17.59	.28
RUMA	-1.00	-.91	-.88	-.93	.02	-.85	-.41	.30	-.19	-.97	-.48	.86	17.34	23.85	–	1.41
HUNG	-1.00	-.98	-.97	-.97	-.41	-.96	-.96	-1.00	-.78	-.99	-.90	3.75	-1.00	-.31	.55	–
RUSS	-.40	-.30	.16	1.47	1.27	-.64	-.69	-.21	-.57	-.93	-.23	-.10	-.33	.69	-.26	-.74

Scores greater than +.15 are underlined.

Table A-4. European Mail Flows, 1920

Receiving Country	Sending Country																
	BRIT	ICEL	NORW	DENM	SWED	FINL	GERM	NETH	BELG	LUXM	ITAL	SWTZ	GRCE	YUGO	BULG	HUNG	POLA
USA	.31	-.59	.65	-.45	.55	1.00	-.42	-.39	-.45	-.63	-.13	-.67	1.98	-.45	.02	.64	2.02
CANA	2.59	-.03	-.87	-.73	-.83	-.62	-.91	-.96	-.84	-.99	-.49	-.90	-.67	-.93	-.46	-.99	-.39
BRIT	—	.39	.60	-.08	.13	-.11	.15	.56	.58	-.80	.47	-.29	-.15	-.92	-.45	-.77	-.78
ICEL	-1.00	—	-1.00	35.60	-1.00	-1.00	-1.00	-1.00	-.72	-1.00	-.92	-1.00	-1.00	-1.00	-1.00	-1.00	-1.00
NORW	.10	5.21	—	9.36	7.03	1.24	.26	.00	-.73	-.97	-.94	-.79	-.70	-.99	-.91	-.92	-.90
DENM	-.17	27.17	7.49	—	8.13	2.74	1.44	.04	-.77	-.96	-.93	-.54	-.79	-.97	-.78	-.89	-.39
SWED	-.37	.12	6.65	13.35	—	7.80	.50	-.16	-.81	-.96	-.97	-.64	-.74	-.99	-.84	-.88	-.89
FINL	.04	.77	1.71	2.07	17.61	—	.57	-.82	-.81	-.96	-.92	-.69	-1.00	-1.00	-.94	-.82	-.69
LATV	-1.00	-1.00	-1.00	3.35	-1.00	16.76	3.68	-.51	-1.00	-1.00	-1.00	-.45	-1.00	-1.00	-1.00	-.47	.88
LITH	-1.00	-1.00	-1.00	-.35	-1.00	-1.00	5.48	-.76	-1.00	-1.00	-1.00	-.74	-1.00	-1.00	-1.00	-.69	-1.00
ESTO	-1.00	-1.00	-1.00	1.52	-1.00	66.10	2.97	-.64	-1.00	-1.00	-1.00	-.49	-1.00	-1.00	-1.00	-1.00	-.12
DNZG	-1.00	-1.00	-1.00	-1.00	-1.00	-1.00	5.73	-1.00	-1.00	-1.00	-1.00	-.92	-1.00	-1.00	-1.00	-1.00	-.95
GERM	-.72	-.40	.64	1.49	1.18	1.60	—	2.57	.39	2.14	-.67	2.40	-.33	.57	.53	.91	3.06
NETH	-.18	-.80	-.46	-.48	-.38	-.53	1.83	—	1.74	-.53	-.96	-.02	-.51	-.98	-.76	-.55	-.85
BELG	.27	-.76	-.66	-.81	-.61	-.66	.82	3.28	—	6.54	-.85	.03	-.34	-.92	-.69	-.92	-.55
LUXM	-1.00	-1.00	-.98	-.98	-.96	-.95	2.87	-.62	4.56	—	-.85	-.68	-.98	-.95	-.95	-.95	-.92
FRAN	-.40	-.83	-.57	-.86	-.66	-.79	-.37	-.63	1.51	1.46	.47	.51	-.29	.33	-.61	-.92	-.69
ITAL	-.21	-.80	-.77	-.80	-.71	-.79	.24	-.45	-.03	-.54	—	2.65	.89	1.04	.97	-.08	-.79
SPAN	.06	-.58	-.43	-.79	-.56	-.70	.31	-.23	-.38	-.83	.03	.06	-.25	-.98	-.74	-.90	-.90
PORT	.42	-1.00	-.52	-.80	-.65	-.94	.51	-.22	-.21	-.96	-.36	-.21	-.54	-.97	-.74	-.94	-.93
SWTZ	-.70	-.84	-.76	-.81	-.65	-.71	1.37	.10	-.09	-.38	3.09	—	-.19	.30	.62	-.38	-.59
AUST	-.88	-.76	-.68	-.63	-.08	-.83	1.19	-.18	-.91	-.80	-.53	.81	-.57	5.41	2.04	9.60	2.71
GRCE	.09	-1.00	-.85	-.89	-.64	-.86	-.21	-.39	-.56	-.97	1.59	.64	—	-.36	14.98	-.89	-.94
TURK	.65	-1.00	-.88	-.89	-.69	-.78	-.41	-.56	-.72	-.95	-.40	.28	12.21	-.46	8.23	-.85	-.78
YUGO	-.73	-1.00	-.98	-.93	-.94	-.84	.70	-.93	-.70	-.90	-.16	.35	60.29	—	19.70	44.91	-.58
ALBA	-1.00	-1.00	-1.00	-1.00	-1.00	-1.00	-1.00	-1.00	-1.00	-1.00	-1.00	1.16	4.16	-1.00	-1.00	-1.00	-1.00
BULG	-.78	-1.00	-.97	-.93	-.87	-.71	.62	-.87	-.67	-.75	-.86	.01	11.88	13.86	—	.64	-.26
RUMA	-1.00	-1.00	-.80	-.90	-.86	-.78	.94	-.39	-.32	-.90	-.58	.62	6.40	1.43	27.83	8.89	3.60
HUNG	-.90	-.15	-.88	-.92	-.85	-.75	.81	-.24	-.92	-.89	-.44	.02	-.69	16.50	2.19	—	.47
CZCH	-.73	-.42	-.75	-.76	-1.00	-.57	2.24	-.26	-.65	-.98	-.89	-.09	-.88	5.07	1.57	-.88	2.93
POLA	-.67	-1.00	-.73	-.46	-1.00	-.09	3.68	-.01	-.42	-.88	-.72	-.15	-.93	.36	-.30	.66	—
USSR	-.99	-1.00	.35	.93	5.39	-.84	-.02	-.74	-1.00	-1.00	-1.00	-.85	-.82	.52	-1.00	.51	.37

Scores greater than +.15 are underlined.

REFERENCES

Buchanan, William, and Hadley Cantril (1953). *How Nations See Each Other: A Study in Public Opinion*. Urbana: University of Illinois Press.

Chadwick, Richard W., and Karl W. Deutsch (1973) "International Trade and Economic Integration: Further Developments in Trade Matrix Analysis," *Comparative Political Studies*. 6:1 (April), 84–109.

Clark, Cal (1973). "The Impact of Size on the Savage-Deutsch RA Statistic," *Comparative Political Studies*. 6:1 (April), 110–22.

Clark, Cal, and Richard L. Merritt (forthcoming). *Mail Flows and the Structure of International Politics*.

Deutsch, Karl W. (1956). "Shifts in the Balance of Communication Flows: A Problem of Measurement in International Relations," *Public Opinion Quarterly*. 20:1 (Spring), 143–60.

Deutsch, Karl W., and Richard W. Chadwick (forthcoming). *Regionalism, Trade, and International Community*.

Deutsch, Karl W., and Walter Isard (1961). "A Note on a Generalized Concept of Effective Distance," *Behavioral Science*. 6:4 (October), 308–11.

George, Alexander L. (1972). "The Case for Multiple Advocacy in Making Foreign Policy," *American Political Science Review*. 66:3 (September), 751–85.

Gibb, Cecil A. (1969). "Leadership," in *The Handbook of Social Psychology* (2d ed.), ed. Gardner Lindzey and Elliot Aronson. Reading, Mass.: Addison-Wesley Publishing Company, vol. iv, pp. 205–82.

Hughes, Barry B. (1972). "Transaction Data and Analysis: In Search of Concepts," *International Organization*. 26:4 (Autumn), 659–80.

Isard, Walter, et al. (1960). *Methods of Regional Analysis: An Introduction to Regional Science*. New York: John Wiley & Sons, Inc., esp. ch. 11, written with David Bramhall.

Linnemann, Hans (1966). *An Econometric Study of International Trade Flows*. Amsterdam: North-Holland Publishing Company.

Merritt, Richard L. (1974). "Locational Aspects of Political Integration," in *Locational Approaches to Power and Conflict*, ed. Kevin R. Cox, David R. Reynolds, and Stein Rokkan. Beverly Hills, Calif.: Sage Publications, Inc.; and New York: John Wiley & Sons, Inc., Halsted Press, pp. 187–211.

Merritt, Richard L., and Donald J. Puchala, eds. (1968). *Western European Perspectives on International Affairs: Public Opinion Studies and Evaluations*. New York: Frederick A. Praeger, Publishers.

Miller, Warren E., and Donald S. Stokes (1963). "Constituency Influence in Congress," *American Political Science Review*. 57:1 (March), 45–56.

Namenwirth, J. Zvi (1973). "National Distinctions: Mass and Prestige Editorials in American and British Newspapers." Paper presented at the 14th Annual Convention of the International Studies Association, New York, 14–17 March. Abstract in: *Growth and Change in the Global System*, ed. Richard L. Merritt. Minneapolis, Minn.: International Studies Association, pp. 24–25.

Pool, Ithiel de Sola, et al. (1970). *The Prestige Press: A Comparative Study of Political Symbols*. Cambridge, Mass.: M.I.T. Press.

Puchala, Donald J. (1966). *European Political Integration: Progress and Prospects.* New Haven, Conn.: Yale University, Political Science Research Library.

Rieselbach, Leroy N. (1966). *The Roots of Isolationism: Congressional Voting and Presidential Leadership in Foreign Policy.* Indianapolis: Bobbs-Merrill Company.

Savage, I. Richard, and Karl W. Deutsch (1960). "A Statistical Model of the Gross Analysis of Transaction Flows," *Econometrica.* 28:3 (July), 551–72.

Schiller, Herbert I. (1969). *Mass Communications and American Empire.* New York: Augustus M. Kelley, Publishers.

Strodtbeck, Fred L. (1954). "The Family as a Three-Person Group," *American Sociological Review.* 19:1 (February), 23–29.

Tinbergen, Jan (1962). *Shaping the World Economy: Suggestions for an International Economic Policy.* New York: Twentieth Century Fund.

Whyte, William Foote (1955). *Street Corner Society: The Social Structure of an Italian Slum* (enl. ed.). Chicago, Ill.: University of Chicago Press.

Zipf, George Kingsley (1949). *Human Behavior and the Principle of Least Effort.* Cambridge, Mass.: Addison-Wesley Publishing Company.

✳ *Part 4*

Toward More Comprehensive Models

✳ *Chapter 18*

Two Kinds of Complexity:
Within Numerical Integration
and Beyond It

Bruno Fritsch

The problem areas most important for the survival of mankind and hence for the political as well as for the economic world order of the future, are the following:

- Prevention of wars.
- A more equitable distribution of wealth both among and within nation states.
- Population growth and food.
- Raw materials.
- Energy and environment.
- Future capital requirements.

   With four billion people and a world GNP of roughly 4755 billion dollars (1973), the development of the population, the economic activity, and the physical life support system cannot be considered independent of each other anymore. They interact on a global level. Although we still lack exact knowledge about the values of the strategic parameters that link the main variables of these various subsystems, we know that the interactions are highly nonlinear. *Globality* and *nonlinearity* of the interrelationships therefore require global modeling and the application of simulation methods. The main questions to be answered focus on the following problems:

- How stable and/or resilient is the overall system?
- What are the relationships between overall stability and regional disequilibria?
- What is the relationship between the slow moving and fast moving variables, i.e. between the parameters determining the "structure" and the state variables characterizing the development of a given system?

- How can complexity be reduced to the strategic variables of the overall system?
- What is the relationship between political and economic variables, and how does this relationship affect the adjustment capability (the learning potential) of the overall system?

We are not going to answer all these questions; our remarks are rather confined to a few points related to the question of complexity within and beyond numerical integration and to the relationship between political and economic variables.

New interdependencies arise between otherwise independent systems under the pressure of an increasing intensity of economic processes, and of an ever-growing population. Dennis L. Meadows, Jay W. Forrester, and Barry Commoner, as well as M.D. Mesarovich and E.C. Pestel, have been among those who first pointed to this process as hazardous for the survival of mankind and deliberately set out to analyse the interaction between systems empirically.[1] Notwithstanding the great methodological differences, their work has provided two decisive answers so far:

1. Interaction processes of importance to the survival of mankind are not confined to economic and technical relations; they also embrace geophysical and ecological, as well as institutional, social, demographic, and cultural processes.
2. The global system consists of subsystems, the texture of which is characterized by highly complicated positive and negative feedbacks which are only partially explored at this time. Often the behavior of this system and its components, in time, depends on minute changes in the constellation of parameters which can be obscured only belatedly, if at all. In other words, the trajectories of the global system, or of one of its parts, are not a linear function of any component's change, but a nonlinear function of the composition of minute partial changes. Empirically well known events, in the sense of sudden extreme alterations of systems (e.g., the entrophication of a lake), can be thus described. The concept is valid for all complex systems, including social ones, which interact with any "environment."[2]

In other words, our socially organized sensors (the statistical offices and the many other "recording units") are not sensitive enough to register with a sufficient degree of accuracy and in time the changes of parameters that determine

1. See Dennis L. Meadows, *The Limits to Growth,*(New York: Universe Books, 1972); Mihajlo Mesarovic and Eduard Pestel *Mankind at the Turning Point* (New York: E.P. Dutton & Co., 1974); Barry Commoner, *The Closing Circle,* (London: Jonathan Cape, 1971).
2. There are serious difficulties in tackling these phenomena theoretically in an accurate way. Description and analysis of trajectories is the subject of topological methods. See, R. Avenhaus, et al., *New Societal Equations,* WP-75-67, International Institute for Applied Systems Analysis (IIASA), Laxenburg, June 1975; further: S. Beer, J. Casti, *Investment against Disaster in Large Organizations,* IIASA, Laxenburg, April 1975. Dixon D. Jones, *The Application of Catastrophe Theory to Ecological Systems,* IIASA, Laxenburg, June 1975.

the separatrix of a system and hence its trajectory. Ever increasing accuracy within economic models, however, will not solve this problem; on the contrary, as long as the interactions between systems of various structures, together with the resulting nonlinearities, are ignored, any advance in statistical accuracy will only increase our blindness vis-à-vis the real problems and perpetuate our incapability to distinguish between important and unimportant variables, parameters, and processes.

At present in the social sciences, three "Worlds of Models" can be distinguished: the *A-World* as represented by linear econometric models, with many hundreds of variables; the *B-World*, represented by nonlinear systems comprising a fair number of variables (dealt with, e.g., by systems dynamics); and the *C-World* comprising only few variables with parameters beyond numerical integration. What matters in these models is not primarily the empirical content (or measurement) of the parameters and state variables, but the topological structure of the system. These three worlds may be located with respect to their relative position to numerical complexity and to the degree of nonlinearity respectively (in somewhat simplified manner) as shown in Figure 18-1.

Alongside the abscissa, we find the *World A* of ever-increasing empirical complexity, i.e., a world with an increasing number of variables, all belonging to more or less the same class of phenomena, e.g., economic phenomena. These models are empirically very demanding, they are linear and "pure" in the sense

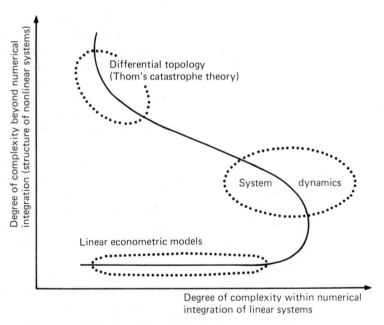

Figure 18-1. The three worlds of models.

that they comprise only such variables as belong to the same "discipline." In the case of econometric models, only "economic" variables are included, whereas all others, such as political ones, are excluded—even if their importance may be recognized. Linearity and "complexity" within numerical integration as well as "purity" are the characteristics of this model world.

Econometric models were, and still are, used for short-term, medium-term, and (wrongly) even for long-term forecasting; they are applied for regions, nation state economies as well as for the world economy, focusing either on the overall economy or stressing particular fields and/or sectors, such as trade, energy, or manufacturing. They are used not only as instruments for forecasting, but also for policy decisions and/or as tools for planning. The structure of these models reveals, in general, a *shock-absorbing capacity,* i.e., they tend to "flatten out" an initial (exogenous) perturbance. In other words, the adjustment mechanisms built into these models, e.g., via price adjustment equations, are predominantly based on negative feedbacks. Since the number and variance of parameters is given, econometric models cannot be used for the analysis of structural problems of the economy. In a nutshell: the high degree of empirical *accuracy,* and the large numbers of variables by no means secure a high degree of *relevance* to real world problems, particularly to those which result from the interactions between the economic system and other systems, e.g., the environment, population, the political system, energy, technology, or values, because they are treated in econometric models as exogenous factors.

The *B-World,* "system dynamics" as developed by J.W. Forrester, is the basic method. So much has been said about this method that I certainly can restrict myself to a few remarks. The first generation of models treated with this method had somewhat fewer variables than the traditional econometric models, but the most important difference remains the nonlinearity of the relationships between the variables and the range (coverage) of the object area, not only economic but many other variables (and ratios) are included, such as, for example, the effects of pollution on mortality, education on fertility, and food per capita on life expectancy.

The systems dynamics interaction approach to global modeling as presented by Dennis L. Meadows in his *Limits to Growth* comprised something like one hundred variables (including ratios). As has been pointed out many times since the publication of this work, the Meadows system includes neither political nor economic adjustments. But this is not a limitation of the method as such, since any kind of adjustment processes can be incorporated into the model without difficulty. More important is the fact that many variables other than economic can be included in the system, and hence the interactions between different types of systems can be analyzed. Contrary to econometric models, which reflect an ideological bias towards "prestabilized harmony" by exaggerating stability-oriented negative feedbacks, the nonlinear system dynamics *B-World* models are not necessarily shock-absorbing. The fast moving variables may reach critical values and the whole system may collapse. The point, however, is that we still do not know why a system collapses and how many ways or types of collapses (or catastrophes) there are.

The answers to these questions are offered by a new mathematical theory which became widely known in recent years as Thom's Catastrophe Theory. In our classification, Thom's Catastrophe Theory represents the *C-World* models. The various applications of Catastrophe Theory to ecological systems was discussed by Dixon D. Jones[3] and its application to urban processes by John Casti and Harry Swain.[4] A popular presentation of Thom's Catastrophe Theory was published by Ian Stewart in the *New Scientist.*[5]

It is too early to say whether catastrophe theory with its extensions will be applicable to real world phenomena; on the other hand, there is no doubt about its cognitive importance. It helps us to understand sudden jumps in the quality of a system, and it may even offer a rigorous theory of ecological niches (Lorenz Attractor). In analyzing the topological structures and properties of a given system, we may learn more about the relevant variables and especially about the critical relationships between the slow moving variables (parameters) and the fast moving (state) variables. It is conceivable to assume that in a social system, a topologically explainable "jump" of a state variable from one level to another may also cause the slow variables (parameters) to "jump," thus changing the topological characteristics of a given system.

Here we then would find a rigorous theory that allows us to determine the transition from, say, economic to political variables and vice versa. Moreover, we would also obtain a basis for a mathematical theory of "cultural revolutions" that are characterized by a "quantum jump" in the parameters of the system caused by a move of the state variable from one level of the manyfold to another.

Looking at linear econometric models from this point of view, one cannot help but consider them as a very poor tool for understanding the intrinsic forces of the world in which we live. Future world modeling efforts, therefore, will have to focus more on the *B-* and *C-Worlds* rather than on the *A-World* models. This will not be easy, since the *A-World* has created its corresponding institutions providing it with the kind of empirical material (statistical offices) it needs in order to operate. Being themselves unimaginative, the *A-World* model builders decreased the learning potential of the social system in which they grew up by focusing society's empirical apparatus to easily determinable, but mostly unimportant events.

3. *Application of Catastrophe Theory.*
4. John Casti and Harry Swain, *Catastrophe Theory and Urban Processes.* April 1975.
5. Ian Stewart, "The Seven Elementary Catastrophes," *New Scientist,* 20 November 1975, pp. 447–54.

✳ *Chapter 19*

When National Security Policies Bred Collective Insecurity: The War of the Pacific in a World Politics Simulation

James P. Bennett and
Hayward R. Alker, Jr.

Chile has occupied the Bolivian littoral and has taken possession of it with the same title with which Germany annexed Alsace and Lorrain, and the United States of North America has taken Puerto Rico.

That the Bolivian sea coast is rich and worth many millions we have always known. We keep it because of its worth; if it had no value there would be no point in keeping it.

Chilean Minister to La Paz, 13 August 1900
(Quoted in Fifer 1972)

1. INTRODUCTION

The War of the Pacific poisoned regional affairs of the Southern Pacific states for more than three decades. On the surface a simple act of territorial aggrandizement by Chile, its causes and consequences illustrate deeper constraints on conflict-management procedures when processes of competitive growth and unilateral pursuit of goals debilitate international collective security structures. Chile found ready justification in contemporary standards of world politics for its seizure and retention of not only the nitrate-rich provinces of Bolivia and Peru but also the materially valueless "buffer" of Peruvian Tacna-Arica, whose subsequent disposition became the focus of an unstable, intermittent, trilateral "cold war."

The Southern Pacific subsystem cannot be entirely isolated from broader world affairs, but its principal external relations with the United States and

The authors gratefully acknowledge their respective sources of support, the Carnegie Endowment for International Peace and the National Science Foundation, Grant GS-2429. We hope this preliminary report will facilitate further international discussion.

215

Great Britain only exacerbated latent local conflicts. Historians differ in their assessment of the roles of the great powers and European financial interests in the region's politics (compare, for instance, Ramirez 1960, 1968 with Kiernan 1955 and Blakemore 1974), although it is certain that they became disturbed when commerce was disrupted for long periods. But it seems equally certain that great power management of regional affairs could not be effective so long as British and American commercial interests remained opposed and autonomous, powerful private parties (whom it is now fashionable to call "transnational actors") such as the great trading-banking house of Antony Gibbs and the "Nitrate King," John North, retained freedom to pursue *their* own interests, often in opposition to one another and to the powers whose favor they sought. External powers found opportunity for the exercise of influence in periodic eruptions of endemic regional international and intranational conflicts. Many regional states took care to manage their external relations to minimize occasions for great power intervention (Burr 1965).

But in fact no party—national or private—consistently controlled outcomes in this subsystem. To focus just on Chile, much of whose development was financed from the spoils of the War of the Pacific, we witness a string of smashing military victories—whose speed and decisiveness emboldened the Chilean government to expand its war aims gigantically—followed by 30 years of insecurity—a defensive effort to forestall alignments against it, first centered on revanchist Peru and Bolivia, but toward the end of the century including, in addition, more rapidly growing Argentina. Examination of nineteenth-century world politics in the Southern Pacific subsystem thus leaves one with the strong impression that each nation's individual pursuit of security has reproduced collective insecurity. This condition, we have found, is not atypical of modern global politics.

Within world politics conceptually we include both weak supranational, including collective, political activities as well as more typically decisive interstate actions and the decision-shaping practices of important transnational actors; often such actions and interactions evidence coherent patterns at a less than global level, thus justifying the delineation of regional subsystems with varying degrees of autonomy, interdependence and dependence vis-à-vis the global system. Our interest in effective collective security mechanisms thus obviously transcends the study of the international politics of any single region. But it is through contextually specific historical analyses that we hope to discover which mechanisms, practices, or security regimes could have produced more jointly desirable outcomes in particular historical situations, and which are more likely to perform durably in structurally uncertain future circumstances. Sometimes the discoveries involved are negative. We have in the past focused principally on the United Nations' collective security "quasi regimes" for handling disputes brought before it (Alker and Greenberg 1971, Alker and Christensen 1972, Alker, Bloomfield, Choucri 1973). Many of the principles developed in those studies have now been incorporated in a more general simulation model that relates actors' problem-solving attempts to systemic outcomes and transformations in the practice of world politics.

In a simulation exercise with a regional focus, we aim at greater historical detail than could easily be accomplished with a highly aggregated world politics model, while retaining a dynamic world environment for the individual actor's policy process. Our level of analysis involves open systems—national or quasi-autonomous organizations—interacting with other open systems as well as with a world environment controlled by the experimenter. It is thus a theoretically focused historical case study that can be replicated in other subsystems and other epochs, or extended toward a global scope by the inclusion of more explicitly modeled actors.

As a topic for a case study, the performance of the nineteenth-century Pacific subsystem suggests four important principles of regional politics that, we believe, are valid in other regions and in other periods. The quotation at the outset of this paper reflects all four.

First, the Pacific subsystem tended in its internal relations to reproduce the larger structures of its contemporary global political system. There are a number of respects in which Chilean manipulation of the economy and politics of Bolivia, for example, replicated British and American manipulation of the economy and politics of Chile. The mode of operation of Chilean regional hegemony after the War of the Pacific resembles the operation of earlier British and subsequent American hegemony over the regional subsystem. In the diplomatic note from which the quotation is taken, the Chilean Minister imperiously rejected Bolivian desire to regain a seaport as far less important to Bolivian security and prosperity than the continuance of Chilean good will.

Second, the Chilean Minister's note illustrates a reliance upon historical examples both to legitimize activities undertaken for other reasons and as precedents or guidance for problem solving. Descriptive and prescriptive aspects of precedents are closely related—we shall devote much attention to this relationship later. In histories of the period, one is struck both by the extent to which legitimacy emanates from practice and the degree to which practicality of policy alternatives is debated in terms of precedents.

Third, the dynamics of Pacific relations indicate that multifaceted growth processes can become politicized in a zero-sum, insecurity-conscious fashion. Chile gained rich nitrate-producing provinces from Bolivia; as a buffer for these conquests it took materially worthless territory from Peru. But Chile's subsequent economic growth, accelerated by its conquests, had always to be compared with the growth and capabilities of those it had defeated. Nazli Choucri and Robert North (1975) have studied the direct impacts of resource requirements and military capabilities on international conflicts. We are exploring an intervening stage of the politicization of growth processes that alters the focus of participants from, for instance, "we are all getting richer," to "they're getting richer than we are." Not merely envy is involved, but also awareness of insecurity and vulnerability.

Fourth, the quotation is indicative of continuing failures by a regional security system within a structurally asymmetric global context peacefully to resolve conflicts instead of shortsightedly trying to contain its localized symptoms. It reflects the point that collective security, without an autonomous framework of authority, must ultimately remain at the mercy of individual attempts to define and achieve it. When placed upon a background of rivalry in the Pacific sub-system, individual efforts to establish a regional order instead tended to stimulate the competition and insecurities they were directed at suppressing.

More generally, the extent to which states large and small, including their subpopulations, are atuonomous or self-steering and achieve their goals has become increasingly problematic. One begins to wonder if "the system" overwhelms the actors. Do influence inequalities, role responsibilities, explosive events, and limited opportunities for policy choice in bureaucratized contexts influence outcomes more than group goals or policies? In other words, how much have international relations turned into group prisoners' dilemma, with weakly adaptive actors always trying to solve tomorrow's security problems using yesterday's structurally inadequate answers?

In principle, such questions are answerable only by those who make a systematic study of the relative impact of policy actions, decision-making structures, and external environments on goal achievements. Explanations of structural change in the international system may well require identifying and explaining failures and pathologies in national foreign policy processes. Our purposes in developing and analyzing a complex computer simulation of restructuring processes in the global political system follow from such concerns. They break down into four major topics.

1. How should we pretheoretically *conceptualize* actors, their goals and the structure of the world political system? What should be considered as possible modes of change in those actors, goals, and structures?
2. How should we *describe* major outcomes and relevant structural transformations in a way appropriate for eventual statistical analyses of empirical fit? Are goal realizations and failures increasing or decreasing, for what kinds of actors? How are they related descriptively to structural transformations? Do policy choices *account* for major outcomes?
3. How should we go about *explaining* the patterns of goal-related changes that have occurred or might occur in response to future actions? Which mechanisms how specified and at what level of analysis, explain observed or possible outcomes?
4. Can one prescribe goal changes, strategy choices, decision-making structures or further transnational structural transformations likely to make group goals

more jointly realizable and at least minimally satisfied without a high level of self-destructive and other-destructive consequences?

The simulation model we are about to describe is designed as a vehicle for answering these questions. In a number of ways it is incomplete, yet the reader may nonetheless find interesting the specifications we have so far developed, as well as some derivative historical postdictions and related prescriptions we have made.

By way of explicating the first two topics, we offer in parts two and three an overview of the rationale for and specifications of the simulation model. In part four we apply these general principles to describe in greater detail the model specifications, enumerating its explanatory mechanisms. In this part of the paper, we also briefly follow the decision processes of an actor to illustrate how the explanatory mechanisms can be integrated. Finally, in part five we begin to explore ways in which some elementary prescriptive applications of the model can be made. We first report one sequence of simulation experiments intended to replicate the relationship of Chilean foreign policy to systemic structural changes in a Southern Pacific subsystem of the nineteenth century. We illustrate the model's usefulness for examining competing explanations of historical outcomes by implementing different histories of the War of the Pacific. We ask if Chilean goals could have been better obtained through radically different approaches to retaining its gains of the war during the last two decades of the century. We argue that, within the set of model specifications, one can discover important structural limitations in the collective management of insecurity when nonunitary organizational entities pursue self-defined objectives with historically derived precedents for problem solving.

2. CONCEPTUALIZATION OF ACTORS, GOALS, AND THE STRUCTURE OF THE WORLD SYSTEM

While not ignoring supranational and transnational actors, we shall focus our modeling on state actors, in particular certain Latin American nation states, and their international (inter)actions. Our conceptualization of the foreign policy processes of state actors and their relations to the world politics system are schematized in Figure 19-1.

The reader will note that the figure differs from the simplest notions of purposiveness in several respects. The strategies (or rules) that actors follow are not assumed entirely to be system given as in Kaplan (1967). They are learned from, and modified by, experience. To the extent that actors start any period with similar rules of behavior and experience then reinforces their relevance as policy precedents, convergence (or polarization) in "system rules" may occur. We also assume that definitions of goals and preference orderings among them may change through a learning process. Rather than assume that every actor seeks the

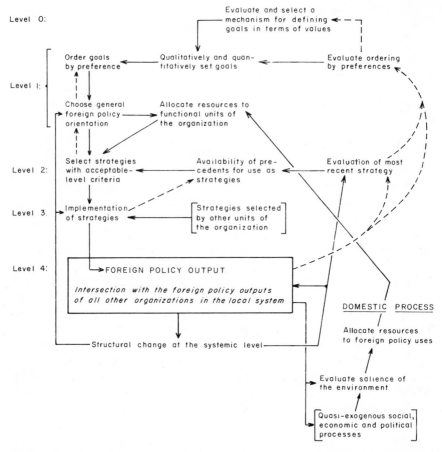

Figure 19-1. A purposive overview of a state's foreign policy process. (Solid lines represent major causal structure-altering relations. Dotted lines represent major cybernetic parameter-altering relations.)

same values (such as wealth, social status, military alliances, and strategic invulnerability), we assume different actors may have or seek such goals according to different foreign policy orientations, which may depend in part on their structural positions in the system's "influence" hierarchies. Status discrepancy equalization, catching up to the leader and relative indifference may be such orientations, either locally or globally defined. Stratification positions (and changes) are also assumed to effect modes of interactions, strategy evaluations, and implementations.

Three concepts in particular require enlargement: the internal structure of actors, the nature of their interactions, and the structure of their international environment.

a. **Internal Structure of Actors.** The actors' internal processes may be differentiated into two levels of analysis in terms of scope or range of authority. (See Bennett 1975 for greater detail.) Within actors at the higher level is a control unit, which sets the order of preference among goals, allocates resources to subunits, and in some instances determines the general foreign policy orientation that is to be followed by the functionally defined subunits. At the lower level, each subunit pursues only one goal constrained by the resources assigned to it. The subunits are, therefore, subordinate to the control unit, but the former are not under all circumstances mere instruments of the latter. Our use of organizational theory permits conflict among and limited autonomy of subunits. It also allows limited hierarchical relations among national units and transnational, transgovernmental, or supranational ones, such as imperial or dependence relationships, collective security organizations, and specialized transnational organizations composed of subnational units.

b. **Interactions and Their Structural Limitations.** In our model, interactions are defined in three ways, each with political significance. One of them we call affective; these produce the "high politics" of war and peace, integration (the merging of old actors), and disintegration (the creation of new ones). In a second, more transactional class of value-seeking efforts, there may occur changes in economic relations, prestige acknowledgements, and military alignments; as a result, relative "influence" positions are maintained or changed. An interesting generalization of state-to-state interactions is the ability, in particular circumstances, of national subunits to develop transnational, functionally specific, cooperative institutions. These constitute a third type of new actors, in addition to the merged and disintegrated ones noted above.

It is useful to consider a third class of anticipatory interactions, although its members are ultimately reducible to the first two classes. This class includes exchanges of instructions about what interactions to engage in, at what level, and with whom. It is more abstract than the former two, and its members may be thought of as higher-order interactions. Especially powerful in the exercise of imperial or hegemonic control, members of this anticipatory class are "strategies" for goal attainment which themselves engender sets of interactions. We shall return to the representation and functions of exchanged "strategies" in part three.

In each class of interactions an opportunity structure of exogenous economic and geostrategic reachability limitations importantly constrains possibilities for voluntaristic or coercive interactions. Influence positions due to previously acquired stratification relations and value–resource positions also limit and shape interaction opportunities.

c. **Stratification Relations.** We need not assume the world system to be a social system (Parsons 1964, pp. 394-96), although it may emergently become one (Smoker 1967). Rather, we assume that within the world political system, corresponding to the second class of transactional interactions defined above, there is a kind of hierarchical social influence system. We define three categories or scopes of influence relations, which are derived from and help engender the interactions previously described. Each influence relation is dyadic and represents one actor's expectations of its capacity to exert general influence over the course of action of another; their pattern suggests and creates the property of "vertical" distance. Influence between two actors may be reciprocal, unilateral, or undefined. We call the net influence between two actors, i and j, the dominance of i over j (which may be negative). Stratification is just another name for the (possibly incomplete) ordering of actors in a three-dimensional influence system.

We take the three dimensions of the stratification system to be the interstate analogues of Weber's class, status, and party (or power) (Gerth and Mills 1958; Bendix and Lipset 1953, Introduction). Weber's concept of stratification identifies classes with the economic order, prestige groups with the social order, and parties with the power order. It is important to note that the groups in the stratification system are defined by their relations with other groups; classes, for example, require a market for their emergence (Gerth and Mills 1958, p. 182). We shall consequently rely on indicators of interactions rather than indicators of attributes of actors in operationalizing the dimensions of stratification.

We follow Lagos (1963) in drawing upon dimensions analogous to those of the social system to structure the stratification system; the concept of class is equated with actors structurally equivalent (in a sense to be made more precise below) in their total economic interactions with others; the concept of prestige is equated with exchange of diplomatic representation and activity; the concept of party is identified with the alliance and alignment structure of the interstate influence system.

3. MEASURING STRUCTURAL CHARACTERISTICS,
THEIR COMPONENTS, CHANGES,
VALUE-RELEVANT CONSEQUENCES

Each of the operationalizations of categories of influence we proposed permits unidirectional, reciprocal, and no-influence relations among actors. In order to describe stratification positions and ranks, we shall first want to compute net potential influence, or dominance, between actors, defined as the difference of the directed influence relations. A network of dominance relations forms a semilattice; the three semilattices define the stratification system, a multimodal structure of expectations.

More complex than a pure hierarchy, or tree, a semilattice is richer in possible configurations and more difficult to grasp in a single mental operation (Alexander 1965). Yet we suggest that it is of direct relevance to actors' perception of their "locations" and "roles" in a vertically partially ordered interstate system. Certainly many foreign ministry officials attribute "declines in control" to increased system complexity. Although we design the dominance rankings, we treat as an empirical question the determinants of greater and less complexity, "equality," concentration, and structural change in the stratification system.

a. Measuring Influence Relations. To operationalize the three categories of influence relations, we require indices that are sufficiently robust to be applicable to long periods, that are analytically simple, and that are reasonably context-free in their validity. We are more interested in the members' general positions in a stratification system than in their specific and situationally evaluated structure of opportunities and constraints, which will be considered below.

The three types of potential influence positions are computed in the same way. In each case, our rationale for assigning actor i a position of net potential influence over actor j is that reductions in the current exchange, or transaction, level between i and j in a particular mode would be more disruptive to j than to i. Put simply, i possesses net potential influence over j if the ratio of their dyadic exchange to the entire foreign exchange of each is smaller for i than for j.

Consider a transaction in some mode, a, between two parties i and j. We first consider the exchange from the perspective of i, whose environment including actor j we denote S. Thus the quantity that i sends to j (i.e., i's "exports") relative to i's total transmittance in this mode is a_{ij}/a_{iS}. To all transmittance in this mode we can assign a weight, w_x, measuring the current relative importance of sending transactions in this mode to receiving them. Thus $w_x \cdot a_{ij}/a_{iS}$ is the weighted relative importance to i of j as a recipient of dyadic transactions in the given mode, a. Similarly, $w_m \cdot a_{ji}/a_{Si}$ is the weighted relative importance to i of j as a source or originator in such transactions. It is natural to assign w_x as the proportion of transmittance to all exchange in the mode

$$w_x = a_{iS}/(a_{iS} + a_{Si}).$$

Similarly,

$$w_m = a_{Si}/(a_{iS} + a_{Si}).$$

From i's perspective, we may take j's total relative importance to exchange in the mode as

$$I_{i/j} = w_x a_{ij}/a_{iS} + w_m a_{ji}/a_{Si}, \tag{19-1}$$

which reduces to

$$I_{i/j} = (a_{ij} + a_{ji})/(a_{Si} + a_{iS}) \tag{19-2}$$

upon substitution into (19-1) of the expressions for w_m and w_x. A corresponding expression can be written from the perspective of j,

$$I_{j/i} = (a_{ij} + a_{ji})/(a_{jS} + a_{Sj}).$$ (19-3)

Equations (19-2) and (19-3) represent what one might call gross dyadic potential influence of j on i and i on j respectively. The net, or directed, dyadic influence of i on j is given by

$$D_{ij} = I_{j/i} - I_{i/j}.$$ (19-4)

Where $a' = a_{ij} + a_{ji}$,

$$D_{ij} = a'/(a_{jS} + a_{Sj}) - a'/(a_{iS} + a_{Si}).$$ (19-5)

Thus if the sum of i's transactions over all others is greater than the sum of j's transactions, we say that i possesses net potential influence over j. If the magnitude of this directed influence exceeds some threshold of salience, as determined individually by i, we say that, in i's perspective, i dominates j with respect to transactions in mode a. This is merely another way of recognizing that the expectable opportunity costs, ceteris paribus, for other transactional possibilities in the environments of i and j, of an interruption of the ij exchange relation are greater for j than for i.

An interpretation of D_{ij} is readily seen by cumulating "import" and "export" transactions over the entire environments of i and j. Letting $a_J = a_{js} + a_{sj}$ and $a_I = a_{iS} + a_{Si}$, we can rewrite equation (19-5) as

$$D_{ij} = \frac{a'}{a_J a_I}(a_I - a_J).$$

The term in parentheses is merely the difference in i's and j's total transaction levels; it is this difference which makes $D_{ij} = -D_{ji}$. The first term measures the relative importance of dyadic exchange to the total exchange product of the two actors. The index, D_{ij}, will approach zero when a_I approaches a_J or when a' approaches zero. If we require the magnitude of D_{ij} to be relatively large before the actors recognize the exchange relation as significantly contributing to the dominance of one over another, then there must exist both disparities in the total exchange levels of the two actors and a substantial portion of their total exchange must be dyadic (but not necessarily reciprocated).

These measures are context-free. That is, they fail to consider peculiarities in the substance of exchange that might limit the alternatives for i and j for transactions with others. They ignore structural limitations in the system, such as "monopolies" of value (for example, an ideological bloc's prestige as "leader") or composition of the transaction (for example, those actors that can consume one million metric tons of sugar annually). Thus, although we define the stratification system in terms of these gross measures of potential, an actor's perceived location in such a stratification system is far from the only contextual determinant or constraint upon the effective influence that it realizes.

Although we would like to consider our measures upon the exchange modes as comprehensive measures of influence positions, data limitations force a much narrower interpretation of stratification when we proceed to validate or measure the performance of the model against history. As an indicator of prestige, we employ Singer and Small's (1966b) weighted scores for diplomatic personnel and a modification of the Singer-Small data that also includes temporary diplomatic missions and mediations.[1] The notion of party or power should encompass informal alignments and highly asymmetric alliances. But systematically collected, high-replicability time series are limited to weighted alliance ties (Singer and Small 1969, Russett 1971). Only a single alliance in the Pacific subsystem during our period of interest meets Singer and Small's criteria for an alliance. That is the Secret Treaty of 1873 between Peru and Bolivia. For a variety of reasons, the Latin American modes of political behavior have not relied upon the European notion of formally constituted, legislatively approved military commitments. Consequently we have relaxed Singer and Small's criteria to include alliances contracted but not ratified by all parties, from the time of their signing until repudiation by a signatory.[2] We also include regularized military cooperation or evident alignment.[3]

Economic exchange, the third type of transaction, should include, inter alia, investments, grants, repatriated earnings, and loans. In many instances these transactions appear to be of a magnitude comparable to that of trade. Their cumulative importance to external penetration and control may be much greater.

1. The modification is: (1) if ambassadorial representation, code three: (2) if other permanent representation which is not purely commercial, code two; if a temporary mission or mediation in a dispute, code one. Furthermore, scores of categories two and three are increased by one unit up to a maximum score of three for each additional mission or mediation in the same year. This admittedly ad hoc calculation attempts to plumb diplomatic activity as well as presence in a subsystem in which there is very little temporal variation in the form of permanent representation. For our purposes, a further improvement would consider diplomatic effectiveness. It is frequently the case, particularly for envoys of the United States, that presence proved aggravating and activity counterproductive. Sources for this and other data are given in the Case Study Bibliography.

2. For example, Argentina was invited to join the Secret Treaty and only narrowly decided to decline. One house of its legislature voted to enter the alliance. During the period of Argentine indecision, Pacific affairs generally were significantly affected by the possibility that Chile might be "encircled" by a hostile alliance.

3. Thus even without a ratified treaty, active military cooperation among Peru, Chile, Bolivia, and Ecuador arose after Spain seized Peruvian guano islands and bombarded Chilean ports. During the ensuing war, a few Peruvian ships were even assigned to defend the Chilean coast.

Data limitations, however, force us to rely solely upon indicators of trade.[4] The measurement of economic—and power and prestige—transactions is very rough. It does, nevertheless, capture the *qualitative* aspects of dyadic transactions for the period under investigation. Moreover, as explained below, the index upon which actors' status comparisons are based is robust against small perturbations in the data, and the actors make only qualitative comparisons among their statuses. It is clear, however, that neither the quality of the data of international transactions nor, in fact, our research objectives permit validation of the model by appeal only to statistical fit with historical data at the systemic level of analysis. We must, in addition, explain systemic outcomes by referring to structures and events within the actors' policy processes.

b. Computing Status Scores. Scores are computed with an index $H_a(i)$, for all actors, i, on a dimension, a. Status is a property of the actor's position relative to some reference group. We do not at this point specify how to delineate the most relevant group of actors. It may be as broad as the entire international system—computation of ranks by ordering magnitudes of actors' attributes make this assumption—or considerably more restricted, limited to the "local" system (as defined by the matrix of geostrategic possibilities). If the reference group varies as a function of the actor's location in the stratification system, then the calculations required to compute the actor's status score are considerably more complex than if the reference group is the entire system for all actors.

The status scores are based on measures of dominance or subordinance in a directed semilattice, $h_a(i) = \sum_k 1/k \cdot n_k$, where in mode a, i has n_k subordinates at level k via the shortest possible path. (Compare Harary 1959 for a similar index intended to assess status considered as hierarchical control.) We create $H_a(i)$ as a difference between i's degree of dominance and its degree of subordinance in a mode of exchange a:

$$H_a(i) = h_a(i)_{\text{downward}} - h_a(i)_{\text{upward}}. \qquad (19\text{-}6)$$

The components $h_a(i)_{\text{downward}}$ and $h_a(i)_{\text{upward}}$ are computed with the formula for $h_a(i)$ while moving up the semilattice from i's location and down from i's location, respectively.

It is necessary to compare status scores of different dimensions in order to compute rank inconsistency. Temporal comparisons are required in operationalizing the notions of gaps between aspirations and achievements. Furthermore,

---

4. Only a few data points were obtainable, particularly in the period before 1880. Many sources of trade data are not comparable across dyads or across years. Data were coded as follows: if the economic flow from actor A to actor B was substantial in several commodities, score three; if substantial in one commodity, score two; if noted by a major historian as greater than "minor" or "insignificant," score one.

the number of actors may vary temporally as well as between modes of exchange. These comparisons require standardization of the status scores. A plot of prestige scores computed across the entire international system from Singer and Small's diplomatic missions data (1969) is given in Figure 19-2. Despite the narrowness of diplomatic exchange as an indicator of prestige, these plots appear reasonably intuitive. Similar plots can be made from alliance data, and, for fewer years, from data on economic exchange. Such plots, while useful for assessing the face validity of our operational measures of status, nevertheless reflect the systemic perspective of the analyst. For purposes of validation of the simulation at the international level of activity, we require status computations of the historical data for more limited or "local" systems about each actor. The extent of each local system is defined by the actor's notion of which are significant other actors on whose behavior its foreign policies are contingent.

By taking the triple of status scores in all modes of exchange, $(H_a (i), H_b (i), H_c (i))$, each actor is located in a three-dimensional space, which we call its stratification system. Since each actor delineates its own local system as well as decides what level of net potential influence constitutes "dominance" and what level "subordinance," in general the stratification system will look different from the perspectives of different actors within it. This perceptual and cognitive disparity is one important source of dynamism in the simulation.

Because the stratification system, as operationalized, concentrates wholly on transactions, capabilities have no influence on position except through their potential for future transactions. Thus a completely "isolationist" actor will have an undefined position in the stratification system, while a second actor, which exchanges only with more transactionally active others, will appear at the "bottom" of the stratification system. One means of increasing an actor's position is to reorient its transactions to others which are generally less active internationally, that is, to carve out spheres of influence.

While this notion of stratification is useful for some purposes, it is nevertheless incomplete. Were actors to key off location in the stratification system entirely, they would ignore actors that were temporarily undefined in its terms. As a rough, first-order attempt to measure capabilities, we employ Arthur Banks' data on government revenue (1974). There are many dangers in relying on a single imperfect indicator, but few other measures are available for Latin America in any part of the nineteenth century.[5] The limitations of using a single variable to reflect generalized capabilities are mitigated by two factors. In our model, actors make comparisons among their capabilities only in terms of quartiles and quintiles of their standardized ranks. General capabilities become specialized

5. The time series of data for government revenue go no earlier than 1860. For earlier years we are forced to make informed guesses about approximate revenue, based upon indirect evidence in a number of sources. This data limitation is not one that can be wholly overcome by more diligent research. In Peru, for example, it was only in 1845 that a governmental budget was first assembled (Pike 1967, p. 94).

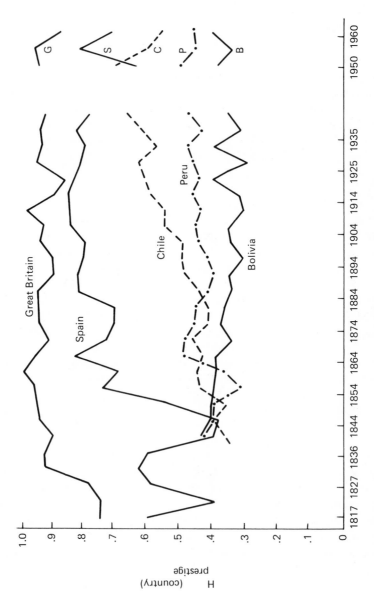

Figure 19-2.   Plot of selected status scores, prestige dimension, from the perspective of the global system.

(Choucri and North 1975) only after they are allocated, as explained below, to subunits of the actor for the pursuit of particular goals.

Actors may identify others both by their relative locations in the stratification system and by their relative capabilities for altering their locations. Both comparisons typically play important roles in the actor's cognition and evaluation of its possibilities for action, as will be seen in part four.

c. Measuring Purposeful Goal Achievement. Two subjects that follow directly from our concern with structural change are the measurement of purposive action at national, supranational, and global levels. We assume, following Ackoff and Emery, that purposive actors can achieve goals using a variety of strategies. The notion of "directive behavior" (Sommerhoff 1969; Alker 1972) can be used to operationalize this notion across different system levels, even those like alliances or international organizations, where it is sometimes difficult to think of unitary actors.

As a first approximation to measuring the degree of goal achievement, we use normalized gaps between the aspired level and the achieved level of acquisition of a particular goal. Deeper problems of measurement arise when goals change not only quantitatively but also qualitatively in terms of the values in which they are defined. In fact, the simulation assumes that actors—whether unitary or not—will redefine goals when they encounter prolonged periods of frustrated goal attainment. Figure 19-1 and our conceptual scheme suggest clues to the comparison of goal achievement among a heterogeneous set of goals. A notion of *interest* is defined at a level of generality higher than that of operational goals. Thus security is operationally interpreted as low vulnerability, but peace and low expectations of future violence have to be treated as important but imputed interests, as defined by system observers.

Interest is evaluated when the experimenter compares the actor's performance at achieving goals with the maximal achievement attainable upon implementation of different precedents for problem solving, keeping fixed both the international environment and the actor's definition of kind and level of goal. This analysis is not always easy to make. It requires altering the actor's search rules over the precedents and observing differences in outcomes. This imputation of interest to the actors is, furthermore, limited in that it fails to consider alternative interpretations of values which the actors might have employed but did not: "interest" is constrained to general measurement of "performance," and not to the variety of ways in which criteria for performance could be operationalized. It is roughly akin to the actor's "national interest," as that term is usually understood.

d. Structural Change at the Systemic Level. Conventional approaches to analyzing multiequation dynamic models usually select one or more variables as relatively "dependent" and others as relatively "independent" and experimentally attempt to observe variations in values of the former in terms of perturbations in the latter.

Our description of international phenomena has been tailored to focus on clarifying determinants and consequences of structural change. This implies a macrohistorical focus, with relatively greater priority given to reproducing major historical restructurings and less priority to approximating intervening periods of stable interaction patterns. Starbuck (1973) has elegantly discussed the analytic requirements of mathematical models of restructuring, which he calls "metamorphosis." Our work is a less formal approach to modeling the political dynamics of multidimensional international systems *that potentially allows restructurings of its actors in selected ways.* These include, in addition to unilaterally achieved realignment of states, *integrative mechanisms*—such as the practice of collective security, alliance building, hegemonic expansion, voluntaristic national integration, and the joint creation of functionally specialized new intergovernmental actors—and *disintegrative mechanisms*—such as breakdown of cooperative regimes, imperial decay, and the emergence to autonomous status of formerly state-subordinate, transnational actors.

To achieve the degree of model flexibility necessary to reproduce historical restructurings, several explanatory mechanisms within the actors' foreign policy processes must themselves be capable of undergoing restructurings internally and in juxtaposition to one another.

4. EXPLANATORY MECHANISMS

In this part of the paper we present a summary of the model's specifications, concentrating on the kinds of analyses that the international actor undertakes in the course of its policy processes. These specifications are designed to be of more general applicability than to only the regional case study of part four. The model is designed to be potentially of global scope. But unlike systems dynamics models of Forrester (1971), Meadows et al. (1972), or Mesarovic and Pestel (1974), it is disaggregated to enable explanations of emergent regional or global phenomena in terms of modes of goal definition and repertoires for problem solving of individual actors and units within them. Furthermore, the fundamental behavioral principles of the actors and their parts are disaggregated and adapted in contextually contingent ways. While the accumulation of behavior of all actors defines the international system in one sense, in another sense the system and its past reside within each actor. When actors disintegrate, their histories of the world reproduce and perhaps subsequently diverge. When they combine or integrate, their histories of the world merge together. The relation whereby the whole lies within each of its parts is not paradoxical, as the model specifications will make clear.

We divide explanatory mechanisms among several topics. The first presents an organizational conception of actors. Its principles importantly constrain the actors' policy processes. The next topic is a series of modules for the definition of goals or objectives. Five topics deal with the actors' memory. "Strategies" are conceived to be precedents for problem solving that relate means to ends and contexts to means. Memory is a complex structure of lists of data which also function as instructions. Dynamics of memory include simplification, concatenation, and "innovation" of new precedents from old. Adaptive rules govern the actor's search for acceptable precedents. New strategies emerge only when the efficacy of old ones is exhausted.

The final three topics concern relations among actors: how one actor may exercise control over another's policy process and thereby induce a crude form of "dependence"; how proposed transactions become effective; how autonomous actors are created and destroyed.

To clarify the interactions among these mechanisms, we follow a simulation trial through one entire policy process of a single actor. In order to emphasize the many ways in which modules of theory of each mechanism may be juxtaposed, we use an entirely hypothetical example. Explanation offered by the model focuses on cross-level linkages and model output as primitive "histories" of the policy process.

The specifications must remain rather summary. The simulation contains over 100 procedures as it is presently designed. More than half the procedures deal with constructing, altering, and interpreting—from the actor's point of view—the numerous lists of data which give the model its considerable flexibility. They are, however, of more interest from the perspective of computer science than of international relations theory, and will therefore not be touched upon here.

a. The Actor as Organization. The behavioral principles of the actors are those presented in Cyert and March's behavioral theory of the firm. (Cyert and March 1963; Cyert, Dill, and March 1958; Alker and Greenberg 1971). In contrast to our conceptualization of the stratification system, we do assume that actors are internally organized in a multiechelon, multisectoral problem-solving structure (Mesarovic et al. 1970) as well as central coordination and task allocation. Were we to model the internal foreign policy processes in greater detail, the presumption of strict hierarchy might well prove untenable (see Friedell 1967; Read 1970). In particular, our specifications do not include the role of opposed groups within a society cutting across functional interests, or the consequent political struggles which may produce revolutionary changes in foreign policy orientations and national or imperial disintegrations. Processes of domestic politics and of growth and development are treated as quasi-exogenous and stochastic as the example below will clarify.[6]

6. By the summary treatment of domestic economic and political phenomena, we are studying only the impact of external systems on autonomous national development. External relations and dependencies may significantly facilitate or constrain domestic efforts to meet basic needs. We are not, however, modeling externally imposed constraints on

A conceptual flowchart of Cyert and March's organizational theory (1963, p. 126) is shown abstractly in Figure 19-3. Functionally equivalent operations are performed by the flowcharts in Figures 19-4, 19-8, and 19-9, and are elaborated below.

The actor is designed to incorporate all four of Cyert and March's assumptions: quasi resolution of conflict (the factoring of large problems into small problems, and subsequent assignment of small problems to individual subunits or sectors such that each can concentrate on the solution of one problem with one goal), uncertainty avoidance (utilizing decision rules that emphasize short-run feedback rather than designing long-run strategies, and avoiding attempts to predict others' future behavior), problemistic search (undertaking search only when motivated by the perception of a problem, and even then seeking alternative solutions as similar as possible to those used in the recent past), and organizational learning (altering goals, attention rules, procedures for search, and types of solutions selected as a function of experience).

We have chosen initially to limit the values which actors may pursue to four that are repeatedly cited in the literature. Actors seek all or some of four values: three of these—security, power, and glory (or prestige)—are suggested by Aron (1966) to be "eternal goals" of foreign policy. The fourth, wealth, may not quite be eternally sought, but appears as a salient feature in the policies of states in recent centuries. Goals are defined in terms of quantities of these values. Note that the stratification system, in which actors are located by their relative value positions, directly parallels these values in the modes of economic (wealth), diplomatic (prestige), and military (power) exchange; security is a composite of modes of exchange in relation to threats from the actor's local environment.

The relative importance of these values varies according to the actor's experience and internal (intraorganizational) and external (systemic) circumstances. Each actor, as organization, contains subunits functionally adapted to the pursuit of a single value. If a particular actor should cease to aspire to increments of a value, we consider the corresponding subunit no longer to be a member of the organizational coalition. Military alliances, for example, if they possess semi-autonomous central direction, might be considered as organizations with one subunit attentive to the value of power.

---

revolutionary domestic transformations. For example, in the case study we treat the Balmaceda Revolution in Chile in 1891 as an exogenously induced change in Chilean foreign policy orientation and not as a consequence of complex struggles between the Chilean legislative and executive, an emerging commercial middle class and an entrenched landholding elite, and domestic and foreign economic interests. (See Blakemore 1974.) Consequently, as the "social problem," centered on the growth of jobless urban migrants, increases in salience in Chile in the 1890s and slightly later in Peru, the international focus of our model becomes gradually but increasingly less important for explaining systemic outcomes than do the domestic dislocations resulting from modernization. This does not necessarily mean that the bulk of present specifications becomes erroneous, but that much more detailed representation of dynamics in the domestic political arena is required as well.

Organizing assumptions:

Quasi resolution of conflict	Uncertainty avoidance	Problemistic search	Organizational learning

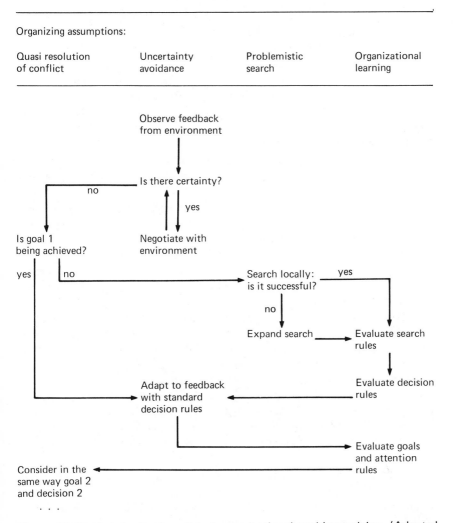

Figure 19-3. A behavioral model of organizational problem solving. (Adapted from Cyert and March 1963, p. 126.)

   In each actor there is a central unit of overall control and coordination that allocates to the subunits quantities of resources appropriate to the pursuit of operational goals defined by the subunit in terms of its particular value. The amount of resources allocated depends upon the current importance of the goal to the organization as a whole. Allocation takes the form of changes from previous levels, so in most cases—that is, when the overall problem-solving processes operate satisfactorily—no internal redistribution of resources among subunits occurs. In addition, the subunit is instructed to propose a set of rules for finding a satisfactory strategy for goal attainment, for searching for and, if unable to find such a strategy, innovating a new strategy, and returning to the control unit with provisional output obtained by implementing the strategy. Subunits search over the organizational experience, and when that proves an insufficient basis for solving a problem, they search over the experiences of other, similar organizations. If still unsuccessful, as a last resort they attempt to innovate a new strategy (as described below, p. 241). The control unit takes the several sets of output as proposed by the subunits, checks to see that they contain no logical contradictions, works out "compromises" giving precedence to the higher priority subunits, and thus generates a foreign policy for the actor as a whole. Foreign policy is operationally defined as the union of problem-solving attempts by specialized parts (or interests) of the organization. More than minimalist, logical resolution of conflict among the strategies proposed by subunits cannot generally be attempted because, as Cyert and March note, that would frequently create excessive strain on the organizational coalition. An exception occurs when one or more subunit encounters problems that are of such magnitude as to be labelled "crises." In this circumstance, the central control unit coordinates search for all the subunits to increase the likelihood (but not guarantee) substantive coherence to the output generated from several strategies.

Each subunit may engage in the whole gamut of interactions with other actors, although each defines its goals in terms of the relative value position in one mode of exchange. There is no structural difference, therefore, between international relations and transnational relations, just as in noncrisis situations there is no unitary determination of policy for each actor.

The continued inability of actors to achieve their desired goals leads—depending upon specific aspects of the situation such as experiences (learning) of the several actors in the local international system—to redefinition of goals, to attempts at policy innovation, or deliberate attempts at restructuring the system to yield better outcomes by removing obstacles perceived to be blocking goal attainment. Different organizational subunits may attempt different kinds of strategies to attain goals at the same time. In the extreme case, the subunits' policies may be mutually self-defeating. Much of what seems to be maladaptive behavior in international history becomes more comprehensible when one considers international politics as inter-organizational politics.

b. Mechanisms of Goal Definition. Organizations are posited to alter their strategies for goal attainment only when they perceive a "problem," or failure, in their current operations. One can easily conceive of a number of ways for identifying "problems," and many of these utilize the notion of gaps or disparities between desired and actualized states. Particular attention is paid to three kinds of gaps which feature prominently in contemporary international relations theory. If goal attainment is thought of as closing gaps between aspirations and achievements, then different definitions of goals arise from attempting to close different kinds of gaps. In addition to three gap-closing modules in the stimulation—all of which undertake the attainment of future states at least as preferable as the present state of the organization—a fourth module defines goals as the avoidance or removal of specific current vulnerabilities in the actor's network of transactions.

Some empirical work suggests basic propositions of rank inconsistency theory may be relevant to international behavior (East 1969, 1972; Wallace 1971, 1973). Little attention has been given (except Wallace 1972), however, to specifying the processes relating perception of inconsistent statuses to responses in foreign policy. Because rank inconsistency theory is fundamentally a theory of preference ordering among values, and because it is becoming increasingly a justification for application of additional theoretical and experimental results of social psychology, we incorporate a variant of it into the organizational model as one module for the definition of goals and the computation of discrepancies between actual and aspired statuses.

The central characteristic of rank inconsistency and related theories (see Kimberly 1970, Geschwender 1967, Sampson 1969, and Galtung 1966a, 1966b) is a focus on comparison across ranks of several modes of value or dimensions of status at a particular time. These cross-status gaps define the problems and thus motivate departures from previous policy. Subordinate concerns, such as the ranks of others in comparison to one's own, the rates of change of particular ranks, and the ascriptive versus achieved characteristics of the relevant status dimensions, constrain response possibilities and shape attempts at problem solving.

By contrast, other gap-oriented theories focus on temporal differences in rank or level. A particularly influential theory of this type is Organski's (1958) power transition theory. Here the motivating discrepancy is between aspired power position and achieved power position. Like the group of rank inconsistency theories, subordinate considerations of relative capabilities, rates of change, and past relations with other actors play important parts in selecting and shaping the actor's attempt at problem solving. The power-transition theory may be generalized to other dimensions of status or modes of value, permitting analogous considerations of aspired versus achieved class and prestige positions to be made by all subunits of the actor.

A third module of problem definition is based on the "traditional" security consciousness of states. Aron (1966, pp. 720–74) suggested that in some circumstances security can become the primary value to states. The security-oriented gap is one of them versus us, in which the capabilities of the actor and others upon which it counts for support are compared with the capabilities of those it perceives as hostile or opposed to itself. At heart, the module computes the difference between expected threat (following Singer's [1958] operationalization of threat as intention times capability) and expected support (following symmetric reasoning), to yield problems defined as insufficient security.[7]

In conjunction with the three modules of goal definition described above, actors define vulnerabilities as required but unrealized transactions with others. The basis of their calculations is a matrix of transactional requirements that reflects the bases of their economic and social development. This matrix is initially exogenous. It is subsequently updated exogenously to mirror technological advances and endogenously to respond to actors' growing dependencies upon long maintained dyadic transactions. For instance, in the Southern Pacific case study, the experimenter intervenes to create a Peruvian requirement for markets for guano in the 1840s. This requirement is a high level of economic transactions with at least one major power. Because the Peruvian government relied upon export taxes for the bulk of its revenue, termination or even prolonged disruption of its guano exports plunge the country into civil strife. A major power which, over a long period, purchases Peruvian guano will, unless it can develop alternative sources of supply, attempt to avert interruption of its trade, because its agriculture has become heavily dependent upon foreign fertilizer. In another context, the major power may define interruption of capital export as a potential source of vulnerability. Central to vulnerability calculations are (1) whether the transaction is significant and (2) whether alternative partners exist for the exchange. A consequence of a high degree of international stratification is the emergence of increasing asymmetries in the vulnerabilities of major and small powers.

Once the actor has satisfied itself that no vulnerabilities demand immediate attention, the simulation permits comparative analyses of these four modules, or analyses of any combination of them when higher-order rules are used (based upon the long-term success of goal attainment when particular mechanisms define goals) to choose among them. Change among these modules corresponds to fundamental revision of a state's world view and of its conception of the nature of international relations. Such changes may occur gradually, but are more frequently associated with domestic upheavals and restructurings of society. In this simulation, they are also empirically found to be frequently associated with the restructuring of the international stratification system, whether intentional or inadvertent.

In Figure 19-1, level one contains the modules for goal definition and relates them to the entire policy process. Figures 19-4A and 19-4B offer more detail

7. In addition to these three principal mechanisms for defining operational goals, the simulation incorporates a "nearly null" module which generates tit-for-tat policies. This module is useful both as a basis for comparison of the performance of the other modules and as a noncoping response mechanism when the magnitude of the problem exceeds that of manageable "crisis" and spasmodic retaliation is the only strategy at hand. (On the opposite side of the coin, preliminary experience with the simulation suggests that only if this module is chosen universally in a generally cooperative and friendly environment, can the simulation guarantee a Kantian world of perpetual peace.)

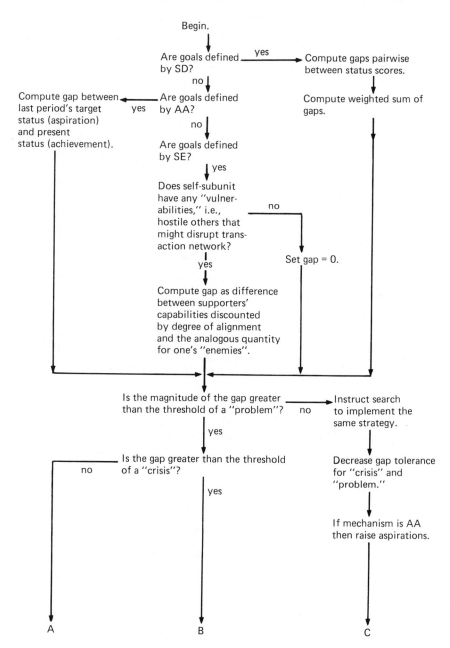

Figure 19–4A. Overview of the goal-definition/problem-recognition module. Mechanisms for defining goals are abbreviated: SD status discrepancy or rank consistency, SE security/vulnerability, AA aspiration-achievement comparisons.

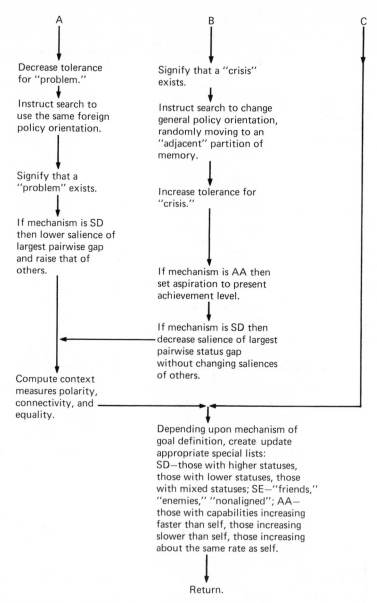

Figure 19-4B. Overview of the goal-definition/problem-recognition module, continued.

about the modules' functioning. In an international environment in which most actors most of the time evaluate important problems of vulnerability or insecurity, their attention—and thus the bulk of their resources—will be devoted to international competition and conflict. Historically, habitual external orientation has led to the development of institutions and allocation of capabilities to tasks that, at the best, offer little support for domestic growth and development. Welfare becomes secondary to survival of the actor's autonomy. The world as a whole fails to respond to the "limits to growth" or to meet basic human needs. By exploring what appear to be systemically imposed obstacles to global improvement, we ultimately hope to learn how collective efforts to diminish obstacles to development may be achieved. Our design of modules for goal definition produces a regionalized problem, which resembles prisoners' dilemmas, requiring integrative resolution if worldwide, as opposed to locally self-reliant approaches to human welfare are to be successful in a short period of time.

    c. **Strategies, Games, Rules.** In designing capabilities by which the organization can interact with others in its environment, we apply the insight of Bobrow (1968) that any actor may simultaneously be playing several different "games" with different sets of others. By "games" Bobrow means "patterned interactions with particular currencies." We equate "games" with sequences of "strategies." A strategy is a set of abstractly defined behavioral rules which have as their object the attainment or furtherance of a particular goal. We refer to strategies that have been implemented as "precedents." A single strategy can call for changes in the levels of economic, diplomatic, and alliance ties. Or it may be limited to one mode of exchange. Since strategies can be constructed from other strategies, our model specifications generate increasing rightness and complexity to the set of available strategies, that is, to precedents for problem solving.

    Figure 19-5 pictures strategies and their components as intersecting circular lists. A decisive advantage of this characterization of learned microtheories for goal attainment is that it offers the flexibility required of the interpretation of these lists at times as *instructions* for international activity and at other times as *data* which can be shaped and adapted by the original processes.

    d. **The Structure of Memory as Intersecting Circular Lists.** Like Shank and Abelson (1975) we believe memory to be episodic, that is, organized around prior experience. There is some evidence that policy makers' collective memories are precedent-bound sets of learned rules for constructing solutions to familiar problems (May 1973). Strategies may be considered *plans*, in the usage of Miller, Galanter, and Pribram (1960), although they are relatively short sighted to obviate the need for long-term planning (Cyert and March 1963, p. 119). Unlike Abelson's scripts (1973, 1975), strategies are stored in a form that accords little attention to means and none at all to the practicability of their implementation. The only real test of practicability—aside from the degree of success they

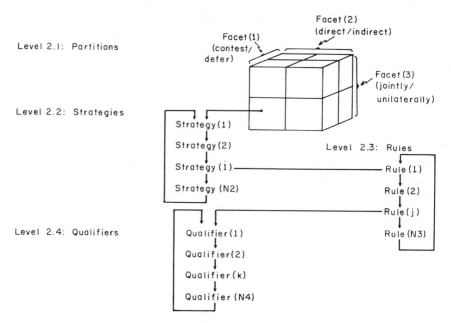

Figure 19-5. Characterization of collective memory composed of lists of strategies.

recorded in previous implementations in similar contexts—is the attempt at implementation.

Strategies are grouped into eight broad classes of policy orientation, as shown in Figure 19-5. Each strategy consists of a node containing information about the most recent implementation, a cumulative success score, and other contextual information which is used in the search process. Each node contains as well a pointer to a singly-linked circular list of information about each previous implementation.

The operational parts of the strategy are one or more abstract *rules* for international activity, usually coded in the form of "self-predicate targets." Each rule is a node in a circular list. (There is no special virtue in using a circular rather than linear list except that it facilitates random access of nodes, which is required for model testing and analysis of performance.) The "targets" are left unspecified by the rule; their identities are found by evaluating the nodes in a subordinate circular list of *qualifiers*. These take the form "others one—in relation to—others two," where "others two" can twice be replaced by phrases of the same form to yield embeddings such as "others which are allies of the enemies of one's principal import sources."

Rules may be more general than prescriptions for particular elementary acts. Special rules may be used for the transmittal of entire strategies or for the acceptance of strategies that others have transmitted. Thus the actor can, in certain circumstances, "instruct" others in their problem-solving attempts. "Instruction" in a coercive context might be associated with foreign penetration and control of one's foreign policy process. We shall return to this aspect of emergent interdependencies.

Qualifiers function to isolate targets according to their location, or generalized roles, in the stratification system (compare Lorrain and White 1971), or to their relative capabilities for specific modes of international activity. The simplest kind of qualifier recognizes seven degrees of eight types of relations. Actors are, in addition, furnished with the means for generalizing these instructions into single relations such as "friend," "colony," "lower prestige," and "others sharing a large number of common transactional linkages with one's principal rival." Since relations may be triply compounded for greater specificity (producing a qualifier which might yield, for instance, "friends of others of lower prestige than those sharing a large number of common economic linkages with the principal rival of oneself"), the actors are, in principle, capable of making a truly astronomical number of discriminations in their local environments.

Strategies may be viewed not only as sets of abstract rules but also as operations to be performed upon the local environment. Each component of a strategy is distinct in what it produces: qualifiers generate sets of actors; rules generate sets of acts; and the strategy as an integral whole yields larger sets of acts. The function of each can be made more specific to illustrate how it may become inoperative and lead to an increased variety of precedents in memory.

Call L the set of actors in A's local system at time t: $L = L(A,t)$. [For convenience we exclude A from $L(A,t)$.] Further, let i index qualifiers, j index rules, and k index strategies. A qualifier $Qkji$ is then simply a reduction of the local system:

$$Qkji \ [L(A,t)] \ = \text{set of other actors.}$$

This set may, of course, be empty.

Similarly, a rule, Rkj, is a mapping of the intersection of its qualifiers into a set of directed dyadic acts of one mode of interaction (viz., wealth or prestige or power or friendliness–hostility):

$$Rkj \ \left\{ \cap i \ Qkji \ [L(A,t)] \right\} \ = \text{set of acts.}$$

By *act* is meant an increment or decrement in the level of interaction of the particular mode. In this respect, acts resemble Abelson's "deltacts" (1975). The set of acts will be empty if the set of targets specified by the intersection among qualifiers is empty.

Finally, a strategy is the union of the acts specified by one or more rules. It may involve acts of several modes, as indicated by its relation to its components.

$SK \left(\cup_j Rkj \ \{\cap_i Qkji \ [L(A,t)]\} \right)$ = set of acts, possibly in several modes.

This notation is awkward but clarifying. It points out how the contents of memory are used as *instructions* for the actors' pursuit of goals. A major contribution of the list-processing representation is that the contents of memory can also be treated as *data* to be adapted to the actor's requirements.

Chomsky and Miller (1963) argue that the "richest source of new plans is our old plans transformed to meet new situations." To produce adaptive goal seeking, the actors must be able to manipulate strategies. "As in the case of grammatical transformations, the truly predictive behavior transformations are undoubtedly those that combine two or more simpler plans into one." (Chomsky and Miller, 1963, p. 488). We can now illustrate that the list structure of memory at least minimally meets these requirements.

e. Simplification of Strategies.   Imagine a very simple strategy that might be called "alliance against a common enemy." Suppose it is chosen by some actor and implementation is attempted.

$S1$ "alliance against common enemy."
$R11$ offer defensive alliance.
$Q111$ those who are not hostile to self.
$Q112$ those who have the same enemy as self.
$Q113$ those who are not already allied with the enemy of self.

To illustrate simplification we assume that when the actor selects $S1$ none of its local system is hostile. In this situation $Q111$ is nondiscriminating: $Q111 \ [L(A,t)] = L(A,t)$. As $Q111$ serves no purpose, it is erased from $R11$.[8]

If all the qualifiers of a rule prove nondiscriminating, the rule will also be removed. (In other words, completely undifferentiated activity directed toward all does not arise in the model.) If, on the other hand, the set of others generated by several qualifiers is empty, the rule is likewise removed. Suppose that the actor implementing $S1$ has, by its own evaluation, no current enemies. Then both remaining qualifiers, $Q112$ and $Q113$, produce empty sets, i.e., for $j=1$, $\cap_i Qkji[L(A,t)] = \phi$. Rule $R11$ produces no acts and is also deleted from $S1$. Finally, since $S1$ has but a single inoperative rule, the strategy is null and without effect. It is erased from memory. (Mechanically more accurately: the altered copy of $S1$ is not placed into memory; the "parent" from which it was copied remains as a valid precedent, but its precedent-related information is not up-

8. A digression on computational procedure: to facilitate subsequent manipulation, a strategy when selected is immediately copied and the copy placed in temporary storage. In the course of implementation, changes may be made upon the copy as parts of it prove inoperative. If changes are not made, the altered copy is erased and the precedent-usage information on the original is merely updated.

dated as a consequence of the totally unsuccessful effort at implementation.) The actor that attempted $S1$ must reinitiate search for an acceptable precedent.

f. Complexity by Concatenation. If the only direction in which precedents could evolve were toward greater simplicity, foreign policy would soon degenerate into simplistic, contextually unqualified, single-mode activities. For this reason, the actors must be given the opportunity to build up complex strategies from simple ones. One plausible occasion in which such a process may occur is during crises, when the control unit of the actor may intervene to try to guarantee coherence and coordination among the strategies selected by its sectors. When the control unit supersedes the functions of the sectors and selects strategies on their behalf, a new strategy is created by concatenating the individual precedents.

Consider two additional elementary strategies:

$S2$ "cut economic ties with enemy and its allies."
   R21 cut economic relations.
   Q211 enemy of self.
   Q212 ally of enemy of self.
$S3$ "withdraw diplomatic relations with enemy and take milder sanctions against those who maintain high level diplomatic relations with enemy."
   R31 cut diplomatic relations.
   Q311 enemy of self.
   R32 reduce diplomatic relations.
   Q321 those with high-level mission to enemy of self.

If the control unit of an actor selected (the original) $S1$, $S2$, and $S3$, the concatenated result, $S4$, would be

$S4$ "attempt to isolate an enemy in all modes"

$R41\ (=R11)$	$Q411\ (=Q111)$
	$Q412\ (=Q112)$
	$Q413\ (=Q113)$
$R42\ (=R21)$	$Q421\ (=Q221)$
	$Q422\ (=Q212)$
$R43\ (=R31)$	$Q431\ (=Q311)$
$R44\ (=R32)$	$Q411\ (=Q321)$

Figure 19–6 shows strategies $S1$–$S3$ in list form. The dotted lines show how $S4$ was constructed from the parts of $S1$–$S3$.

Neither simplification by deletion nor concatenation is likely to permit the very frequent emergence of truly novel strategies. A theory of policy innovation is required.

g. **Toward Innovation of Strategies.** One approach to innovation is exemplified by the efforts of Fogel, Owens, and Walsh (1966) to evolve "intelligent" automata. The "intelligence" involved was chiefly the prediction of the next in an input sequence of symbols, and the predicting devices were small, minimally structured automata. "Evolution" was produced by fast-time mutation–evaluation–selection sequences using the most promising automata, in between trials of predicting the next symbol. Their automata correspond approximately to our strategies and their task of prediction to our criterion of successful goal attainment. But strategies typically consist of more than a couple of parts, offereing a large variety of points at which random disturbances ("mutation") could be induced. The processes of implementation and evaluation are, moreover, so time consuming and difficult that it is hard to rationalize repeated trials as analogous to any processes in foreign policy bureaucracies. Mutation would be acceptable only if a very long time were available and if the structure of strategies were very simple.

An alternative approach would be empirically to discover and systematize those heuristics that statesmen and others might presumably employ to shape and adapt precedents to changed conditions. One would thus wish to record policy makers protocols, in much the same fashion as Newell and Simon (1972) study the problem-solving steps of subjects confronted with cryptarithmetic or logic problems. Because formulations of strategies are generally collective decisions, reconciling personal as well as organizational interest and ambitions, it is likely that the individual's protocol would poorly describe organizational choice.

A pragmatic approach to a theory of innovation that is compatible with capabilities for organizational learning posited by Cyert and March (1963) further constrained by incomplete learning cycles (March and Olsen 1975) could combine advantages of the two extreme courses: selection would be blind and heuristics would be extremely simple. One might suppose that an organizational unit searching for a strategy would more readily forsake that part of its matching criterion which described the current international context than that part which demanded a level of successfulness of precedents for problem solving. Such a consideration leads to an approach to policy innovation that works fairly well if strategies are generally highly differentiated and specific. The actor finds the N most successful precedents, and concatenates them into a new strategy. The magnitude of N is allowed to vary as a function of the actor's past experience with different values: since concatenation is similar to union, too small an N and the actor produces nothing really new, but too large an N and the resultant strategy is likely to be too encompassing to address specific problems. A second, more promising procedure is to select only those rules most frequently associated with successful (yet, in the current context, inappropriate) precedents and

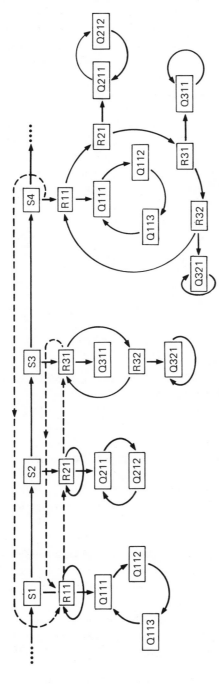

Figure 19-6.   Concatenation of strategies to create a new strategy.

to combine them in a new strategy. This procedure assures neither coherence nor consistency (so that the mechanisms for simplification must be applied as a final step in the creative sequence), but it has given interesting experimental results.

Let us consider a simple example actually produced by an early simulation experiment. Suppose that there are only two precedents available, neither of which is prohibitively unsuccessful in previous implementations but neither suitable to the matching criterion. One strategy attempts to isolate an enemy (1) by cutting direct economic relations, (2) by rewarding other smaller actors that are generally hostile toward the enemy and not economic partners of it, and (3) by offering alternative opportunities for economic exchange to those smaller actors engaged in low levels of economic activity with the enemy. The second policy is to increase economic relations with regional actors while avoiding extremes of uneven concentration of economic activity.

$S5$ "isolate enemy activity."

$R51$ increase economic exchange slightly.

$Q511$ those currently engaged in low levels of economic exchange with enemy of self.

$Q512$ those of lower economic status than self.

$Q513$ those not engaged in high levels of economic exchange with enemy of self.

$R52$ cut economic relations.

$Q521$ enemy of self.

$R53$ increase economic exchange moderately.

$Q531$ those hostile to enemy of self.

$Q532$ those not involved in economic exchange with enemy of self.

$Q533$ those having lower economic status than self.

$S6$ "increase and deconcentrate regional economic activity."

$R61$ increase economic exchange slightly.

$Q611$ those proximate to self.

$Q612$ those not engaged in very high levels of economic exchange with self.

Only one rule appears more than once: $R51 = R61$ increase economic exchange slightly. A strategy created from this rule, concatenating its list of qualifiers is $S7$:

$S7$ "increase economic exchange slightly with regionally inferior others."

$R71$ increase economic exchange slightly.

$Q711$ those currently engaged in low levels of economic exchange with enemy of self.

$Q712$ those of lower economic status than self.

$Q713$ those not engaged in high levels of economic exchange with enemy of self.

$Q714$ those proximate to self.

$Q715$ those not engaged in very high levels of economic exchange with self.

At the time of innovation of $S7$, the implementing actor evaluated none in its local system as an enemy, simplifying $S7$ to $S8$ (Figure 19-7 shows the list structures of $S5$, $S6$, and the simplified $S8$):

$S8$ "increase economic exchange slightly with regionally inferior others."

$R81$ $(=R71)$
   $Q811$ $(=Q712)$
   $Q812$ $(=Q714)$
   $Q813$ $(=Q715)$

A strategy such as $S8$ encompasses policies such as concentrating trade with neighboring actors with weaker economies to induce economic dependence. Commodity dumping, of which Hirschman accuses Germany in the 1930s, is a typical example: "as good an instance as could be desired to illustrate the general principles of a power policy using foreign trade as its instrument." (1945, p. 95).

This example is not intended to suggest that strategies $S5$ and $S6$ were the historical "parents" of German economic policy toward the Balkans. Rather, it shows how strategies with qualitatively new impact may be fashioned when the lists of precedents in memory are treated as data to be restructured. The example is weak because relatively homogeneous "parents" were involved, but strong because the generated strategy was at least interpretable. In the course of experimentation with this procedure of innovation we find strategies are commonly generated that are very rich in number and in variety of their parts. Some of them are intelligible and/or prove relatively successful in goal attainment. The greater number is hopelessly incoherent and even disastrous. It is nevertheless becoming clear that the elementary devices for simplification, concatenation and frequency-directed innovation are together capable of maintaining and even expanding the variety of policy alternatives available in the memory.

h. Selection of Precedents from a Common Memory. Each sector in the simulation has "experienced" the full history of the simulation, but each has perceived and evaluated that history differently. We find it convenient to model a memory common to all actors, but with actor-specific evaluations on the precedents that each has used and with subunit-specific search instructions for choosing precedents in specified situations. Thus, while each actor's experience is part of the system's history—the whole—the system's history resides in the memory of each part. Using a differentiably accessible common memory is convenient from an experimental point of view because it allows us to investigate the consequences of altering actors' search rules and evaluations of their and others' histories.

There are three aspects by which access differs. First, actors are not presumed to "know" the evaluations that others have made of strategies' usefulness. Second, precedents are not available to actors unless they possess the rough level

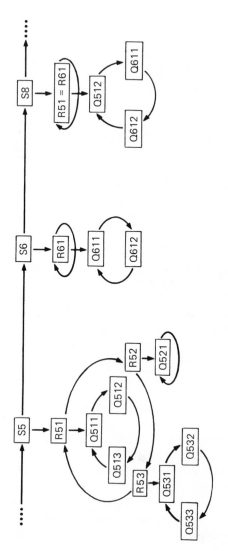

Figure 19-7. Frequency-directed innovation of a new strategy.

of capabilities required for implementation. Third, even when actors "know" information relevant to the selection of a precedent, they generally differ in assessing the significance of portions of that information. These considerations lead to the notion of selecting strategies according to matches made between an actor's criteria and attributes of a strategy generated from previous experience (Alker and Christensen 1972).

The three properties of search activity can be explicated by reference to Figure 19-8 which presents the process of local search. Taking search instructions that have been shaped by search experience and by decisions earlier in the policy process, the actor's subunit initially chooses a set of other actors from which it is willing to borrow precedents. The searching subunit is restricted to the evaluations of this set of others when it evaluates a precedent's prior successes.

Although the cost of strategies—in terms of the magnitude of transactional changes that will result from its implementation in a contemporary local system—is generally unknowable to the actor, its subunit can predict the scope of activity the strategy might entail by comparing roughly the level of capabilities of others that have used the strategy in the past with its own. Subunits are free to select precedents whose previous users lie in the same or lower capability quartile. There is no mechanism in the model that guarantees that actors will not, for example, export 150 percent of their GDP. In fact, we wish to examine the conditions under which such pathologies occur to improve model specifications. But four features—(1) the relatively greater extent of the local systems of great powers, (2) cost constraints on the selection of precedents, (3) actors' individual attention to a matrix of priority transactions against which vulnerabilities are defined (p. 235), and (4) the removal during implementation of undifferentiated rules in strategies (p. 239)—effectively combine to stratify the scope and efficacy of actors' problem-solving attempts in much the same way that the actors are stratified by statuses.

A fourth restriction to accessing precedents in a common memory arises from adjustable latitude in matching precedents with regard to the international context for which they are intended. Context is operationalized by indices of polarity (the number of separate alignment groups of high-capability others), connectivity (the density and completeness of the exchange network [Harary and Miller 1970]), and equality (the variance in status scores)—all evaluated with respect to the value dimension of most relevance to the search subunit. When a strategy is created, the indices of context of the then current local system are recorded upon it. Stored among the subunit's matching criteria are tolerances within which the contemporary context must correspond with any acceptable precedent. The tolerances are dynamically adjusted, as shown in Figure 19-8, as a function of how discriminating each facet of context proves. This is done to increase the likelihood that all subunits will find only a few precedents applicable to a particular environment, and that no precedent will appear applicable

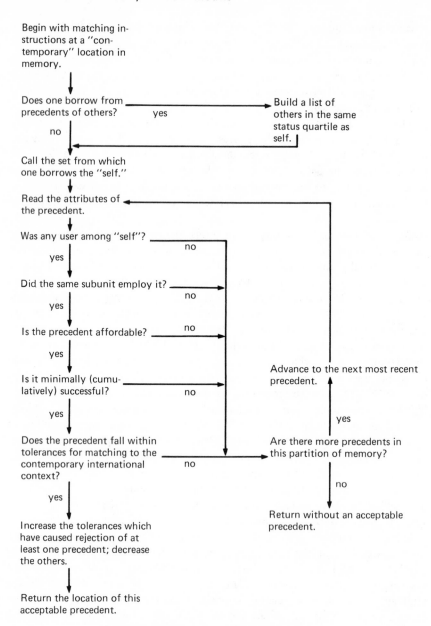

Figure 19-8. Process of local search.

(during initial, local search) to truly novel environments, such as might follow sudden, structural transformation of the system. Consequently, even though all actors match on abstractly the same attributes of a precedent, their effective matching criteria generally differ sufficiently to cause them to find different historical precedents applicable to the same problem situations. This is just one manner of operationalizing the observation that an organization's understanding of means–ends relations is ultimately shaped largely by its particularistic history.

i. Extended Search and Creation of New Strategies. Our use of organization theory leads the actor to prefer to search locally for precedents, that is, to seek an acceptable strategy for problem solving of the same general type as most recently applied. To partition collective memory into general types, or policy orientations, we borrow loosely the distinctions from Miller, Galanter, and Pribram (1960) between policies that are contentious or deferential, direct or indirect, and unilaterial or joint in their implementation. These three dichotomous facets partition memory into eight general orientations. Local search is restricted to a single partition. When local search fails to reveal an acceptable precedent or when decisions earlier in the policy process indicate a change of orientation, the actor moves randomly into a "neighboring" partition, i.e., one which differs only in respect to one of these facets. Once the partition is changed, local search begins anew. (See Figure 19-9).

The facets defining partitions of memory refer to differences in gross style of, or orientation to, legitimate modes of transacting international relations. The dichotomy contest–defer is similar to Wolfer's (1962) distinction between policies of self-extension, on the one hand, and self-abnegation and (frequently) self-preservation, on the other. Very roughly, it characterizes the degree of belligerence implicit in an actor's approach to problem solving. The tendency to contest others' aspirations proves empirically frequently, although not necessarily theoretically, to be associated with positions of dominance in the system of stratification. The tendency to defer to others is more typical of positions of subordination or deferrence.

The distinction between direct and indirect strategies refers to relative emphases on unconditional (unreciprocated) changes *versus* conditional (reciprocated) changes in transactions, and on initiating new transactional linkages with others in the local system *versus* incrementing existing linkages. The former are activities typical of relatively high capability actors. Indirect strategies require reciprocation by those to whom they are directed to become operational. We have in mind a distinction like that between a grant of economic aid and a proposal to undertake balanced economic exchange. (Note that both types of transaction may confer influence on the initiator, directly through the index defining stratification orderings or indirectly through created dependencies, future obligations, and bases for threatening revocation of the exchange relation.)

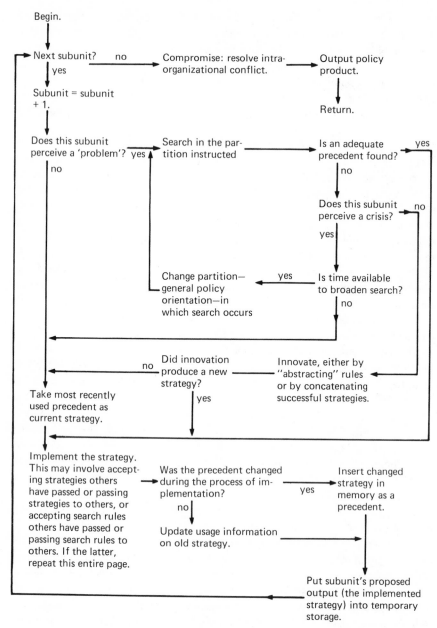

Figure 19-9. Overview of the strategy search–implementation process.

Joint strategies are typically undertaken with others, often by including rules that instruct the transmittal of entire strategies for others to implement, as well as by more conventional increments of transactions and events. Unilateral strategies do not require opportunities for collective action and thus may be implemented alone. "Collective security" can be interpreted either as a joint strategy or as a unilateral strategy which the vast majority of actors happen to implement simultaneously. The institutionalization of collective action is achieved by joint strategies which create new actors (see p. 254).

To an extent, rules can be evaluated differently, depending upon the partition, or general foreign policy orientation, in which they reside. For instance, opportunities are operationalized differently for "direct" strategies than for "indirect." "Direct" opportunities are formed from the intersection of up to four kinds of lists, each of which is identified by the kind and degree of transactions others have with the implementing actor. "Indirect" opportunities are formed from lists of others which share "structurally similar" locations in the transactional system with the implementing actor. By "structurally similar" we mean that the implementing actor and others share a large proportion of their exchange relations with the same set of third parties (Schofield 1971). The first sort of "opportunities list" references other actors which presently engage in a wide variety of transactions with the implementing actor, and which therefore are candidates for augmentation or diminution of exchange relations. The second kind of references those others which are not presently in one's exchange network but which might favorably respond to initiatives for collective action by virtue of sharing similar problems and contextual evaluation.

Clusters of similar strategies constitute generalized foreign policy orientations. Strategies are initially assigned to different partitions depending upon their relative emphasis toward the three facets. However, actors may adapt precedents to alter these emphases, and the precedents are not reassigned among partitions. Any strategy produced from one or more precedents in a partition remains in the same partition, even though it may bear little resemblance to its antecedents. Consequently, entire partitions may atrophy or expand, depending upon the preferences actors develop for precedents within them. Furthermore, the original distinctions among partitions can, from the perspective of the behavioral implications of their precedents, be eroded or sharpened in the course of a simulation. To the extent that major wars represent breakdown in great power management of international politics (Modelski 1971, 1972), one would expect to witness increasing divergence in partition preferences among high capability actors. Conversely, convergent ideological trends should be reflected in increasing agreement upon which partitions of precedents are most fertile sources of acceptable problem-solving precedents.

The supposition that actors' subunits prefer to search locally means that their precedents tend over long periods to originate in a single partition of memory. As long as the selected precedents prove moderately satisfactory, the search rules that a subunit uses within a partition will change only incrementally. Thus particular precedents—which may differ from one another only marginally from attempted implementations in varying environments—and sequences of precedents frequently recur historically as the basis of individual actors' policies.

Abelson calls "themes" the "often repeated, perhaps even stylized, interactions between individuals or organizations or nations." (1973, p. 325) These arise in our simulation if one actor's selection of a particular precedent or sequence of precedents regularly evokes in another actor the selection of another precedent or sequence of precedents. We find that our model occasionally produces such stable interaction patterns in situations in which the actors are mutually very salient, pursuing goals that are interdependent (or exclusive). If the possibilities for enriching the repertoire of precedents is limited by reduced opportunities for innovating or borrowing strategies from others, the theme-like interactive sequences may recur in different contexts much later in the simulation experiment. Occasionally, sequences of themes appear. Abelson terms these "scripts": they are marked by one theme following another, regardless of the cause.

Abelson's representation of belief systems is rich, involving distinctions among types of concepts, their functions, and relations among them. Our representation of precedents as generalized strategies is much less developed. Nevertheless, complex sequences of behavioral rules for generating foreign policy emerge from the operation of our simulation from the combination of the elementary representation of precedents, the prevalent search rules in a context, and the availability of precedents produced by previous operation of the simulation. We find it encouraging to the endeavor of capturing process of international restructuring in the long term that sophisticated interdependent sequences of abstract policy generators occasionally emerge—if not always in historically accurate contexts—from an initially confused, unorganized mass of primitive rules and qualifiers.

This emergent property encourages us to believe that the very rough, partially empirically problematic specifications of the foreign policy process are sufficiently rich to yield, in certain circumstances, new regimes of systemic organization and, when these ultimately erode or collapse, qualitatively different regimes of reorganization. In other words, we identify the emergence of script-like generalizations for policy with a partial explanation of international restructuring, one which points to the antecedents of actors' international behavior in their implicit understandings of "how the world works" as reflected in explicit representations of "how the world can be manipulated" to particular ends.

The approach to modeling dynamics of restructuring described above is radically different from, and we think a valuable complement to, the emphasis on capability-constrained global political behavior in the dynamic models of Choucri–North or Mesarovic–Pestel. Our memory-oriented approach takes the problem of disaggregating historical phenomena as more than successively restricting the spatial and temporal domains of action. It also requires stages of translation, or concretion, of historically generated and abstracted instructions in contextually sensitive ways. Translation, nevertheless, is frequently severely constrained by others' capabilities or influence. An important kind of constraint is dependence.

j. **Dependence and the Acceptance of Others' Proposals.** We hypothesize that all international exchange leads to dependence, but that dependence is mutual (interdependence) if the exchange occurs among actors structurally equivalently located in the stratification system. The effects of dependence should, moreover, be cumulative—both in accumulation and in decay. Because we do not explicitly model the actor's internal center-periphery conflicts or government-opposition competitions, dependence is behaviorally consequential in two ways, both relating to the propensity of one actor to accept the initiatives of another. We are aware that there remains considerable room in our model for further elaboration of dependence mechanisms; we have heretofore studied only some of the impacts of external systems on the possibilities for autonomous national development. We have not, however, modeled constraints on revolutionary transformations within the national actors.

An actor's transactions may be made conditional upon reciprocation by another. Such conditional exchange is definitionally "equal," as accounts are kept in the matrix of current transactions. But the implications of the terms under which it is begun and the consequences for internal structures of the participants differ as functions of the relative influence positions of the participants and of the importance of their dyadic transactions (Emmanuel 1972; Buckley, Burns, and Meeker 1974).

The more important of two consequences of a dependence relation operates through the dependent actor's acceptance and implementation of strategies that others transmit to it. We express the propensity to acceptance as a probability. In effect it is the probability of pursuing policies that are complementary to another's goals and not necessarily to one's own. A plausible specification of the dependence relation—where $P_{ijt}(a)$ indicates a probability that subunit a of actor i will accept a strategy from actor j (if transmitted) in period t—is

$$\hat{P}_{ijt}(a) = (1-d) P_{ij,t-1}(a) + r I_{i/j,t}(a) [1 - P_{ij,t-1}(a)] \qquad (19\text{-}7)$$

and

$$P_{ijt}(a) = \hat{P}_{ijt}(a) \text{ if } P_{ijt}(a) \leqslant 1,$$
$$P_{ijt}(a) = 1 \text{ if } \hat{P}_{ijt}(a) > 1,$$

with $I_{i/j}(a)$ given by equation 19-2. Here d is a decay rate and r is an accumulation rate which depends upon how vital the transactions between i and j in mode *a* are. Specifically, we suppose *r* to be twice as large for those transactions rated "essential" in the quasi-exogenous "requirements" matrix than for those transactions that are "nonessential." (The "requirements" matrix is initially exogenous, and is occasionally exogenously updated to reflect "discovery" of alternative resources and technological developments, but it also responds slowly to existing transactions with the effect of making all transactions "essential" if they persist long enough, ceteris paribus.) Parameter values which produce reasonably appearing dependence relations when applied to historical transactional data are about $d = .15$ and r(essential) $= 3.0$. The exact values of these parameters are crucial to policy outcomes only when transactions become very highly dyadically concentrated for prolonged periods.

Strategies accepted by an actor are "internalized," that is, concatenated with other strategies currently being implemented. They subsequently become part of the accepting actor's behavioral repertoire and may thus serve to prolong or deepen the dependence relation. In the model, the practice of imperialism entails transmittal of strategies to others whose acceptance is highly probable. In one sense, imperialism is a learned metastrategy, for it requires the metropole to know not only to whom to transmit instructions but also which strategies to send. In this way imperial practice is subject to disruption from such structural changes in the international system as a disintegrating dependence network and self-redefinition of the dependent actors. As in the nationally disaggregated models of Mesarovic-Pestel and Choucri-North, an underlying grid of transactions generates systemic outcomes. But importantly and variably mediating between transactions and systemic outcomes are the actors' processes of problem identification, goal setting, and strategy choice, implementation, and transmission.

When a low probability of accepting a transmitted strategy nevertheless results in a decision to accept, one might characterize the situation as "instruction" or "imitation." When the probability of acceptance is high, the situation is more typical of foreign penetration or "coercion." In either case, the accepting actor undertakes a policy that can be expected to be irrelevant (and, at worst, inimical) to the attainment of its own goals: repetitive acceptances almost always force the actor to drastically reduce the level of aspiration for goals or to abandon altogether the mechanism by which goals are defined. Some fundamental internal reorganization usually ensues.

The second consequence of the dependence relation is to condition the dependent actor to accept individual acts, or "residual" changes in transaction levels, from others. This general orientation to others' atomic proposals is more easily understood within a broader discussion of types of international transactions.

k. Current Transactions, Conditional and Unconditional Proposals: From Policy Proposal to Policy Output. The status ordering and indeed the international status quo is determined by a matrix of *current transactions* and friendliness-hostility interactions among all the actors in the system. In addition there are two matrices of *proposed changes* in transaction and interaction levels. One contains *conditional* proposals, whose consummation is dependent upon reciprocation of the activity by the target. The other contains *unconditional* proposals which require acceptance by their targets but not reciprocation.

If all transactions were conditional, international exchange would be exactly dyadically balanced. We identify unconditional economic transactions with aid, loans, and investment; unconditional military transactions with asymmetric alliance obligations and treaties of guarantee; unconditional prestige transactions with diplomatic delegations, state visits, and the like. Conditional transactions include trade, symmetric alliance obligations and the exchange of embassies.

The two matrices of proposed transactions constitute part of the input to the organization, or feedback from the systemic level to one actor's policy process. The organization is forced to respond in some manner to these inputs, if only to reject them. Many responses may be subsumed with the implementation of strategies. In this case, the organizational response occurs directly from the pursuit of its goals. But other proposed activities may not receive attention during the strategy implementation phase; these become, in a sense, residual stimuli.

The model recognizes three responses to residual stimuli: outright rejection of the proposed changes; acceptance at reduced magnitudes of change, and acceptance of the full proposals. The organizational response disposition is selected for each set of residual stimuli dyadically. It is guided by a generalized orientation to each member of its local system: dominance suggests rejection, dependence suggests acceptance, and an undefined or ambiguous relationship leads to reduced acceptance. The portion of proposed changes that the organization accepts is added to the matrix of current transactions, and a new international status quo thereby emerges.

Organizational output produced in pursuit of its own goals consists of proposed conditional and unconditional changes in relations with other actors and does not directly enter the current transaction matrix. It must await others' analyses and policy processes and the possibility of being reduced or rejcted by its intended targets. An exception is made in interactions: "unconditional" changes in levels of friendliness-hostility enter the current transaction matrix directly. ("Conditional" interactions have no operational significance except as expressions of good or ill will. Actors can express crude "threats" by means of conditional increments in hostility.) Thus, war is ultimately a unilateral act, while peace requires acquiescence, if not cooperation. In our model, very hostile events define war, but very friendly ones do not suffice for integration.

1. Processes of Growth and Decay: the Creation and Dissolution of Actors. The number of actors can increase by the creation of new ones and by the disintegration of existing actors. It can decrease by "conquest" of one actor by another and by integration of two or more actors. We assume throughout that political integration and the creation of new, autonomous actors are not merely results of repeatedly augmenting transactions but require, in addition, specific decisions or purposes for their achievement. But if integration is not an undirected process, neither may it emerge from political decisions without a transactional foundation. Rules that prescribe integration as part of a strategy must therefore have qualifiers which demand high transactional levels in all modes between the implementing actor and potential targets.

Strategies can create actors jointly or unilaterally. In addition, a unilaterally created actor can subsequently broaden its base of support and resources, perhaps gaining autonomy from its creator. New intergovernmental actors are still-born if they fail to receive enough resources to enable them to select and implement strategies of their own. Loss of support is equated with decay. As Ruggio (1971) has emphasized, intergovernmental actors are likely to encounter built-in limitations to their capabilities for autonomous action when that begins to run counter the interests of their creators.

Disintegration is caused by the failure to sustain dependence relations that induce one actor to accept and implement the strategies suggested by another. Rather than attempt to predict the geographic divisions that emerge from disintegrative processes, we highly constrain the variety of disintegrative outcomes by a design which requires prior specification of which areas are susceptible to separatism, liberation or conquest (see below, page 270). We have not dealt with imperial disintegration because of the growth of independence movements in colonies: explanation here lies primarily in the realm of endogenous social processes despite the prominence of diffusion or contagion effects in selection of liberation strategies.

New actors can prove beneficial to their creators in two important situations. The first is that the new actor, if it remains dependent upon its creator alone, will execute strategies transmitted to it, thus increasing the effective per-period repertoire of its creator. The second is that a subordinate new actor directly improves its creator's stratification position by the positive contribution of a new dominance relation to the creator's status scores. Without experimenter-imposed constraints on the model's development, those strategies which create new subordinate actors tend to become relatively popular and to contribute toward greatly expanded complexity of the system. Countervailing tendencies toward systemic simplification and reintegration will obviously depend upon the variety and efficacy of strategies at the disposal of the newly created subordinate actors. Newly created actors encounter a precarious existence if they transgress the standards of the great powers. But if there are no widely recognized standards, they might successfully employ strategies of clientelism, nonbelligerent nonconformism, balancing rivals, and so on. Their primary obstacle is the timely borrowing of or innovating strategies adequate to their needs. Experience with the model suggests that few of the rapidly proliferating new actors with only a single subunit—that is, few that are specialized to pursue a single kind of goal—can prove viable in a rapidly changing system. Integrated actors retain the memories of their antecedents, however, and prove more robust.

m. **Histories of the Foreign Policy Process as Partial Explanations of Outcomes.** Although we have discussed the explanatory mechanisms in the model, a better comprehension of the kinds of analytic and cognitive activity in which actors may engage is obtained from following in condensed form the policy process of an arbitrary organization through one period. In order to incorporate a wide variety of model features in a short description, our illustration is hypothetical: the description below corresponds to no particular experimental trial, but all its features are frequently observed in simulations. To continue this paper's focus on international vulnerabilities, we assume that the actor defines goals in terms of perceived security.

Despite the existence of "simultaneous" causal structures and multiple paths in the conceptual outlines of Figures 19-1 and 19-3, all computerized models must ultimately perform sequentially, one task at a time. It is convenient to divide this computational sequence into four major stages:

1. examination of the international context,
2. domestic processes,
3. qualitative and quantitative setting of goals, and
4. operationalization of goals, quasi-resolution of intraorganizational conflict, and policy output.

We shall, of course, give relatively less attention to model features already discussed.

1. Examination of the International Context. The organization's first task is to examine if it exists as an autonomous actor and to reevaluate its status. If it is not autonomous, we go immediately to the next organization. Among possible statuses are:

"state," a fully articulated, autonomous organization,

"colony" or "disputed territory," a fully articulated nonautonomous organization,

"transnational economic entity (MNC)," an autonomous organization with no control unit and one economically specialized subunit,

"intergovernmental economic entity," an autonomous organization with a control unit and one economically specialized subunit, and

"alliance secretariat," an autonomous organization with a control unit and one militarily specialized subunit.

By "autonomous" we mean "capable of making one's own decisions," not "independent of external influences." Some statuses impose severe constraints on the foreign policy process. For instance, an intergovernmental organization dependent upon states for its annual appropriations cannot tolerate even temporary disruptions of the transactions that represent its resources. For such an actor, transactions in the prestige mode are equated with membership; those in the economic mode with contributions. Our example follows the policy process of a state, which is more interesting from an organizational perspective.

The organization next inquires if it is engaged in any "absorbing" processes that demand priority attention. In particular, is it involved in a major war or in the final stages of integration with other organizations? The finding of major war requires it to increase the priority of foreign as opposed to domestic matters (see below, p. 250) and to allocate more resources to the foreign policy subunits. The severity, extent, and outcome of the war can be determined stochastically from specifications in the regressions of Starr (1972). It is often more efficient, from the experimenter's point of view, to intervene in the simulation and direct wars to desired or interesting outcomes (which is the course followed to study the consequences of the War of the Pacific, below).

The finding of integration means that authority is to be located in a new actor as a consequence of an explicit decision—that is, selection and implementation of an "integrationist" strategy—and not merely that there exist high transaction levels among organizations. Creating a new actor involves nothing more mechanical than setting aside some additional space inside the computer, giving it a name, and assigning it the resources and subunits of its components. In addition, its identity incorporates those of its component organizations in the sense that their precedents for problem solving become its own. Deletion of actors follows the reverse process: they are simply erased from the system.

The actor then updates the set of others it considers relevant to international activity, that is, its local system. If the current transaction matrix includes exchange with a new actor, or if the partially exogenously determined matrix of geostrategic proximities indicates that other actors are "reachable" as a function of technological developments or improved capabilities, then these are added to the local system. Conversely, members are deleted that have lost their autonomy or ceased to exist. All of the actor's subsequent analysis is limited to, and its location in the stratification system calcuated in terms of, local system members.

The organization computes its status scores for each mode of exchange in which it participates (see p. 226). Over the local system it also computes indices of polarity, connectivity and equality (see p. 244), which are used to direct the search for precedents. Finally, it "cleans house" by erasing miscellaneous lists from past contextual analysis, reading the stored data which function as "parameters" during the current policy cycle, and writing, for the experimenter's benefit, a substantial record of its internal state and its perception of the local international system.

2. Domestic Processes. The second stage in the policy process deals with domestic social, political, and economic processes, although in very abstract and abbreviated form as these are not the focus of our investigation. Without structural models like Hibbs' (1973), specified for individual national experiences or a broad spectrum of historical periods, we are forced to represent domestic processes largely stochastically. Probabilities for decisive events, such as revolution and mass unrest, are taken from historical relative frequencies (Banks 1974) and slightly altered in response to extraordinary events and conditions produced within the simulation itself.

The actor reads a historical long-term probability of domestic instability and determines—to continue our illustration—that instability does not occur in this period. But a similar, randomly generated revolution does occur. Since the actor is not involved in major war, a historically adapted long-term growth rate is taken as the baseline for incrementing capabilities. We compute the growth rate by exponentially decaying the simulation-adjusted rates and averaging the result with the historical rate corresponding to the current period.

These are very crude devices. But the model's performance appears very insensitive in the short and middle term—up to about 50 iterations—to the quantitative adjustments made in domestic processes. Actors key off quartiles of capabilities, not off the values of capabilities directly. Thus considerable change in capabilities can occur before others alter their evaluation of whether the actor possesses higher, lower, or similar capabilities to themselves. In effect, we attempt to compensate for very incomplete processual specification by using very robust decision thresholds.

The effect of both mass unrest and revolution occurring simultaneously is randomly to change the general foreign policy orientation, that is, to change the partition of memory in which search is initiated. Governmental change alone is, especially in the Pacific case study of section four, often inconsequential for foreign policy. Only if mass unrest accompanies it are sufficient replacements of personnel and, possibly, ideologies likely to result (Eckstein 1964).

The sole remaining function of domestic processes in the model is to allocate a proportion of organizational resources to all foreign activities. Ordinarily the control unit would limit its responsibilities to allocating resources among the specialized subunits. Priority is normally accorded the domestic sector of the organization. Foreign activity receives residual resources, treated as a percent of GDP. A cumulative priority for foreign activity is incremented, however, if the actor engages in major war or the terminal stages of integration. Furthermore, the priority of international activity increases when the environment becomes very salient, that is, when a great number of problems and crises arise, as discussed below.

We consider domestic resources simply in economic terms, aware that this represents a substantial oversimplification. From the proportion of GDP allocated to foreign activity as a whole, the control unit reallocates amounts to each subunit individually. There is, in the model, no recognition of the difficulties of converting from one type of capability to another. Subunits are constrained in selecting precedents by the quartile of their (economic) capabilities. Greater attention to differentiation among capabilities (see Choucri and North 1975) would involve much more explicit representation of internal dynamics of organizations. For the present we have opted for greater temporal and contextual applicability at the price of less detail.

Subunits are permitted to select precedents that involve all modes of activity. In principle, the prestige subunit can involve the actor in war and the power subunit can engage in foreign trade. What differentiates subunits is not any intrinsic character of the resources they employ but the definition of their goals with respect to individual values. It is this goal attainment, and the preferences developed in its pursuit, that constitutes their ultimate guide to international activity and their basis for differentiation within the organization.

3. Qualitative and Quantitative Setting of Goals.   The actor first examines its exchange network for specific vulnerabilities. These are identified by disparities between its matrix of current transactions and its matrix of "requirements" (page 235). Special recognition is given to that set of other actors to which the organization is vulnerable: strategies subsequently selected by individual subunits frequently refer to targets with this designation. They become, in effect, the principal foci of the actor's goal-oriented policies.

Goals are expressed as disparities between actualized and aspired statuses. The most fundamental policy option available to the actor is how qualitatively to define a goal. The principle for choice is to continue to use the current mechanism until it produces a string of disastrous outcomes. Very slow parameter-altering feedback from systemic outcomes to the choice of mechanism for goal definition connects the topmost level of the model with the bottommost level in the conceptual flowchart of Figure 19-1 (dotted lines).

The control unit reallocates resources among subunits in response to their "needs," which are expressed as the magnitude of problems they encountered in the most recent period. Relative "need" is equated with subunit priority in the organizational coalition, which below becomes a basis for resolving intraorganizational conflict.

Our hypothetical actor continues to be security oriented. Its decision process can be traced through Figure 19-4. The description that follows applies to each subunit separately, though we shall not repeat it. The subunit first attempts to discern any coalition which might be arrayed against it. For the largest set of mutually friendly "enemies," the actor computes their total capabilities, discounting the contributions of each by its degree of hostility to others in the group, to arrive at an estimated total "threat." It similarly computes an estimated "support" and compares the two quantities. The subunit uses this very crude calculation, not as a basis for attempting to "balance power," but to evaluate subjectively the likelihood that members of this coalition will challenge the actor's status attainment.

Following Organski (1958), subordinate considerations involve sorting the members of the local system according to their several relations with the actor. The subunit seeks to identify those whose statuses are rising relatively more rapidly than, relatively less rapidly than, and at about the same rate as its own. It also sorts the system into those of relatively equal, of much greater and of much less capabilities than itself. From among those of relatively equal capabilities, whose status is rising faster, and who are hostile to the actor, the subunit selects a "rival." The constraints and opportunities for the actor and its rival then become the focus of analysis.

If the rival is among those to whose disruptive activity the actor is vulnerable, a serious "crisis" exists. Normal organizational disaggregation of tasks is suspended, and the control unit intervenes to manage the policy process directly. (The finding of a "crisis" results also in an increased priority being given to foreign as opposed to domestic policy.)

We suppose a "crisis" not to be the case of our hypothetical actor. The subunit nevertheless finds that it has not satisfactorily reduced the gap between aspirations and achieved status set during the last policy cycle. The failure constitutes a "problem." Its significance is that the strategy implemented last period is rated a "failure." The precedent is updated accordingly and search activity is instructed to begin from the unacceptable strategy but remain within the same partition of memory.

Since a "problem" was found the subunit's level of aspiration of its goal is left qualitatively unchanged. Had the disparity between aspiration and actuality been substantially larger, the level of aspiration would have been reduced, but never below the current achieved level. To this point, the subunit's goal has been set quantitatively and qualitatively. But it remains to be operationalized by finding a strategy that promises to contribute to achieveing the goal more completely.

4. Operationalization of Goals, Quasi Resolution of Intraorganizational Conflict, and Policy Output. Figure 19-8 traces the subunit's process of local search for an acceptable precedent for problem solving. Our subunit is willing to borrow from all nonhostile others in the same status quartile. Because we discussed local search above (p. 245), we suppose that no acceptable precedent is found in the given partition. Consequently, the tolerances about the contextual matching criteria are not altered and the subunit is forced to broaden its search activity.

In Figure 19-9, the next test is whether a "crisis" was found earlier in the policy process. As it was not, the subunit can perform under relatively relaxed conditions, and innovation may be attempted from precedents in the same partition. This subunit has learned to prefer innovation by concatenating the three most successful precedents, regardless of the context under which they were employed previously. A new strategy is produced and implementation of its rules is attempted.

Rules contain two types of qualifiers. The first identifies targets directly by reference to their current transactions or capabilities. The second identifies them by reference to special lists of roles and role occupants, that is, by a more general set of relations to the evaluating actor. An example of the first type is "those currently demonstrating a high level of friendship." A similar set of targets might be identified by "(those in the list of) friends." Operationally, the latter role designation requires the targets to have a history of friendliness with the evaluating actor. Such sets are updated whenever referenced. An actor in the model can recognize up-to-ninety odd roles, ranging in complexity from "self" (that is, "others from which precedents may be borrowed") to "others which share similar prestige relations with the rival of oneself." Which roles will be defined and referenced depends upon the actor's mechanism for goal definition and the requirements of particular strategies. Table 19-1 is a partial enumeration of roles known to one actor at one point in the simulation experiment discussed in part four. Apparent ambiguities and anomalies can arise because reevaluation of role membership occurs irregularly and cumulatively—note in Table 19-1 that the organization "Brazil" is deemed simultaneously to have consistently lower statuses and mixed statuses.

The richer the organization's experience in terms of the variety of precedents available to it and the scope of cognitive activity it has undertaken, the greater the number of roles it can recognize and—therefore—the greater the potential complexity of its policies. Newly created actors lack the "deep pasts" of older actors that tend to generate simpler behavioral patterns. This does not mean new actors will necessarily be less successful in goal attainment, but only that their borrowed strategies may not fulfill their aspirations.

The particular strategy involves both transmitting a second strategy to one's "friends" who are also "dependents" and accepting any strategy transmitted by all of one's "allies" upon which the actor is dependent. Implementation is accomplished by first taking the intersection of the sets of "friends" and "dependents" which we suppose not to be empty. The address of the strategy to be transmitted is placed in a message to the "dependent friends." Its fate must await the targets' evaluations of the sender: it is by no means necessary that the targets will perceive the dependency relationship as being of the same degree, or even running in the same direction, as does the sender. The result of this precedent may be no change at all!

We further suppose that the subunit has no "allies" in the given mode, rendering the second rule null. The inoperative rule is erased from the strategy, thus establishing a new precedent. The new, adapted strategy acquires the attributes of the context in which it was created—the polarity, connectivity, and equality of the local system—and the identities of the creating subunit as well as its quartile of capability ("cost"). No "success" score can be assigned until the strategy's effects are observed and evaluated in the next policy cycle.

The search–adaptation–implementation process is repeated for each other active subunit. When all are finished, the control unit again intercedes to resolve

Table 19-1. An Actor's View of Its Local System—Roles Recognized by Chile in the Third Experiment, Iteration 4 (1887)

Local system members: Peru, Ecuador, Bolivia, Gibbs, Britain, United States, North, Argentina, Colombia, Brazil
Enemies: Bolivia, Peru, Argentina
Friends: Britain, Gibbs
Rivals: Peru
Major powers: United States, Britain, Argentina
Neutrals: United States, Britain (sic), Gibbs, Ecuador, Colombia
Higher status than self in all modes: Britain
Mixed statuses: Argentina, United States, Brazil
Lower status than self in all modes: Bolivia, Ecuador, Brazil (sic), Gibbs
More rapidly increasing capabilities (power): Britain, United States
Less rapidly increasing capabilities (power): Bolivia, Ecuador, Colombia
More rapidly increasing capabilities (wealth): Argentina

Adjacent to self: Peru, Bolivia, Argentina, Britain, United States, Gibbs, North
Proximate to self: Peru, Ecuador, Bolivia, Argentina, United States, Britain, Gibbs, North
Others dependent upon self (wealth): Bolivia, Peru, Tarapaca, Tacna-Arica
Others vulnerable to self (wealth): Bolivia, Tarapaca, Tacna-Arica
Others upon which self is dependent (wealth): Britain, Gibbs
Others to which self is vulnerable (wealth): Britain, Gibbs

Colonies ("disputed territories") of self: Tacna-Arica, Tarapaca
Others which share similar prestige relations with self: Argentina, Peru
Others which share similar prestige relations with rival: Bolivia, Ecuador, Chile (sic)
Others which share similar alliance relations with self: None
Others which share similar alliance relations with rival: None

Others from which one will accept "residual" proposals (wealth): Gibbs
Others from which one will accept "residual" proposals (prestige): Britain

---

(A variety of lists of the complement of the roles above with the set of local system members, i.e., "others not having higher statuses than self in all modes.")

---

logical inconsistencies in the combined proposals. We might suppose that the highest priority subunit has proposed to decrease economic transactions with one of the same targets with which a lower priority subunit has proposed increasing economic transactions. The highest-priority subunit gets its way. But had two low-priority subunits disputed proposals, the control unit would have insisted on the minimalist resolution (Cyert and March 1963, p. 118): the smaller degree of proposed change would be accepted unless the proposals called for change in opposite directions, in which case no change at all would result.

The organization as a whole has now completed a logically consistent set of acts which become its output. It does not attempt to assure that they are substantively compatible. To do so would demand conformance by the subunits to a metastrategy. This would deny to the functionally specialized subunits the autonomy to solve the disaggregated problems they were assigned. Coherence might perhaps be achieved, but at the cost of increased internal conflict. The absence of any organization-wide standard of coherence permits the subunits to end up playing their most exciting "games" with each other rather than with other organizations in their (external) environments. (The procedures for handling output and responding to "residual" acts of others are treated on p. 253).

The final step in the actor's policy process is the attempt to generalize the qualifiers in its strategies by replacing direct references to matrices of transactions or capabilities with references to particular roles. One qualifier in the strategy selected above indicated "friends." Had it instead indicated "those currently highly friendly" in terms of the matrix of transactions, the actor would—immediately *after* implementing the strategy—have searched through its list of known roles for one whose members were identical to those given by the qualifier. It would replace the direct reference in the qualifier with the matching role designation. When this actor subsequently implements the same strategy, it would determine the targets of its activity by evaluating the occupants of the role.

Actors' capabilities to generalize the targets of their activities are a powerful application of organizational learning. One can begin a simulation experiment with a common memory consisting entirely of strategies whose qualifiers reference only transactions and capabilities. The dynamics of the policy processes of the several actors will rapidly increase the sophistication and generality—that is, the level of abstraction—of the historical precedents. When coupled with the actors' mechanisms for concatenating and innovating strategies, generalization of qualifiers permits actors to reevaluate their own pasts in an ongoing quasi-adaptive fashion. Records of the past may also undergo structural change; "lessons" of the past are themselves dynamic.

The actor terminates its policy cycle at this point. It will not know the consequences of its acts until it evaluates the international context in the next period. Because the order in which actors enter their policy processes is determined randomly each period, the next actor encountered in the simulation may be the same one. Or it may have to wait until all the others have "gone twice." When it finally does reflect on the efficacy of its output during this period, the international system may be unchanged, or it may appear completely transformed. Consequently, its task of diagnosing the causes of success or failure will not be easy.

One capacity which organizations in the model lack—and which "real" organizations quite probably generally lack as well—is that of modeling itself. Without a causal understanding of why policies succeed or fail to achieve their objectives, the feedback in Figure 19-1 to lower organizational levels from several higher levels is confounded. The organization is forced to attempt to learn under ambiguity (March and Olsen 1975). Did the strategy fail to achieve its goal because the aspiration level was unrealistic? Or because policy was based upon an unsuitable historical precedent? Or because the precedent-directed activities could not be carried out in the existing international context? Or because the policy of one subunit conflicted with that of other subunits pursuing different goals in a quasi-autonomous manner? Or because the activities which did emerge elicited opposition from other organizations? Or for a combination of these reasons? Strategies may be abandoned, aspirations lowered or goals changed when a more appropriate solution would be to attempt to reduce intraorganizational conflict. Alternatively, structural reforms may be attempted in pursuit of impossible objectives.

5. ALTERNATIVE PASTS AND A PROGRAM OF DIAGNOSTIC AND NORMATIVE ANALYSIS

In this section, we describe the output of three consecutive simulation experiments, the first of which is preparatory to estimating "parameters" and establishing a memory for the subsequent two. These we diagnose from the point of view of (1) historical adequacy or external, contextual validity, (2) developmental potential of the model itself to grow and become more complex, to structurally transform itself, and—most important: (3) possibilities within the simulated histories for "better" outcomes by changing goals, strategy choices, and decision-making structures. We do not intend this as a substitute for thorough, statistical analysis of model performance, but rather to point out missed opportunities, assuming specificational validity, for actors' realization of long-term interests. Table 19-2 presents the historical and simulated protocols to which we shall refer.

a. Comparison of Simulated and Historical Chronologies. We present summaries of international transactional changes and events produced by some (of the more successful) simulation experiments from the perspective of the Chilean foreign policy process from 1832 through 1904. The Chilean local system initially includes only Argentina (abbreviated in the protocols as Arge), Bolivia (Boli), Peru (Peru), Ecuador (Ecua), and Great Britain (Brit). Of these, the international behavior of Argentina and Great Britain is exogenous; to this extent the Chilean environment corresponds with the historical one. After 1850, New Granada (Colo), the United States (USA), and Brazil (Braz) also enter as exogenously controlled system members. Periodically, several nonnational actors are created by the simulation—a weak supranational, intergovernmental actor identical in membership to the stillborn Congress of Plenipotentiaries of 1846 appears—or introduced by the experimenter—a "Spanish fleet" enters in simulated year 1864.

Little data on national capabilities is available before 1860, necessitating our use of very crude estimates. Time series of economic exchange is also lacking, although some years' transactions appear in Platt (1968), IBAR (1892, 1909),

Centner (1942), and other sources. Because the standards for historical validation of transactions are weak, in the protocols we indicate changes in transaction levels simply as - and +. Our interests in understanding structural systematic change prescribe an attempt at replication of historical transactions of the appropriate mode, direction, and approximate time; the exact magnitude and time are rarely crucial to systemic restructurings.

Table 19-2 presents five columns of data with which to appraise three sequential simulation experiments. Columns one and two relate important historical events. Column three represents historical transactions in terms of a simple accounting scheme. Column four lists the iteration number of the corresponding simulation experiment. Column five represents simulated transactions, as well as events crucial to understanding other simulated outcomes. In the experiments prior to calendar year 1884, the protocols were obtained by repeatedly running the simulation and adjusting parameters and contents of memory until a satisfactory fit to the historical protocols was obtained. With more effort we could assuredly have improved this fit. As the commentary upon these protocols will make clear, we do not seek to validate the model only, or even principally, by comparison with historical transactions—more important are crucial events, such as the onset of war and creation of new or dissolution of old actors, and the *processes* by which policies were formulated and outcomes produced. The model can report in detail upon the types of analyses and sequence of steps taken within an actor's policy process. It is important that these be compatible with historians' accounts of the determinants and constraints of Southern Pacific politics of this period. Only a little of this information is reported in column five of Table 19-2; additional comparisons arise in the commentary. Prior to 1883 the protocols are essentially curve fittings and in no sense a test of the model. In the last two decades of the nineteenth century, we allow the simulation to write alternative histories.

Chilean foreign policy output is the focus of our discussion because (1) the policy process of Bolivia, Ecuador, and Peru are often dominated for long periods by stochastic terms for internal instability and revolution (see Barton [1968] and Klein [1969] for illegal transfers of power in Bolivia, Blanksten [1964] on Ecuadorean instability, and Pike [1967] for Peru's unsettled history), (2) Chilean foreign relations are relatively more completely contained by the local system as operationalized, and (3) we were not able to replicate the historical record quite as well for the other actors.

The experiments confine actors to defining goals in terms of security.[9] The common memory is initialized with 24 precedents prominent in the historical

---

9. Using all three modules of goal definition permits the actors choice among ways to operationalize values. It usually yields more historically accurate simulation experiments when adequately initialized. But it greatly increases the complexity of discussion of the experiments since more "parameters" can vary and since actors can use different mechanisms in the same period.

Table 19-2. Comparison of Historical and Simulated Protocols for Three Sequential Experiments

1	2	3	4	5
1832	Chile halts imports from Peru.	+H(Peru),-E(Peru)/R:+M(Boli)/	01	-E(Peru,Arge),revolution(Ecua,Peru),failure(DE)
1833	Chile increases hostility towards Peru.	+H(Peru) //	02	-E(Peru),+D(Ecua)
1834		-H(Peru) //	03	-E(Peru)
1835	Chilean–Peruvian commercial treaty	+E(Peru) //	04	+E(Peru,Ecua),revolution(Boli,Ecua), success(DE)
1836	Emergence of Peru–Bolivia Confederation	-E(Peru),+H(Peru,Boli)//A:-E(Peru)	05	+E(Peru,Ecua),+D(Peru,Ecua),revolution(Boli),success(D),failure(M)
1837	Chile seeks alliance with Argentina against Peru–Bolivia	+M(Ecua,Arge)/R:+D(Ecua)/	06	+H(Peru,Boli),-D(Peru,Boli),success(E), failure(M)
1838	Chilean leader Portales assassinated.	+M(Ecua,Arge),+H(Peru,Boli,Brit)//	07	+H(Peru,Boli),-D(Peru,Boli),failure(M)
1839	Chile renews war against Peru–Bolivia. Chile seeks alliance with Ecuador which suggests partition of Peru. Destruction of Peru–Bolivia Confederation.	-H(Peru,Boli,Ecua,Arge),+M(Peru, Boli,Ecua) //	08	+H(Peru,Boli,Ecua),-D(Peru,Boli), success (M)
1840		+D#(Peru,Boli,Ecua)/R:+M(Ecua)/	09	+H(Peru,Boli),success(M)
1841	Peru in war against Bolivia.	+D#(Peru,Boli,Ecua) //	10	+H(Peru,Boli),success(M)
1842	Chile demands that Bolivia restore status quo ante bellum. Potential of guano deposits recognized.	+D(Peru,Boli),+E(Brit) //	11	-H(Boli),+D(Arge),revolution(Ecua,Boli), success(M)
			12	+D(Arge,Brit),+E(Arge,Brit),-H(Peru,Boli), revolution(Peru),failure(EM)
			13	-E(Arge,Brit),-H(Boli),+H(Peru),success(E), failure(M)

(continued)

Table 19-2 continued

1	2	3	4	5
1843		//	14	+H(Peru),-H(Boli),failure(M)
1844		//	15	+H(Peru,Boli),-H(Brit)
1845	Peru is isolated by hostility of its neighbors.	+D#(Peru,Boli,Ecua) //A:+E(Peru)	16	-H(Peru,Ecua,Brit),+E(Brit)
			17	-H(Peru,Ecua,Brit),+E(Brit,Peru)
1846	Flores expedition threatens Ecuador from Spain and Britain.	+H(Brit),-E(Brit) //	18	+E(Brit),failure(M)
			19	-H(Peru),+E(Brit,Boli)
			20	-H(Peru,Ecua,Boli),+E(Boli),failure(DM)
			21	+E(Boli),+H(Peru),+H(Brit),-D(Brit),-E(Brit)
1847	Peru hosts Congress of Lima of Peru, Chile, Bolivia, Ecuador and Colombia. Peru begins to enlarge navy with nitrate revenues.	+H(Arge) // A:+D#(P)	22	+E(Boli),revolution(Boli),failure(D)
			23	+E(Boli),revolution(Boli),failure(D)
			24	+E(Boli),create(intergovernmental diplomatic actor, by Peru, Boli, Chile, success (E)
			25	-H(Brit),create(intergovernmental diplomatic actor, by Peru,Chile)
1848		/ R:+MD(Congress of Lima) /	01	-D(Arge), +E(Arge,USA),-H(Brit)
1849	"Radicals" come to power in Colombia.	//	02	-D(Arge), -H(Brit),revolution(Ecua)
1850	Ecuador begins decade of anarchy, during which its international effectiveness is miniscule. Clayton-Bulwer Treaty between U.S. and Great Britain.	+H(USA) //	03	+E(Boli,Arge,USA),failure(D)

No.	Year	Event	Code	Code
04	1851		+H(USA,Colombia) //	+E(Boli,Arge,USA)
05	1852		// A:+M(Peru)	+E(Arge,Brit),revolution(Ecua)
06	1853		//	+E(Arge,Brit),revolution(Ecua)
07	1854	Possible U.S. hegemony over Ecuador seen as threat by Chileans.	+DEH(Ecua) //	+E(Arge,Brit),+H(USA,Ecua),+M(Ecua), failure(M)
08	1855	Colombia experiences internal chaos through end of decade.	-H(USA) / R:+M(Ecua) /	+E(Arge),+H(USA,Ecua),-E(Peru),failure (M),success(E),revolution(Peru)
09	1856	Continental Treaty	+D(Peru,Ecua,Arge),+E(Boli),-H(USA) / R: +M(Peru),+D(Peru,Ecua) /	+E(Boli,Arge),+D(Peru,Ecua),-H(USA, Ecua)
10	1857	Chile demonstrates de facto control over much of Antofagasta.	+H(Boli),+E(Boli) //	+E(Boli,Arge),+D(Peru),-H(Ecua), +H(Boli, Peru)
11	1858		+E(Boli),+H(Boli) //	+H(Boli,Peru),+E(Boli,USA,Brit),failure (M),revolution(Boli)
12	1859		+H(Peru) //	+H(Boli,Peru),+E(Boli,Brit),+D(Arge), -H(Arge),revolution(Boli)
13	1860	Ecuador cedes territory to Peru.	-D(Peru),+H(Peru) //	+H(Boli),+E(Boli),+E(USA,Brit,Arge), success(D)
14	1861		+E(Boli) / R: +M(Ecua) /	+H(Boli),+E(Boli,USA,Brit)
15	1862		+E(Boli) //	+E(Boli,Brit),+D(Arge,Ecua)
16	1863	Spanish fleet reaches Callao.	+E(Boli),+H(Boli) //	+H(Boli),+E(Boli,USA,Ecua),-M(Arge), failure(M)
17	1864	Spanish fleet seizes Chincha Islands from Peru. Second Lima Congress to oppose Spain. Paraguayan War begins.	+D#(Peru,Boli,Ecua,Arge),+M (Peru,Ecua,Boli,Arge) //	-H(Ecua,Arge,USA),+D(Arge,Boli,Peru), +H(Peru),-M(Arge),failure(M)
18	1865	Quadruple Alliance (Chile, Ecuador, Peru,Bolivia) against Spain. Argentina declines to join.	+M(Peru,Ecua,Boli,Arge),-H(Boli), +E(Boli,Ecua),+H(Spain),+D(Arge) //	+M(Peru),+E(Boli,Brit,Ecua),+H(Spain, Arge),revolution(E),failure(DM)

(continued)

Table 19-2 continued

1	2	3	4	5
1866	Increasing tension between anti-Spain coalition and Argentina-Brazil, which resupply Spanish fleet. Secret treaty to partition Paraguay revealed.	+E(Boli),+D(Boli,Arge),-H(Boli), +H(Arge) //	19	-E(Arge),+E(Boli,Peru,Brit),+M(Peru), +H(Spain,Arge),+D(Boli,Peru,USA),failure (M),success(E)
1867	Increasing Chilean influence over Bolivian nitrate industry.	+H (Arge,Braz), +E (Boli,Brit) //	20	-H (Boli), +H (Peru), +E Boli Arge), revolution(Boli), failure (D)
1868	Continuation of dispute between Peru and Bolivia over Puna de Atacama.	+H (Peru, Boli), +E (Boli,Brit) //	21	-H (Boli), +D (USA,Braz), +E (Brit,USA, Boli), failure(D)
1869	Peru borrows heavily abroad, creating fiscal difficulties in 1870s.	+H (Peru,Boli) //	22	+H(Arge,Peru,Boli), revolution(Peru), failure(E)
1870		+D (Arge) //	23	+H (Arge, -E (USA), failure (E)
1871	Chile authorizes increase in Navy	+E (Boli) //	24	+E (Boli,Brit), -H (Boli,Brit,Arge)
1872	Superior Peruvian Navy demonstrates in support of Bolivia during brief crisis between Bolivia and Chile. Argentina and Chile dispute boundary. New Bolivian government agrees to joint administration of littoral with Chile.	+H (Arge,Peru,Boli), +D (Boli), +E (Boli) / R: +E (Boli) /	25	+M (Arge), +H (Peru,Boli), -E (Boli), success(E,M) (Note: precedent that ultimately leads Chile into War of the Pacific is innovated at this point.)
1873	Secret Treaty signed by Peru and Bolivia. Argentina narrowly declines to join. Bolivian-Chilean relations again deteriorate. Brazil withdraws from Paraguayan War.	+D (Boli), +E (Boli), -D (Arge), +H (Arge,Boli) //	26	+H (Boli,Peru), -E (Boli), failure(M)

Year	#	Event		
1874	27	Chile proposes alliance with Brazil to counter Peru–Bolivia–Argentina; Brazil declines. New treaty over use of Atacama. New ironclad arrives in Chilean Navy; delivery of a second is imminent.	+D (Arge,Boli), +H(Braz), +M (Braz) // A: +D (Boli), +E (Boli)	+E (Ecua,USA,Boli,Brit), +M (Braz,Arge), +H (Peru), failure(E)
1875	28	Increased salience of boundary dispute between Chile and Argentina.	+D (Arge), +H (Arge) //	+H (Peru,Arge), –E (Peru,Boli), +D (Braz), failure(E)
1876	29	Anti-Chilean sentiment increases in Bolivia. End of Paraguayan War.	//	+H (Arge), –H (USA), –E(Peru,Boli), +D (Braz)
1877	30		//	+H (Arge), +E (USA), –E (Boli), +D (Braz)
1878	31	Chile and Argentina at brink of war in border incident. Bolivia begins to enforce higher export duties in shared littoral. Chile occupies Antofagasta to 23rd parallel. Peru is unprepared for war.	+H (Boli,Arge), +D (Arge) //	+H (Peru,Arge), –E (Peru,Boli), revolution (Peru), failure(E,M)
1879	32	Despite treaty, Peru initially avoids support for Bolivia. Chile declares war on Bolivia and Peru.	+H (Peru,Boli), +D (Braz,Arge,Colo), –H (Colo) / R: +D (Peru,Ecua) / A: +D (Arge)	+H (Peru,Boli), –D (Peru,Boli), –E (Boli), –H (Ecua,Colo), revolution (Ecua), success (EM)
1880	33	War of the Pacific	–E (Arge), +D (Arge), +H (Colo,Peru, Boli) //	Not simulated.
1881	34	War continues	+E (Boli), +D (Arge), –H(Arge) / R: +D (Brit,Arge) / A: +D (USA,Colo)	Not simulated.
1882	35	Belligerency continues; less military activity.	//	Not simulated.
1883	36	Treaty of Ancon with Peruvian faction formally ends war with Peru.	+E (Peru,Boli), –H (Peru,Boli), +D (Arge) // A: +D (Arge)	Not simulated.

(continued)

Table 19-2 continued

1	2	3	4	5
1884		+E (Boli), –H (Boli), +H (Arge) // A: +E (Boli)	01	+E (Boli,Arge), –H (Boli,Peru), +H(Arge, Brit), +D (Brit)
1885		+E (Boli) // A: +D(USA)	02	+E(Boli,Arge,Brit), +D (Brit,USA), –H (Arge)
1886		+E (Peru) //	03	+E (Peru), –E(Brit,USA),+H(Brit,Peru,USA), revolution(Peru)
1887	Chile begins program of military expansion.	+H(Peru), +E(Ecua) //	04	+E(Peru,Ecua,Colo),+H(Peru,Brit), failure (E,M)
1888	Chile seeks to purchase Tacna-Arica. Increasing Chilean rivalry with Argentina.	+E(Peru,Boli), +H(Boli) //	05	+E(Peru), +D(Peru), failure(M)
1889	First International American Conference at Washington.	+D(Arge), +E(Ecua,Brit) // A: +D# (USA)	06	+E(Brit,Colo,Ecua), +H(Peru), –H(Brit, USA), failure(M)
1890		+E(Peru,Boli), +D(Boli) / R: –E(Boli) /	07	+E(Peru,Boli), –H(Peru), +H(Arge)
1891	Congressionalists revolt against Balmaceda's administration.	+H(USA,Brit), –E(Brit) / R: –E(Boli) /	08	+D(Boli,Arge,Ecua), +H(Arge), +M(Boli)
1892		+H(Peru,USA,Arge), +D(Arge) / R: –E (Boli) /	09	+H(Peru), –H(Arge), +D(Arge,Boli), revolution(Ecua), success(D)
1893		+M(Ecua), +E(Ecua), –H(Arge) / R: –E(Boli) /	10	+E(Ecua,Brit), –H(Boli,Brit),failure(E)
1894		+D(Peru), +H(Peru,Arge) //	11	
1895	Treaty with Bolivia to counter growing Argentine power and Peruvian hostility.	+H(Peru), –H(Boli), +D(Boli, Braz), +E(Boli) // A: +D(Boli), +E(Boli)	12	+H(Peru), +E(Ecua,Boli), –H(Brit,Boli,USA), +D(Arge), success(M), failure(E)

275 When National Security Policies Bred Collective Insecurity

Year	Description		No.	
1896	Attempt at treaty with Peru.	+E(Brit), +H(Arge) / R: +E(Brit) /	13	+E(Boli,Brit), -E(Peru)
1897	Collapse of above treaties. War scares between Chile and Argentina are frequent.	+H(Peru,Arge), +D(Boli)//	14	+H(Arge,Boli,Peru), -E(Peru,Arge)
1898	Chile engages in arms race with Argentina.	-H(Peru), +H(Arge) // A: +D(Peru)	15	+H(Arge), +E(Peru,Brit), +D(Peru), -D(Arge), revolution(Ecua), failure(E)
1899		+D(Boli,Arge), +H(Boli), -H(Arge) / R: +D(Arge) /	16	+H(Arge), +E(Brit), +D(Boli,Arge, Peru)
1900		-D(Boli), +M(Colo,Ecua), +D(Colo, Ecua) // A: +D(Peru,USA)	17	+H(Peru), -H(Arge), -D(Peru)
1901	Break in relations with Peru. Chile faces possible combination of Argentina, Peru and Bolivia.	+E(Arge), -D(Peru) //	18	+H(Peru)
1902		+D(Arge), +E(Arge,USA), -H(Arge) / R: +E(Arge) / A: +D(Arge)	19	+H(Brit), +E(Arge,Brit,USA), -E(Peru)
1903		//	20	-H(Peru), +E(Brit,USA)
1904		// A: +E(Arge)	21	-H(Arge,Peru)

literature.[10] The precedents chosen are sufficiently complex to serve both as a source of historically realistic strategies and as a basis for adaptation and innovation to yield many more strategies recognizable in the model.

In columns three and five, subunits and their corresponding transactions are abbreviated:

D diplomatic/prestige (D# indicates a proposal for a multiactor meeting)
E economic/wealth
M military/power
H hostility–friendliness continuum.

Increments of modes D, E, and M indicate larger transactions; increments of mode H indicates greater hostility. Column three, the summary of historical exchange, has three components separated by /'s: the first list of transactions records Chile's output; the second list (beginning "R") records those proposals of other actors to Chile which Chile rejected; the third list (beginning "A") is those proposals which Chile accepted. Transactions in the fifth column of the table are those which in the simulation Chile produced. Proposals of others which Chile rejected are not shown because they are too numerous. In this last column, two additional types of information are coded. "Revolution" indicates that the specified actor experienced sufficiently severe internal disturbances to change its general foreign policy orientation, that is, to begin search for an acceptable precedent in a different partition of memory. Although stochastically generated, such events are important to systemic outcomes because they often suddenly change the Chilean international position. When a subunit of the Chilean actor evaluates a strategy as a "success" or "failure," this fact too is noted, for it entails renewed search within the Chilean organization.

The protocol for 1832 may be interpreted as follows. That year Chile interrupted imports from Peru, an important sanction because much of Peruvian trade with Europe passed through Chilean ports. In column three, this interruption is indicated by "-E(Peru)." In addition, the same column indicates that Chilean hostility to Peru increased and that Chile declined a Bolivian overture for a military treaty. The entry in column four means merely that this is the first iteration of the simulation experiment. Column five shows that, in the simulation, Chile reduced economic exchange with both Argentina and Peru, that a revolution occurred in both Ecuador and Peru, and that both the prestige- and wealth-seeking subunits of the Chilean actor evaluated their contemporary strategies as failures. Consequently, both subunits renewed search for an acceptable precedent in the following iteration.

Because important parts of the model are stochastic, one must repeat the experiment reported in column five from the same initial conditions to get a dis-

10. The interpretations of Burr (1965) and Dennis (1931) are major sources.

tribution of outputs whose central tendencies can more adequately be compared with the historical protocol in column three. For present purposes, however, it is sufficient to focus on a single experiment to illustrate and diagnose the kinds of alternative histories the model generates. For instance, in 1838 the Chilean strongman, Portales, was assassinated. It could not have occurred in the simulation; historically the assassination only briefly deflected Chile from its attempt to break up the Peru–Bolivia Confederation. On the other hand, the simulated protocols for iterations six through ten indicate progressive increases in hostility directed at both Peru and Bolivia; in the corresponding historical summary, Chile implacably seeks the destruction of its neighbors' union. The simulated Chilean actor perceives the same threat as did statesmen of the historical Chilean nation. Portales observed

> . . . the confederation must forever disappear from the American scene. By its geographical extent; by its larger white population; by the combined wealth of Peru and Bolivia, until now scarcely touched; by the rule that the new organization, taking it away from us, would . . . exercise in the Pacific; by Lima's larger number of cultured white people closely connected with influential Spanish families; by the greater intelligence, if indeed inferior character, of its public men, the confederation would soon smother Chile. . . . We must rule forever in the Pacific. (Quoted in Burr 1965, p. 38)

Chilean General, Mariano Egana, made clear the historical precedent for opposing the union of the neighbors:

> The incorporation of the two republics into one . . . clearly endangers neighboring states. . . . We do not care whether General Santa Cruz rules in Bolivia or in Peru; what we do care about is the separation of the two nations. . . . If Austria or France seized Spain or Italy . . . to form a single political body, . . . would the other nations be indifferent? (Quoted in Burr 1965, p. 40)

Not only did the simulation produce Chilean policies similar to those historically recorded, it also reinforced the attractiveness of war as a preventive to the union of one's neighbors. Note in column five that the power subunit of Chile counted its strategy of continually increasing the level of hostility with Peru and Bolivia a success in iterations eight through eleven. Chilean military status increased in this period, satisfying the aspirations of its power-oriented subunit. In the twelfth iteration of the simulation, however, the same strategy no longer satisfied the international context (in particular, the polarity and power equality of the local system changed markedly with the dissolution of the Peru–Bolivia Confederation), forcing Chile's power-oriented subunit to seek a new precedent. Thus the strategy calling for hostility toward confederating neighbors remained with the evaluation of "highly successful" when applied to the appropriate context.

Ecuador's irresponsibly adventurous historical policies are faithfully reproduced by the simulation. But in conformance with the historical record, Chile declines involvement with Ecuadorean schemes for dismemberment of one or more of its neighbors: in its restricted system, no outcomes or combinations that far from its borders (specifically, in noncontiguous actors) constitute a threat to security. On the other hand, the exogenous introduction of the "Flores expedition" into the simulation does constitute a danger to all the littoral states, because it is associated with dangers of great power intervention (and sea-capable great powers are defined as contiguous to all but landlocked actors). This association is operationalized when both Peru and Chile simultaneously place Britain in lists of "enemies," "major power," and "others to which one is vulnerable." (To keep things as simple as possible, Spain does not appear until simulated 1864).

A third notable event is the emergence of Chile's proposal for an intergovernmental diplomatic actor not initially present in the system. This emerges when Chile's prestige-specialized subunit changes strategy to respond to a changed international prestige structure. A common explanation of the historical proposal (which was the product of a joint Congress and not unilateral as in the simulation) is the promotion of cooperative efforts against external intervention and regularization of the habitually chaotic Pacific subsystem through institutionalized arbitration of disputes. In the simulated Chilean policy process, the explanation is somewhat different. Witnessing more rapid growth of Peruvian capabilities and external activities, Chile's prestige-oriented subunit encounters a "problem" in relatively decreasing status (iterations 20 and 23). Search in its original partition of "contest/directly/unilaterally" is unable to uncover an acceptable precedent. An attempt at policy innovation fails (i.e., no strategy whatsoever is produced). A random shift to a different partition yields "contest/directly/jointly," and the first (and only) acceptable precedent encountered created, however briefly, an intergovernmental organization.

Chile's new actor shared the fate of the historical Congress of Plenipotentiaries: it failed to gain acceptance, much less financial support, from its intended members. At this period of the simulation, Peru, Ecuador, and Bolivia are predisposed to reject any diplomatic proposals by third parties that are not completely compatible with the pursuit of their individual goals. Chile's actor is stillborn because it lacked the resources with which to implement any strategies. When the experiment ended, Chile was persisting in its proposal for the intergovernmental diplomatic actor. Examination of its memory and search criteria later revealed that it was "locked in" upon that infeasible policy choice: until the international context changed markedly, no other precedent would be acceptable.

In this first simulation example, which we equated with the years 1833–1847, historical Pacific politics were perhaps too chaotic to expect a very high degree of replication. Domestic instabilities and petty rivalries dominated outcomes in the historical system; to a large extent the former dominated the simulated system. The next experiment to examine, from 1848 through 1879, illustrates a variety of different performance characteristics of the model. Most "parameters" are retained as they emerged from the first experiment, except that the search rules for all actors are adjusted in the hope that they will select more realistic strategies. In addition, the pre-1848 collective memory is brought into line with historical experiences. But by this point the simulation's collective memory has grown to 128 complex precedents (from the initial 24, so that it becomes more difficult to make adjustments consistently in the intended directions.

As in the previous experiment, we are not "testing" the model's performance. We continue to control the "marginal" actors of Great Britain, Argentina, Colombia, Brazil, and the United States. We also introduce two nonnational actors in—for the present—very minor roles: "Gibbs" as a surrogate for the British trading houses, and "North" to represent the nitrate interests abroad. When the magnitudes of feedback channels are "tuned," we attempt to fit the historical protocol of transactions rather than the significant events of the period.

Two important events of the verbal chronology in column two do not, by design, appear in the simulation. The first is the European revolutions of 1848, whose shock waves reached the Pacific system via the emergence of a "radical" government in Colombia. These revolutions created a new sense of danger among the conservative Pacific oligarchies which does not appear in the simulation. It is notable, however, that when an aggressive foreign policy is experimentally grafted onto Colombian inputs into the Pacific system, Chile does not react—events at that distance remain irrelevant to Chilean security unless they involve the machinations of a great power.

The second neglected event is the Paraguayan War, in which Brazil, Argentina, and Uruguay eventually decimated belligerent Paraguay. We controlled the Argentine policies of this period to reflect their preoccupation with their own local affairs, but the important precedent for international practice of that war— that a group of American allies might agree to partition their opponent—is lost upon the simulated history.

We count some significant successes of this experiment. At least by the seventeenth iteration, the Pacific states have learned that it is best through cooperative action that they can oppose interventionist policies of great powers. When the experimenter introduces a "Spanish fleet" in 1864, Chile, Peru, and Bolivia more or less simultaneously begin a series of proposals for greater local cooperation and exchange, reducing their mutual levels of hostility, and directing their attention outward from previously salient local disputes. The military cooperation that emerges from the simulation in iterations eighteen and nineteen is, however, only between Peru and Chile. And the Chilean power-oriented subunit rates this strategy as a failure (see Frazer 1949) because, while it dissipates the external threat, Peruvian capabilities and activity abroad are increasing more rapidly than those of its rival.

Upon a background of traditional mutual suspicion, the differential growth rates of Peru—first with the exploitation of nitrates—and Chile—later with policies more attractive to European capital—provided opportunities, however transient and uncertain, for aggrandizement by one or the other of the rivals. The increasing integration of the Pacific system into European economic and political affairs only aggravated these opportunities: decisive military advantage could hinge on the acquisition of a single ironclad. As the effective distance between the Pacific subsystem and external powers diminished, events began to unfold at rates characteristic of European politics, a development for which Latin governments were unprepared (Sherman 1926). As the capabilities of Pacific states expanded differentially, the political horizons of their leaders followed (Platt 1973, p. 111), so that fundamental revision of the Bolivarian equilibrium became imaginable. Historical precedents that had been successfully adaptive began to fail. In Table 19-2 it is apparent that the range of strategy failure increases for Chile after about 1860. In this experiment, failure increases also for Peru, Ecuador, and especially, Bolivia.

But neither historically nor in the simulation does a major war in the Pacific system occur until the end of the 1870s. In the simulation, a combination of factors averts the selection and implementation of a war-producing strategy by Chile. First, as long as no combination of its neighbors emerges the precedent with which Chile destroyed the Peru–Bolivia Confederation remains contextually inappropriate. This constraint is, however, removed in 1873 and iteration 25 when (not shown in Table 19-2) Peru and Bolivia exchange military commitments and begin to implement compatible, if not coordinated, policies. Second, in the simulation Peruvian difficulties with Ecuador and Britain preclude attention toward Chile during much of the period it possesses military and diplomatic advantage. It is noteworthy that the Chilean initiation of war in iteration 32 is only one aspect of a military strategy that involves the removal of outstanding disputes with Argentina. Third, although the strategy which leads to war in iteration 32 is innovated (by selecting successful rules from three contextually inappropriate but generally successful precedents) by Chilean power-oriented subunit in iteration 25, Chile's local environment in the earlier period does not yield qualitatively the same results as it will later.

The strategy innovated in iteration 25 can be summarily described as "substantially increase the level of hostility with the rival; in all three modes of exchange attempt to isolate the rival by increasing economic exchange and friendliness with external powers, lessening hostility with the rival's dependents and with other proximate actors not allied with the rival." While Chile recognizes the role of "rival" throughout these decades, that role is empty in iteration 25 (1872) but occupied by Peru in iteration 32 (1879). Other rules of the strategy cannot be implemented in the earlier year. Because other strategies in the 1870s fail to satisfy Chilean aspirations for increased power status or become contextually inappropriate in a rapidly changing international environment, Chile's subunit returns to the precedent of iteration 25 when seven iterations later it confronts a serious threat from Bolivia, Peru, and (more ambiguously) Argentina.

In the simulation, actors in the Pacific system remain tolerably insecure through the 1860s and most of the 1870s without resort to war, chiefly because they are distracted by a large number of petty disputes and because they tend to pursue policies unilaterally. It is only when Chile perceives the emergence of a combination of all the bordering states against it that the severity of the problem and restructured environment combine to lift the restraint of previous years. This simulation-generated explanation of the War of the Pacific places more emphasis on the breakdown of security–management practices and less on positive Chilean aspirations for economic gain than do many historians.

The acquiescence of Chile's wealth-oriented subunit was nevertheless necessary for the power-oriented subunit to lead the actor into war. From iteration nineteen onward, the economic subunit is accorded higher priority than the military one. Had the economic subunit selected strategies which conflicted with those of the military subunit, the Chilean actor would have resolved this internal conflict by denying the proposals of its military arm. In fact, the contemporary policies of the economic subunit only amplified the military subunit's proposals. In iteration 32, for instance, the economic subunit proposed to decrease economic exchange with Bolivia, increase exchange with Ecuador (which the latter rejected), and increase hostility toward Peru.

Kiernan has summarized the proximate causes of the War of the Pacific:

> Bolivia had nitrate deposits in her coastal province in the Atacama desert; Peru, her ally since 1873, had guano and nitrates in the Tarapaca province bordering it on the north. Chile, to the south, with few deposits of her own, had invested in the development work in Bolivia and to some extent in Tarapaca. All three countries were hard up, and run by oligarchies which disliked paying taxes and looked to revenue from these fertilizers as a substitute. Peru set up a state monopoly, taking over private enterprises in exchange for certificates. Bolivia put an export tax on the Chilean company at Antofagasta. Chile denounced this as a breach of agreement, and in February, 1879, seized the port. Bolivia declared war on Chile, and Peru supported her ally. (1955, p. 14)

As Kiernan recognizes, however, such a description ignores the "exceedingly tortuous" evolution of interests and advantages which created the occasion for reordering the structure of Pacific power relations. In this complex of factors, Bolivian weakness (Adolfo Ballivian, 1872, quoted in Dennis 1927, p. 53), international finance (Dennis 1931, p. 64), European capitalists' desires for Latin stability (Rippy 1959), Peruvian political rivalries (Markham 1882), Argentine disputes with Brazil (Burr 1955), and a host of others must be included. Our model emphasizes in addition the inadequacy of historical precedents to solve novel political problems in a security-conscious subsystem undergoing differential rates of growth. If, to understand the restructuring occasioned by this war, it is unquestionably necessary to look at the totality of systemic experience with security-management problems—as that experience is contained within each organization through its access to and evaluation of the set of precedents—it is also possible to identify crucial points in the development of precedents, significant changes in aspirations, and critical problem-definitions which channeled the actors' problem-solving efforts toward war.

Peru's attempts to solve its own security problems by creating a triple alliance with Argentina directly elicited Chilean adamancy concerning economic exploitation of Bolivian nitrates (Yrigoyen 1921). Had the Chilean military subunit not felt threatened in iteration 31, it would have reimplemented again in the next period the same moderately hostile strategy toward Peru and Bolivia. War would have been, if not averted, at least postponed. It is interesting that both historically and in the simulation, Peru desired an overhwhelming alliance against Chile. Peruvian Chancellor Riva Aguero invited Argentine participation in these terms:

> It is much to the interest of the Argentine Republic as to Bolivia's, and indeed to that of all American countries whose boundaries have not yet been defined, to become members of the Defensive Alliance. . . . With the strengthening of the Alliance, by the entry of other republics, wars for territorial expansion will become impossible in America, because the exaggerated ambitions of any one of these Republics would have to be restrained when confronted by the firm and unyielding attitude of the Allies. (Quoted in Dennis 1931, p. 61)

This differs from an appeal for a system of collective security because the identity of the potential aggressor was assumed, unalterably, to be Chile. That all the interested powers, except perhaps Bolivia (Klein 1969, p. 13), anticipated an imminent clash between the incompatible aspirations of Peru and Chile foreclosed the possibility that either Peru or Chile could initiate a successful collective solution to their mutual security problem. An examination of the Pacific actors' aspirations and available precedents in the simulation suggests that the only realistic possibility for avoiding war was to indefinitely postpone it until other problems of higher priority arose to focus their attention elsewhere. In this sense, there may be some truth to the claim that Chile's victory over Peru helped to avert war between Chile and Argentina (Espinosa 1969).

In the decades after 1860, nonnational actors and disputed territories take on increased importance in Pacific politics. Although private economic actors—Gibbs and North in the simulation—receive the same treatment as states, it is convenient to impose restrictions upon the activities of disputed territories, such as Antofagasta and Tarapaca. They serve, in effect, as stakes in disputes, contributing to the economic capabilities of their possessors but unable to engage in autonomous problem solving.[11]

b. Latin American Dependence and European Instigation of War: Possibilities for Reinterpretation. Prior to the War of the Pacific, both Peru and Chile had enormous outstanding debts. Peru had already nationalized its guano industry, most of which had been controlled by French capitalists. Chilean government bonds in London were down to 64 on a par of 100. The financial strain of Chilean naval programs compromised the nation's ability to borrow additional funds abroad (Sherman 1926, pp. 116-17). Because British capitalists in the long run benefited most from the war (see Kiernan 1955 and Blakemore 1974), it is tempting to impute to them importance in its initiation. That the Chilean oligarchy was possibly enabled to postpone domestic social reform with the gains of conquest (Fifer 1972, p. 75) supports the hypothesis that British investors together with the Chilean elite sought war for economic gains. Britain sold ironclads to Chile; Bolivia was refused credit; the delivery schedule of Chile's ironclads heavily influenced Argentine policy and Peruvian timing (Burr 1955). The British government imposed neutrality laws to prevent Peru from acquiring warships once war began (Dennis 1927, p. 126). Much other evidence can be adduced to support the thesis that Chilean aggression was the product of an opportunistic alliance between British capital and the Chilean elite.

> . . . A few days before declaring war the (Chilean) government published in the official daily a long description of the desert not only to parallel 23°, but to the boundary of Peru. It was written in glowing terms of a prospectus of a stock company's mine. (Dennis 1927, p. 77)

(At least an equally weighty case can be made for the contrary, though we lack the space for it here.)

Within the confines of the simulation, how adequately does this alternative explanation account for historical outcomes? Two issues are central: (one) to

11. Boundary disputes play a central role in Pacific politics well into the middle of the twentieth century (see, for example, Zook 1964, Juaregui 1938 and Burgos 1966). Treatment of important disputed territories is rather ad hoc: they are considered "passive organizations." They function as stakes in disputes and as references in strategies (e.g., "those proximate to Antofagasta"). They can neither initiate activities of their own nor reject activities directed to them by others. Their geographic extent is immutable and known to all. Their resources are controlled by other autonomous organizations. This control may be shared. If control is shared, each controlling organization proposes strategies for the disputed territory in each mode of value separately. Which strategy is implemented depends stochastically upon the proportion of the disputed territory's total transactions in the mode with each controlling actor. Prior to the War of the Pacific, Chile exercised affective control over Antofagasta in the economic mode (its proportion is .8 in iteration 22), but Bolivia exercises control in the modes of prestige and power. Disputed territories include Tacna-Arica, Puna de Atacama, Patagonia, the Amazon Basin, the Acre River Vicinity, and Ecuadorian Oriente.

what extent can Chile's economic subunit be considered to have functioned as an agent for the interests of either Britain or the economic actors Gibbs and North? (two) how adequately does an economic emphasis account for postwar Chilean policies?

For iterations 25 through 32 the cumulative dependence of Chile's economic subunit upon Britain (which is the probability that Chile's subunit will accept a transmitted British strategy) is about .12. The dependence index of Chile upon Gibbs is only .11 and upon North .02 (although the latter skyrockets after the war). There is little evidence from the model's performance in the middle of the nineteenth century that the preponderance of influence of British capital was in Santiago and not London (Kiernan 1955): we strongly suspect that important facets of foreign penetration are ignored by any purely transactional index. One can, however, repeat the simulation experiments until stochastically Chile does accept a strategy transmitted either from Britain or from Gibbs. That strategy will be added to the Chilean repertoire although it may have little impact upon outcomes until it is substantially reshaped by implementation in a differering context. The transmitted strategy may function in Chilean policy more or less as a contingency plan. Hence it is difficult to argue that, within the simulation model, Britain could not have instigated the Chilean economic subunit to undertake a war of conquest. Furthermore, any strategy that Britain transmitted would interact with other precedents in Chilean experience and with the many other environmental factors that dynamically alter the actor's policy repertoire: "it should be kept in view that anyone who may possibly have encouraged Chile at the outset may have intended no more than a war with Bolivia alone, especially as there was a prevalent notion that the Chilean army was weaker than the Peruvian." (Kiernan 1955). Yet the level of dependence—as operationalized here—is small enough that anyone attempting externally to influence Chilean policy could not reasonably expect to provide coordinated guidance on a regular basis. It is noteworthy that, to pay for the war, the Chilean government increased export duties on nitrates several times over what it had complained of during Bolivian administration (Dennis 1927, pp. 169-70).

To better appreciate the scope and nature of alterations in the experiment required to generate a British-instigated war, we restarted the simulation semi-interactively from iteration 25 (1872). One must make a number of ad hoc adjustments in the policies of both Chile and Peru before the protocols reveal both major war and reasonable resemblance to historical transactions. We found, in short, that reinterpretation of the War of the Pacific requires deeper and earlier revision of the system's history. The germ of "cooperation" between Britain's economic subunit (or Gibbs) and Chile's economic subunit must be established a decade or more before the war.

The second question can be answered less tentatively if one continues to assume the model's specificational adequacy. It is difficult, regardless of the number of ad hoc interventions made by the experimenter to adjust parameters, to replicate even the broad outlines of postwar Pacific politics if one assumes Chile's economic subunit initiated a successful war in 1879 to acquire economic resources. In the model, the war-provoking strategy must be evaluated as a great success in the short term (and there is no mechanism for revising this evaluation subsequently): it substantially enlarged Chilean economic status and resource base. But there is no contextual reason why Chile's economic subunit will not, later in the century, resort to war in its rivalry with more rapidly growing neighbor, Argentina. To avoid the reimplementation of the war strategy, one must direct Chile to search for precedents in a different partition of memory, that is, to adopt a different general orientation to foreign policy. Yet such a redirection generates significant departures from Chilean policy in the power and prestige modes. Chile's power-oriented subunit, by contrast, will eventually be forced to accept parity with Argentina, but it will not fall decisively behind any of its continental neighbors as it subjectively did in the mid-1870s.

We have not argued that *no* adjustments of the model can suffice to support the alternative explanation of economic motivations and British (or Gibbs') instigation as primary causes of the War of the Pacific. But it does appear that, although economic considerations supported the primary security-conscious Chilean decision, considerations of regional constellations of potential military power form a more natural and parsimonious basis for reproducing the most salient historical events of the period. Without claiming to have definitively resolved the historians' disputes over the origins of the War of the Pacific, we have tried to elucidate the applicability of the model to the exploration and evaluation of competing historical interpretations.

c. Long-Term Consequences of Chilean Alternatives to War. It is possible to intervene in the experiments to impose upon actors different preferences among precedents and different levels of aspirations for security. Such interventions can decidedly alter systemic outcomes. Rather than inquire here what difference perturbations make in general, we ask, could Chile have done any better, given its repertoire of precedents and international context? By "better" we mean simply, could it have improved its statuses and lessened its vulnerabilities? To deal with this question concretely, we compare radically different Chilean approaches to goal-attainment from the end of the War of the Pacific to 1905.

Table 19-2 reports the continuation of the simulated protocol beyond the War of the Pacific. To obtain this we imposed a "historical" settlement upon the war, evaluated the strategies that brought the losers into the war as "failures," and resumed the simulation experiment in 1884. We did not iteratively fit the postwar simulation experiment to historical events or transactions. Although we continued to exogenously control the Pacific system's environment of Britain, Brazil, and other peripheral actors, no intervention is exerted over the policies of Chile, Peru, Ecuador, or Bolivia. To this extent, the post-1884 simulated protocols "test" the model's adequacy.

The simulated protocols in column five of Table 19-2 continue in 1884 (iteration one of the third in the sequence of reported experiments). The experimenter has intervened to bring the War of the Pacific to a historically realistic close, but then allowed the simulation unhindered operation[12] for 21 subsequent iterations, through 1904. Highlights of the simulated protocol of this experiment are repeated in the first column of Table 19-3, where alternative Chilean approaches to managing security in the postwar system are compared.

In broad terms, the simulated and historical systems show similar principles of operation, although divergences tend to cumulate. By the beginning of the twentieth century, however, increasing mobilization of the Chilean populace constrains the oligarchy's traditional freedom in foreign policy. This is not to claim that the executors of policy become truly democratically accountable—much less do they in Peru, Bolivia, or Ecuador—but the era of *inter*-actor political predominance wanes as Pacific politics exhibit more the character of external projection of domestic political conflicts, especially of the "social issue" concomitant with urbanization (Rippy 1968, Pike 1963). By this time, our model's specifications become, not so much wrong as irrelevant: more attention must be given to the explicit representation of domestic processes than to that of foreign stimuli.

Immediately after the War of the Pacific, the simulation rather faithfully reproduces the mutual suspicion among Peru, Bolivia, and Chile. As long as Bolivia lacks access to the sea and as memory of the military disaster persists, Bolivia counts both Peru and Chile as others to which it is vulnerable. Chilean problems become increasingly frequently defined in terms of Argentina's more rapid growth, so that even with Peru and Bolivia incapable of challenge individually or together, permanent security is unattainable. The conquered territories of the war also appear as foci of the Pacific states' attention. In iterations four, five, and seven, Chile seeks accommodation with Peru along lines similar to its historical attempts to buy Tacna-Arica.[13] The Chilean strategy applied during this period is a variant of that which led to war against Peru and Bolivia in the preceding experiment. But in the postwar environment, the primary Chilean rival is Argentina, and Bolivia's support is sought as a counter. Bolivia, as the "rival's dependent," is offered closer ties in iterations eight through fourteen (except

---

12. As in the first two experiments, historical policies of the United States, Britain, and peripheral Latin countries were input quasi-exogenously. That is, these actors were constrained to select among historically observed strategies, unable to innovate, concatenate, or borrow strategies from others. The frequency and order with which they implemented these strategies was, however, dependent upon events generated within the simulation.

13. In the model Tarapaca, not Tacna-Arica, is the focus of the actors' dispute. We have not modeled the demographic characteristics of the disputed territories. Hence the initially preponderant Peruvian population in Tacna-Arica cannot serve to legitimate efforts to return it to Peru; nor is the prewar Chilean migration to either Tarapaca or Antofagasta a basis for Chilean efforts to retain these gains. On the former's resistance, see Maurtau (1901); on the latter, Encina (1963).

iteration twelve when intraorganizational conflict consumes all Chilean initiatives!). Peru remains too hostile to Chile to qualify as one "not allied with the rival." Because Bolivian support, which is gained only intermittently, contributes little to Chilean security, all three Chilean subunits encounter frequent policy failures (iterations four through six, ten, twelve, and fifteen), resorting often to attempts at innovation. Yet since their repertoire of historically successful precedents is limited to direct confrontations with the rival while marginal support is sought from nonaligned neighbors (lessons of the conflicts against the Peru–Bolivian Confederation and the Peru-Bolivian Secret Treaty), the innovated strategies produced nothing usefully new. Chile's only other consistent successes are variations on the theme "unite with neighbors in a common effort against a threatening great power." Elements of this clearly fail in applicability to the postwar world. The reader will note that the variety of Chilean initiatives diminishes in the last decade of the experiment: a more detailed examination of the simulation's performance indicates that Chilean problem-solving activity is diminishing, its entire foreign efforts "running down," basically because its variety of positively rewarded experiences is too small. Important sources of precedents are lacking: European experience (especially events associated with the Franco–Prussian War which find frequent reference, as in the quotation at the beginning of the paper), intellectual currents of internationalism, a resurgence of the Hispanic tradition, and simply more penetratingly foresightful policy planning all enriched the historical Chilean repertoire.

Neither historically nor in the model do Chile and Argentina go to war, although in both protocols they occasionally reach the brink. As we noted above, Chile tries essentially the same strategies toward Argentina as is directed toward Peru in its earlier rivalry. The simulation does produce transactions suggestive of the historical arms race of the late 1890s. And Argentine growth alone constitutes a threat of a similar magnitude to that jointly formed by Peru and Bolivia. Two conditions avert war. First, the preexisting level of hostility between Chile and Argentina is much lower than that which earlier held between Chile and Peru. Second, the policies of Chile's diplomatic and economic subunits repeatedly subvert those of its military subunit—with some exceptions, such as in iteration twelve when the economic subunit augments the military subunit's economic transactions with Ecuador and Bolivia and its hostility with Peru. In iterations seven, eleven, thirteen, fourteen, and eighteen, intraorganizational compromises severely constrain proposed output. In each, the actual output is more moderate than that proposed by the military subunit. In other words, the policies of the Chilean organizational parts diverge. Within the simulation, the economic and diplomatic subunits learn to moderate their goals—specifically to seek smaller increments of wealth and prestige statuses and to tolerate larger shortfalls—before the military subunit does. This result is not, we think, intrinsic to the model's performance; rather, the military subunit is relatively more circumscribed in its choice of precedents because it had the greatest success in goal attainment in the past.

Table 19-3.   Four Alternative Chilean Approaches to Postwar Security Problems

1	"Historical" 2	"Conciliatory" 3	"Peru–Chilean Coalition" 4	"Belligerence" 5
1883			Return of Tacna-Arica and Tarapaca; joint exploitation of minerals.	
1884	Peru accepts Treaty of Ancon.			
1885		Peru given Tacna-Arica and Tarapaca. Bolivia given diplomatic influence in Antofagasta while Chile retains economic and military control.	Peru–Chile joint military force. Alliance between Argentina and Bolivia.	War between Chile and Peru.
1886		War between Peru and Bolivia.		
1887		Argentina given Puna de Atacama.	War between Peru–Chile and Argentina–Bolivia.	Argentina joins Peru against Chile.
1888	Chile seeks to purchase Tacna-Arica. Increasing rivalry with Argentina.			Chile evokes hostility of Britain.
1889		War between Bolivia and Argentina.		
1890				
1891	(Balmaceda Revolution)	(Balmaceda Revolution)	(Balmaceda Revolution)	(Balmaceda Revolution) Alliance of Argentina, Peru and Bolivia.
1892		Gibbs emerges as a dominant economic actor.		

Year				
1893		Argentina given Patagonia.	Peru–Chile coalition strained by second crisis with Argentina.	Chile encounters perpetual insecurity, cannot find acceptable historical precedent.
1894		Despite concessions from Chile, crisis with Peru and Argentina.	End of Peru–Chile coalition; Chile alone on brink of war with Argentina.	Chile reduced to tit-for-tat behavior in modes of wealth and power. Experiment ended.
1895	Treaty with Bolivia to counter Argentine power and Peruvian hostility.	Continued crisis with Argentina.		
1896	Treaty with Peru.			
1897	Collapse of treaties.			
1898	Arms race with Argentina.			
1899				
1900			Break in diplomatic and economic relations with Britain.	
1901	Break with Peru. Chile faces combination of Peru, Bolivia and Argentina.		War with Britain.	
1902	Britain effectively manages disputes in Pacific system.			
1903	Crises with Argentina.	Chile plays minor role in Pacific system.		
1904				
1905		Creation of new military actor by Peru and Argentina; Chile's military and economic subunits perceive threat.		

Twice in the simulation experiment after 1884, scriptlike sequences of strategies emerge from Chilean policy. The first occasion occurs in iterations nine through twelve and fifteen and sixteen when the prestige-oriented subunit applies two strategies in succession with different results because the targets of its activities have changed. In iteration nine, the diplomatic subunit selects a strategy (let us call it "A") which directs Chile to send or augment a diplomatic mission to those actors enjoying close diplomatic and economic ties with Chile's most hostile "enemy." The most hostile "enemy" is Peru, and both Argentina and Bolivia satisfy the other qualifications. But in the next iteration, the diplomatic subunit attempts to repeat this strategy (because it was a "success"). On this occasion, Bolivia has reduced its economic ties to Peru, leaving the subunit's proposal to be +D(Arge). However, in the same period, the economic subunit proposed –D(Arge); neither has priority; no output is generated. However, the strategy is not rated a "failure."

Strategy A fails to satisfy the precedent-matching criteria in iteration eleven. Instead, a precedent (call it "B") prescribing an increase of diplomatic representation with "enemies" of others with high capabilities (that is, with great powers) meets search criteria. But there are found to be no such targets, and the consequent output is null. In Figure 19-10, Chile's prestige can be seen to remain constant over these three iterations, once again satisfying the subunit's aspirations at least to the extent that strategy B cannot be considered a "failure."

Strategy B fails to satisfy the matching criteria in the following iteration. A third strategy (call it "C") is found, and its implementation proves more successful. This strategy directs Chile to augment its diplomatic mission to its "rival's" neighbors having less prestige than Chile. Only Bolivia satisfies the qualifications for the economic transaction. Argentina is Chile's current "rival."

Further systemic evolution precludes the repetition of strategy C. In iteration fifteen, however, renewed search leads the subunit to strategy A once more. On this occasion, the most hostile "enemy" is Argentina. Argentina and Bolivia have decreased transactions since iteration nine. The only output is +D(Peru) because Peru alone retains diplomatic and economic ties with Argentina. Chile's environment continues to change rapidly, requiring renewal of local search. As before, the next acceptable strategy found is B. But once again there are no "enemies" of great powers, and no output results. The subunit rates the strategy neither a "success" nor a "failure."

With local search renewed in iteration seventeen, strategy C is passed by because the level of systemic connectivity in the diplomatic mode has exceeded the threshold beyond which C is judged inappropriate. It is apparent, nevertheless, that were the experiment continued beyond iteration 21, sequences of strategies, such as AB, AAB, AAAB, . . . , ABB, and so on, remain probable consequences of Chile's diplomatic subunit's search criteria, measures of systemic context, and available repertoire of precedents.

Very little output results in Table 19-2 from the second occasion on which scriptlike sequences of strategies emerge. In iterations eleven through thirteen and

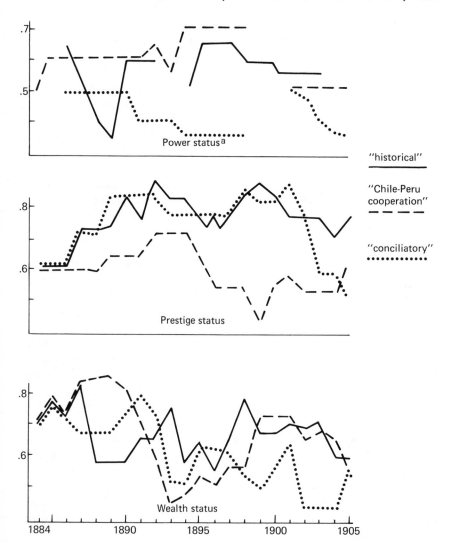

aStatus is undefined for several years.

Figure 19-10. Comparisons of alternative Chilean approaches to postwar regional politics. (computations by Chilean subunits.)

seventeen through twenty, the military subunit proposes sequences which can be abbreviated DEF and DEEF, respectively. Even though strategy E produces as output merely +H(Peru) in iterations twelve and eighteen, a fortuitous improvement in military status makes it a "success" in the earlier period. By iteration 21, sufficient changes occurred in the international military context—specifically, the degree of inequality in power statuses has risen—that additional sequences of the DEF-type are unlikely.

The emergence of recurring sequences of strategies depends on no functional relation among them. They are not produced purposively by the subunits, but arise from recurrent conjunctions of (1) sufficiently rapidly but incrementally changing international context to necessitate frequent renewal of local search, (2) relative stability in search criteria (that is, neither excessively frequent "successes" not excessively frequent "failures" of problem-solving attempts), (3) a limited variety of precedents appropriate to the contemporary context, and (4) stability of the subunits' priorities within the actor (so that resolution of intraorganizational conflict is more or less repetitive). All of these conditions are more likely to occur in periods of relatively unchanging international stratification than in periods of rapid and novel reorganizations. Moreover, because in the model, sequence of strategies occurs contingently without the emergence of specific instructions of the kind "now that you have implemented strategy A go on to strategy B . . . ," disorganization of transactional networks and breakdowns of status orderings are likely to irrevocably destroy the associations among strategies. Scriptlike strategy sequences thus tend to be particular to periods of systemic stability. One should note that, in the experiments reported here and in many others, strategy sequences that emerge tend to be particular to individual actors. We have not investigated whether great powers might produce characteristic strategy sequences: their available memory of precedents is limited to historically realistic strategies. But the sequences of Chile differ from those of Peru, just as Ecuador's and Bolivia's differ. We witness the limited emergence of multiiteration regularities in actors' approaches to problem solving. But we have not observed the model to generate shared sequences of strategies, such as the operational rules explored by Kaplan (1967).

d. Long-Term Consequences of Chilean Alternatives to War. We explore the question, could Chile have done any better in the postwar world by adopting a radically different approach to security management? Departing from the protocols produced by the post-1883 attempt to replicate historical developments (Table 19-2), one can ask if, by 1905, the Chilean position in its stratification system can be appreciably bettered if its search criteria and evaluations of precedents are altered, ceteris paribus. Three alternative approaches are a basically conciliatory policy built around concessions to avert hostility, a coalition of Peru and Chile to counter the growth of Argentina, and a rather extreme policy of unilateral belligerence which seeks supremacy over any combination of neighbors. Figure 19-10 presents a comparison of statuses produced by the first three approaches. The third is omitted for reasons that will become apparent. Highlights of events in all four experiments are found in Table 19-3. In each experiment we intervened only to create a revolution in 1891, in which a Congressional party toppled President Balmaceda. Intervention is useful here to reflect a temporary reduction of Chilean power and, more important, a longer-lasting change in Chilean relations with the United States and Britain (Blakemore 1974).

A quick glance at Figure 19-10 suffices to indicate the relatively equal wealth

statuses produced by each policy. The prestige status of Chile-Peruvian cooperation is generally substantially lower than that of either the "historical" or "conciliatory" policies, although the latter drops sharply in the last few iterations. It
is harder to evaluate the power statuses; under the three approaches Chile is
isolated for periods, removed from all alignments, lacking defined status. Nevertheless, the "conciliatory" approach appears generally inferior.

Our assessment of the alternative differs somewhat if we turn to major
events of each approach. "Belligerence" is a disaster. Here Chile is involved in a
series of wars (whose cost is assessed stochastically from the regressions of Starr
[1972, pp. 121-23], exhausts acceptable precedents by "1893," and effectively
withdraws from international relations by "1894," when we terminate this
fiasco of policy).

A coalition with Peru is almost equally disastrous. Blocs quickly arise in Latin
America between Peru-Chile, on the one hand, and Bolivia-Argentina, on the
other. When the Peru-Chilean coalition suffers defeat, it dissolves (because the
strategies necessary for its continuation are discredited), and Chile, left alone,
gradually withdraws from external involvements. In this experiment, Chilean
aspirations for increased status, in all but the mode of power, fall to nearly
zero, while its tolerances for frustration in goal attainment enlarge. We recognize
that this approach to the postwar Pacific system is influenced to a degree greater
than the others by stochastic outcomes. It is very possible that repetition of the
experiment could reveal Peru-Chilean cooperation to be more successful than we
report in Table 19-3.

The "conciliatory" approach, whereby Chile selects strategies exclusively
from the partitions of memory characterized by "deference," proves little
better. Chile loses control over its gains of war without achieving security: the
previous record of almost uninterrupted hostility with Peru is too deeply etched
on the Peruvian memory. For example, Chile remains in Peru's list of "enemies"
until 1900 despite a series of concessions. Nor do deferential strategies toward
Argentina avert rivalry. Gibbs becomes a high-status economic actor because its
overtures to Chile are usually accepted; in effect, it gains a monopoly on Chilean
foreign trade. By "1903" Chilean strategies yield few initiatives toward
expanded foreign exchange, and its transactions are almost wholly determined
by the initiatives of others.

By comparison, Chile's "historical" policies appear relatively sound. Its
power-oriented subunity acknowledged Argentine military parity only after an
expensive and ultimately futile arms race, but it averted war. Its wealth-oriented
subunit acquiesced to heightened stature of both Gibbs and North but avoided
interruptions of mineral exports and manufactured imports. Its prestige-oriented
subunit escaped diplomatic isolation by undertaking policies designed to prevent
combinations of neighbors against it. This comparison does not, of course,
definitively demonstrate that no alternative to postwar security management
would not have been superior. For instance, had we systematically fitted the
model's performance in earlier periods to accord with a presumption of the

"conciliatory" or "belligerent" approaches, the repertoire of precedents upon which postwar policies could have been built would have differed, perhaps vastly.

Yet the essential point of comparison remains that, were Chile to have departed upon a radically different orientation to achieving security *after* having initiated and won the War of the Pacific, it would have had to acquire additional powerful precedents for solving the postwar problems. These precedents would, furthermore, have had to transcend Chile's own experiences as well as those of its immediate neighbors. The collective memory produced by the simulation experiments up to the War of the Pacific is insufficiently rich to enable Chile more successfully to pursue new directions of security management.

e. Sensitivity of Simulation Performance to Variations of Parameters and Precedents. We have not yet undertaken detailed, quantitative sensitivity analysis of the model, except to study informally the robustness of the types of structural transformations to changes in model assumptions. For instance, if goals are defined in terms of capabilities rather than statuses, performance is generally much the same, except where several high-capability actors are or become "isolationist." However, defining goals in terms of capability increments tends to lessen the degree of conflict in the simulated politics whereas the use of status indices makes mobility in the stratification system objectively a zero-sum situation—one's own gain is at least one other's loss. It is important to note that the actors do not necessarily perceive international mobility to be zero sum: they frequently mitigate competitiveness by parochial measurement of status and by adjustment of their own goals. When the actor aspires merely to maintain its existing value position, status quo–preserving strategies definitionally become "successes."

To explain outcomes, one must give special attention to the search-strategy adaptation–implementation stages of the policy process. A wide range of experience with the model indicates that the variety of precedents in the common memory and the search rules used to select precedents are, taken together, vastly more important to the determination of outcomes for both the actor and the system than, for example, the rapidity of adjustment in setting aspiration levels, intraorganizational compromise among policy proposals or the several subunits, or even the choice of mechanisms for defining goals. *The significance for outcomes of whether the actor seeks to equalize status ranks, avoid vulnerabilities in its security structure, or realize successive increases of status is less than the significance of the set of historical precedents from which the actor must seek solutions to its self-defined problems.* If continued experimentation leads to increased confidence in the major model specifications, these behavioral implications suggest that more important to systemic restructuring than what values an international agent seeks, or even how much it seeks, are the means available with which to seek them.

This conclusion stems in part from model design and is not entirely a synthetic observation. We never get anything more out of our model than we build in, intentionally or not. But the conclusion aggravates problems of selecting and coding historical data, such as means–ends relations, strategic microtheories of historical precedents. Were the model more robust in this respect, adequacy of data and its abstract representation would be less vital. Histories are not usually written as the implementation of abstract behavioral rules by poorly coordinated, internally functionally differentiated actors. Even to the extent of determining the initial states of an experiment, we are forced to make sometimes tenuous inferences from historical accounts to the processes that underlie them.

Actors bear simple and multiple relations to one another. The analyst's choice of which relations to code in a precedent and which to omit strongly influences future outputs of the simulation when the same precedent is implemented in a radically different international context. If one's "enemy" is also a "dependent" of a "friend" of another actor "similarly economically situated" in the stratification system, there arises an inherent ambiguity—when judged from a historical record of international interactions alone—in the decision of which relation was the more salient to the actor's problem-solving attempts. Accurate, reliable coding of precedents requires detailed knowledge of how the responsible statesmen evaluated contextual possibilities and constraints, and how they built the many "lists" of abstract relations, such as "friends," "dependents," and "similarly economically situated."

When our model is employed as a device for generating dynamic implications of various combinations of theoretic modules, difficulties of historical strategic attribution and insufficient data of other kinds are less important. But when it is employed to gain a causal understanding of particular historical events and processes—in the manner of our Pacific case study—the analyst's historical interpretations are crucial.

The lack of robustness to variations in the common interorganizational memory may arise in large part because the model is self-restructuring. Thus unlike many simulations of social and economic processes whose qualitative behavior remains the same despite considerable variation of parameters and input data, structural transformations of our simulated systems can differ as a function of very slight differences in the initial memory. Structural flexibility is permitted the actor not only in the ways in which it solves problems but also in the ways in which it defines them.

6. BIBLIOGRAPHY

Abelson, R.P. (1973). "The Structure of Belief Systems." *Computer Models of Thought and Language,* ed. R.C. Schank and K.M. Colby, San Francisco: Freeman, 1973.

Abelson, R.P. (1975) "Concepts for Representing Mundane Reality in Plans." *Representation and Understanding: Studies in Cognitive Science,* ed. D. Bobrow and A. Collins, New York: Academic, 1975.

Ackoff, R.L., and F.E. Emery (1972). *On Purposeful Systems.* Chicago: Aldine, 1972.

Alexander, C. (1965), "A City Is Not a Tree." *Architectural Forum,* 122, 58–62 April, 58–61 May, 1965.

Alker, H.R. Jr. (1971). "Le Comportment Directeur." *Revue Française de Sociologie.* 1971.

Alker, H.R. Jr. (1973) "On Political Capabilities in a Schedule Sense: Measuring Power, Integration and Development." H.R. Alker, Jr., K.W. Deutsch and A.H. Stoetzal, ed. *Mathematical Approaches to Politics.* San Francisco: Jossey-Bass, 1973.

Alker, H.R. Jr. (1974) Are There Structural Models of Voluntaristic Social Action? *Quality and Quantity* 8, pp. 199–246, 1974.

Alker, H.R. Jr. and W.J. Greenberg (1971) "The U.N. Charter: Alternate Pasts and Alternate Futures." Fedder, ed. *The UN: Problems and Prospects.* St. Louis: University of Missouri, 1971.

Alker, H.R. Jr. and C. Christensen (1972) "From Causal Modeling to Artificial Intelligence." J. LaPonce and P. Smoker, eds. *Experimentation and Simulation in Political Science.* Toronto: University of Toronto, 1972.

Alker, H.R. Jr., Bloomfield, Choucri. "Analyzing Global Interdependence." C.I.S., MIT, 1973.

Aron, R. (1966) *Peace and War: A Theory of International Relations.* Garden City, New York: Doubleday, 1966.

Banks, A. (1971) "SUNY-Binghamton's Cross-National Time-Series Data Archive." *Public Data Use,* 2, 32–39, 1971.

Banks, A. (1974) "Time Series Data," Technical Report 1, 1974.

Bendix, R. and S. Lipset, eds. (1953). *Class, Status and Power.* New York: Free Press, 1953.

Bennett, J.P. (1975a). "Foreign Policy as Maladaptive Behavior: Operationalizing Some Implications." Peace Science Society, Papers 25, 85–104, 1975a.

Bennett, J.P. (1975b). "Describing Fundamental Structural Change: Conceptual Contributions to International Relations Theory of List Processing and Catastrophe Theory." Paper presented to the Meeting of the International Studies Association, 1975b.

Bobrow, D.B. (1968). "Ecology of International Games: Requirements for a Model of the International System." Peace Research Society, Papers 11, 67–87, 1968.

Brams, S.J. (1969). "The Structure of Influence Relationships in the International System." *International Politics and Foreign Policy,* ed. J.N Rosenau, New York: Free Press, 1969.

Bueno de Mesquita, B. (1975) "Measuring Systemic Polarity." *Journal of Conflict Resolution,* 19 187–216, 1975.

Chomsky, A.N. and G.A. Miller (1963) "Finitary Models of Language Users." In R.D. Luce et al, ed. *Handbook of Mathematical Psychology,* 2. New York: Wiley, 1963.

Choucri, N. and R.C. North (1971) "Alternative Dynamics of International Conflict: Population, Resources, Technology, and Some Implications for Policy." *World Politics,* Special Issue, 1971.

Choucri, N. and R. North (1972) "In Search of Peace Systems: Scandinavia and the Netherlands." In B.M. Russett, ed. *Peace, War and Numbers,* Beverly Hills, Calif.: Sage, 1972.

Choucri, N. (1975) *Nations in Conflict: Population, Expansion and War.* San Francisco: Freeman, 1975.

Cyert, R.M., W.R. Dill, and J.G. March (1958) "The Role of Expectations in Business Decision Making." *Administrative Science Quarterly* 3, 307-340, 1958.

Cyert, R.M., and J.G. March (1963) *A Behavioral Theory of the Firm.* Englewood Cliffs, N.J.: Prentice-Hall, 1963.

East, M. (1969) "Bank-Dependent Interaction and Mobility: Two Aspects of International Stratification." Peace Research Society, Papers 14, 113-127, 1969.

East, M. (1972) "Status Discrepancy and Violence in the International System: An Empirical Analysis." In J.G. Rosenau, McDavis and M.A. East, eds. *The Analysis of International Politics: Essays in Honor of Harold and Margaret Sprout.* New York: Free Press, 1972.

Fogel, L.J., A.J. Owens, and M.J. Walsh (1966) *Artificial Intelligence through Simulated Evolution.* New York: Wiley, 1966.

Forrester, J.W. (1971) *World Dynamics.* Cambridge: Wright-Allen Press, 1971.

Friedell, M.F. (1967) "Organizations as Semilattices." *American Sociological Review* 32, 46-54, 1967.

Galtung, J. (1966a) "International Relations and International Conflicts: A Sociological Approach." Paper presented to a meeting of the International Sociological Association, 1966a.

Galtung, J. (1966b) "Rank and Social Integration: A Multidimensional Approach." In J. Berger, M. Zelditch and B. Anderson, eds. *Sociological Theories in Progress, 1.* Boston: Houghton-Mifflin, 1966b.

Galtung, J. (1971) "A Structural Theory of Imperialism." *Journal of Peace Research,* 81-118, 1971.

Galtung, J., M. Mora y Araujo, and S. Schwartzman (1972) "The Latin American System of Nations: A Structural Analysis." In B. Hoglund and J.W. Ulrich, eds. *Conflict Control and Conflict Resolution.* Copenhagen: Munksgaard, 1972.

Gerth, H.H. and C.W. Mills, eds. (1958) *From Max Weber: Essays in Sociology.* New York: Oxford University Press, 1958.

Geschwender, J.A. (1970) "Continuities in Theories of Status Consistency and Cognitive Dissonance." In E.O. Laumann et al, eds.' *The Logic of Social Hierarchies.* Chicago: Markham, 1970.

Gurr, T.R. and R. Duvall (1973) "Civil Conflict in the 1960's: A Reciprocal Theoretical System with Parameter Estimates." *Comparative Political Studies.* 1973.

Harary, F. and H. Millier (1970) "On the Measure of Connectedness in a Social Group." *General Systems* 15, 67-69, 1970.

Harary, F. (1959) "Status and Contrastatus." *Sociometry* 22, 23-43, 1959.

Hibbs, D.A., Jr. (1973) *Mass Political Violence: A Cross-National Causal Analysis.* New York: Wiley, 1973.

Hirschman, A.O. (1969) *National Power and the Structure of Foreign Trade.* Berkeley and Los Angeles: University of California Press, 1969.

Isnard, C.A. and E.C. Zeeman (forthcoming) "Some Models of Catastrophe Theory in the Social Sciences." In L. Collins, ed. *Use of Models in the Social Sciences.*

Kaplan, M.A. (1967) "Some Problems in International Systems Research." In *International Political Systems: An Anthology.* Garden City, N.Y.: Doubleday, 1967.

Kaplan, M.A. (1957) *System and Process in International Politics.* New York: 1957.

Kimberley, J.C. (1970) "The Emergence and Stabilization of Stratification in Simple and Complex Social Systems." In E.O. Laumann ed. *Social Stratification Research and Theory for the 1970's.* Indianapolis: Bobbs-Merrill, 1970.

Lagos, G. (1963) *International Stratification and Underdeveloped Countries,* Chapel Hill: University of North Carolina Press, 1963.

Linnemann, H. (1966) *An Econometric Study of International Trade Flows.* Amsterdam: North Holland, 1966.

Lorrain, F. and H.C. White (1971) "Structural Equivalence of Individuals in Social Networks." *Journal of Mathematical Sociology* 1, 49–80, 1971.

March, J.G. and J.P. Olsen (1975) "The Uncertainty of the Past: Organizational Learning under Ambiguity." *European Journal of Political Research* 3, 147–71, 1975.

May, E.R. (1973) *"Lessons" of the Past: The Use and Misuse of History in American Foreign Policy.* New York: Oxford University Press, 1973.

Donella H. Meadows et al. (1972) *The Limits to Growth.* Washington, D.C.: Potomac Associates, 1972.

Mesarovic, M. and E. Pestel (1974) *Mankind at the Turning Point.* New York: E.P. Dutton, 1974.

Mesarovic, M.D., D. Macko and Y. Takahara (1970) *Theory of Hierarchical, Multievel Systems.* New York: Academic, 1970.

Miller, G.A., E. Galanter and K. Pribram (1960) *Plans and the Structure of Behavior.* New York: Holt, Rinehart and Winston, 1960.

Modelski, G. (1971) "War and the Great Powers." Peace Research Society, Papers 18, 45–59, 1971.

Modelski, G. (1972) *Principles of World Politics.* New York: Free Press, 1972.

Moll, K. (1974) "International Conflict as a Decision System." *Journal of Conflict Resolution* 18, 555–557, 1974.

Myers, R.H. (1971) *Response Surface Methodology.* Boston: Allyn and Bacon, 1971.

Newell, A. and H.A. Simon (1972) *Human Problem Solving.* Englewood Cliffs, N.J.: Prentice-Hall, 1972.

Nye, J.S., Jr. and R.O. Keohane (1972) "Transnational Relations and World Politics: An Introduction." In *Transnational Relations and World Politics.* Cambridge: Harvard University Press, 1972.

Organski, A.F.K. (1958) *World Politics.* New York: Knopf. 1958.

Parsons, T. (1964) *Essays in Sociological Theory,* Revised Edition. New York: Free Press, 1964.

Read, W.R. (1970) "The Decline in the Hierarchy of Individual Organizations." In W.P. Sexton, ed. *Organizational Theories.* Columbus: Merrill, 1970.

Ruggie, J.G. (1971) "The Structure of International Organization: Contingency, Complexity and Post-Modern Form." Peace Research Society, Papers 18, 73-91, 1971.

Russett, B.M. (1971) "An Empirical Typology of International Military Alliances." *Midwest Journal of Political Science* 15, 262-289, 1971.

Russett, B.M. and W.C. Lamb (1969) "Global Patterns of Diplomatic Exchange." *Journal of Peace Research* 37-58, 1969.

Sampson, E.E. (1969) "Studies of Status Congruence." *Advances in Experimental Psychology* 4, 225-, 1969.

Schank, R.C. and R.P. Abelson (1975) "Scripts, Plans and Knowledge." Paper presented at the 4th International Joint Conference on Artificial Intelligence, 1975.

Schofield, N.J. (1971) "A Topological Model of International Relations." Peace Research Society, Papers 17, 93-111, 1971.

Scott, A. (1965) *The Revolution in Statecraft: Informal Penetration.* New York: Random House, 1965.

Simon, H.A. (1962) "The Architecture of Complexity." Proceedings of the American Philosophical Society 106, 467-482, 1962.

Singer, J.D. (1958) "Threat Perception and the Armament-Tension Dilemma." *Journal of Conflict Resolution* 2, 90-105, 1958.

Singer, J.D. (1970) "Escalation and Control in International Conflict: A Simple Feedback Model." *General Systems* 15, 163-173, 1970.

Singer, J.D. and M. Small (1972) *The Wages of War 1816-1965: A Statistical Handbook,* New York: Wiley, 1972.

Small, M. and J.D. Singer (1969) "Formal Alliances, 1816-1965, an Extension of the Basic Data." *Journal of Peace Research* 3, 257-282, 1969.

Sommerhoff, G. (1971) "Abstract Characteristics of Living Systems." In F.E. Emory, ed. *Systems Thinking.* Baltimore: Penguin, 1971.

Starbuck, W.H. (1973) "Tadpoles into Armageddon and Chrysler into Butterflies." *Social Science Research* 2, 81-109, 1973.

Starr, H. (1972) *War Coalitions, the Distribution of Payoffs and Losses.* Lexington, Mass.: Heath, 1972.

Thom, R. (1972) *Stabilité structurelle et morphogénèse, essai d'une theorie generale des modèles.* New York: Benjamin, 1972.

Wallace, M.D. (1971) "Power, Status and International War." *Journal of Peace Research* 8, 23-35, 1971.

Wallace, M.D. (1972) "Status, Formal Organization, and Arms Levels as Factors Leading to the Onset of War, 1820-1964." In B.M. Russett, ed. *Peace, War and Numbers,* Beverly Hills: Sage.

Wolfers, A. (1962) *Discord and Collaboration.* Baltimore: Johns Hopkins Press, 1962.

Zinnes, D.A. (1967) "An Analytical Study of Balance of Power Theories." *Journal of Peace Research* 4, 270-288, 1967.

7. CASE STUDY BIBLIOGRAPHY

Barton, R. (1968) *A Short History of the Republic of Bolivia,* 2nd ed. La Paz: Editorial los Amigos del Libro, 1968.

Bemis, S.F. (1943) *The Latin American Policy of the United States, an Historical Interpretation.* New York: Harcourt and Brace, 1943.

Bizzarro, S. (1972) *Historical Dictionary of Chile.* Metuchen, N.J.: Scarecrow Press, 1972.

Blakemore, H. (1974) *British Nitrates and Chilean Politics, 1886-1896: Balmaceda and North.* London: Athlone Press, 1974.

Blanksten, G.I. (1964) *Ecuador: Constitutions and Caudillos.* New York: Russell and Russell, 1964.

Bollinger, W.S. (1971) "The Rise of United States Influence in the Peruvian Economy, 1869-1921." University of California, Los Angeles, unpublished M.A. thesis, 1971.

Brown, J.R. (1958) "The Chilean Nitrate Railways Controversy." *Hispanic American Historical Review* 38, 465-81.

Brown, J.R. (1963) "Nitrate Crises, Combinations and the Chilean Government in the Nitrate Age." *Hispanic American Historical Review* 43, 230-246, 1963.

Burgos Ortega, E. (1966) *Bolivia y su derecho al mar.* Potosi: Universidad Tomas Frias, 1966.

Burr, R.N. (1955) "The Balance of Power in Nineteenth-Century South America: An Exploratory Essay." *Hispanic American Historical Review* 35, 37-60, 1955.

Burr, R.N. (1965) *By Reason or Force: Chile and the Balancing of Power in South America, 1830-1905.* Berkeley: University of California Press, 1965.

Bustamente Munoz, A. (1960) *Lista de los instrumentos internacionales concludios por el Ecuador.* Quito: Editorial Casa de la Cultura Ecuatoriana, 1960.

Calderon Cousiño, A. (1920) *Short Diplomatic History of the Chilean-Peruvian Relations 1819-1879.* Santiago: Imprenta Universitaria, 1920.

Centner, C.W. (1942) "Great Britain and Chilean Mining, 1830-1914." *Economic History Review* 12, 76-82.

Dennis, W.J. (1927) *Documentary History of the Tacna-Arica Dispute.* Iowa City: University of Iowa Press, 1927.

Dennis, W.J. (1931) *Tacna and Arica: An Account of the Chile-Peru Boundary Dispute and the Arbitration of the United States.* New Haven: Yale University Press, 1931.

Donald, M.B. (1936) "History of the Chile Nitrate Industry." *Annals of Science* 1, 29-47 and 193-215, 1936.

Encina, F.A. (1963) *Las relaciones entre Chile y Bolivia 1841-1963.* Santiago: Nascimento, 1963.

Espinosa Moraga, O. (1969) *El precio de la paz chileno-argentina, 1810-1969.* Vol. 1. Santiago: Nascimento, 1969.

Evans, H.C., Jr. (1927) *Chile and Its Relation with the United States.* Durham: Duke University Press, 1927.

Ferns, H.S. (1960) *Britain and Argentina in the Nineteenth Century.* Oxford: Clarendon Press, 1960.

Fifer, J.V. (1972) *Bolivia: Land, Location and Politics since 1825.* Cambridge: At the University Press, 1972.

Frazer, R.W. (1949) "The Role of the Lima Congress, 1864-1865, in the

Development of Pan-Americanism. *Hispanic American Historical Review* 29, 319–48, 1949.

Ganzert, F.W. (1934) "The Boundary Controversy in the Upper Amazon between Brazil, Bolivia and Peru, 1903–1909." *Hispanic American Historical Review* 14, 427–49, 1934.

Griffin, K. (1969) *Underdevelopment in Spanish America: An Interpretation.* Cambridge: M.I.T. Press, 1969.

Hancock, A.U. (1893) *A History of Chile.* New York: AMS Press, 1971 reprint, 1893.

Hardy, O. (1948) "British Nitrates and the Balmaceda Revolution." *Pacific Historical Review* 17, 171–181.

Heath, D.B. (1972) *Historical Dictionary of Bolivia.* Metuchen, N.J.: Scarecrow Press, 1972.

International Bureau of the American Republics (1909) *Chile, a Handbook.* Washington: IBAR, 1909.

International Bureau of the American Republics (1892) *Peru, a Handbook.* Washington: IBAR, 1892.

Ireland, G. (1938) *Boundaries, Possessions and Conflicts in South America.* Cambridge: Harvard University Press, 1938.

Juaregui Rosquellas, A. (1938) "Bolivia's Claustrophobia." *Foreign Affairs* 16, 704–13, 1938.

Keeble, T.W. (1970) *Commonwealth Relations between British Overseas Territories and South America 1806–1914.* London: Institute of Latin American Studies Monographs, No. 3, 1970.

Kendall, L.C. (1936) "Andres Santa Cruz and the Peru–Bolivian Confederation." *Hispanic American Historical Review* 16, 29–48, 1936.

Kiernan, V.G. (1955) "Foreign Interests in the War of the Pacific." *Hispanic American Historical Review 35,* 14–36, 1955.

Klein, H.S. (1969) *Parties and Political Change in Bolivia, 1880–1952.* Cambridge, Cambridge University Press, 1969.

Marett, R. (1969) *Peru.* New York: Praeger, 1969.

Markham, C.R. (1882) *The War between Peru and Chile.* London: 1882.

Matthew, W.M. (1970) "Peru and the British Guano Market, 1840–1870." *Economic History Review* 23, 112–128, 1970.

Maude, W. (1958) *Merchants and Bankers, 1808–1958.* London: Antony Gibbs and Sons, 1958.

Maurtua, V.M. (1901) *The Question of the Pacific.* Philadelphia: G.F. Lasher, 1901.

Mercado Moreira, M. (1930) *Historia internacional de Bolivia,* 2 ed., Ampliada. La Paz: "Atena" -deCrespi, 1930.

Millington, H. (1938) *American Diplomacy and the War of the Pacific.* New York: Columbia University Press, 1938.

Mitchell, B.R. (1975) *European Historical Statistics 1750–1900.* New York: Columbia University Press, 1975.

Nuermberger, G.A. (1940) "The Continental Treaties of 1856: An American Union Exclusive of the United States." *Hispanic American Historical Review* 20, 32–55, 1940.

Parks, E.T. (1934) *Colombia and the United States 1765-1934.* Durham, N.C.: Duke University Press, 1934.

Pastoriza Flores, A.M. (1921) *History of the Boundary Dispute between Ecuador and Peru.* New York: Columbia University Press, 1921.

Pike, F.B. (1963) *Chile and the United Sates, 1880-1962: The Emergence of Chile's Social Crisis and the Challenge to United States Diplomacy.* Notre Dame, Ind.: Notre Dame University Press, 1963.

Pike, F.B. (1967) *The Modern History of Peru.* London: Tavistock, 1967.

Platt, D.C.M. (1968) *France, Trade and Politics in British Foreign Policy 1815-1914.* Oxford: Clarendon Press, 1968.

Platt, D.C.M. (1973) *Latin America and British Trade 1806-1914.* New York: Harper and Row, 1973.

Ramirez Necochea, H. (1960) *Historia del Imperialism en Chile.* Santiago: Editoria Austral, 1960.

Ramirez, N.H. (1969) *Balmaceda y la contrarevolucion de 1891.* 2nd edition Santiago: Editorial Universitaria, 1969.

Rippy, J.F. (1948) "Economic Enterprises of the Nitrate King and his Associates in Chile." *Pacific Historical Review* 17, 1948.

Rippy, J.F. (1959) *British Investments in Latin America, 1822-1949: A Case Study in the Operations of Private Enterprise in Retarded Regions.* Minneapolis: University of Minnesota Press, 1959.

Rippy, J.F. (1968) *Latin America, A Modern History,* revised edition. Ann Arbor: University of Michigan Press, 1968.

Sherman, W.R. (1926) *The Diplomatic and Commercial Relations of the United States and Chile, 1820-1914.* Boston: Richard G. Badger, 1926.

Wilgus, A.C. (1922) "James G. Blaine and the Pan American Movement." *Hispanic American Historical Review* 5, 662–708, 1922.

Yrigoyen, P. (1921) *La alianza peru-boliviano-argentina y la declaratoria de guerra de Chile.* Lima: Sanmarti, 1921.

Zook, D.H., Jr. (1964) *Zarumilla-Maranón: The Ecuador–Peru Dispute.* New York: Bookman Associates, 1964.

Chapter 20

Machiavelli in Machina: Or Politics among Hexagons

Stuart A. Bremer and
Michael Mihalka

1. INTRODUCTION

I wonder if any one of you in this audience watches and notes the steps by which Philip, weak at first, has grown so powerful. First he seized Amphipolis, next Pydna, then Potidaea, after that Methene, lastly he invaded Thessaly. Then having settled Pherae, Pagasae, Magnesia, and the rest of that country to suit his purposes, off he went to Thrace, and there, after evicting some of the chiefs and installing others, he fell sick. On his recovery, he did not relapse into inactivity, but instantly assailed Olynthos. . . . If he takes Olynthos, who is to prevent his marching further?

—Demosthenes

Demosthenes describes above the destruction of a multistate system and the creation of an empire, a pattern that has been repeated throughout history. This paper will describe a computer model which should help us understand how and under what conditions multistate systems achieve stability, or alternatively, are transformed into empires.

Let us begin by defining what we mean by a multistate system. Conceptually, a multistate system is a regionally bounded and territorially contiguous set of autonomous and sovereign political entities that recognize no higher secular authority. Waltz (1959) describes it as follows:

. . . many sovereign states, with no system of law enforceable among them, with each state judging its grievances and ambitions according to the dictates of its own reason or desire. Because each state is the final judge of its own cause, any state may at any time use force to implement its policies. Because any state may at any time use force, all states must constantly be ready either to counter force with force or to pay the cost of weakness (pp. (159–60).

Other scholars have designated such systems as stateless societies (Masters 1964), subsystem-dominant systems (Kaplan 1957a), or balance of power systems (Wright 1965). We have selected Walker's (1953) term "multistate system" because it carries fewer connotations and is thus a more neutral term. As we see it, the ideal multistate system lies on one end of a continuum with empire on the other end. In its purest form, a multistate system would be composed of a large number of states that are approximately equal in power. A few historical examples which come close to this form are ancient China during the Chou dynasty; northern India prior to Chandragupta's unification; ancient Greece; Renaissance Italy; and Europe in the years following the Peace of Westphalia.

Systems of this nature have prompted a great deal of theoretical speculation on the part of international relations scholars and practitioners, both classical and modern. One of the primary theoretical concerns has centered on the question of how stability is achieved in systems of this type. There is, though, some confusion as to what stability means in this literature: one view equates it with a low level of violent conflict, while another designates a system as stable if the number of states and distribution of power remains relatively constant. Since war itself may serve to preserve states and a distribution of power, the second definition is more acceptable to us because it does not set a priori limits on the level of violence.

The problem of stability in such systems has been succinctly stated by Wright. In multistate systems

> . . . Governments have a tendency to struggle both for increase of power and for self-preservation. Only if the latter tendency checks the first will all the governments continue to be independent. Whenever one increases its relative power, its capacity to increase it further will be enhanced. As a consequence, any departure from equilibrium tends to initiate an accelerating process of conquest (1965, p. 744).

It is precisely this "accelerating process of conquest" about which Demosthenes was concerned.

Leaving aside those strategies for achieving or maintaining stability that rest upon the creation of central authorities or institutions of some nature—such as collective security systems and world government—one finds a set of theories that are often subsumed under the general rubric "balance of power." Under this rubric, Claude (1962) has identified three different processes that various authors have put forth as a means to achieve stability in multistate systems. These are the *automatic* process, the *semiautomatic* process, and the *manually operated* process.

The automatic stabilizing process assumes that powerful feedback loops are intrinsically present in the system, and that these loops insure the stability of the system. As Kaplan has put it, ". . . Should any nation desire to become predominant itself, it must, to protect its own interests, act to prevent any other nation from accomplishing such an objective. Like Adam Smith's 'unseen hand' of competition, the international system is policed informally by self-interest." (1957b, p. 690). Authors such as Rousseau, Toynbee, Butterfield, and A.J.P. Taylor have expressed similar views.

The semiautomatic process requires that one major state be committed to the preservation of the stability of the system; that is, there must be a "balancer" for the system to work. The classic case, of course, is Britain's alleged balancing behavior in Europe. Claude (1962) sums up this position in the following way:

> The ordinary members may do what comes naturally—no dedication to the ideal of equilibrium is required of them—but the automatism of the system is supplemented by the calculated operations of the unique participant, the state committed to the process of equilibration (p. 48).

The third variant, the manually operated process, requires that most, if not all, of the major states subscribe to a set of superordinate principles regarding the conduct of interstate affairs. Prominent among these is the belief that "the best way to preserve the individual state [is] to preserve the system of which it [is] a part." (Gulick 1955, p. 31). Words and phrases such as the general good, self-discipline, survival for the group, moderation, and the like figure prominently in this approach. Von Gentz, Kissinger, and Gulick tend to support this view as to how stability can be achieved in multistate systems.

As we can see, the main difference between these three models is the degree to which major actors pursue the preservation of the state system as one of their primary objectives. In the automatic version, no major actor need be so oriented; in the semiautomatic version, one major actor needs to have such a goal; and in the manually operated model, most, if not all, of the major states must be pledged to system preservation. This presents an interesting theoretical result, as well as an interesting theoretical problem: starting from rather different premises about the goals of states, these theories produce the same deduction—a stable multistate system. It may be that all three are correct, but this seems unlikely to us. It may be that each process produces stability under a different set of conditions that are not specified. Or it may be that these deductions are not logically correct. Since the models are not well defined or rigorously specified, it is, as a result, difficult to check the logic involved in the deductive process. It is this latter explanation which seems most likely to us.

One way to discover whether deductions follow from assumptions is to translate the verbal descriptions into a more precise representational language, such as a mathematical or a computer model. Once this is done, one can then determine whether the conclusions reached by those working with mental models—in which assumptions, definitions, and specifications are not explicitly articulated—conform with those obtained by more rigorous methods. This, in effect, is what we are in the process of doing with respect to the three processes outlined above.

At this point in our research, we have completed the construction and preliminary testing of a working version of the automatic stabilization model. Drawing principally upon the writings of observers, such as Machiavelli and Kautilya, who were present when a multistate system was in operation, as well as historians who have studied such systems extensively, such as Walker (1953) and Mattingly (1955), we attempted to extract and synthesize a set of conditions and decision rules that seem to capture the essence of the process. The next two parts of this paper are devoted to describing the model that resulted from these efforts. Before we turn to this, however, three points need to be made. First, the model that we have developed is generally consistent with the prescriptive statements put forth by writers like Kautilya and Machiavelli, but it is not the only model that would be consonant with their less-than-complete and inconsistent observations. Second, resting as the model does on a large component of prescriptive literature, we do not claim the replication of observed behavior as one of our main objectives. Our central concern at this stage is answering the question: what are the logical consequences of states acting according to a particular set of decision rules? Finally, we should hasten to add that we are not prepared at this time to offer any more than a very tentative answer to that question. Thus, this paper should be viewed as a preliminary report.

2. THE MULTISTATE SYSTEM

A multistate system has three essential characteristics. First, it is composed of a relatively large number of states, by which we mean not fewer than ten and usually more than 20. Second, at any point, each of these states has a certain amount of military power and a defined territorial base. Third, each state knows the geographical position of every other state and is able to estimate, with varying degrees of accuracy, its own power and the power of other states. Since the simulation model allows for a variety of initial configurations, we need to discuss these characteristics in more detail.

Turning first to the geography of a simulated system, we need to make several simplifying assumptions. First, we assume that the system is closed; that is, there are no relevant actors outside of, or adjacent to, the region that the system occupies. Second, the territorial space is finite and limited to the total area that is initially specified. Thus, a state may not expand by adding territory from outside the region. The third simplifying assumption is that the territory within the region is not infinitely divisible, but rather it is composed of a fixed number of indivisible blocks.

Figure 20-1 indicates a system which satisfies these assumptions. As one can

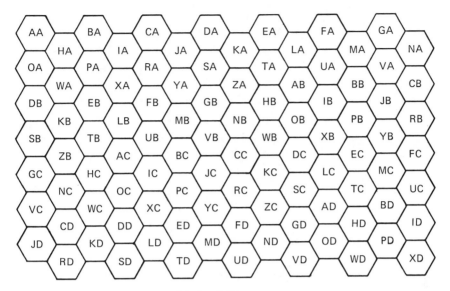

Figure 20-1. A 98-state system.

see, this particular region is rectangular in shape and composed of 98 hexagons, each corresponding to a block of territory. The rectangular shape of the region is merely a matter of convenience. At this point in the development of the model, we can specify any shape we wish. The number of indivisible territorial blocks is also arbitrary and could easily be expanded or reduced. The hexagonal block shape was chosen because it maximizes the number of borders a block can have without creating gaps within the map, and it is the shape that is conventionally used in war games. States are identified by two letter combinations, and Figure 20-1 portrays the situation in which each state is composed of a single block of territory. This 98-actor system has been the starting point for several simulation runs. We can, however, specify different initial spatial configurations by aggregating blocks to form larger entities. Figure 20-2, for example, illustrates a different initial configuration that has also been used several times. In principle, then, we can duplicate the geography of a wide variety of multistate systems. In the early stages of our research, however, we have restricted ourselves to the abstract systems shown in Figures 20-1 and 20-2.

In addition to territory, each state has an initial amount of military power. These values may be assigned or generated randomly. In the runs to date we have used a normal distribution with a mean of 100 and a standard deviation of 20 to generate the initial power values for the 98-state system of Figure 20-1. By changing the probability distribution itself or changing the parameters governing the distribution, we can produce systems with varying degrees of power concentration at the outset of a simulation run. This is one of the areas that we are interested in investigating in future analyses.

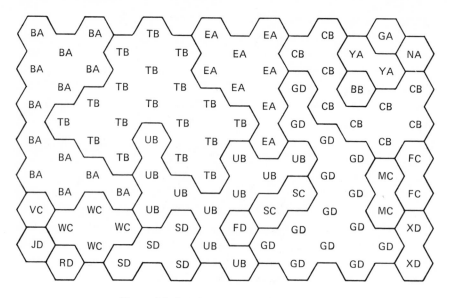

Figure 20-2. An alternate state system

As we shall see shortly, many of the decisions that the simulated states make in the course of a simulation run require that they know the power of their own state as well as the power of other states. Thus, as noted above, we need to bestow upon each state the ability to estimate power. This is a notion which figures prominently in the realist literature and one which we are particularly interested in examining. A central issue involves the accuracy of the power estimation process; and in constructing the simulation model, we chose to include a set of parameters which determine how accurate or inaccurate the states are at estimating power. Assigning these parameters different values allows us to create systems where the states are prone to underestimate power, overestimate power, or a mixture of the two, as well as to estimate power accurately. We are particularly interested in discovering the theoretical implications of accurate and inaccurate power estimation for the system as a whole and for individual states. For example, is the interstate system more stable when its component states are very *good* power estimators or very *bad* estimators? Or, is there a relationship between the accuracy of a state's power estimation process and its chances of survival? Later on in this paper we will report some results of a few experiments dealing with some of these questions.

Having outlined the fundamental structural givens that define a simulated multistate system at the outset of a run, we turn now to a description of the decision rules that guide the actions of states during a simulation run.

3. DECISION-MAKING RULES

A run of the simulation model is composed of a series of iterations, which, in turn, are composed of actions and reactions by actors in the system. An iteration always begins with the selection of one of the system's members as an initiating actor, but it may be terminated, as we shall see, in a variety of ways.

a. Initiator Selection. An action round, or iteration, begins with the selection of an initiating actor. Initiators are selected stochastically, the probability of selection for any particular entity being equal to that fraction of the system's power it possesses. For example, an actor with 11 percent of the total amount of power in the system at the beginning of an iteration has a probability of .11 of being selected as the initiating actor for that round.

For several theoretical and empirical reasons this seems to be a reasonable selection rule. If we take seriously the theoretical notion that actors that find themselves in a multistate system should take advantage—whenever possible— of favorable power disparities to extend their territory and enhance their power, then, other things being equal, the more powerful an actor is relative to others, the more opportunities it will have to expand.

On the empirical side, there is ample evidence to suggest that more powerful states have been more active, and have exhibited more initiative, in interstate relations than less powerful states. Rummel (1969), McGowan and Shapiro (1973), East (1973), Salmore and Hermann (1969), and Bremer (1975) are only a few of the large number of scholars who have assembled supportive evidence. This selection mechanism produces behavior that is in accord with these empirical observations.

b. Target Selection. The next action in an iteration of the model is undertaken by the actor chosen as the initiator. At this point, the initiator must determine whether it has an opportunity for expansion. It does so by comparing its own power with that of each of the actors with which it shares a common border. This, in turn, requires a power estimation algorithm. Again, a persistent issue within much of the balance of power debate centers on the ability of actors accurately to estimate their respective strengths. If the actors cannot estimate power accurately, so the argument runs, the balance of power system cannot function as it is supposed to. As it turns out, this is precisely one of the several central theoretical questions the simulation is designed to address. Thus the power estimation routine contains the option of varying the amount of proportionate error that enters into the power calculations. That is, by varying a set of parameters we can set up actors that tend to underestimate or overestimate the power of other actors, or we can, as we have in the run described below, give the actors perfect information about the amount of power possessed by other actors.

The power comparison procedure may have one of two overall outcomes. First, the initiator may find that it is surrounded by neighboring actors it estimates to be more powerful than itself. In this eventuality, the initiator declines to take action, and the iteration ends. If, on the other hand, the initiator discovers that it has a power advantage over one or more neighboring actors, it will decide to take action against the actor which is the least powerful neighbor. The initiator's action is analogous to a threat; that is, it is a warning to the target actor that the initiator intends to take hostile action against it shortly.

The rationale for this process rests principally upon the basic tenets of the classical, geopolitical, realist school of thought regarding such matters. A rational actor should not initiate conflict with a more powerful state, but it should not hesitate to undertake activities that will enhance its power when it has the advantage. Although the morality of this prescription is open to question, the assertion that nations have actually behaved in precisely this manner is less open to question.

It should be noted, however, that in spite of the rational character of the target selection process, miscalculations may still occur. In particular, when error is introduced into the power estimation process, an initiator may be led to take action against a target that it erroneously believes to be less powerful than itself. Or, conversely, it may pass up an opportunity for expansion if it incorrectly judges that a neighboring actor is more powerful. We can control the level of such miscalculations by altering the power estimation error rates described above.

c. Target Responses. The action now shifts to the target actor, which must decide how to cope with the initiator's threat. The target actor immediately compares its own power with that of the initiator, relying, once again, on the power estimation routines. These estimates may or may not be subject to error. If the target perceives that it is more powerful than the initiator, the target actor will decide to do nothing with respect to the initiator's threat. If this happens, action shifts back to the initiator, and action continues.

More frequently, however, the target actor finds itself at a disadvantage in the power comparison and decides that some defensive action is necessary. Under these circumstances the target actor attempts to construct a defensive coalition with approximately the following characteristics:

1. All members are contiguous to the initiator.
2. The combined power of the coalition is greater than the power of the initiator.
3. The combined power of the coalition is the smallest power total that still satisfies the second condition.

The rationale for these requirements is as follows. The first condition stems from the traditional view that the most militarily effective alliances are those which encircle or directly block the opponent. The contiguity criterion embodies this traditional wisdom.

The second and third conditions together represent the essential features of the minimum-winning coalition notions advanced by William Riker and others (Riker 1962). We should hasten to note that this is by no means the only criterion that could be advanced for evaluating alternative coalitions. For example, one might hypothesize that an actor should attempt to construct the largest coalition possible in order to obtain maximum deterrence. This is sometimes referred to as the "grand coalition" strategy. Or one may prescribe that the preferred coalition is the one containing the fewest actors while still retaining superior power. Our selection of the minimum-winning criterion was based upon our theoretical preference and its prominence in the literature. One of the key questions we are interested in examining in the future concerns the impact of substituting different coalition criteria, such as those discussed above, for the one currently employed.

The specific actions of the target actor entail estimating the power of each of the actors contiguous to the initiator and evaluating various candidate coalitions in order to find the coalition that best satisfies the three conditions outlined above. It is possible, of course, that no satisfactory coalition can be constructed. This would be true if the initiator were more powerful than all of its neighbors combined. When this occurs, the target actor ceases its considerations, and action shifts back to the initiator. Usually, however, there is a candidate coalition that satisfies the three conditions, and the target actor sends out alliance bids to the relevant actors.

d. Ally Response. Each of the actors contacted by the target actor must decide if it will ally with the target actor. Each is assumed to follow the same decision process, and their decisions are considered independent of one another. The question each asks is, "Does the proposed coalition have more power than the initiator?" If so, the coalition will be joined; if not, the bid will be rejected.

This decision requires each of the potential allies independently to estimate the power of the relevant actors. If the power estimation error rates are set at zero, then all will decide to join the coalition, since their power estimates will be identical to those of the target actor. If, however, these parameters are assigned different values, then potential allies may conclude that the coalition proposed by the target actor does not contain sufficient power, and consequently they will decline membership. Since each potential ally makes its decision independently, some may decide to join while others may decline. Thus, the target nation may experience degrees of success in constructing its defensive coalition.

After the potential allies have communicated their answers to the target actor, action shifts back to the initiator.

e. Initiator Response. The initiator at this point in the action sequence may or may not be confronted with a new situation vis-à-vis the original target actor. If the target has not acquired allies, either because it deemed them unnecessary or unavailable or found the search for allies unfruitful, then the initiator, taking advantage of its perceived power advantage, will go to war against the target actor. When this happens, action shifts back to the target, and the action round continues.

Usually, however, the target nation has been able to assemble at least a partial defensive coalition, and the initiator must therefore reassess its situation. The initiator estimates the power of the target's newly acquired allies and derives the total power of the coalition now arrayed against it. If the initiator still feels that it has superiority, it will proceed with the attack on the target without additional action, and it is the target nation's turn to reassess the situation.

If, on the other hand, the target actor has been successful in assembling a defensive coalition that the *initiator* judges to be superior to itself in terms of power, then the initiator decides that some further action is required before a determination can be made whether it should attack the target. More specifically, the initiating actor that perceives itself at a disadvantage attempts to construct an offensive coalition more powerful than the defensive coalition. This search for alliance partners is subject to the same constraints and evaluated by the same three conditions outlined above. In this case, however, the relevant comparisons are based upon the estimated power of the target and its allies and the estimated power of the initiator and different candidate coalitions. If it is impossible at this stage for the initiator to design a superior coalition, it decides to break off action against the target, and the iteration ends.

If, on the other hand, it finds a coalition that satisfies the three conditions, alliance bids are sent to the relevant nations. Each of the potential allies then evaluates the proposed coalition in terms of power and decides whether or not to join, using the above criteria. After the initiator has received replies from each of its potential allies, it then reevaluates the situation. If it has received support from actors whose combined power, together with its own, is larger than that of the defensive coalition, an attack will be launched against the target nation. Action then shifts to the target nation.

If, on the other hand, the initiator's efforts to secure allies do not result in a more powerful coalition, the initiator breaks off action against the target, and the iteration ends.

f. Final Target Response. If the initiator follows up his threat with an attack upon the target, the target may, if the situation requires, appeal for additional allies. Thus, after an attack, the target nation immediately reassesses the power of the initiator and its allies, if it has acquired any, and the power of its own defensive coalition. If the target feels that it has an edge over the opposing coalition, it will not seek to add any additional allies to the current defensive coalition.

If the overall balance of power has shifted in favor of the initiator because of the addition of allies, the target actor will attempt to enlarge its defensive coalition. Once again the standards of contiguity and minimum winning are applied to the candidate enlarged coalitions, and alliance bids are sent to the appropriate actors, if a qualified enlarged coalition is determined to exist. Action then passes to those actors receiving bids, and they evaluate the proposed coalition vis-à-vis the opposing coalition, and decide to join or not to join, depending on their evaluation of the relative strengths of the two coalitions. A superior coalition will be joined; an inferior one will not. After the target nation has received answers to any alliance requests it may have sent out, the war begins in earnest.

g. War Outcomes and Costs. The outcome of the war is stochastically dependent upon the relative capabilities of the initiator and its allies and the target and its allies. This power comparison is based upon the actual power of the two sides rather than the estimated power of the opponents. The likelihood of victory for the initiator is curvilinearly related to the ratio of the power of the initiator's coalition to the power of the defensive coalition in the manner illustrated in Figure 20-3.

This figure shows three different likelihood functions generated when a controlling parameter is assigned different values. Perhaps the best way to see the effects of this parameter is to take a particular initiator–defender power ratio— three to two, for example—and note what happens to the initiator's likelihood of victory as the controlling parameter is varied. The following table gives these values.

Parameter Values	Likelihood of Victory For the Initiator
.01	.99
.05	.98
.10	.84
.20	.69
.30	.63
.50	.58
1.00	.54
10.00	.50

As we can see, increasing the parameter decreases the likelihood of victory for the initiating side with a 3:2 advantage over the defending side. There are two interpretations of what this parameter represents. It may be viewed as reflecting the importance of factors other than sheer power in the determination of war outcomes, or, to take a less deterministic view, it is the amount of inherent uncertainty in the process and outcome of war.

Once the outcome of the war has been determined, the assessment of war

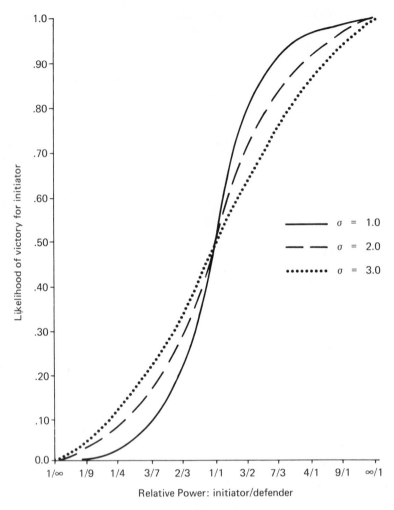

Figure 20-3. Likelihood of victory as a function of relative power.

costs begins. All participants are assessed war costs, and all suffer a decrease of power of equal proportion. The proportionate decrease in power is a function of two factors: (one) a parameter specifying the maximum level of war costs, and (two) the power parity between the opponents. The first of these factors enables us to create systems which vary in terms of the destructiveness of war. A small value would generate systems where only limited wars were possible, while a larger value would make very severe wars possible, although not inevitable.

The second factor affecting the costs of war is the relative power of the opponents. The general argument is that the more evenly matched the opponents, the more destructive the war will be (Cannizzo 1976), and hence, the higher the war costs. The particular function used is depicted in Figure 20-4. The interpretation of this function would be as follows: if the power ratio were two to one, for example—which could represent superiority for either the initiating or defending side—the war costs would be 67 percent of the maximum permissible war costs. If this latter value were 10 percent, then each participant's power base would be depreciated by 6.7 percent. The equation that generates this function is:

$$\text{Cost} = \left(1 - \frac{LSR - .5}{.5}\right) \times \text{War Costs Maximum,}$$

where LSR = $\dfrac{\text{Power of Larger Side}}{\text{Power of Smaller Side} + \text{Power of Larger Side.}}$

After each participant's power base has been depreciated, the determination and division of spoils commences.

h. Assessment and Division of Spoils. The spoils of war are composed of two conceptually distinct factors: territory and indemnities, the latter being a payment in power units. There is a critical difference between these two, in that a piece of territory has a power-producing capacity; thus, a state that receives only an indemnity acquires only a single, one-time increment in its power; but a state

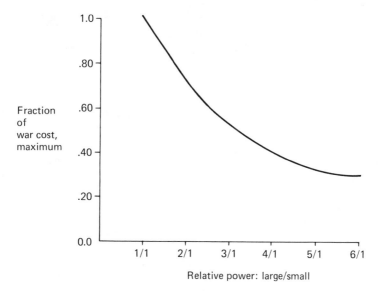

Figure 20-4. War cost function.

that acquires territory receives increments in power for as long as it holds that territory.

Turning first to the more simple indemnification process, we note that two things have to be determined. The first is the size of the indemnity and each loser's share of the indemnity. At this time, we merely postulate that each loser contributes an equal proportion of power units, as determined by the value assigned to the spoils parameter. An initial value, which has been used in several runs, for example, is 10 percent, which means that each member of the losing side contributes 10 percent of its power base to the "pot." Higher or lower values would represent harsher or more lenient terms of peace.

The next task is to divide the indemnity among the victors. Here we assume that the proportion of the indemnity a victorious state receives is equal to its proportionate share of the total power present in the winning coalition. Thus, more powerful members of the coalition receive more of the spoils than less powerful members.

The process of determining how much territory is to be lost and acquired is much more complicated than the indemnification process. In order to make the problem of territorial change manageable, we assume that only the initial member of the losing side suffers a loss of territory; that is, either the state that precipitated the conflict or the state that was the target initially. Thus, although the allies of the defeated state lose power, they do not yield territory. The amount of territory that the losing state must cede depends upon its size and the decisiveness of the defeat. If a state is composed of only one territorial unit, it loses all of its territory and ceases to exist. On the other hand, if a state is composed of many units and is only narrowly defeated in a war, it may have to give up only one or two of its units to the victors. Of course, if a large actor suffers a dramatic defeat, it will lose a substantial portion of its territory. Once the number of territorial units to be ceded is computed, the distribution of this territory among the victors begins.

The division of territorial acquisitions is guided by two principles. First, as with the division of the indemnity, more powerful members of the winning coalition receive proportionately more of the ceded territory than less powerful members. Thus, if a state constitutes one-half of the power in a coalition, it will receive roughly one-half of the territory. This guideline provides us with a desirable division of territory, but often it is not possible to achieve this because of the indivisibility of the basic territorial units and the limitations imposed by the second basic principle.

The second principle is difficult to state succinctly. It stems from Gestalt considerations of "good form." Perhaps the best way of explaining this set of constraints is to outline some of the territorial configurations we did not consider "good form." First, we did not want states to emerge that were composed of many noncontiguous pieces; therefore, a state is permitted to annex only contiguous territories. Second, we did not want states that were spread out and not compact, such as "serpentine" states; therefore, the algorithm seeks to minimize the length of a state's borders for a given area. After considerable effort, we were able to develop a set of heuristic rules that seem to produce territorial configurations with a significant amount of face validity.

    i. Power Adjustments.   The final step in an iteration of the simulation model involves increasing the power of each actor in the system, regardless of whether or not a war has occurred. Each territorial unit is considered to have a power-generating capability of 3 percent per iteration. Thus, whatever state controls a particular territorial unit at the end of a particular iteration receives an increment in its power equal to 3 percent of the unit's *initial* power value. After these power adjustments have been made, a new initiator is selected and another iteration begins.

    Let us now turn to the question of what type of behavior these decision rules produce.

4. A TYPICAL RUN

Pending the completion of a rather extensive set of simulation runs, our conclusions about the behavior of the model must be very tentative. It may be useful, however, to examine a single run of the model in some detail in order to provide some sense as to the nature of the model's dynamic properties.

    Figure 20-1 shows the starting 98-state geographical configuration used for this run. The initial power values were stochastically generated according to a normal distribution with a mean of 100 and a standard deviation of 20, thus making the initial power disparity rather small. For this run, the power calculation error rates were set to zero, which has the effect of giving each state the ability accurately to estimate the power of all others.

    The parameter governing the outcomes of wars was given the value of .10. This introduces a relatively low amount of uncertainty in the outcome of wars; that is, relative capability is considered to be a very important factor in the determination of victory or defeat. The maximum war cost parameter was assigned the value of .10 for this run, thus permitting only moderately severe wars. Similarly, the spoils parameter was set at .10, which prescribes that the terms of peace will be only moderately severe. The power increment factor was set at 3 percent of the initial power per iteration.

    Figures 20-5 through 20-15 show the territorial configurations that developed over the course of the 268 iteration run. By the end of the first 50 iterations, as illustrated in Figure 20-5, some territorial expansion has occurred. The number of states has dropped from the original 98 to 64, and a few actors, notably JB and UC, have been substantially enlarged. The unification process continues, and by iteration 100, seen in Figure 20-6, 41 actors remain in the system. At this point, about ten major actors are emerging: EB, NB, PB, GB, OB, UC, GD, FD,

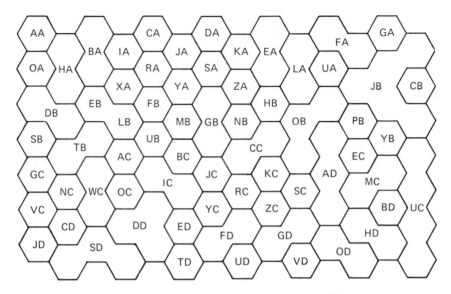

Figure 20-5. Map of system at iteration 50.

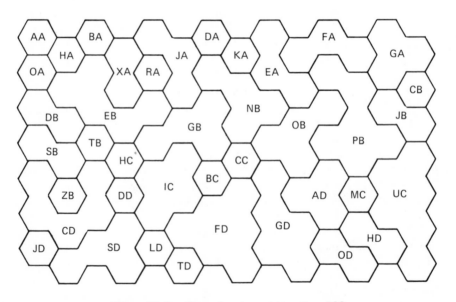

Figure 20-6. Map of system at iteration 100.

IC, and CD. Note that JB has declined in territory since the fiftieth iteration. This ebb and flow phenomenon is common during the first 100 or so iterations of a run.

Figure 20-7 portrays the territorial configuration after 125 iterations. Ten states have five or more territorial units–CD, PB, GD, FD, EB, NB, UC, GB, OB, and SD. CD has gained the most territory in the intervening 25 iterations. As we can see from Figure 20-8, there have been dramatic changes in the territorial configuration by iteration 155. Two actors, NB and CD, have grown dramatically; together they control about one-third of the total space. Other actors, such as SD, EB, GD, and UC, have remained relatively large or made significant acquisitions. At this stage, 26 actors remain in the system.

Six iterations later, the situation revealed in Figure 20-9 has changed in slight but significant ways. NB and SD have both lost substantial territory to CD and GD, but most noteworthy is the surrounding of YA by CD. This can occur because of the rule that only the initiator or the primary defender may lose territory in a war. Since YA was not in that position during the intervening six iterations, it retains its territorial integrity. What is most interesting about this situation is that for the next 80 or so iterations, CD persistently attempts to capture YA but is deterred by the defensive coalition that YA is able to put together from those states surrounding CD. It is almost as if YA is under siege from CD and is able to continue its independent existence thanks to continued pressure from CD's other neighbors. At one level of abstraction, this simulated situation is not unlike the status of West Berlin.

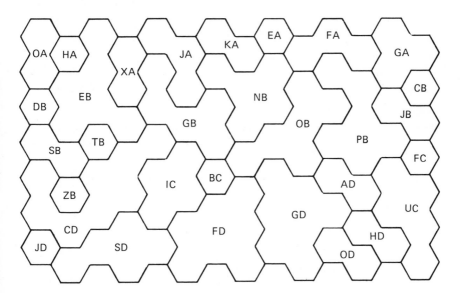

Figure 20-7.   Map of system at iteration 125.

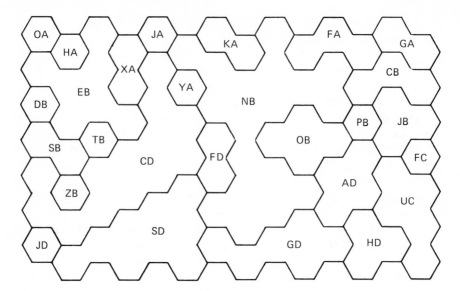

Figure 20-8. Map of system at iteration 155.

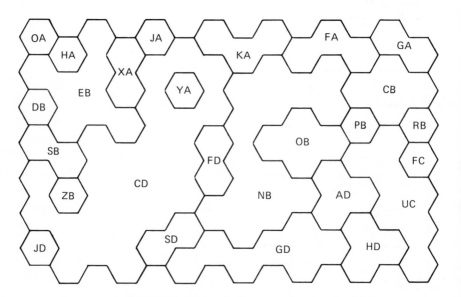

Figure 20-9. Map of system at iteration 161.

By iteration 193, shown in Figure 20-10, NB has been able to recover some of its territory and expand into new areas. CB, KA, AD, OB, and GD are the states that yielded a large part of their territory to NB, while UC and FA have made minor acquisitions. By contrast, CD has acquired only one territorial unit during the 32 iterations between Figure 20-9 and Figure 20-10. As indicated above, CD's main effort during this time is directed against YA, and this effort is continually blocked.

Figure 20-11 reveals the geographical situation ten iterations later. FA and UC have seized much of NB's newly acquired territory, with FA exhibiting the most dramatic growth. Once again, CD has not made any acquisitions during the intervening iterations.

Figure 20-12 shows the situation at iteration 217, and it shows FA at the peak of its territorial control, acquired largely at the expense of NB.

The ebb and flow nature of the action of the model is quite clear if Figures 20-12 and 20-13 are compared. By iteration 230, FA has been substantially reduced, with GA, UC, OB, and FD the principal beneficiaries.

Moving on to iteration 244, we note that the territorial configurations in Figures 20-13 and 20-14 are quite similar, but there is a crucial difference. YA has at long last been conquered by CD. This is an important transition point, because it means that YA was no longer able to put together a coalition with sufficient power to block CD. One explanation for this is that the defenders of YA have, through the course of their struggles with one another, weakened themselves significantly. As we can see, even at this point FA has succumbed to CD's assaults.

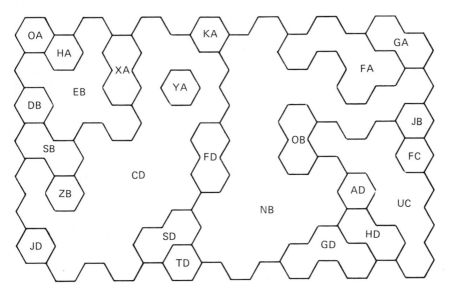

Figure 20-10.   Map of system at iteration 193.

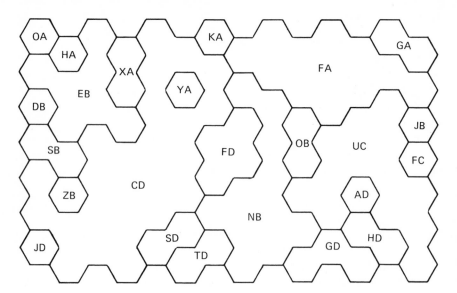

Figure 20-11.   Map of system at iteration 203.

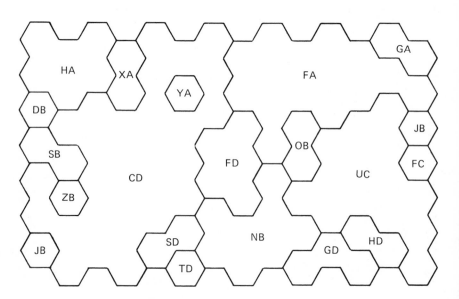

Figure 20-12.   Map of system at iteration 217.

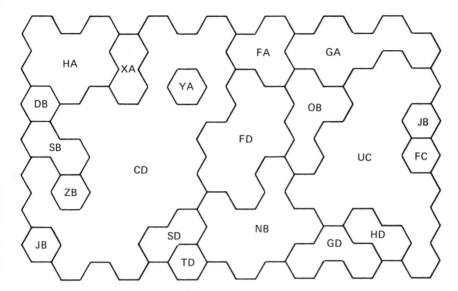

Figure 20-13. Map of system at iteration 230.

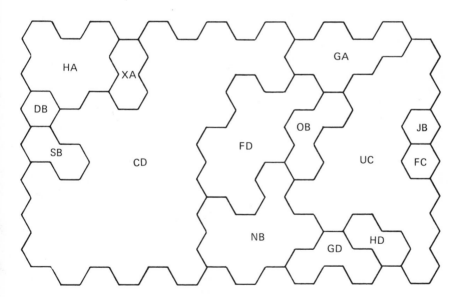

Figure 20-14. Map of system at iteration 244.

The remaining figures, 20-15, 20-16, 20-17, and 20-18, reveal what might be called CD's "end game." It is a kind of mopping-up operation where CD absorbs the remaining thirteen states. In Figure 20-16 we see HA alone confronting CD, and in Figure 20-17 HA scores a significant victory over CD. But, alas, Figure 20-18 reveals that HA's efforts ultimately proved to no avail.

The empire of CD is established.

(CURTAIN DESCENDS.)

It is difficult to appreciate fully the nature of a dynamic process by merely examining the status of the system at a few time slices. It is rather like trying to understand what a film is about when all one has is a handful of frames drawn from various points in the picture. We hope, nevertheless, that the more modest objective of conveying a sense of how the model behaves has been achieved.

In the next section we will consider some statistical profiles of the simulation run in order to illuminate some macrodynamics of the simulation model.

5. SOME TENTATIVE GENERALIZATIONS

Our purpose here is to put forth some tentative generalizations about the overall behavior of the model. They must be tentative in nature, since only a limited number of runs of the model have been completed as of this writing. In the future we plan to conduct a larger set of runs, and at that point we will be

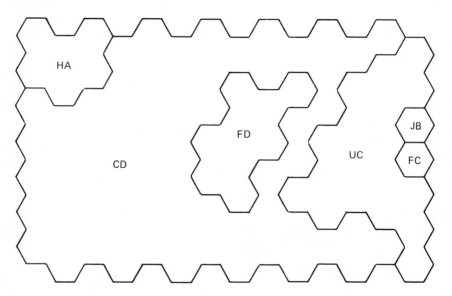

Figure 20-15.   Map of system at iteration 248.

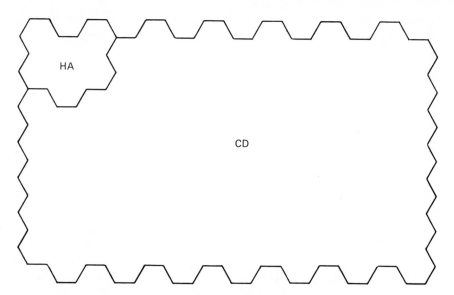

Figure 20-16. Map of system at iteration 263.

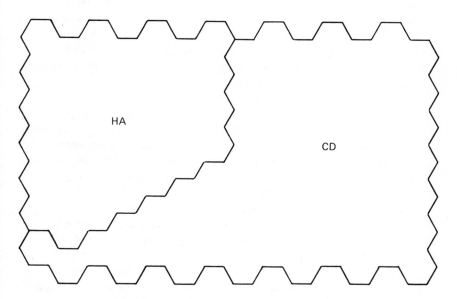

Figure 20-17. Map of system at iteration 264.

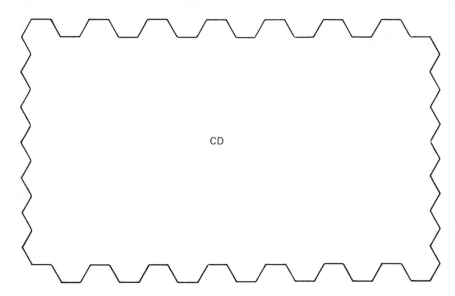

Figure 20-18.   Map of system at iteration 268.

in a better position to evaluate the general statements that follow. With this caveat in mind, let us turn to the generalizations.

The first and most obvious observation we have been able to make is that our simulation model, if permitted to run its full course, almost always ends in empire, and it is our experience that it usually occurs before iteration 300. In one sense, this is not surprising since all closed dynamic systems will reach a steady state of some kind eventually, including, of course, the total destruction and disintegration of the system itself. The fact remains, however, that most of the theorists who provided the basic elements of the model's structure believed that faithful adherence to their rules of conduct was essential to the prevention of imperial domination. The model's behavior suggests that the conditions under which a multistate system will retain its multistate nature for an extended period of time are unique. It also suggests that if political entities act according to the dictates of "realism," the consequence for the vast majority is extinction, not survival. The seemingly inexorable movement toward empire may be similar to the tendency for laissez-faire economic systems to move from open competition toward monopoly. By some economists' reasoning, this movement toward monopoly capitalism can only be prevented by the intervention of an outside agent, such as government.

One might inquire at this point as to how realistic this movement toward empire is, in light of historical phenomena. Several of the multistate systems of the past did in fact culminate in empires. During the period of approximately 700 B.C. to 200 B.C., the multistate system of ancient China underwent a transformation not unlike the one portrayed above. The ultimate rise of the Ch'in dynasty and the subsequent integration of China brought an end to centuries of incessant war and ushered in a golden age of Chinese culture. In a similar but less dramatic way, the pattern was repeated in northern India during the period of roughly 550 B.C. to 250 B.C. Again a long period of intense interstate rivalry and conflict was brought to an end by Chandragupta's establishment of the Maurya dynasty, uniting northern India for the first time from Herat in the west to the Ganges delta in the east. Both of these systems were relatively isolated from outside extrasystemic actors and were, therefore, able to reach what may be called their equilibrium states.

Several multistate systems did not move inexorably toward empire. The Greek city state system and the Italian Renaissance system are two cases where the "normal" process of integration was retarded for a long period of time. It is noteworthy that these systems were both penetrated by powerful external actors during their balance of power periods. Often these external actors were invited to intervene in the system's affairs by one of its members in order to redress a perceived imbalance of power within the system. The disruption that resulted from the relatively sudden introduction of a powerful actor or actors took several forms. The Greeks found themselves dominated by a succession of empires, while the Italians were caught up in the major power intrigues of France, Spain, and Austria.

These historical sketches do not by any means demonstrate that the computer model is valid. Our intention is merely to show that there are historical parallels to the kind of behavior that the simulation model produces. It appears that one critical difference between those multistate systems that end in empire and those that do not is that the former are allowed to develop in isolation while the latter are not. We should hasten to add the obvious point that empires do not last forever, and our model, in its current level of development, says very little about the dissolution of empires. We will return to this consideration below. Let us turn now to the second set of general observations concerning the behavior of the model.

A typical run of the simulation model can be divided into three fairly distinct phases. Each phase has a different set of emergent properties, and, to a significant extent, each phase corresponds to a different type of interstate system. Before we present a rather detailed examination of how these phases differ from one another, it will first be useful to consider a general overview of each.

Phase one is a period of *political unification,* and it is characterized by the slow but steady growth of many states by small territorial acquisitions. This process seems to be quite similar to the stage of political development Organski refers to as primitive unification. He notes that in Europe, for example, the problem of "establishing central political rule" was "generally solved brutally and unimaginatively through military conquest" (1965, p. 8). There is also a strong similarity between Phase one of the simulation run and the nation-building activities described by Tilly (1975).

Phase two of a simulation run has many of the characteristics associated with a *balance of power* system. The slow process of political unification yields five to seven states that are significantly more powerful than the remaining states in the system, and the action of the simulation is largely dominated by the parrying and thrusting of this major power oligarchy. Very often during this phase a power that threatens to dominate the system is blocked by a coalition of opposing powers, which, as Gulick (1955) notes, is a behavioral manifestation of a balance of power system. Eventually, however, the blocking coalition loses its power advantage, largely because of conflict within the coalition itself. At this point, the third and final phase begins.

Phase three, which might be called the period of *imperial consolidation,* is characterized by a series of large territorial conquests by the dominant state that has emerged from the balance of power phase. Following the strategy of divide and conquer, the imperial state is able to eliminate and absorb the remaining states in the system.

Before turning to an examination of quantitative indicators of the transformations sketched above, we want to pause to discuss some of the broader implications of these transformations. Kaplan (1957a) postulated a set of international systems, each characterized by a unique set of decision rules. According to Kaplan, system transformations occur when these rules are violated and are followed by a new set of decision rules that specify a new system. Our research suggests that a shift in decision rules is *not* necessary for a system transformation to occur. That is, the simulation model is able to produce a series of systems that are quite different structurally and behaviorally *without changing any of the decision rules* that guide the behavior of individual states.

This point is worth emphasizing, since all too often we are led to believe that a marked alteration in the appearance of an interstate system stems from a change in the characteristic behavior—i.e., decision rules—of the component states. This research suggests another interpretation. A given set of decision rules operating over time will modify the environment in which they operate, and the conjunction of the altered environment and the unaltered decision rules produce a transformation of the system. Having laid out the overall developmental sequence in one simulation run and suggested why we think these changes are important from a theoretical point of view, let us turn to an examination of the statistical profile of the simulation run described above.

a. The Size of the System. By size we simply mean the number of independent actors that are in the system at the beginning of any particular iteration. Figure 20-19 reveals the number of states present in the system at each iteration of the 268–iteration run described above. From iterations one through 150, we see a rather steady decline in the size of the system. This is the political unification phase discussed above, and it represents the gradual aggregation of individual units into compound states. This contrasts quite sharply with the period

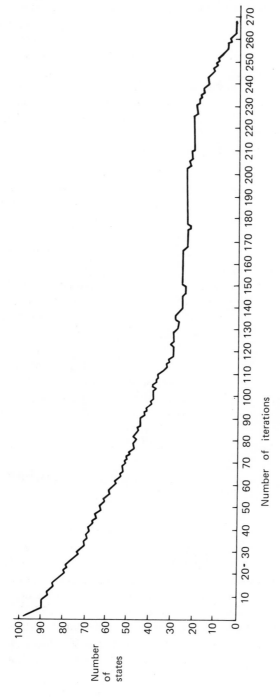

Figure 20-19.   Size of system over time.

that follows, when the size of the system seems to stabilize between iterations 150 and 230. This corresponds to the balance of power phase, with approximately 25 states present throughout the period. The final phase, covering iterations 231 through 268, is the period of imperial consolidation, when CD absorbs the remaining actors.

Clearly the most interesting aspect of this figure is the relatively stable system size during the middle period. As we indicated earlier, this period is characterized by five to seven major powers, and the interruption of the gradual process of integration is due to the tendency for these powerful actors to block any attempts at territorial acquisition by other powerful actors.

b. The Relative Frequency of War. The relative frequency of war differs markedly over the three phases. In the first phase, war occurs in 119 of the 150 iterations, revealing that war takes place in slightly under 80 percent of the action rounds in the political unification phase. During the balance of power phase, corresponding roughly to iterations 151 through 230, the incidence of war drops markedly. War takes place in only 30 of the 80 iterations, or somewhat under 40 percent of the action rounds. The last period reveals a rise in the frequency of war. During the imperial consolidation phase, war occurs in 26 of the 38 iterations, yielding a relative frequency somewhat under 70 percent.

When we turn to the question of whether the initiating or defending side tends to be victorious when war occurs, we find that the initiating side won 54 of the 119 wars, or 45 percent, in the political unification phase, and fourteen of the 30 wars, or 47 percent, in the balance of power phase. In the final phase, however, the initiating side won 21 out of the 26 wars, or about 81 percent.

Taken together, then, these results reveal three distinct patterns. In Phase one, war is frequent and the defending side has marginally greater probability of victory. In Phase two, war is decidedly less frequent, but the defending side still has a slight edge with respect to the probability of victory. In Phase three, however, war increases in frequency and the initiating side is substantially more likely to be victorious than the defending side.

c. Alliance Activity. During the first 150 iterations of the simulation run, which roughly corresponds to the political unification phase, a state decides to take action against another 126 times. In each of these cases, the defending state is successful in building a defensive coalition. The average size of this coalition, not counting the target nation itself, is 2.3 states. The initiator is joined in 119 of the action rounds, and on the average 1.1 states ally with the initiator. The modal alliance pattern during this first phase is two initiating states against three defending states. The largest defending coalition during this phase is composed of six states, and occurs only once. The largest initiating coalition is composed of three states.

During the Balance of Power phase, a state decides to take action against another in 67 of the 80 iterations. In 65 of these 67 instances, the defending state assembles a coalition and is joined, on the average, by 3.6 states. The initiating state, however, is much less likely to gain allies during this phase; it is joined in 28 of the 67 confrontations that occur during this phase, or about 42 percent, and rarely do these alliances involve more than the addition of a single state. The modal alliance pattern is two initiating states facing four or five defending states. The largest initiating coalition is composed of four states and occurs once. The largest defending coalition, in contrast, is composed of nine states, and coalitions of approximately this size are relatively common.

Alliance activity is significantly lower in the imperial unification period, as might be expected. A state undertakes action against another state in 35 of the 38 iterations, and this action is met by the construction of a defensive coalition in only twelve instances, or about one-third of the time. When the defender is joined, the average number of states joining is 1.8. The initiator seeks and acquires allies in only three instances, twice adding one ally and once adding two.

In sum, then, alliances are frequently constructed during the political unification phase, although they tend to be relatively small. In the balance of power phase, defensive coalitions tend to be large and frequently formed, while initiating alliances are less frequent and smaller, and in the final phase, alliances tend not to occur at all.

A review of the above indicators reveals that there are discernible differences between the behavioral profiles of the phases of the simulation run. During the period of steady incremental integration, wars and alliances are frequent, but involve relatively few members of the state system. At some point, the pace of expansion and integration slows, apparently when five to seven major powers have emerged, and the system becomes significantly more peaceful. Alliances are primarily defensive in nature and tend to be large. Ultimately, the balance of power is upset, and the period of imperial consolidation begins. In this last period, wars are a frequent occurrence, but alliances are not. Only future experimental work will reveal whether this pattern characterizes the behavior of the simulation model in general. At this point, we would like to reflect on some of the theoretical concerns raised in the introduction. A primary concern was with the means by which stability can be achieved in multistate systems and, in particular, the process that assumes automatic stabilization. Our tentative conclusion is that, for a limited period of time, stability can be achieved in a multistate system without any actor in the system having as its objective the maintenance of that stability. Thus, it appears that the automatic process can work for a limited period of time. Further research is needed to discover whether the period of relative stability is lengthened or shortened under different initial conditions and/or parameter settings.

As we indicated earlier, an extensive set of experiments on the model has not yet been conducted, but in the next section of the paper we will report some findings derived from a set of simulation runs designed to explore the implications of different degrees of accuracy in power estimation.

6. A PRELIMINARY EXPERIMENT

A model with many parameters, such as ours, offers a variety of experimental options, and in this preliminary report we chose to focus upon some simple variations in the accuracy of the power estimates made by states. We selected this area for two reasons; first, the need to estimate power accurately is a prominent theme in the literature that served as an inspiriation for the model. Realist thinkers, both classical and modern, emphasize that the effective statesman is, among other things, a shrewd power estimator. Our second reason for focusing on this process stems from our intimate knowledge of the structure of the model. A large number of critical decisions made by simulated actors—most important, to attack or not to attack and to ally or not to ally—depend heavily upon the estimation of power.

For this experiment, we chose to use as our initial configuration, not the 98-state system presented in Figure 20-1, but rather the 20-state system pictured in Figure 20-2. This latter configuration was obtained as an intermediate result of a 98-state run and is typical of simulated systems passing from the political unification phase into the balance of power phase. For this set of simulation runs, the parameters of the model were assigned the same values as those given above, with the exception of the power estimation error rates.

The experimental design for the simulation runs was as follows: six runs, using different random number seeds, were conducted under each of three power-estimating conditions, yielding a total of eighteen runs of the simulation. The first six runs were assigned a zero error rate in the power estimation process, while the second and third sets of six runs were conducted with 5 percent and 10 percent error rates, respectively. A zero error rate, as we indicated above, means that all power estimates are correct. The 5 and 10 percent error rates require some further elaboration, and perhaps the easiest way to provide this is by example. Let us assume that state A is trying to estimate the power of state B, and state B's true power is 100 units. If state A is operating under a 5 percent error rate, this means that the standard error of its prediction would be (.05 × 100) or five units. We assume in the model that power estimates are normally distributed, and in this example, A's estimates of B's power would have a mean of 100 and a standard deviation of five. Thus, the probability that A will arrive at an estimate of B's power that is between 95 and 105 units is about two-thirds. The actual value is determined by a normal random generator. If a 10 percent error rate is in force, then the standard error in the above example would be one-tenth of the true power, or ten power units. It should be noted that a larger error rate produces a wider dispersion of power estimates and that overestimation and underestimation are equally likely. As it presently stands, the model permits us to set the relative likelihoods of under- and overestimation at any ratio we desire, and for this set of runs we decided to make them equally probable results.

Quite obviously we can not present a detailed discussion of each of these eighteen runs, but we can outline the essential differences between the three sets of simulation runs.

1. If error is present in the power estimation process, actors selected as initiators are marginally less likely to threaten neighboring states than if power estimates are accurate. The relative frequencies of initiator action per iteration are .869, .853, and .857 for the 0, 5, and 10 percent error rates respectively. The effect is slight and apparently not directly related to the magnitude of error introduced.

2. If a state is threatened by another, its response, when error is introduced into power estimates, is to seek *fewer* alliance partners than when no error is present. The average number of alliance bids sent for the 0, 5, and 10 percent rates of error are 1.58, 1.32, and 1.44. Once again, the magnitude of the difference is not directly related to the amount of error.

3. When error is present in the power estimation process, the rate of alliance bid acceptance in the first round of alliance formation is *lower* than when error is absent. The rates for the 0, 5, and 10 percent conditions are 1.00, .86, and .83, respectively, indicating that the decline is directly related to the magnitude of error. The net result of this finding and the previous one is that the defending state's initial coalition is *smaller* when error is present in the power estimation process.

4. The initiator's subsequent response when estimation error is introduced is to seek *fewer* allies than when it is excluded; the average number of alliance bids sent by initiators is .64 for no error and .49 and .50 for the 5 and 10 percent error conditions. The rate of acceptance for these alliance bids is noticeably *lower* with the estimation error. The relative acceptance frequencies for the 0, 5, and 10 percent rates are 1.00, .91, and .86. Once again, the overall result is that the assembled coalition is *smaller,* on the average, when error is allowed to enter the power estimation process.

5. If the initiating state decides to follow up on its threat with war, then the defending state has an opportunity to add additional allies to its coalition. Interestingly, the average number of alliance bids sent by the defending state in this last round of coalition activity is directly related to the magnitude of error. The averages are .65, .76, and .83 for the 0, 5, and 10 percent error rates, respectively. This effect is offset by the reduced likelihood of bid acceptance under the error conditions. The mean acceptance rate is 1.00 for no error, .87 for 5 percent error, and .83 for 10 percent error.

6. The relative frequency of war is *lower* in systems with error in the power estimation process. Wars occur in about 64 percent of the iterations with no error, while this figure drops to 60 and 59 percent for the 5 and 10 percent error conditions, respectively. This drop is attributable to a decrease in the probability that a state, if selected as an initiator, will threaten another and to

an increase in the probability that an initiating state will break off action after the first round of alliance-building activity by the defending state. It is noteworthy, however, that if a war does occur, the probability that the initiating side will be victorious is greater when error is present in the power estimation process. The relative frequencies of victory for the initiator's coalition are .568 for no error, .572 for 5 percent error, and .621 for 10 percent error.

7. Given the above findings, it is not surprising that simulation runs with error in the power estimation process are *longer,* on the average, than those without error. Runs without estimation error end in empire after 90 iterations, while the inclusion of error extends this to an average lifespan of 103 iterations. Given that there is relatively little variation in the length of the imperial consolidation phase, this finding suggests that the inclusion of error in the power estimation process prolongs the balance of power phase; or, to put it a different way, the period of system stability is *longer* when the decision-making units are *less accurate* in estimating the power of states. We should hasten to add, however, that the difference between the length of the 5 and 10 percent error runs is negligeable, indicating that the presence of a moderate degree of error may be more important than the degree of such error.

The pattern that emerges when all these findings are considered together is that states appear to behave in a "cautious" manner when power estimation error is present. They take action less often, participate in alliances less frequently, and terminate conflicts at a stage short of war more often, with the result that international systems with poorer power estimators are less conflictual and are stable for a longer period of time, than those comprising better power estimators. This conclusion must remain tentative until we undertake additional simulation runs; nevertheless, we think it is an interesting discovery since it suggests that "traditional wisdom" is in error when it implies that peace and stability follow from shrewd power estimation. Indeed, the preservation of a multistate system may depend more on folly, ignorance, and error than on prudence, intelligence, and precision. It is a hypothesis worth considering.

7. DIRECTIONS FOR FUTURE RESEARCH

At this moment, we see four main avenues for future research, and although they are, in principle, not mutually exclusive, time and resource constraints make it unlikely that we will be able to explore all of them in the near future.

The first alternative open to us, and the one we intend to follow in the near future, is to freeze the development of the model as it presently stands and conduct a more extensive set of simulation runs. This would serve two purposes. First, given that the model relies upon stochastic factors in several important areas, a single run of the model under a particular set of conditions may not be a reliable indicator of its overall behavior. Thus, in order to establish the veracity of the tentative generalizations offered above, it is necessary to conduct several replications of each simulation run.

The second purpose to be served by an extensive set of simulation runs is to be able to ascertain the effect of different initial conditions and parameter values on the behavior of the model. Among the factors we are interested in varying are the initial distribution of power, the power calculation error rates, the initial spatial configuration, and those parameters that govern such factors as victory determination, war costs, and spoils. In our view, each of these variations represents an interesting theoretical problem.

A second avenue for future research would involve empirically estimating the parameters of the model and assessing its validity with respect to a particular spatial-temporal domain. This would in turn depend upon the existence of a large data base, and, given available data, this would restrict our time perspective to the post-Napoleonic years. Unfortunately, the century and a half, 1816-1970, does not appear to have many truly multistate systems that remain isolated for a relatively long period of time.

In spite of these problems, some initial work has been done that can serve as a basis for future estimation efforts. Mihalka (1976a, 1976b) has conducted research on the effects of power, alliances, and contiguity on the likelihood of interstate hostilities and war for the states of Europe during the period 1816-1970. Gochman's (1975) research on the major powers during the same period has a similar focus. Cannizzo (1976) has investigated the impact of power, alliances, and spatial factors on the duration and deadliness of interstate wars during the same 150-year period, as well as the relationship between relative capability and victory. Sabrosky's research (1975) on the circumstances under which alliances are honored or not would also be relevant, and Starr's (1972) study of war coalitions and the postwar distribution of spoils might be helpful. The estimation of war costs could be based, in part, upon Wheeler's (1975) work on the effects of war on certain sectors of economic activity.

As impressive as this partial list of relevant studies might be, it is not simply a matter of incorporating their results directly into the simulation model. For one thing, these studies, understandably, do not provide answers to the questions in precisely the way in which we need them, and therefore, considerable effort would have to be directed toward integrating these empirical results with the theoretical structure of the model. This research possibility does, however, have a high priority on our agenda.

Another avenue of research available to us is to create alternate theoretical structures for certain processes that are presently in the model. Our objective would be to discover the consequences of different sets of decision rules for the overall behavior of the model. One example that comes immediately to mind is the rules which govern the coalition process. At present, these are of a quasi-minimum winning nature; but many other formulations could be distilled from the sizable theoretical literature on coalition formation. As intriguing as this endeavor might be, it is not something we contemplate undertaking in the immediate future.

The last main direction for future research entails extending and expanding the present structure of the model to include processes and behaviors not now present, and we have received a large number of suggestions along this line. In terms of our theoretical concerns, one of the most interesting areas for development would be the addition of actors that behave in accordance with decision rules that incorporate system-preserving norms. As we indicated in the introduction, the principal difference between the three stabilization processes is the number of such actors required to maintain a stable system. If we were able to develop and program a set of decision rules for system-preserving actors, we would be able to compare the three models under identical conditions. There are, of course, a large number of other modifications that have occurred to us (and others) at one time or another, but we think we need to know more about the model as it presently stands before we follow this avenue of research.

We began this paper by noting that this was only a preliminary report on a research project that is in its early stages. In spite of this, we think the model has great potential for both integrating and synthesizing our empirically based knowledge and enabling us to better understand the dynamic nature of complex international systems.

8. REFERENCES

Bremer, Stuart A. (1975). "The Powerful and the War-Prone: Relative National Capability and War Involvement, 1820–1964." Ann Arbor, Michigan: Mental Health Research Institute, mimeo.

Cannizzo, Cynthia A. (1976). "The Costs of Combat: A Statistical Model for Predicting the Cost and Outcome of Interstate War, 1916–1965." Ann Arbor: University of Michigan, unpublished Ph.D. Thesis.

Claude, Inis L., Jr. (1962). *Power and International Relations.* New York: Random House.

East, Maurice (1973). "Size and Foreign Policy Behavior: A Test of Two Models," *World Politics* 25:4 (July), pp. 556–576.

Gochman, Charles S. (1975). "Status, Conflict, and War: The Major Powers, 1820–1970." Ann Arbor: University of Michigan, unpublished Ph.D. Thesis.

Gulick, Edward V. (1955). *Europe's Classical Balance of Power.* Ithaca, N.Y.: Cornell University Press.

Kaplan, Morton (1957a). *System and Process in International Politics.* New York: John Wiley and Sons.

Kaplan, Morton (1957b). "Balance of Power, Bipolarity, and Other Models of International Systems," *American Political Science Review* 51:3 (September).

Masters, Roger D. (1964). "World Politics as a Primitive Political System," *World Politics* 16:4 (July), pp. 595–619.

Mattingly, Garret (1955). *Renaissance Diplomacy.* London: Jonathan Cape.

McGowan, Patrick J. and Howard B. Shapiro (1973). *The Comparative Study of Foreign Policy.* Beveraly Hills, Calif.: Sage Publications.

Mihalka, Michael (1976a). "Hostilities in the European State System, 1816–1970." *Peace Science Society (International) Papers* 26.

Mihalka, Michael (1976b). "Hostilities and War in the European State System, 1816–1970." Ann Arbor: University of Michigan, unpublished Ph.D. Thesis.

Organski, A.F.K. (1965). *The Stages of Political Development.* New York: Alfred A. Knopf.

Riker, William H. (1962). *The Theory of Political Coalitions.* New Haven: Yale University Press.

Rummel, Rudolph J. (1969). "Some Empirical Findings on Nations and Their Behavior," *World Politics* 21:2 (January), pp. 226–241.

Sabrosky, Alan N. (1975). "The War Performance of Peacetime Allies." Washington, D.C.: Paper presented. International Studies Association Annual Meetings.

Salmore, Stephan A. and Charles F. Hermann (1969). "The Effect of Size, Development, and Accountability on Foreign Policy," *Peace Research Society (International) Papers* 14, pp. 15–30.

Starr, Harvey (1972). *War Coalitions and the Distribution of Payoffs and Losses.* Lexington, Mass.: D.C. Heath, Lexington Books.

Tilly, Charles, ed. (1975). *The Formation of National States in Western Europe.* Princeton: Princeton University Press.

Walker, Richard L. (1953). *The Multi-State System of Ancient China.* Hamden, Conn.: The Shoe String Press.

Waltz, Kenneth N. (1959). *Man, the State, and War.* New York: Columbia University Press.

Wheeler, Hugh G. (1975). "The Effects of War on Industrial Growth: 1816–1965." Ann Arbor: University of Michigan, Unpublished Ph.D. Thesis.

Wright, Quincy (1965). *A Study of War.* Second Edition. Chicago: University of Chicago Press.

✳ *Chapter 21*

Societal Development as the Quintessence of World Development

P.N. Rastogi

This paper advances the thesis that national societies are the logical units of analysis in a study of the world system. Salient elements of this thesis may be outlined as follows:

1. National societies are the coherent socio-politico-economico-cultural collectivities of mankind. They serve as the anchors of self-reference and identification for the populace of the globe.
2. Problems and predicaments of mankind are the problems and predicaments of specific societies and groups of societies facing similar problems.
3. These problems and predicaments involve a complex interaction of demographic, economic, ecological, military, political, psychological, and social factors. This interaction differentially affects different societies. The problems of each society are, to that extent, unique and specific. Problems of energy and pollution, food and natural resources, capital and technology affect different societies unequally. No two societies face identical problems.
4. Sources of mankind's many and diverse problems lie in the internal functioning of national societies and their relationships with one another. Military tension and conflict, increasing price and scarcity of vital commodities and materials, deteriorating terms of trade, pressures of population growth, poor administration and internal divisive schisms induce and aggravate the constraints of vulnerable societal systems. Poverty, unemployment, inflation, public unrest, and social tensions afflict large sections of mankind in consequence.

This paper was contributed to the Tenth World Congress of Political Science at Edinburgh in August 1976.

5. Implementation of solution measures on global, regional, and societal scales has to be carried out ultimately by the national governments. The ability of these governments to undertake and execute long-term programs of development in a sustained manner depends on their stability. Governmental stability is a precondition for the solution of severe and chronic problems that require difficult, long-range decisions and actions. Stability of governments (*GS*) is affected by and affects the dynamics of system processes within societies.

6. Stability of governments is a part of the larger problem of political instability in societal systems. Political stability cannot exist in societies with low viability (*Z*). High levels of politico-military pressure, population growth, unemployment, inflation, internal divisiveness, and civil unrest and low levels of administrative efficiency, political leadership, economic growth, and education lower the viability of societal systems. The lower the viability of a society, the more serious the problem of political instability and the resultant indigenous incapacity for development there.

7. Goals of world development are made of the goals of societal development. Human welfare at the world level is synonymous with the development of the world's societies.

8. The concept of societal development is generically different from, and more inclusive than, the concept of economic development. Societal development incorporates social, political, and psychological facets in addition to economic ones. It stands for the movement of societal systems toward peace and cooperation among themselves, economic well-being and communal harmony among their citizens, political stability and administrative effectiveness of their governments and the advancement of their knowledge base for the service of mankind.

9. Validation of the diagnosis and prognosis of the world's future course(s) can come only from the verifiable predictive inference and retrodictive confirmation of the events and processes occurring in specific societies of the global regions. Gaps in knowledge, errors of estimation, and incomplete availability of required information render any attempt in this direction inherently speculative unless it consistently meets the criteria of time-specific confirmation in the past, present, and near future of specific societies.

This paper is accordingly based on the following three orienting principles:

1. The status and course of the world and its regions require for their proper study a knowledge of the statuses and courses of their constituent societal systems.

2. A world system of development must be based on the generic concept of societal development including the intersocietal relationships of peace and cooperation.

3. Validation of theory, methodology, and results of a world model depends on an unambiguous and time-specific confirmation of a comparable set of events and processes in all societal systems of a region and the globe.

In what follows, an invariant cybernetic model of societal systems is outlined. The nature of the verifiable inferences obtainable is illustrated with reference to past, present, and future time paths (1960-1980) of four very diverse societies— Brazil, India, Nigeria, and the United States.[1] The concept of societal development and its relation to world development is discussed briefly. Performance panels for societies are presented, based on the output of system simulation and depicting the time-varying course of societal variables and viability (Z). They can perform the task of status monitoring, planning, and early warning systems for societies and mankind. A world model, then, is seen as a composite of the performance panels of societies, the classification of societies according to their viability status, and the time-varying indices of regional and global viability.

1. THE DYNAMICS OF SOCIETAL SYSTEMS: A BRIEF OVERVIEW OF THEORY AND METHODOLOGY

Society is a complex adaptive system of interacting institutional processes. Government, as the regulatory subsystem of society, is confronted with a number of internal and external disturbances and stresses that strain its regulating capacity. Together these disturbances and stresses constitute a destabilizing politicomilitary pressure (PMP) on the system regulator. This pressure results in a nonproductive diversion of available economic resources toward the requirements felt for internal public support and military security. In capitalist systems, the pressure also leads to a lessening and cessation of private investment in national economies. Capitalist societies, in this context, may be interpreted as distributed control systems in comparison to the centrally planned economies of the socialist societies. Politicomilitary pressure hence reduces the quantum of investible resources (IR) for productive input to the economy.

Available resources permit a potential rate of economic growth, which is, however, subject to a society's relative capability in the utilization of its resources. This capability factor, termed administrative effectiveness (AE), is seen to be determined by two major elements: education (ED) and government stability (GS). The higher the educational level and knowledge base of a society, the more efficient its administration. Similarly, for the administrative processes to be carried out effectively, governmental stability is vital. Administrative effectiveness acts as a filter on IR to determine the actual rate of economic growth (EG). Economic growth may also be affected by the exogenous impacts of weather, global trade relations, and inflows of economic resources. EG affects unemployment (UE) and price rise (PR) in conjunction with the rate of population growth (PG). Unemployment and price rise lead to public unrest (PU) and produce an impact on ethnic tension (ET) or the internal divisiveness within a social order.

1. The case of France has been discussed elsewhere (Rastogi 1974.)

Public unrest, ethnic tension, and the politicomilitary pressure on government determine the total magnitude of institutional pressure on government (*TPG*) and determine the extent of its stability or viability (*GS*) during any particular period. The latter expresses the relative capacity of a societal system to withstand stresses and strains, i.e., its strength. It affects, as such, the standing of ruling leadership and the evaluation by the citizenry of the conduct of their government concerning their society's most pressing problems (*ES*).

Mass standing of a leader is given by a leadership factor (*LDF*). Stature of a ruling leader is affected by the performance of the government (i.e., system viability) managed by him. Hence, the actual value of *LDF* may vary from period to period. The expectations of the citizenry during a period depend on the actual value of *LDF* and *GS* during that period. When the value of *ES* approaches a critically low level, it signals an impending change of government. The leadership factor explains situations where societies, confronted with tremendous stresses of war, poverty, and privation, stand up to their problems and survive. Charismatic leaders like Gandhi, Ataturk, Ho Chi Minh, and Lenin illustrate the type of situation in question. On the other hand, the chronic political instability of postwar France and Italy may also be interpreted in terms of a low leadership factor, despite these countries' relative affluence as "developed" industrial societies.

The foregoing variables and processes are seen to be organized into six positive feedback loops. Exogenous impacts affect the system along the boundaries of the relevant loops. (See Figure 21-1.) The dynamic operation of these loops may be discussed as follows:

1. Loop one shows that politicomilitary pressure (*PMP*) resulting from the impact of other societies and the internal problems of unrest and divisiveness (*PU,ET*) reduces the level of investible resources (*IR*) for productive input to the economy. The higher the pressure, the lower the quantum of available resources. The level of resources, along with administrative effectiveness (*AE*), determines the level of actual economic growth (*EG*). The latter is also affected by a number of random exogenous factors. The impact of weather on agricultural production and of terms of trade on national income are, for example, marked. Other exogenous factors may affect economic growth by increasing investible resources and national product through external investment and commodity aid. The rates of economic growth and population growth (*PG*) determine the level of unemployment and price rise (*UE,PR*) during a given period. Economic growth reduces unemployment and price rise; population growth increases them. The magnitude of unemployment and price rise determines the level of public unrest and ethnic tension. Internal divisiveness within a society is also affected by its history. *PU* and *ET* affect politicomilitary pressure. The loop is complete at this point. It is a self-reinforcing positive loop, i.e., *PMP* will go on continuously increasing after each

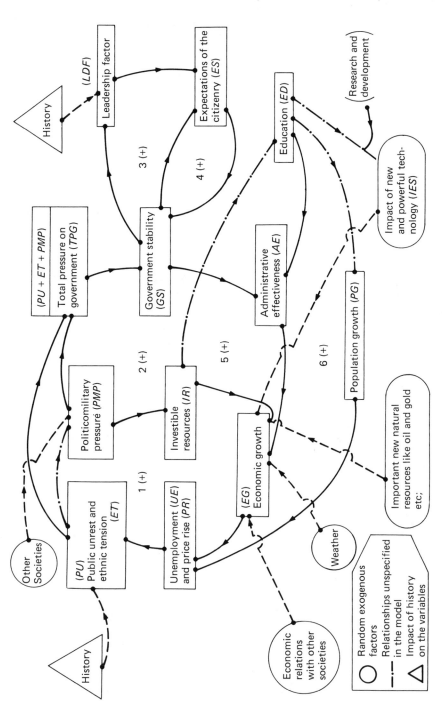

Figure 21-1. Dynamics of societal systems.

loop cycle unless there is a reduction in the internal and/or external pressure from other societies. Foreign economic and military aid may help reduce it temporarily. In the reverse phase, *PMP* will go on decreasing with each successive loop cycle leading to increases in economic growth.

2. Loop two shows that total pressure on government (*TPG*), which is determined by *PU, ET,* and *PMP*, determines government stability (*GS*). *GS*, along with education (*ED*), determines administrative effectiveness (*AE*). The latter then constrains *EG*. The remainder of the loop proceeds as before and terminates at *TPG*. It is also a positive loop. It seeks to increase *GS* with each loop cycle through increase in *EG* and reduction of *TPG*. Loop two includes Loop one within its boundary.

3. Loop three shows the mutually reinforcing relationship of government stability, leadership factor and expectations of the citizenry. *LDF* is determined by contemporary historical factors and affected by the changes in *GS*. In turn it affects *ES*, which influences *GS*. Higher and lower value of any loop variable affect the remaining variables in a corresponding manner.

4. Loop four shows a similar, mutually reinforcing relationship between *GS* and *ES*. The higher the government stability, the greater the *ES* and vice versa. Expectations of the citizenry refer to the citizens' evaluation of their government. It is also a self-exciting, positive loop.

5. Loop five shows that a higher level of *IR* for *ED* serves to increase *AE*. The latter, in return, increases *EG*, reduces *UE, PR, PU, ET,* and *PMP*, and thence increases IR. It is a positive loop seeking continually to increase *IR* via increases in *ED* and *AE*.

6. Loop six shows that higher investible resources (*IR*) increase education (*ED*), which reduces *PG*.[2] Reduced population growth then reduces *PR* and *UE*, which in their turn reduce *PU, ET,* and *PMP* and hence result in increasing the investible resources and *ED*. It is also a positive loop. It seeks to increase the level of investible resources progressively through increased education and reduced population growth.

The fact that all the six loops are positive demonstrates an inherent growth orientation of the normal societal processes. They move toward continuous development and stability of societal systems. Only when they fail to function in their natural growth mode does one find a society beset with crises (i.e., high *PR, UE, PU,* and *ET;* low *GS, AE,* and *EG*) and despair (i.e., low *ES*).

2. SYSTEM SIMULATION AND VIABILITY

Simulation of dynamic system processes generates time-varying values of the loop variables. The latter may then be compared with the relevant data and in-

2. Contingent factors like strength of religious beliefs may serve to reduce the impact of ED on PG in some societies.

formation from the concerned periods of the simulated societies. Confirmable inference—retrodictive and predictive—for the societal systems thus becomes possible.

Government stability (*GS*) in the multiloop system dynamics measures the viability of the total society system. System viability is, however, also measurable through another procedure. The latter is based on the regulatedness or viability (λ) of the system variables. High and low values of variables such as unemployment, price rise, economic growth, and public unrest signify the higher and lower regulation (λ) of their performance by the system governor, i.e., government. Accordingly, they reflect the regulatory effectiveness or viability (*Z*) of the societal system concerned.

Viability (λ) of system variables is measured by mapping their performance values into a viability continuum ranging from zero to one. The λ poles of zero and one correspond to perfect regulation and maximal disorder respectively. Division of this range into four equal parts defines the four λ zones. Performance values mapped into the boundaries of the four λ segments may be interpreted as the quantified levels of the variables corresponding to the sampling intervals of 0.25λ. The pattern of measurement may be presented as follows:

Viability continuum.

Zone of chaotic conditions	Zone of disturbed conditions	Zone of viable performance.	Zone of maximally viable performance.	
* I (λ)	* II (λ)	* III (λ)	* IV (λ)	*
0.0 disruption of regulatory process	0.25 poor regulation.	0.5 high level of regulatedness.	0.75 highest level of regulatedness.	1.

pmp. $\longrightarrow$				
* IV (λ)	* III (λ)	* II (λ)	* I (λ)	*
0.0	0.25	0.5	0.75	1.

ae. $\longrightarrow$				
* I (λ)	* II (λ)	* III (λ)	* IV (λ)	*
0.0	0.25	0.5	0.75	1.

eg. $\longrightarrow$				
* I (λ)	* II (λ)	* III (λ)	* IV (λ)	*
0.0%	0.5%	3%	9%	13%

pu. $\longrightarrow$				
* IV (λ)	* III (λ)	* II (λ)	* I (λ)	*
0.0	0.25	0.5	0.75	1.

and so on.

a. **Mapping of λ Zones into the Performance Zones of System Variables.** The schema shows the mapping of quantified performance values of variables into the four zones of a viability continuum. Any given value of a system variable may be transformed into its λ measure and vice versa via this mapping schema.

The mathematical expression for computing the value of system viability (Z) through the viabilities of its regulated variables is given by

$$Z = \sum_{i=1}^{n} |\lambda_i|/N$$

where $|\lambda_i|$ are the spectra of the regulatedness of the ith performance vector and N is the number of the regulated performance vectors. Both λ and Z vary between zero and one. The values of Z and GS are found to be in close agreement, as expected on a theoretical basis.

The algorithm for system simulation is based on Wiener's law of the entrainment and matching of frequencies (Wiener 1958, 1962). According to this law, the constituent parts of a dynamic system work synchronously so that their frequencies match one another. This matching principle leads to the following basic equation types used in the simulation algorithm:

$$\int_{t-1}^{t} \int_{0}^{1} \lambda x \, d\lambda \, dt \pm \int_{t-1}^{t} \int_{0}^{1} \lambda \, ex \, d\lambda \, dt = |\lambda x|t$$

$$\int_{t-1}^{t} \int_{0}^{1} \lambda y \, d\lambda \, dt \pm \int_{t-1}^{t} \int_{0}^{1} \lambda \, ey \, d\lambda \, dt = |\lambda y|t \tag{21-1}$$

$$|\lambda x| \longrightarrow |\lambda y| \ldots \tag{21-2}$$

$$|\lambda x|t \equiv |\lambda y|t \ldots \tag{21-3}$$

For a variable

$$u = P\{a, b, \ldots, m\},$$

$$|\lambda u|t = \sum_{j=a}^{m} |\lambda_j|t/M, \ldots \tag{21-4}$$

where x and y are system variables (vectors), ex and ey are random exogenous impact vectors on x and y, $|\lambda x|t$ and $|\lambda y|t$ are the viability spectra of vectors x and y at time t, t–1 to t is the system's cycling time (one year) and 0 to 1 is the range of λ continuum. Equation (21-2) represents the precedence and covariation relationships between the viabilities of x and y. Equation (21-3) represents the equivalence relationship between them at time t. P ( ) in equation

(21-4) represents the set of M precedent variables of u. The normalized additivity of their viabilities determines the viability value of u. Viability spectra $|\lambda x|$ refer to the differential regulatedness of the constituent and cognate parts of the performance vector x and their resolution into a point estimate.

The overall framework of the theory and methodology discussed so far is synoptically outlined in Figure 21-2.

3. THEMES OF INFERENCE AND VALIDATION

Simulation of system dynamics permits the following themes of retrodictive confirmation and predictive inference for all societal systems:

1. By estimating politicomilitary pressure through a maximum likelihood procedure, a preview of the system state for a period, $t + n$, with reference to the present period, t, may be obtained. This knowledge of the future system state would be presented in terms of the whole configuration of variables given in the system's multiloop structure. The supplementary requirements here would be a knowledge of Z or GS for period $t + n - 1$ and the values of education (in terms of literacy and emphasis on research and development), population growth, and potential leadership factor (LDF).

2. Insofar as government as a societal institution is the control subsystem of society as an adaptive system, the passage of any directly regulated variable into the "collapse zone" of the viability continuum ($0 < \lambda \leqslant 0.25$) would signal an impending state of government instability, i.e., a failure of the system regulator in a principal area of system performance. Such a period would be associated with major policy and structure changes in the government and the political system.

3. The mode of political instability and/or government change may be orderly or disorderly, depending upon the closeness of Z or GS values to the polar limits. Systems in higher λ zones would display orderly change, owing to their higher innate vitality, while those in the lower zones, i.e., $GS < 0.5$ may be disorderly. The probability of violent changes, revolutions, coups, and chaos would increase directly with the approach of GS values toward the collapse zone.

4. The same would be the case with the duration of political instability. The periods of political uncertainty may be short lived or prolonged depending upon the Z or GS values. In the case of higher system viability values, Wiener's law would rectify the unstable situation(s) depending upon the (relatively short) period required for the equilibrial matching of frequencies. Higher λ variables would pull the lower λ variable(s) up. The reverse would be the case in societies with low values of Z or GS. Here, low λ variables would pull the higher ones down. Themes (3) and (4) provide a basis for understanding the absence of such a class of situations, i.e., prolonged

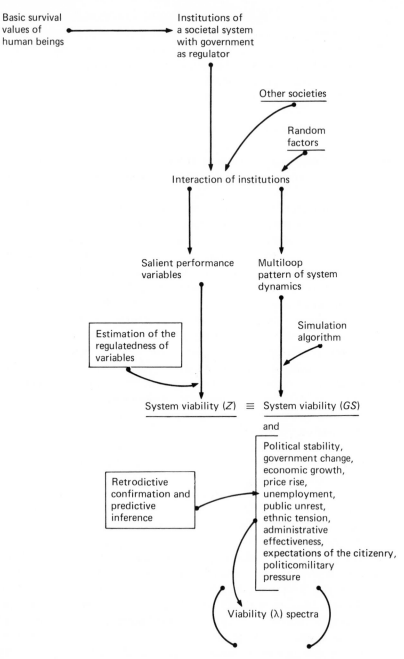

Figure 21-2. Logical structure of cybernetic approach to the study of societies.

and disorderly instability in the political systems of developed societies. The reverse is the case with some undeveloped societies of Africa, Asia, and Latin America.

5. In the case of societies in higher λ zones, where most of the variables may be performing viably, the change of government would be exclusively predicated around the variable *ES* unless it is overwhelmed by sudden external military pressure.

6. Government change in stable societies, i.e., $GS > 0.5$, is explicable in terms of the *GS* and *ES* values during electoral periods. A sequential decrease of *GS* values, i.e., $GS_t < GS_{t-1}$ and correspondingly $ES(\lambda)_t < ES(\lambda)_{t-1}$ during an electoral period would provide a basis for prediction regarding the lack of success of the ruling party. In the case of marginal differences, the situation would be one of *close* electoral contest. Higher *GS* and *ES* values favor the stability of the regulator unambiguously.

7. Values of economic variables like economic growth, unemployment, and price rise generated by the model are directly testable against the reported values of these variables for the corresponding periods.

8. Values of qualitative variables like administrative effectiveness, public unrest, and ethnic tension are indirectly confirmable. A consistent correspondence between their variation in the system's simulated course and comparable situations (corruption, inefficiency, mass protests, violence, riots) in the societies concerned during those periods would serve to validate the model results.

9. Values of leadership factor variable are also similarly confirmable. Periodic public opinion surveys on the popularity of the ruling leadership may help in the validation of this variable.

10. Expectations of the citizenry are most directly confirmable. If the value of this variable comes down to $0.25\ \lambda$ or less, it signifies an imperative change of the society's government.

4. THE COURSES OF FOUR SOCIETAL SYSTEMS

Time paths of Brazil, India, Nigeria, and the U.S. from 1961 to 1975 are depicted in Tables 21-1 through 21-8. They have been generated by the same simulation algorithm. Time-varying values of the same set of variables for all the four systems are outlined. Economic variables are given as percentage variations over the preceding year. Others are given in the scaling range of zero to one.

Validation of simulation results is indicated by the Tables 21-2, 21-4, 21-6 and 21-8, respectively, representing the four societies. Each of these tables compares the reported figures of economic growth at constant prices *EG*(R), unemployment *UE*(R) (where available), and price rise *PR*(R) with their values gen-

Table 21-1. The Course of Brazilian Society (1961-1975)

Variables	1961	1962	1963	1964	1965	1966	1967	1968	1969	1970	1971	1972	1973	1974	1975
Politicomilitary pressure	0.38	0.57	0.67	0.70	0.53	0.50	0.40	0.25	0.24	0.23	0.20	0.19	0.18	0.21	0.25
Administrative effectiveness	0.48	0.49	0.46	0.435	0.45	0.470	0.56	0.60	0.63	0.64	0.66	0.67	0.69	0.635	0.62
Economic growth	4.3%	2.6%	2.0%	3.6%	2.6%	4.8%	4.9%	7.8%	9%	9.5%	10.0%	10.8%	11%	10.3%	8.7%
Unemployment	21.8%	24.3%	23.5%	24.3%	20.3%	18.8%	16.3%	14.8%	10.8%	10.3%	9.3%	8.8%	7.9%	10.3%	11.3%
Price rise	34%	50%	72.4%	86.8%	50%	46.5%	25.2%	22.8%	24%	23.4%	20.4%	18%	16.8%	23.4%	25.2%
Public unrest	0.68	0.71	0.72	0.74	0.69	0.68	0.62	0.58	0.58	0.58	0.56	0.55	0.54	0.58	0.59
Ethnic tension	0.53	0.54	0.545	0.555	0.53	0.525	0.495	0.475	0.475	0.475	0.47	0.46	0.455	0.475	0.48
Total pressure on government	0.53	0.61	0.645	0.660	0.58	0.570	0.50	0.44	0.430	0.43	0.41	0.40	0.392	0.423	0.44
Government stability	0.47	0.394	0.36	0.340	0.42	0.430	0.50	0.56	0.57	0.57	0.59	0.60	0.61	0.58	0.56
Z	0.45	0.397	0.367	0.347	0.410	0.440	0.49	0.542	0.56	0.564	0.58	0.595	0.607	0.570	0.55
Leadership factor–actual	0.49	0.48	0.46	0.45	0.49	0.50	0.50	0.53	0.54	0.54	0.55	0.55	0.56	0.54	0.53
Expectations of the citizenry	0.23	0.19	0.17	0.15	0.21	0.22	0.25	0.30	0.31	0.31	0.325	0.33	0.34	0.31	0.297

Table 21-2. Time Series Validation of the Simulated Course of Brazilian Society (1961–1975)

Year	GS	Z	EG(R) (percentage)	EG(S) (percentage)	PR(R) (percentage)	PR(S) (percentage)	UE(R)	UE(S) (percentage)	ES	Regulator Change
1961	0.47	0.45	5.0	4.3	35	34	—	21.8	0.23	Kubitschek replaced by Quadros.
1962	0.39	0.40	1.6	2.6	50.2	50	—	24.3	0.19	Quadros quits. Goulart faces political turmoil.
1963	0.36	0.36	3.1	2.0	71	72.4	—	23.5	0.17	Conditions of civil war.
1964	0.34	0.34	3.9	3.6	87	86.8	—	24.2	0.15	Military government by General Branco.
1965	0.40	0.396	2.8	2.6	50	50	—	20.3	0.18	Repudiation of Branco administration in elections. Rapid and radical changes in political institutions.
1966	0.42	0.43	5.1	4.8	44.1	46.5	—	18.8	0.19	Military regime of General Silva.
1967	0.50	0.49	4.8	4.9	24.9	25.2	—	16.3	0.25	Political stability under military government.
1968	0.56	0.54	8.3	7.8	23.6	22.8	—	14.8	0.30	
1969	0.57	0.56	8.5	9.0[a]	23.1	24	—	10.8	0.31	
1970	0.57	0.564	9.3	9.5	22	23.4	—	10.3	0.31	
1971	0.59	0.58	11.3	10	20.5	20.4	—	9.3	0.325	
1972	0.60	0.595	10.5	10.8	18.3	18	—	8.8	0.33	
1973	0.61	0.607	12	11	16.5	16.8	—	7.9	0.34	
1974	0.58	0.57	12.5	10.5	23.8	23.4	—	10.3	0.31	
1975	0.56	0.55	—	8.7	24.3	25.2	—	11.3	0.297	

R indicates reported figure.
S indicates simulated figure.
[a] Economic growth of 1 to 2 percent per year from 1969 on remains unassimilated in the economy, i.e., does not affect UE and PR.

Table 21-3.   The Course of Indian Society (1961–1975)

Variables	1961	1962	1963	1964	1965	1966	1967	1968	1969	1970	1971	1972	1973	1974	1975
Politicomilitary pressure	0.47	0.56	0.50	0.50	0.53	0.59	0.56	0.56	0.47	0.47	0.47	0.56	0.47	0.47	0.50
Administrative effectiveness	0.42	0.41	0.51	0.41	0.41	0.395	0.38	0.39	0.42	0.42	0.42	0.415	0.40	0.385	0.51
Economic growth	2.8%	2.3%	3.3%	5.6%	2.4%	2%	2.1%	8.2%	4.8%	3.8%	2.8%	2.27%	0.44%	0.40%	5.6%
Unemployment	9.3%	11.8%	8.2%	7.8%	11.3%	13.3%	12.8%	5.3%	7.2%	7.8%	9.3%	11.8%	22.3%	23.3%	7%
Price rise	7.2%	10.2%	5.9%	9%	9.6%	12%	11.4%	4.0%	5.4%	5.6%	7.2%	10.2%	22.8%	24%	4.9%
Public unrest	0.510	0.54	0.49	0.48	0.53	0.55	0.54	0.40	0.46	0.48	0.51	0.54	0.64	0.65	0.47
Ethnic tension	0.47	0.48	0.46	0.46	0.48	0.49	0.48	0.42	0.45	0.465	0.47	0.485	0.54	0.55	0.45
Total pressure on government	0.483	0.53	0.48	0.48	0.51	0.54	0.526	0.46	0.46	0.473	0.483	0.530	0.55	0.556	0.473
Government stability	0.517	0.47	0.52	0.52	0.49	0.46	0.474	0.54	0.54	0.527	0.517	0.47	0.45	0.444	0.527
Z	0.516	0.482	0.532	0.517	0.480	0.452	0.46	0.561	0.535	0.527	0.508	0.48	0.43	0.42	0.53
Leadership factor—actual	0.70	0.67	0.69	0.54	0.53	0.55	0.55	0.59	0.59	0.605	0.60	0.61	0.60	0.595	0.64
Expectations of the citizenry	0.36	0.315	0.36	0.28	0.26	0.253	0.26	0.318	0.32	0.32	0.31	0.28	0.27	0.264	0.34

Table 21–4. Time Series Validation of the Simulated Course of Indian Society (1961–1975)

Year	GS	Z	EG(R) (percentage)	EG(S) (percentage)	PR(R) (percentage)	PR(S) (percentage)	UE(R)	UE(S) (percentage)	ES	Regulator Change
1961	0.517	0.516	3.5 Avg.	2.8	6.0	7.2	—	9.3	0.36	Nehru government.
1962	0.47	0.482	1.9	2.3 Avg.	6.0[a]	10.2	—	11.8	0.315	India's defeat by China reduces Nehru's popularity.
1963	0.52	0.532	5.5 Avg.	3.3 Avg.	6.2[b]	5.9	—	8.2	0.36	Nehru regains national standing.
1964	0.52	0.517	6.6[a]	5.6[a]	10[b]	9.0	—	7.8	0.28	Shastri succeeds Nehru after latter's death.
1965	0.49	0.48	-5.0	2.4	8.9[b]	9.6	—	11.3	0.26	Shastri government meets war and drought.
1966	0.46	0.452	1.8	2.0	10.5[b]	12	—	13.3	0.253	Mrs. Gandhi succeeds Shastri after his death.
1967	0.47	0.46	2.4	2.1	11.3[b]	11.4	—	12.8	0.26	Mrs. Gandhi's government.
1968	0.54	0.56	8.6[e]	8.2[e]	3.6[a]	4.0	—	5.3	0.318	
1969	0.54	0.535	5.3	4.8	6.5[c]	5.4	—	7.2	0.32	Mrs. Gandhi emerges as supreme leader of Congress Party.
1970	0.527	0.527	4.9 Avg.	3.8 Avg.	5.5[d]	5.6	—	7.8	0.32	Mrs. Gandhi's government.
1971	0.517	0.508	1.4	2.8	4.0[d]	7.2	—	9.3	0.31	Mrs. Gandhi manages Bangla Desh Crisis.
1972	0.47	0.48	-0.9	2.3	9.9[d]	10.2	—	11.8	0.28	Difficult economic situation.
1973	0.45	0.43	3.1	0.44	22.6[d]	22.8	—	22.3	0.27	Difficult economic situation.
1974	0.44	0.42	1	0.4	23.4[d]	24	—	23.3	.264	Prelude to the declaration of emergency.
1975	0.53	0.53	5.5[e]	5.6[e]	4.3[b]	4.9	—	7.3	0.34	Mrs. Gandhi manages economic and political crises.

R indicates reported figure.

S indicates simulated figure.

Avg. indicates average.

[a]Food items.

[b]Consumer price index—all items.

[c]Wholesale price index—manufactures.

[d]Wholesale price index—all items.

[e]Impact of monsoon on economic growth.

Table 21-5. The Course of Nigerian Society (1961–1975)

Variables	*1961*	*1962*	*1963*	*1964*	*1965*	*1966*	*1967*	*1968*	*1969*	*1970*	*1971*	*1972*	*1973*	*1974*	*1975*
Politicomilitary pressure	0.41	0.44	0.44	0.44	0.50	0.56	0.81	0.81	0.53	0.44	0.44	0.41	0.44	0.50	0.59
Administrative effectiveness	0.38	0.38	0.385	0.38	0.37	0.37	0.34	0.285	0.28	0.34	0.37	0.46	0.48	0.39	0.36
Economic growth	3%	4.2%	4.7%	2.7%	5%	2.1%	0.6%	0.48%	1.8%	2.5%	2.7%	3.8%	7.0%	2.4%	0.9%
Unemployment	10.3%	8.3%	7.9%	12.3%	7.7%	16.3%	23.8%	24.3%	16.3%	13.3%	12.3%	9.3%	5.9%	13.8%	16%
Price rise	8.4%	7.2%	6%	8.4%	5.7%	17.2%	24.6%	26.4%	18.0%	13.8%	14.4%	5.7%	5.6%	16.8%	25.8%
Public unrest	0.52	0.50	0.50	0.53	0.48	0.58	0.65	0.67	0.59	0.56	0.55	0.50	0.46	0.56	0.62
Ethnic tension	0.525	0.515	0.52	0.53	0.54	0.56	0.59	0.60	0.56	0.545	0.54	0.52	0.495	0.545	0.575
Total pressure on government	0.49	0.483	0.49	0.50	0.51	0.57	0.68	0.69	0.56	0.515	0.51	0.48	0.465	0.53	0.59
Government stability	0.51	0.517	0.51	0.50	0.49	0.43	0.32	0.31	0.44	0.485	0.49	0.52	0.535	0.47	0.41
Z	0.49	0.502	0.506	0.48	0.50	0.43	0.335	0.315	0.41	0.46	0.47	0.51	0.55	0.45	0.40
Leadership factor—actual	0.54	0.54	0.54	0.53	0.53	0.47	0.41	0.405	0.47	0.52	0.525	0.54	0.55	0.515	0.485
Expectations of the citizenry	0.275	0.28	0.275	0.265	0.26	0.202	0.13	0.21	0.21	0.255	0.261	0.28	0.30	0.244	0.201

Table 21-6. Time Series Validation of the Simulated Course of Nigerian Society (1961-1975)

Year	GS	Z	EG(R) (percentage)	EG(S) (percentage)	PR(R) (percentage)	PR(S) (percentage)	UE(R) (percentage)	UE(S) (percentage)	ES	Regulator Change Observed
1961	0.510	0.490	3.3	3	8[b]	8.4	—	10.3	0.275	Continuity of Belewa government.
1962	0.517	0.502	4.7	4.2	6.5[b]	7.2	—	8.3	0.28	
1963	0.510	0.506	4.6	4.7	(—)	6	—	7.9	0.275	
1964	0.50	0.48	2.6	2.7	2.5	8.4	—	12.3	0.265	
1965	0.49	0.50	5.16	5	4.7	5.7	—	7.7	0.260	
1966	0.43	0.43	2.6	2.1	18.2[b]	17.2	—	16.3	0.202	Military coup and counter coup.
1967	0.32	0.335	0	0.6	(—)[c]	24.6	—	23.8	0.13	Bitter civil war.
1968	0.31	0.315	0	0.48	1[c]	26.4	—	24.3	0.13	
1969	0.44	0.41	26.7[a]	1.9	17.3[b]	18.0	—	16.3	0.21	
1970	0.485	0.46	24.4[a]	2.5	13.6	13.8	—	13.3	0.255	Collapse of secession.
1971	0.49	0.47	11.97[a]	2.7	13.5	14.4	—	12.3	0.261	Continuity of Gowan government.
1972	0.52	0.51	3.8	3.8	2.9	5.7	—	9.3	0.280	
1973	0.535	0.55	7.1[a]	7	3.6	5.6	—	5.9	0.300	
1974	0.47	0.45	—	2.4	16.9	16.8	—	13.8	0.244	Coup conditions against Gowan government.
1975	0.41	0.40	—	0.90	24.1	25.8	—	16.0	0.201	Coup against Gowan government.

R indicates reported figure.
S indicates simulated figure.
[a] Oil revenue increase.
[b] Food items.
[c] Artificially proclaimed official prices, exclude the situation in Biafra.

Table 21-7.   The Course of U.S. Society (1961–1975)

Years	1961	1962	1963	1964	1965	1966	1967	1968	1969	1970	1971	1972	1973	1974	1975
Politicomilitary pressure	0.64	0.50	0.59	0.53	0.47	0.47	0.65	0.59	0.68	0.70	0.57	0.50	0.50	0.59	0.53
Administrative effectiveness	0.68	0.67	0.695	0.68	0.70	0.705	0.71	0.665	0.68	0.655	0.645	0.68	0.69	0.67	0.65
Economic growth	3.2%	5.1%	4.2%	5%	5.9%	6.2%	3.5%	4.0%	3.0%	2.8%	3.8%	5.2%	2.4%	1.4%	2.1%
Unemployment	6.4%	5.4%	4.8%	5.5%	4.6%	4.05%	5.0%	4.8%	5.5%	6.1%	6.4%	5.7%	5.5%	6.4%	8.8%
Price rise	3.5%	2.9%	3.3%	2.8%	2.6%	3.5%	3.8%	4.0%	4.4%	5.0%	4.0%	3.8%	5.8%	10.8%	7.2%
Public unrest	.40	0.37	0.39	0.38	0.35	0.365	0.40	0.40	0.41	0.43	0.41	0.40	0.45	0.49	0.51
Ethnic tension	.405	0.39	0.40	0.395	0.38	0.39	0.40	0.40	0.41	0.42	0.41	0.405	0.43	0.45	0.46
Total pressure on government	0.48	0.42	0.46	0.44	0.40	0.404	0.48	0.463	0.500	0.510	0.46	0.43	0.46	0.51	0.50
Government stability	0.52	0.58	0.54	0.56	0.60	0.596	0.52	0.537	0.500	0.490	0.54	0.57	0.54	0.49	0.50
Z	0.55	0.596	0.558	0.585	0.616	0.615	0.558	0.561	0.538	0.520	0.557	0.586	0.552	0.488	0.505
Leadership factor—actual	0.51	0.54	0.52	0.53	0.55	0.55	0.51	0.52	0.50	0.49	0.52	0.55	0.48	0.42	0.50
Expectations of the citizenry	0.265	0.313	0.28	0.29	0.33	0.33	0.27	0.28	0.252	0.24	0.29	0.314	0.26	0.21	0.25

Table 21-8. Time Series Validation of the Simulated Course of US Society (1961-1975)

Year	GS	Z	EG(R) (percentage)	EG(S) (percentage)	PR(R) (percentage)	PR(S) (percentage)	UE(R) (percentage)	UE(S) (percentage)	ES	Regulator Change
1961	0.52	0.55	2.0	3.2	1.1	3.5	6.7	6.4	0.265	Kennedy government.
1962	0.58	0.59	6.5 Avg.	5.1 Avg.	1.9	2.9	5.5	5.4	0.313	Johnson succeeds Kennedy after latter's assassination in November 1963.
1963	0.54	0.57	3.9	4.2	1.2	3.3	5.7	4.8	0.28	
1964	0.56	0.58	5.2	5.0	1.3	2.8	5.2	5.5	0.30	Johnson elected.
1965	0.60	0.616	5.9	5.9	2.2	2.6	4.5	4.6	0.33	Johnson government.
1966	0.596	0.615	6.5	6.2	3.9	3.5	3.8	4.05	0.33	
1967	0.52	0.558	2.8	3.5	3.0	3.8	3.9	5.0	0.27	Johnson renounces candidacy.
1968	0.54	0.56	4.5	4.0	4.1	4.0	3.6	4.8	0.28	Nixon narrowly elected.
1969	0.505	0.538	2.8	3.0	5.3	4.4	3.5	5.5	0.26	Nixon government.
1970	0.49	0.52	1.5 Avg.	2.8 Avg.	5.4	5.0	4.9	6.1	0.24	Further gains by the Democratic Party in the Congress.
1971	0.54	0.56	4.0	3.8	4.0	4.0	6.0	6.4	0.29	Nixon re-elected by large majority.
1972	0.57	0.586	5.0	5.2	3.5	3.8	5.6	5.7	0.314	Nixon loses stature because of Watergate scandal.
1973	0.54	0.55	5.6 Avg.	2.4[a] Avg.	6.0	5.8	4.9	5.5	0.27	
1974	0.49	0.49	-2.2[a]	1.4[a]	10.6	10.8	5.6	6.4	0.21	Nixon resigns. Ford succeeds him.
1975	0.50	0.505	—	2.1	7.6	7.2	8.6	8.8	0.25	Attempts on the life of Ford.

R indicates reported figure.
S indicates simulated figure.
Avg. indicates average.
[a]Reduced *EG* figures owing to inflationary impact of oil crisis. The original figures for 1973 and 1974 are 5.3 percent and 3.9 percent, respectively. They affect *UE*, but the reduced figures affect *PR*.

erated by system simulation, i.e., $EG(S)$, $UE(S)$, and $PR(S)$.[3] Comparison of GS and Z is also given to indicate the similarity of the two estimates of system viability. Marked declines of their values attest to the presence of political instability during the given periods. Decline of Z, GS, and ES in an election year accounts for the electoral reverses of the ruling political regime. Increase of Z, GS, and ES in an election year accounts for the electoral success of the ruling political leadership in an analogous manner. Values of ES at 0.25 and less stand for change of government or its equivalent phenomena, irrespective of the nature of a society's political system. Evidence for the indirect validation of other variables is available but is not shown here.

5. THE PROBLEM OF PREDICTION IN SOCIETAL SYSTEMS

Prediction of the future course of a society is based on an extension of the simulation algorithm up to the desired period. Methodologically the problem is simple; empirically it is not. Exogenous impacts on the system are of a random nature, and unless their values are specified, the course of the system cannot be generated. The values of politicomilitary pressure, population growth, and education are also subject to variation, and their estimation over the period concerned also needs resolution. Accordingly, the prediction of societal future can be made under a specified set of conditions. Sets of possible courses for the four societies from 1976 to 1980 are outlined below. The assumptions under which these courses have been generated are also stated.

A course of Brazilian society has been outlined under the assumption of the continuation and development of current trends. The salient aspects of these trends are a continuing decline in politicomilitary pressure, rising levels of economic growth and investment of external capital, and the continuing high level of the population growth rate. An economic growth rate to the extent of 2 percent per year is deemed to be created by large external investments, but it remains unassimilated in the national economy insofar as its impact on inflation and unemployment is concerned. The impact of the high rise in petroleum prices has not been taken into account as a significant factor. The societal course under these assumptions is shown in Table 21-9.

An inspection of Brazil's course shows society moving toward greater viability. However, it will not be able to solve its inflation and public unrest problems. Under these conditions, random exogenous and endogenous factors may lead to an increase in the level of politicomilitary pressure. If this happens, society will relapse into the chaotic pattern of the early 1960s. An alternative course of Bra-

---

3. Reported figures for Brazil, Nigeria, and the U.S. are mostly taken from the U.N. monthly Bulletin of Statistics. Indian figures are reproduced from annual economic surveys issued by the government of India. Simulated figures refer to normal calendar year whereas some of the reported figures pertain to "fiscal year."

Table 21-9. A Course of Brazilian Society (1976-1980)

Variables	1976	1977	1978	1979	1980
Politicomilitary pressure	0.18	0.18	0.17	0.16	0.15
Administrative effectiveness	0.65	0.67	0.68	0.69	0.70
Economic growth	10.8%	11%	11.2%	11.4%	11.6%
Unemployment	8.8%	8.3%	8%	7.8%	7.5%
Price rise	21.6%	21%	20.4%	19.8%	19%
Public unrest	0.565	0.56	0.555	0.55	0.54
Ethnic tension	0.467	0.465	0.46	0.46	0.45
Total pressure on government	0.40	0.40	0.395	0.39	0.38
Government stability	0.60	0.60	0.605	0.61	0.62
Z	0.59	0.59	0.60	0.594	0.61
Leadership factor—actual	0.55	0.55	0.553	0.56	0.56
Expectations of the citizenry	0.33	0.33	0.333	0.34	0.35

Table 21-10. An Alternative Course of Brazilian Society (Years t+1 to t+5) (Impact of high politicomilitary pressure)

Variables	t + 1	t + 2	t + 3	t + 4	t + 5
Politicomilitary pressure	0.37	0.43	0.43	0.46	0.48
Administrative effectiveness	0.65	0.62	0.60	0.60	0.595
Economic growth	8.0%	7.5%	5%	4.8%	4.5%
Unemployment	14.3%	15.8%	16.3%	17.5%	17.8%
Price rise	27.6%	30%	31%	33%	34%
Public unrest	0.62	0.64	0.645	0.65	0.66
Ethnic tension	0.495	0.505	0.51	0.51	0.52
Total pressure on government	0.495	0.525	0.53	0.54	0.55
Government stability	0.515	0.475	0.47	0.46	0.45
Z	0.51	0.485	0.476	0.465	0.458
Leadership factor—actual	0.51	0.49	0.485	0.48	0.475
Expectations of the citizenry	0.265	0.24	0.23	0.22	0.216

zilian society from year $t + 1$ to $t + 5$ under the impact of high politicomilitary pressure could be represented as shown in Table 21-10.

An examination of this course shows a continuing rise in inflation, unemployment, public unrest, and ethnic tension accompanied by a continuing decline in economic growth, government stability, leadership factor, and expectations of the citizenry. External investments cease from the third year (assumption). Serious political instability and recurrent changes of government are evidenced in the system from the second year onward.

A course of Indian society is outlined under the following assumptions: a gradual decline in the level of politicomilitary pressure, contribution of indigenous oil production to the economic growth rate from 1978 onwards, and the occurrence of a serious drought in 1979 and 1980. Table 21-11 outlines the course of Indian society under these conditions. An inspection of the societal course reveals the continuing problems of low economic growth, unemployment, price rise, public unrest, and ethnic tension. The system, however, maintains its stability because of its high leadership factor. The specter of political instability and recurrent changes of government is not evidenced in the course of this system.

A course of Nigerian society is outlined under the assumption of the continuation of present trends. A further assumption is the absence of large-scale external capital investments. Higher oil production directly contributes to the economic growth rate in 1977 and 1979. The societal course is represented by Table 21-12. An inspection of the societal course here reveals the continuation of its earlier problems, i.e., administrative ineffectiveness, low economic growth, unemployment, inflation, public unrest, ethnic tension, and a continuing instability of the government. Values of *ES* persist at their low threshold level. An abortive coup took place in early 1976, confirming the low value of *ES* during the period. The coming years also presage such unstable situations in both covert and overt forms.

The solution to problems of a great and complex society like Nigeria is not easy. However, if the country manages to reduce its population growth rate even a little, i.e., to 2 percent annually and improves its administrative efficiency, it could be able to avoid the specter of recurrent instability and change of government. An alternative course for years $t + 1$ to $t + 5$ is given in Table 21-13. The value of *ES* here stays above 0.25 throughout the five-year period.

A course of U.S. society is similarly outlined under the assumption of the continuation of present trends. The impact of the oil crisis is deemed to have

Table 21-11. A Course of Indian Society (1976-1980)

Years	1976	1977	1978	1979	1980
Politicomilitary rpessure	0.47	0.47	0.44	0.41	0.41
Administrative effectiveness	0.475	0.43	0.43	0.44	0.44
Economic growth	3.1%	2.8%	3.5%	2.7%	1.9%
Unemployment	8.3%	9.3%	8%	9.8%	13.8%
Price rise	6%	7.2%	5.8%	7.8%	12.6%
Public unrest	0.50	0.51	0.49	0.52	0.56
Ethnic tension	0.465	0.47	0.46	0.475	0.50
Total pressure on government	0.48	0.483	0.463	0.47	0.49
Government stability	0.52	0.517	0.537	0.53	0.51
Z	0.526	0.515	0.533	0.523	0.50
Leadership factor—actual	0.635	0.63	0.644	0.64	0.63
Expectations of the citizenry	0.33	0.33	0.346	0.34	0.32

been absorbed and a declining trend of politicomilitary pressure is assumed. Table 21-14 outlines the societal course. Its inspection reveals that the U.S. will overcome its present problems of unemployment and inflation in the coming years and move toward increasing system viability.

The predictive inferences outlined above are indicative in nature. They are meant to demonstrate the realizability of unambiguous predictive inference for widely varying societal systems. Definitive and reliable predictions are, however, fully realizable depending upon the availability of accurate estimates of random exogenous factors and certain parameters. They require an adequately developed and sensitive system for monitoring relevant exogenous and endogenous factors.

Table 21-12. A Course of Nigerian Society (1976-1980)

Years	1976	1977	1978	1979	1980
Politicomilitary pressure	0.50	0.50	0.47	0.47	0.47
Administrative effectiveness	0.33	0.43	0.43	0.37	0.38
Economic growth	4.2%	3.7%	2.8%	3.5%	2.6%
Unemployment	8.3%	9.3%	11.8%	9.8%	12.3%
Price rise	10.2%	7.2%	9.6%	7.8%	11.4%
Public unrest	0.515	0.51	0.53	0.51	0.54
Ethnic tension	0.52	0.52	0.53	0.52	0.53
Total pressure on government	0.51	0.51	0.51	0.50	0.513
Government stability	0.49	0.49	0.49	0.50	0.487
Z	0.48	0.49	0.48	0.484	0.47
Leadership factor—actual	0.50	0.50	0.495	0.50	0.49
Expectations of the citizenry	0.245	0.245	0.243	0.25	0.24

Table 21-13. An Alternative Course of Nigerian Society (Years $t + 1$ to $t + 5$)

Variables	$t + 1$	$t + 2$	$t + 3$	$t + 4$	$t + 5$
Politicomilitary pressure	0.50	0.50	0.47	0.47	0.47
Administrative effectiveness	0.42	0.47	0.47	0.47	0.48
Economic growth	4.6%	3.9%	3%	4%	3.2%
Unemployment	8%	8.8%	10.8%	8.3%	10.3%
Price rise	4.8%	5.2%	5.6%	4.2%	5.4%
Public unrest	0.465	0.48	0.50	0.48	0.49
Ethnic tension	0.50	0.51	0.515	0.505	0.51
Total pressure on government	0.49	0.50	0.495	0.485	0.49
Government stability	0.51	0.503	0.505	0.515	0.51
Z	0.51	0.51	0.50	0.514	0.504
Leadership factor—actual	0.505	0.50	0.50	0.51	0.505
Expectations of the citizenry	0.26	0.252	0.253	0.26	0.26

Table 21-14.   A Course of U.S. Society (1976-1980)

Variables	1976	1977	1978	1979	1980
Politicomilitary pressure	0.53	0.56	0.53	0.50	0.47
Administrative effective- ness	0.66	0.68	0.68	0.685	0.69
Economic growth	4.6%	4.2%	4.9%	5.2%	5.5%
Unemployment	6.1%	5.6%	5.0%	4.9%	4.2%
Price rise	4.6%	3.7%	3.4%	3.2%	3.0%
Public unrest	0.43	0.40	0.385	0.38	0.36
Ethnic tension	0.42	0.405	0.40	0.40	0.385
Total pressure on government	0.46	0.46	0.44	0.43	0.41
Government stability	0.54	0.54	0.56	0.57	0.59
Z	0.56	0.57	0.58	0.59	0.61
Leadership factor—actual	0.52	0.52	0.53	0.535	0.55
Expectations of the citizenry	0.28	0.28	0.30	0.31	0.32

6. A PERFORMANCE PANEL FOR SOCIETAL SYSTEMS

The courses of individual system variables together depict the successive changes in system states. The system states reflect the differential performance of the system over a given period. The collective trajectories of system variables along with those of Z and GS would then serve to represent the course and performance of the system during a simulation period. The composite schema of such trajectories may be designated as the performance panel of the system. An example of such performance panel for Indian society for the 1970-1980 period is illustrated in Figure 21-3. A panel may also display the changing values of population, population growth rate, population density, per capita income, size and composition of GNP, number of unemployed persons, expectancy of life, and the educational level of a society.

Performance panels depict past problems and future prognoses. Directions for changing the course of a system may logically be determined on their basis. A collection of performance panels for a neighboring group of societies may serve as a performance panel for that global region.

7. THE CONCEPT OF SOCIETAL DEVELOPMENT

Development of societies as a whole is a concept operationalized by the present cybernetic model. It stands for the rising λ trajectories of all the system variables along with the increasing viability of the total system (Z and GS). The task of *societal planning* accordingly involves an integration of administrative, economic, educational, military, political (external and internal), and social policies for sys-

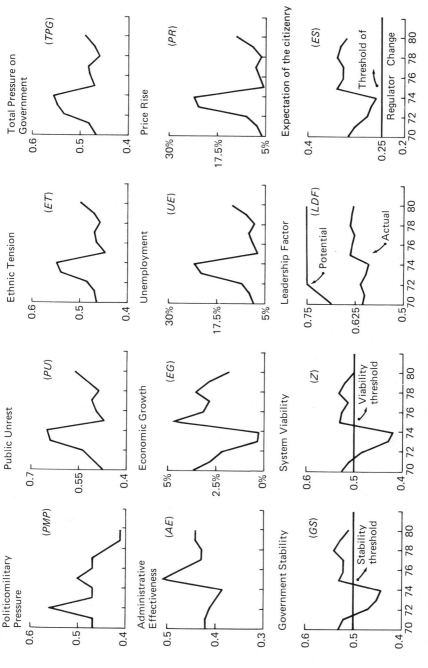

Figure 21-3. Performance panel for indian society (1970-1980) (Lower level of pmp and the impact of oil production).

tem development. The integration is required to augment the viability values of all the system variables concomitantly. The prime objective is to ensure that λ values of the variables and system viability remain at a level higher than 0.5 and never go down to 0.25. The various patterns of societal stability and instability as a function of λ values may be represented as shown in Figure 21-4.

The figure shows that a societal state will be unstable if any of its given variables is in the HI cell, irrespective of the status of other variables and *GS*. Political instability will be evidenced in the system if the values of *GS* are in any of the I cells. Marked political instability will increasingly prevail as the value of *GS* goes down into the hI cell. Persistence of *ES* values in 0.25 λ block will denote a societal state involving the change of its regulator, irrespective of the value of the status of *GS* and other system variables. Values of *ES* in the S cells denote a continuing state of high system stability. They are incompatible with the existence of hI and HI values of the other system variables. Permutative combination of the diagnostic status of *GS*, *ES*, and other variables define the diverse patterns

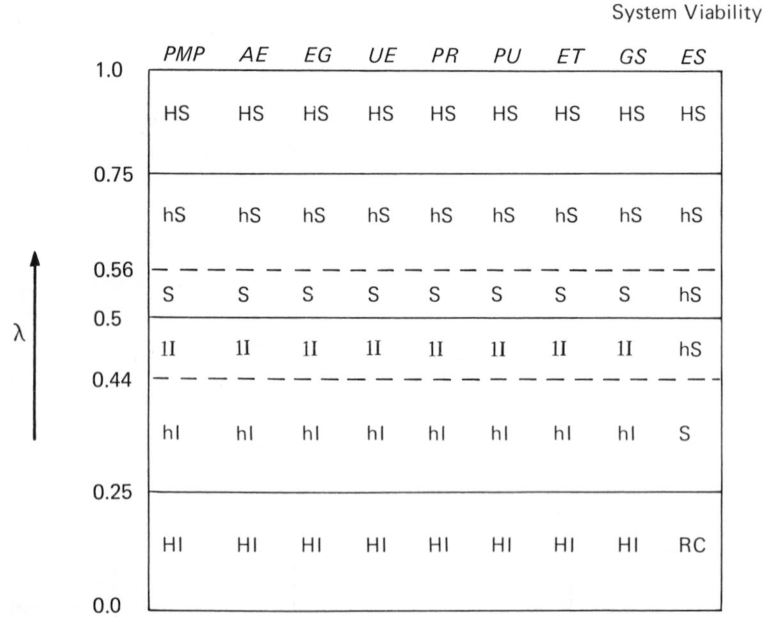

System Viability

	PMP	AE	EG	UE	PR	PU	ET	GS	ES
1.0	HS	HS	HS	HS	HS	HS	HS	HS	HS
0.75	hS	hS	hS	hS	hS	hS	hS	hS	hS
0.56 / 0.5	S	S	S	S	S	S	S	S	hS
0.44	II	II	II	II	II	II	II	II	hS
	hI	hI	hI	hI	hI	hI	hI	hI	S
0.25									
	HI	HI	HI	HI	HI	HI	HI	HI	RC
0.0									

λ

HS – Hyper-Stability, hS – High Stability

HI – Hyper-Instability, hI – High Instability

S – Stability, II – Low Instability,

RC – Regulator Change

Figure 21-4. Diagnostic status of system variables.

of system instability. Efforts toward sustained societal development will become increasingly difficult and ineffective depending upon the degree of system instability.

The planning priorities are logically indicated by the order: HI > hI > II > S. If any variable is in a hyper-instable state, it must have an overriding priority in the marshalling of the society's planning effort.

The pattern for planning is defined by the dynamics of system structure. Each system variable outputs [Ov] and receives [Iv] a set of links to and from other variables. The set of inputs links received [Iv] by a variable is the set of output links [Ov] from some precedent variable, and so on throughout the interacting system. Input and output sets of links provide a basis for identifying the *control interaction* among a cluster of variables, and thence an insight into the problems of regulating a given variable. Suppose one is interested in the control of price rise (*PR*). Figure 21-1 shows that it is receiving two links—population growth (*PG*) and economic growth (*EG*). But *EG* is also an output from investible resources (*IR*). Hence control interaction factor *C*, between *PR* and *IR* is given by

$$C\,(PR, IR) = \frac{|Oir \; \Omega \; Ipr|}{|Ipr|} = \frac{|EG \; \Omega \; EG, PG|}{|EG, PG|} = 1/2,$$

where *Oir* is the set of output links from *IR*, *Ipr* is the set of input links to *PR*, the numerator denotes the cardinality of the intersection set of *Oir* and *Ipr*, and the denominator, the cardinality of the input set, *Ipr*. Examining the interaction pattern of *PR* throughout the system, we find that control of *PR*, interacts with the control of *IR*, *AE*, *PMP*, *ED*, and *TPG*. The relative magnitudes of control interaction factors[4] computed with respect to them are given as

Variables   *AE, ED, IR, PMP, TPG*

Control
interaction
factor   ½, ½, ½, ⅔, ⅔

Precedent
variables   *EG, PG*

Control interaction factors signify that any attempt to regulate price rise would involve the *conjoint* regulation of the above five variables in a consistent and compatible manner, in addition to that of the precedent variables. Inconsistencies between the policies for their regulation and the regulation of price rise would make the regulatory process ineffective. If any of them is in the HI or

---

4. Multiplication of a control interaction factor with the salience weight of the variable concerned would serve to bring out its relative importance further. Salience weight of a variable is given by the total number of links—incoming and outgoing—associated with it.

hI diagnostic category, it may disclose an important source of the problem. The analysis here therefore shows that in order to control inflation, a government has to undertake conjointly a number of relevant measures concerning economic growth, population growth, administration, communication with citizens, investments in the economy, reduction of politicomilitary and total pressure on the government in a *coordinated* and *mutually consistent* manner. Relative emphasis among them would be determined by their diagnostic status, i.e., HI > hI > lI.

The inflationary situation in Brazil, for example, is a much discussed problem. In terms of our analysis, a definitive answer to this problem emerges. An inspection of the course of this society from 1970 to 1975 reveals that none of the problem-associated variables, i.e., *AE, ED, IR, PMP, TPG,* and *EG,* are in HI and hI status. This leaves only the population growth rate which indeed is very high. It is in the magnitude of 3.5 percent annually, inclusive of immigration. Accordingly, the unambiguous inference that emerges here is that rapid population growth is the primary cause of inflation in this society. Analysis of the situation by simulation algorithm supports this inference and leads to following definitive conclusions about this problem:

1. Brazil will not be able to solve its inflation problem if its current rate of population growth, i.e., ⩾ 3.5 percent per year (inclusive of immigration), continues.
2. Brazil would be able to bring down its annual rate of price rise to 6 percent if it were able to reduce its population growth rate (including immigration) to as little as 3 percent. This, however, presupposes the continuance of the economic growth rate at 9 percent annually in real terms.
3. Brazil would be able to attain high price stability, i.e., *PR* = 2.6 percent only provided it were able to reduce its *PG* rate to 2.3 percent and increase its *EG* rate to 10 percent annually.
4. Brazilian society would relapse into the chaotic pattern of inflationary spiral and political instability of the early 1960s if the politicomilitary pressure on it increased along with the continuance of the present *PG* rate.

Figure 21-5 compares the two possible time paths of Brazilian society showing both continuation and development of current trends and the impact of higher politicomilitary pressure. The problems of inflation and public unrest continue in the first case, but they amplify menacingly in the second case, leading to recurrent political chaos and economic crises.

The Achilles Heel of Nigerian society is ethnic tension, i.e., its internal tribal divisiveness. Its destabilizing role stems from history (i.e., History as an exogenous impact variable on *ET* in Figure 21-1) which is aggravated by the socioeconomic problems of price rise and unemployment. The latter are, in turn, bound up with administrative effectiveness, population growth, education, and political stability in an interlocking pattern. Despite its oil wealth, Nigeria may

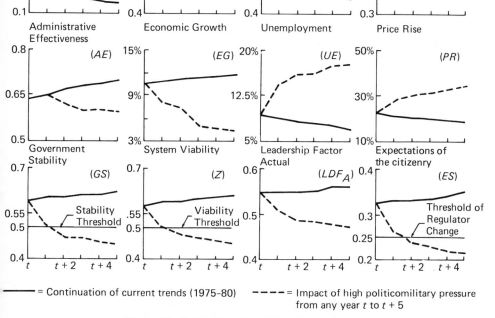

Figure 21-5. Two paths of Brazilian society.

not be able to solve any of the major problems shown in Table 21-11. On the other hand, if it is able to reduce its population growth to 2.3 percent and improve its *AE*, it would be able to avoid the specter of recurrent political instability, i.e., the value of *ES* would stay at a level higher than 0.25 λ. The two time paths are shown side by side in Figure 21-6.

Blocking factors of societal development are revealed by the recurring and persisting values of variables in the II, hI and HI categories in the time path societal systems. These blocking factors are at once the causes and consequences of a society's lowered viability. They may differ from society to society. Among the four societies discussed here, the blocking factors are identified below:

Brazil
1. Inflation.
2. Public unrest.
3. Unemployment.

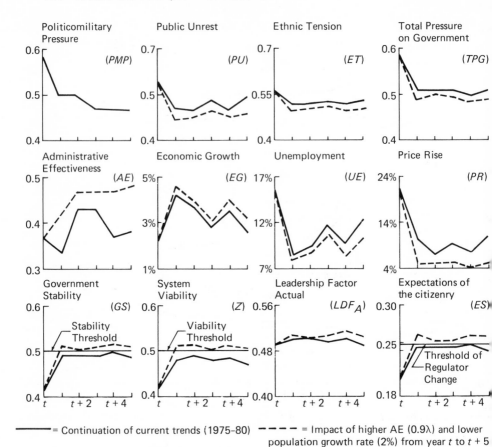

Figure 21-6. Two paths of Nigerian society.

India
1. Politicomilitary pressure.
2. Low administrative effectiveness.
3. Low economic growth (including agricultural development).
4. Unemployment.
5. Inflation.

Nigeria
1. Ethnic tension.
2. Politicomilitary pressure (primarily endogenous stresses).
3. Public unrest.
4. Unemployment.
5. Inflation.
6. Leadership factor.

United States
1. Politicomilitary pressure.
2. Low economic growth (engendered by energy crisis).

Planning for societal development would hence aim at eliminating the blocking factors that impede the progress of a society toward higher viability. The methodological paradigm for the planning process is summarized in Figure 21-7.

The implementation of this planning paradigm for societal development would require the creation of a sensitive and adequate management information system for monitoring a system's status and behavior.

8. SOCIETAL DEVELOPMENT AND ECOLOGICAL FACTORS

The energy crisis, pollution, population growth, droughts and shortages of non-renewable resources are important ecological factors affecting mankind.[5] They are potentially capable of leading to catastrophic population crashes within the vulnerable systems. In the dynamics of societal systems outlined here, all these factors are seen to affect the variable economic growth (EG), which has the highest salience weight in the system. The impact of population growth on EG is indirect, but it is direct on unemployment and inflation that are the destabilizing sources of internal crises. Droughts come under weather, an exogenous variable. Pollution problems, where present, would constitute auxiliary exogenous variables. The energy crisis, i.e., an inordinate increase in the prices of crude oil coupled with shortages of vital materials, comes under the exogenous variable, "economic relations with other societies." The impact of these factors therefore can be accounted for within the present context for any given society or group of societies.

The important point, however, is the differential and unequal impact of ecological factors on different societies, as mentioned earlier. Societies like Indonesia and Nigeria are relatively free from the "energy crisis" and possess larger national incomes through higher revenues from crude oil. Yet, they are not able to solve their chronic problems of unemployment, inflation, public unrest, and internal divisiveness. Other countries, like Ethiopia, Chad, and Niger, were in a vulnerable position even before the advent of the energy crisis. On the other hand, oil rich Arab nations have been able to overcome the problem of their chronic political instability and are unlikely to encounter the cruel dilemmas of poor societies in the coming decades. They are, however, vulnerable to the crises of inflation and militarism. The basic conclusion here is that there are no undifferentiated global predicaments. The blocking factors of societies constitute the real verities of life for mankind living within its societal arrangements.

5. Two reports of the Club of Rome—the Forrester and Meadows and Mesarovic and Pestel world models—accord primacy to this aspect of the global crisis.

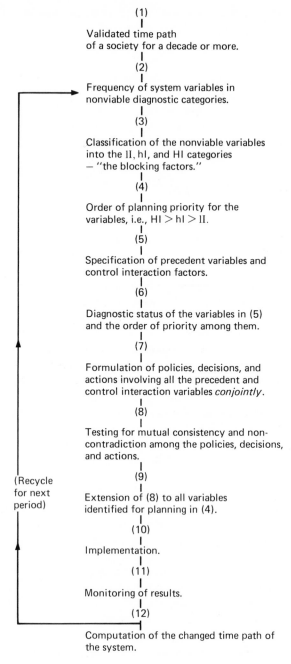

(1)

Validated time path
of a society for a decade or more.

(2)

Frequency of system variables in
nonviable diagnostic categories.

(3)

Classification of the nonviable variables
into the II, hI, and HI categories
— "the blocking factors."

(4)

Order of planning priority for the
variables, i.e., HI > hI > II.

(5)

Specification of precedent variables and
control interaction factors.

(6)

Diagnostic status of the variables in (5)
and the order of priority among them.

(7)

Formulation of policies, decisions, and
actions involving all the precedent and
control interaction variables *conjointly.*

(8)

Testing for mutual consistency and non-
contradiction among the policies, decisions,
and actions.

(Recycle
for next
period)

(9)

Extension of (8) to all variables
identified for planning in (4).

(10)

Implementation.

(11)

Monitoring of results.

(12)

Computation of the changed time path of
the system.

Figure 21-7. Methodological paradigm for the planning process.

Unsolved ecological problems represent the current limitations of human knowledge. Their solution would come from basic advances in the relevant fields of knowledge. Alternative sources of energy, reduction of pollutants, simple and effective contraceptives, and the recycling and substitution of scarce materials do not pose insoluble problems for man's creative ability. What is more important is the capability of societies to develop, accept, implement, and disseminate the solutions to ecological problems for their own and mankind's benefit. For developed societies, this capacity means the development and diffusion of solutions through sustained and collaborative efforts. For the weaker societies, this capacity means the capacity to accept, absorb, and implement these solutions on a societywide plane with minimal delays. Both types of capacities fundamentally depend on the high levels of political stability of the societies concerned. Political stability is the characteristic of viable societies (i.e., $0.5 < Z < 1$) only.

9. THE QUALITY OF SOCIETAL LIFE

The quality of societal life is a cognate concept of societal development. It differs from such related economic concepts as standard of living and per capita income. It is, rather, an integration of some basic societal factors that shape the nature of social living in a society. Lives of masses are affected by social tensions engendered by inflation, unemployment, and internal communal disharmony. Health and educational statuses of a society, as defined by the life expectancy and literacy levels of its citizens, are other important characterizers of citizens' lives in a society. Government stability affects societal living as a determinant of administrative and political processes. Quality of societal life (QSL) may then be defined as a function of these five variables:

$$(QSL)_t = \int_{t-1}^{t} \int_{0}^{1} (HL + ED + GS + PU + ET) d\lambda \, dt$$

The value of this variable reflects the conjoint impact of these five variables. It changes in accordance with the changes in the dependent variables. Computations of QSL for the four societies from 1961 to 1975 are given in Table 21-15 and shown graphically in Figure 21-8.

The table shows the time-varying behavior of this variable for the four societal systems. The viability threshold of this variable is also 0.5 λ. Accordingly, a prime task of world development may be defined as an increase in the value of this variable for the weaker systems.

10. SOCIETAL MODELS AS THE BASE OF REGIONAL AND WORLD MODELS

Delineation of the performance panels of societal systems would serve to characterize the status and course of a region they constituted. The statuses and courses

Table 21-15.   Quality of Societal Life in Four Societies (1961-1975)

Year	Brazil	India	Nigeria	U.S.
1961	0.470	0.462	0.394	0.680
1962	0.446	0.440	0.404	0.698
1963	0.44	0.470	0.405	0.686
1964	0.43	0.472	0.396	0.696
1965	0.466	0.454	0.410	0.712
1966	0.474	0.442	0.374	0.712
1967	0.508	0.448	0.332	0.682
1968	0.534	0.502	0.326	0.686
1969	0.540	0.486	0.380	0.672
1970	0.544	0.480	0.402	0.662
1971	0.558	0.476	0.408	0.682
1972	0.570	0.456	0.430	0.690
1973	0.576	0.422	0.450	0.670
1974	0.560	0.416	0.410	0.650
1975	0.560	0.490	0.386	0.644

of the regions collectively would depict the status and course of the world. In an analogous manner, the maximally viable trajectory of societal systems would serve to define the goals of regional and world development. Problems faced by the societies within a region, i.e., population growth, energy crises, food shortages; paucity of economic and technical resources, military pressure, and internal stresses, would identify the constraints on regional development. Developmental possibilities available through peace and cooperation in different fields would similarly identify the opportunities for regional and global development. A comprehensive and flexible framework for the modeling of global regions and the world hence appears to be realizable through the society-based approach. In its comprehensive form, the world model would consist of the performance panels of the concerned societal systems. Summation of the viability values (Z, GS) of the societies weighted by their respective populations would serve to define the viability status of the region or the world during any given period. Population weighting serves to underscore the equality and unity of mankind. The world is as good or as poor as the mass of mankind inhabiting it. Normalized values of the regional and global viabilities would also range between null and unity. The viabilities of societal systems, regions, and the world as a whole would hence vary between null and one in an analogous manner.

Viability of a region could, for example, be represented as

$$R\lambda = \sum_{j=1}^{M} Z_j P_j / \sum_{j=1}^{M} P_j,$$

where $R\lambda$ is the viability of region R, Z_j is the viability of the jth society in the region, P_j is the population weighting of the jth society, and M is the number of societies in the region.

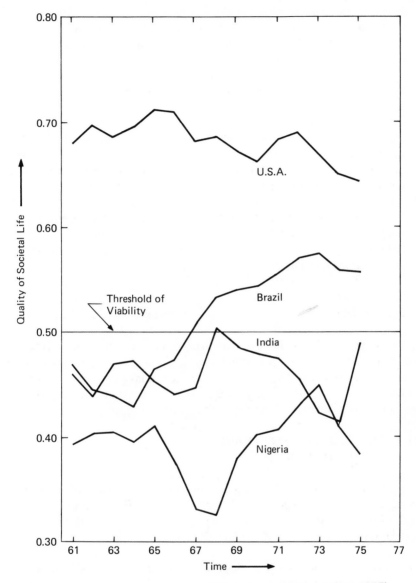

Figure 21-8. Quality of societal life in four societies (1961–1975).

Viability status of the world as a whole could similarly be represented as

$$W\lambda = \sum_{k=1}^{X} R_{\lambda k}\, P_k \Big/ \sum_{k=1}^{X} P_k,$$

where $W\lambda$ is the viability of the world, $R_{\lambda k}$ is the viability of the kth region, P_k is the population weightage of the kth region, and X is the number of global regions of the world. A synoptic review of the discussion so far leads to a definition of the world model along the following lines:

1. Performance panels of societal systems within global regions, i.e., regional performance panels.
2. Exogenous impacts on each system from other systems consisting of (a) politicomilitary tension and conflict relationships, (b) relationships of close political, economic, and military cooperation, (c) critical economic relationships involving crucial imports and exports, and (d) economic relationships involving the inflows of technology and investment resources.
3. The impact of ecological variables in the context of the relationships in (2).
4. Identification of unstable systems and their potential for impeding peace, cooperation, and development within a region and the world.
5. Display of aggregative regional data regarding population, per capita income, life expectancy, and literacy in the regional panels.
6. Time-varying course of the index $R\lambda$.
7. Time-varying course of the index $W\lambda$.
8. Societies falling within different viability zones over the successive periods.

Items one to eight would depict the changing course of global regions and the world as a whole. $R\lambda$ and $W\lambda$ would serve as the time-varying measures of the level of development or "overall health" of the regions and the world. The basis of the validity of the present schema is provided by the verifiable prediction and retrodictive confirmation of the course of its constituent societal systems.

11. SOCIETAL DEVELOPMENT AND
WORLD DEVELOPMENT

The present approach finally leads to a definition of the goals of regional and world development in a logically deductive manner. They emerge as the basic goals of human living in the world's societies. The maximally viable behavior of societal systems (i.e., $0.75 < Z < 1.0$) reflects these goals as

1. Human living in a world of peace and cooperation (low and null values of politicomilitary pressure).
2. The creation of material values for human consumption (high values of economic growth).
3. Freedom from economic pressures and insecurity (low and null values of price rise and unemployment).
4. Efficient and capable administration (high values of administrative effectiveness).

5. High level of knowledge and techniques in the societies (high values of education in a catholic sense).
6. The absence of social misery and unrest (low and null values of public unrest).
7. Communal harmony and social solidarity (low and null values of ethnic tension).
8. A social climate of hope and optimism (high values of expectations of the citizenry).
9. Political stability (S cell(s) values of ES).
10. System viability (high values of Z and GS).
11. Highly regarded ruling leadership (high values of leadership factor).
12. An uncrowded world (very low and null values of population growth rate).

At regional and global levels, the overall goal of world development would be to increase the viability of all constituent societies. The greater the number of viable societies and the greater their degree of viability, the greater would be the level of mankind's development.

The fundamental factor in this context is the cooperative relationship of societies with one another. It implies a continuous decline in the values of *PMP* for all the societal systems of the globe. Declining values of *PMP* would release rising levels of investment for productive growth. Increased resources and world peace would stimulate the development of appropriate scientific knowledge and technologies for the solution of population, pollution, productivity, and energy problems. Regenerative processes would become dominant in the behavior of societal systems leading them toward higher trajectories of system viability (Z).

World peace and cooperation would further help in a nonrestrictive dissemination of new technologies and innovations. They would also lead to increasing transfers of economic and technical resources saved from military preparations to the least developed societies. Solution of the problems of war and poverty on the globe would facilitate material existence, foster human—and humane—interdependence and ultimately form the basis for individual and collective happiness. Furthermore it will prepare mankind to enter a wider role in the Cosmos as a whole.

12. BIBLIOGRAPHY

Afanasyev, V. (1971). *The Scientific Management of Society,* Moscow: Progress Publishers.

Ashby, W.R. (1956). *An Introduction to Cybernetics,* London: Chapman & Hall.

Beer, Stafford (1964). *Cybernetics and Management,* New York: Wiley, Science Edition.

Beer, Stafford (1975). *Platform for Change,* London: Wiley.

Buckley, Walter (1967). *Sociology and General Systems Theory,* Englewood Cliffs, N.J., Prentice Hall.

Deutsch, Karl (1963). *The Nerves of Government,* Glencoe, Ill., Free Press.

Easton, David (1965). *A Systems Analysis of Political Life.* New York, Wiley.

Forrester, Jay (1969). *Urban Dynamics,* Cambridge, M.I.T. Press.

Kovach, Ladis, "Life Can Be So Nonlinear," *American Scientist,* 48:2.

Klir, J. and M. Valach, (1967). *Cybernetic Modelling,* London: Iliffe Books Ltd.

Maruyama, M. (1963). "The Second Cybernetics: Deviation–Amplifying Mutual Causal Processes." *American Scientist* 51:2.

Pekelis, V. (1974). *Cybernetics A to Z,* Moscow: Mir Publishers, (Trans. from Russian Edition published in 1970).

Rastogi, P.N. (1967). *A Cybernetic Model of Total Indian Society,*–An Introductory Framework., M.I.T., Cambridge: C.I.S. Monograph No. C/23–67.

Rastogi, P.N. (1969a). "Protracted Military Conflict and Politico-Economic Stability," *Simulation,* 11:7.

Rastogi, P.N. (1969b). "Cybernetic Approach to Organization Effectiveness," *Cybernetica,* 12:1.

Rastogi, P.N. (1970). "The Problem of Prediction in Social Systems." *Revue Internationale de Sociologie* Series 2, 5:3.

Rastogi, P.N. (1971). "The Dynamics of Government Stability." Paper contributed to the International Political Science Association Conference on Quantitative Methods & Political Substance, Mannheim, W. Germany.

Rastogi, P.N. (1976). "The Dynamics of Government Stability" revised version to be published in *Sozial-Wissenschaftliches Jahrbuch für Politik* Vol. 5. Munich: Olzog Verlag.

Rastogi, P.N. (1972a). "Cybernetic and Dialectical Approach to Social Phenomena–Toward a Theoretical Convergence." Paper contributed to International Conference on Systems & Cybernetics, Oxford.

Rastogi, P.N. (1972b). "Prediction & Measurement in Total Society Systems." *Yearbook of General Systems* Volume 17, 1972.

Rastogi, P.N. (1972c) "Time path of Total Society Systems–the Case of US Society (1951–1972). *Simulation,* 16:7.

Rastogi, P.N. (1972d). "The Course of Indian Society (1951–75) Cybernetic Analysis and Predictive Inference." Paper prepared for XII All India Sociological Conference, Varanasi.

Rastogi, P.N. (1973a). "Structure, Function and Process-Cybernetic Approach to Social Phenomena." Paper contributed to IV International Conference of American Cybernetic Society, Washington, 1970; Revised version published in *Sociological Bulletin* 22:2, 1973.

Rastogi, P.N. (1973b). "Performance Panels for Societies: The Concept and the Methodology." *International Review of Sociology* 9:1–2.

Rastogi, P.N. (1974a). "The Course of French Society, (1955–73)." *Simulation* 18:4.

Rastogi, P.N. (1974b). "Cybernetic Analysis of the Behaviour of Urban Systems." Paper contributed to the Seminar on Urban Development, I.I.M., Calcutta; Revised version to appear in *Kybernetes* (1976).

Rastogi, P.N. (1975). *The Nature and Dynamics of Factional Conflict.* Delhi: Macmillan.

Rastogi, P.N. (1975). "Time Path of Indian Societal System." Project report prepared for Centre for Policy Research. New Delhi: November, 1975.

Rastogi, P.N. (1976). *The Behaviour of Societal Systems.* I.I.A.S., Simla, forthcoming.

Rastogi, P.N. (1976). *The Behaviour of Societal Systems and Course of the World.* Paper contributed to a working seminar on Global Opportunities and Constraints for Regional Development organized by IPSA, UNESCO & World University at Harvard University, Cambridge, February 18–22, 1976.

Schon, Donald (1971). *Beyond the Stable State.* London: Temple Smith.

Singh, Jagjit (1966). *Information Theory, Language and Cybernetics.* New York: Dover.

Tustin, Arnold (1953). *The Mechanism of Economic Systems.* London: Heinemann.

Tustin, Arnold (1955). "Feedback," in *Automatic Control,* Volume 2. New York: 1955.

Wiener, Norbert (1948). *Cybernetics.* New York: Wiley.

Wiener, Norbert (1958). *Nonlinear Problems in Random Theory.* Cambridge, Mass.: The MIT Press, Lecture 8.

Wiener, Norbert (1962). "The Mathematics of Self-Organizing Systems." In *Recent Developments in Information & Decision Processes,* ed. R. Machol and P. Gray. New York: Macmillan.

✳ *Chapter 22*

Information Systems for World Models*

Manfred Kochen

1. INTRODUCTION

Wide publicity has been given to plans for information systems to
help top management in public and private organizations evaluate
programs, formulate and test alternative policies. "But no data bank has been
found in civilian agencies of city, county, state, or federal government that is in
fact delivering on such promises" (Westin 1972, p. 60). Decision makers often
use data to support a position they have already taken and seek to support than
to reach a position in the first place. Masses of data are little used, perhaps with
good reason.

Even wider publicity has been given to "world models" and their use to support the limits-to-growth and similar movements. The conclusions and methodologies associated with these models have generated controversy rather than the
consensus and confidence initially expected from the application of powerful
methods of systems theory to socially important problems. The impact of these

*I am indebted to several people, some of whose ideas are incorporated here and who
helped me improve this paper. The participation of I. de Sola Pool, J. Forrester, K.W.
Deutsch, and M. Mesarovic in a very stimulating panel session on this topic at the Annual
Meeting of the General Systems Research Society in Boston on February 20, 1976, supplied
me with several important ideas reported here, and these are gratefully acknowledged. So
are K.W. Deutsch's comments and the help of R. Crickman and H. Frederick on an earlier
draft, as well as useful discussions with K. Chen and L. Kazda. A. Markovits' transcribed
version of my presentation at the conference on "Global Opportunities and Constraints for
Regional Development," at Harvard on February 21, 1976, is incorporated into this version.
A valuable suggestion, by M. Marien, was received too late to incorporate into a revision.
It is to insert another category of discussants into Figure 22-1, between groups two and
three, called "Other Commentators," to include historians, philosophers, leaders from business and labor, natural scientists, humanists, and others who are not social scientists (group
two).

models is not known, and if it is not yet great, that too may be an unintended blessing.

For many reasons, there are no information systems in use where plans are formed and decisions made. The most evident is the need for time series data "which for the most part we do not presently have" (Michael 1973, p. 54). A deeper reason for the lack of adequate information systems to support planning is that we have not yet developed models to help us decide which data it is important to collect. Forrester (1971), believing that anyone who proposes a policy does so on the basis of a model (or mental image), initiated a line of model development for calculating world levels of population, pollution, usage of natural resources, and capital investment. As intended, *World Dynamics* stimulated a series of studies—critiques, alternate models, tests (Chen 1972; Mesarovic and Pestel 1974; Meadows et al. 1972) of which the present volume is the latest contribution.

Critics of world models—and there are many in the scientific as well as the policy-making communities—might reflect not only about the rate at which model development has been maturing but also about the learning potential inherent in newer forms of communication within a community as a means to improve and accelerate model development by an order of magnitude. To be sure, present models are still more appropriately used as toys than as tools to help shape important policies.

We try to show in this paper how the imaginative and novel use of computer conferencing could help create a community and a climate in which a series of better models, the data bases to support them, and improved mechanisms of utilization emerge as outputs of a continuing learning process.

We suggest that highest priority be given to building an information system that significantly advances the development of models in a direction that will make them actually be used by planners, resulting in wiser planning. By wiser planning we mean policies and decisions based on (one) a deeper understanding of the key issues; (two) reliable predictions about likely consequences, at least having and heeding a reliable early warning system for major impending disasters that are avoidable; (three) humanitarian values that reflect the long-term best interests of many of the world's people; and (four) the courage and resolve to execute such policies consistently. It is, of course, better to have a good and valid model that is as yet unused than a poor model that is used. Our thesis is that, in this area of investigation, where what is to be modeled includes the likely behavior of planners and decision makers, good models *evolve;* this *requires* their being used. Only when such models begin to evolve can we rely on them to help us decide which important time series data to collect.

The most important information is about the goals of a social system, its controls, the consistency between the two, and the goals and attitudes of its human components. "The conventional internal accounting and reporting systems of management and the traditional general-purpose, general-parameter information systems conventionally employed by social science do not generate information of these kinds" (Dunn 1971, pp. 254-255). The major limitation of management science is increasingly recognized as "our inability to effectively sort out conflicting objectives" (Hertz 1971, p. 14). This applies equally to "system theory," whether that is interpreted by electrical engineers, general system theorists, operations researchers, or decision theorists, some of whom are still incredibly naive about the power of their methodologies in dealing with complex problems that cannot be divorced from their own political and socioemotional aspects.

The main point of this paper is that it is most important to inject information into the process of building world models to help key planners improve their problem representations and ask better questions. One example of a "better" question is one based on an intuitive understanding of something previously counterintuitive. Only secondarily should information systems help planners to use the best models available and to validate them. But these functions are necessary, too.

2. DESIDERATA FOR AN INFORMATION SYSTEM TO IMPROVE LEARNING IN THE MODEL-BUILDING COMMUNITY

Seven assumptions about the properties an information system and its community of users must have if it is to improve communication and productivity within a scientific community by an order of magnitude are presented below. The first two are attitudes toward modeling not now widely held in practice. An important consideration for the proposed information system is that it helps its users to acquire these attitudes.

1. Models are useful primarily to answer specific questions. These questions usually have to be decided a priori and formulated at a given level of specificity. Models are used secondarily to raise questions in some framework, with a point of view that would not have occurred to users. People are thus helped to ask questions, to represent problems in ways they would not have done without having had hands-on experience with a certain model.

   General purpose models are rarely a reliable tool in solving specific problems. Experience has shown repeatedly that methodological advances in a specialized area of knowledge lead to better problem solving in that area than general methods; attempts at theorem proving in logic by heuristic methods and symbolic integration by computer are two examples.

2. World models are not total. They tend to be broad and shallow, rather than deep and narrow. Yet, the word *world* should not mislead people into thinking that these are complex models that take everything into account. Some deal with problems, such as pollution of air or water, that transcend national

boundaries. Others deal with problems such as solid waste disposal, that occur, with minor variations, in many regions or cities of the world. All recognize that variables cannot simply be divided into first-order and higher-order effects, that feedback loops can give rise to systemic effects such as instabilities and pseudorandom behavior.

3. There is an important distinction, made by J. Forrester, among three types of information bases. The first are numerical data bases. They help us assess the state of the world. Today, they consist mostly of economic, technical, and demographic data. A potentially large part of this type of information base is to be found in various data archives of public opinion, but these need to be made far more accessible than at present. The second kind of data base is the scientific and social science literature, both primary and secondary. The third kind of information base has traditionally been in our heads, and it reflects what we know and learn about how decisions are made, how models are shaped, and how the images that guide our actions are really formed and used. It contains more attitudinal and social data, representing peoples' beliefs, ideas, and symbols. This third information base is to be made explicit as the record of an ongoing computer conference.

4. Professer Ithiel de Sola Pool has suggested that social scientists will increasingly want to use some of the data that are operational, for instance, in the national accounts, at a highly disaggregated level. Many years ago, when people were confined to hand calculations or desk calculators, it was impossible to keep highly disaggregated data, and people made their living aggregating them, which is why we have them in such aggregated form. But present-day computer processing capabilities free us from the burden of having to live with highly aggregated data. Not all data collected for operational purposes will be useful for social science purposes since data collected for one purpose are often not useful for another. This observation does not imply that we should drop the concept of highly aggregated variables, such as those used in many world models, because we now have enough computing capacity. We want the ability to zoom rapidly between highly aggregated and a highly disaggregated version of the same set of variables and to see both simultaneously. We want to be able to take a worm's eye view and work our way through the data, the paths in the forest, as well as the eagle's eye view, to see what the entire shape of the forest is, even while we are in it.

5. A model will not predict reality far enough in advance as a reliable basis for action or decisions under uncertainty. It may not be a realistic expectation to forecast to the year 2050. It would be quite a feat to make accurate short-range forecasts in some essential details. In the case of weather forecasting, for example, it is not difficult to predict tomorrow's weather much of the time as an ad hoc linear extrapolation of yesterday's and today's. To put it on a scientific basis required seven-layered models of the atmosphere to get a 24-hour forecast; and not too many years ago it took more than 24 hours to compute that forecast by solving a vast system of partial differential equations

with moving boundary conditions. Another reason for lowering expectations about models capable of long-range forecasting is that the kind of world system we are trying to predict is inherently unpredictable. For example, most of us hope that this conference, with its human components, will make a difference in the shape of world models to come, which in turn may make a difference in the shape of the world to come. We cannot even predict accurately what conclusions we will reach by the end of this conference. Perhaps Church's theorem has some bearing on this. It says that in any system our creativity outstrips our ability to anticipate the outcome of that creativity. There are propositions, which we cannot enumerate beforehand, that we can eventually invent.

6. Good models evolve with use. This is a critical assumption. Good models are not made by one person and then sold for use by others. They evolve within a community of people who get hands-on experience with one another's models and criticize them.

7. The most important kind of information concerns the goals of social systems, their controls and constraints, and the consistency between the goals and the controls, in order to help us sort out conflicting objectives. It follows that an information system should provide such help in three ways. First, it should help in the model-building process, so that planners, social scientists, and others will be able to ask questions based on an intuitive understanding of what was previously counterintuitive. Second, it should help its users make decisions in simple cases, in small steps, where it serves their short-term self-interest. Third, it should, at the same time, help them to perceive the world more imaginatively and more resourcefully; it should help people come up with richer problem representations with a longer time horizon and a broader interest scope. It should help them select the key variables and concepts and assumptions with more specificity and depth than they have today.

It is very important to help not only scientists but also the general public to *use* models. In June 1976, the voters of California were asked to decide if the development of nuclear energy should be banned, and they had little information, imagination, or experience relating to what they were asked to judge. Perhaps it is too ambitious to expect today's policy and decision makers to change their images and modes of behavior so immediately as to become receptive to systems thinking. But there is hope for the next generation. Courses involving sophisticated games and simulation are now successfully offered in universities. Fifth graders are able to learn some of the key concepts of systems theory with the help of a program called "Systems Analysis for the Classroom," created by K. Boulding.

It seems worth making explicit what we should *not* expect of an information system supporting the development of world models. Some social scientists tend to view world models as analogues of physical models, such as those for planetary motion, and to expect world models to be validated by social science data by statistical inference techniques. As suggested earlier, we should not, as a rule, expect models of the social world to have good predictive power. The primary purpose of world models has not been to predict, and emphasis on prediction in social science modeling has been unproductive, because, as Forrester has shown, social systems are broadband, the opposite of what is epitomized by a clock. The complex systems that are the objects of world models are characterized by a great deal of noise; the search for simple laws—or perhaps any laws that appear as sharp signals or regularities in the noise, such as Kepler's three laws—may be fruitless. The most help that we have a right to expect from a world model is that it exhibit the same kind of periodicity, stabilities, instabilities, or other phenomena as the system being modeled and that these global properties of the model be quite insensitive to exact numerical values of estimated parameters. Thus, use of data for estimating parameters, regression analyses, or the like is not an important function of the information system needed.

These seven assumed desiderata imply two main kinds of problems. The first deals with how to improve the model-building process. A key problem is how to improve the exchange and improvement of ideas, not data or their use; to help us become more conscious of what we can do well now, what we cannot yet do, and what, perhaps, we are not likely to do at all. We need to realize, for example, that we lack methodologies for measuring closeness of fit between historical accounts of decisions and the protocols of a computer program simulating such a historical process.

The second class of problems deals with model use, with closure of the widening gap between what is already known and understood and its utilization in real situations. We can identify four specific information bases that need to be created for each of these two classes of problems.

For the first class of problems, these are

1. Registers of who is doing what. Ever since Forrester's book appeared, scientists in many centers created variants of his models. DYNAMO, the computer programming language in which his 1970 world model was expressed, became available for public use in FORTRAN. Such models proliferated with the great publicity given to world models by Meadows et al. (1972) and the availability of ever-higher-level programming languages in which to express new models, at the same time that some of those experienced with these models became convinced that they had no impact. Until recently, people who wrote such programs would know about similar programs written by colleagues only within the same insular intellectual community. Since the convenient and increasingly widespread use of networks (usually of "mini" computers), investigators in over a dozen intellectual centers can more easily communicate about their models. Documentation of programs—their existence and how to run them—still leaves much to be desired, and the potential of computer conferencing over these networks for mutual criticism and constructive sugges-

tions of one another's models is far from being tapped. In the area of world models there will probably soon be a half-dozen centers throughout the world, involving perhaps 100 people who should be included in such a register or directory. Also included should be several hundred potential users and critics. A register that makes it easier for the members of this invisible college to be aware of, and in touch with, one another's work can be viewed as a need.

2. Key findings or conditions that world models are to explain and with which they should be consistent. A great deal of research has been done on the various specific problems that are part of a world model. These findings are scattered throughout the literatures of a great variety of disciplines, including anthropology, sociology, political science, various branches of engineering, biomedicine, and even law, to mention but a few. They were reported by authors using vastly different conceptualizations, styles of investigation, and even languages. It may be difficult to recognize that a finding obtained by a sociologist can be used in conjunction with a finding obtained by an engineer. Yet world model developement should build upon, and be consistent with, relevant findings from these disciplines to the extent that these findings can be restated in the same language and conceptualization. There is a need to evaluate, synthesize, and bring to bear on world model development what is relevant and significant in the 2682 social science sources listed in 1964 (White and associates) plus probably twice that number published since then.

3. Key questions and issues of concern to those responsible for steering the course of nations and regions. This could take the form of questions that planners and decision makers have actually raised. Astute political analysts could add to this list questions and issues that probably occupied decision makers although they were unwilling to raise them publicly.

These concerns, overt and covert, need to be juxtaposed with issues they *should be* concerned with, according to various value orientations. What is probably most needed are means to help actual decision makers expand their horizons, their options for problem representation. It is desirable that they become more aware of their models, the degree of consistency between the priorities they assign, or think they assign, to issues and the priorities displayed in their behavior as observed by others. At the same time, there must be data relevant to the real constraints in the exercise, of options, as well as data that reflect imagined constraints, such as a balanced budget.

4. Key implications in the form of briefings or recommendations that can be used by decision makers. These should include a clear statement of the assumptions a decision maker must accept if he adopts the conclusion. It should also include an indication of how sensitive the conclusion is, at least qualitatively, to the most questionable assumptions.

Busy decision makers seldom deal with models at a level of specificity greater than that presentable in a short briefing with summarizing graphs or charts of highly aggregated data. Nor are they notably receptive to devices that would broaden and deepen their problem representation, perspectives, and world views. Advisers have been generally ineffective in influencing the decision makers they advise, but they often exert influence on the next generation of decision makers. Thus, the assumptions and implications of world models may be expected, at best, to change the perceptions and premises of the planners who will replace those on the job now.

The second kind of information needed by world modelers is that which fosters utilization of the more accepted existing models. Four specific information bases that appear to be needed are

1. The documentation necessary actually to obtain, run, and possibly change the computer programs embodying various world models. This would include such evaluations of, and experiences with, the models as are available. It would provide an annotated subject index to available operational programs. By that we mean a kind of thesaurus, combined with a glossary, to help a user decide whether or not he wants to use a particular program, and if so, what step to take next. It differs from the directory to the investigators who are in the process of developing models, but there is a great deal of overlap between these two.

2. Documentation generally aimed at helping other computer programmers to run or revise a program. There is also a definite need to help people who cannot acquire or maintain any kind of computer expertise to run programs embodying some world models. This requires aids to learning, and "friendly" prompting, especially for novice, nonfluent computer users. It must start with elementary details, such as the location of a terminal, how to get to it, how to get an account on some computer, how to turn the terminal on, call the program, what button to press, and when, and other such basics. Names and telephone numbers of people to call for help are also of great value.

3. The value of certain input data and parameters needed to use a model. This requires an index to sources containing such data and, eventually, the data themselves. Such a data base must be organized so that relevant data can be readily retrieved in a form suitable for input to models. Such data include indicators about the state of the world, including estimates of the reliability of both the data and their source.

   Since we cannot yet specify what time series we need, we can estimate only roughly how many data indicative of the state of the world exist. Data relevant to food come from periodic FAO sources that add up to about 40,000 title issued from 1945 to 1974. If about a third of these contain data, they total about 4×10^9 characters (at 1000 characters per page, 100 pages per publication). Some of the current annual publications producing data likely to be relevant to world models includes *State of Food and Agriculture*

(3 × 10^5 characters per year), *Animal Health Yearbook* (3 × 10^5), *Monthly Bull. Agric. Econ. & Stat.* (3 × 10^6), *Trade Yearbook* (5 × 10^5), *Production Yearbook* (8 × 10^5), and *Commodity Reviews* (2 × 10^5). The ILO has data on the health, welfare, employment levels, retirement of workers, training, and forecasts for all countries. *International Labour Documentation* probably generates about 6 × 10^8 characters per year, the *Yearbook of Labor Statistics* about 8 × 10^5, and there are several others. WHO issues *Epidemiol. and Vital Statistics Report* (10^6 characters per year), *Technical Reports* (10^6 characters per year), an annual report (2 × 10^5). Since 1952, UNESCO has published the yearly *Basic Facts and Figures* covering literacy, educational attainment, school populations, and the like, on 215 territories, and UCLA has produced the annual *Statistical Abstract for Latin America* since 1955 (area, population, social organization, economic characteristics). The Council of Europe's annual *Donne és Statistiques* has been covering transportation, GNP, and the like, since 1954. The *Stat. Int'l des grand villes* of the International Statistical Institute, the publications of the U.N. Statistical Office, and the U.S. Bureau of the Census give an idea of the data volumes available. Very roughly these contribute another 4 × 10^9 characters of accumulated data, totaling perhaps 10^{10}, growing at an annual rate of 10^9 per year.

The latest U.S. Census is now stored on the trillion-bit mass, on-line memory of the Berkeley Radiation Laboratory, of which it fills about half. Data from satellite photographs such as EROS are publically available and, if accumulated, would constitute an enormous data base of potential value for some models.

The problems of creating a data archive from such a vast miscellany of sources are well known (Bisco, 1970). It is less clear whether the cost of solving them does not exceed the magnitude of the need to do so.

4. The information processing requirements for the analysis of world models. Many of the models use systems of plain or differential equations whose solutions require the inverting of large matrices. It is known (Ralston and Wilf 1960) to require a n^3m seconds of computer time for an n × n matrix with a computer that multiplies two numbers in m seconds; here a is between 2 and 3. With $a = 2$, $n = 1000$, $m = 10^{-7}$ seconds, it would take 200 seconds or about $10 per run at $.05 per second. With $n = 10,000$, $a = 2$, and $m = 10^{-8}$ sec. (10 nanoseconds), it would take 20,000 seconds or about five hours of computer time ($1000 per run). Thus, for the kinds of models now in use, rather large and fast computers, with vast auxiliary storage capacities, would be needed.

3. A SUGGESTED INFORMATION SYSTEM

What kind of information system, if any, has these properties, so that it could foster a sufficiently coherent regional outlook to effect wise action? Cognitive understanding alone will probably not suffice. Emotional understanding is required as well. Mesarovic and Pestel (1974, p. 147) want to foster a change in outlook whereby a famine in tropical Africa is considered as relevant and disturbing to a German as a famine in Bavaria. For this to occur, a necessary condition may be that those whose outlook is to be changed must be sufficiently secure in essential respects. If the information system does nothing for him—or even threatens his security—if it clashes with his basic intuitions on major issues, he will, at best, not use it at all. Given that he does use some kind of information system, then the artful use of television holds promise of bringing a more vivid perception of others, of bringing about such changes in outlook (Platt 1975). But will the native of tropical Africa consider the massacre of athletes in Munich as reprehensible as an act of terrorism in his own land?

Despite the potential of information technologies to bring people's world images closer together, the evidence appears to point toward increases in the socioemotional distances among groups of people. Increasing energy costs affect those in developing countries more harshly than they affect those in industrialized regions. The difference in vulnerability to shock thus increases. So does the difference in the confidence people have in controlling their own fates rather than believing them to be governed by chance. While a few continue to believe in the methods of science as a reliable path to an understanding even of social systems, a larger multitude begin to distrust methods of the mind and trust their feelings more than their reason. The gap between those who rely on reason and those who harken to their hearts seems to increase.

Feelings are of many sorts. They can brake or amplify reasons. They can become polarized, and it is possible for both self-reinforcing human networks of inhumanity as well as networks of compassion and solidarity to emerge under certain conditions.

Some of those committed to reason are convinced of the merit and value of world models. Yet, few scientists would place their entire trust in a model as a basis for decisions about a spouse, a career, financial investment, business, or even medical treatment. They, like their nonscientific colleagues, would place some weight on clinical judgment, intuition, and subjective feelings. The decisions, on which hang the fate of the world or a region, are of a similar nature.

Feelings and moods are subject to swings and fashions. That is the case for reason as well. The concern with world models initiated by Forrester seems to have given rise to the cognitive fad, "Limits to Growth," at least in the United States. At the same time, there may also have been a moodswing expressed by "Limits to U.S. Control," that is also widely felt. Both feelings and thoughts have such transient components, but they also carry the germ of something of lasting value, one that can be built upon.

It may just be possible to persuade builders of world models to accomodate affective aspects that are not in the traditional mainstream of science. It may be equally possible to persuade anti-intellectuals, the scientifically untrained, and some of those with strong feelings about how to right wrongs, to accommodate some of the objective and scientific thinking inherent in world models. One way to do this may be to help everyone to learn a common language, a new language in which each person can express what is most important to him.

The new language probably ought to be a pictorial one, suitable for presentation to people over television. It should be adequate for stimulating people to form useful mental images that blend their feelings with their reason. It should help them cope with their immediate individual problems *at the same time* that it helps them become concerned about problems affecting the larger community. It is not enough merely to inform a person so that he can look out soley for his own short-term interests, that may eventually hurt him as well as all the others, as in "The Tragedy of the Commons."[1] The consequences of ignoring longer-term, more communitywide traps or opportunities must be dramatized to the point where the necessary compromises or trades will be made. Thus it is most important to increase consciousness about the need to make such trades.

The Tragedy of the Commons is easily avoided by a centralized authority, a powerful manager who acts in the interests of the community as a whole. Indeed, the world models developed by Forrester or Mesarovic-Pestel may be used by some *leader* with the power to change world events. He may attempt to act with these models' help to try to steer a wise course. This method of relying on benevolent leadership is fraught with peril, even if it reflects consensus among key executives. Its success depends crucially on the quality of the world model. If, consciously or not, the leader places personal or short-range interests in top priority, or if he does not make the necessary compromises or trades, or is not able to marshal the appropriate knowledge, understanding, and wisdom at the right time and translate it into the action indicated by them, catastrophes of great magnitude can result.

A safer, though perhaps slower and less efficient, course is to allow a network of several information systems at various levels, each tailored to the needs of some individual user, to grow. We should assume, conservatively, that each user will put his own short-run interests first. He will not use or trust an information system that does not help serve those interests well. If, *in addition,* such an information system raises his level of consciousness and active concern about traps and opportunities of import to a larger community over the longer run, then this may not detract from the information system's utility to him. Moreover, if the component of the information system that represents the social dynamics of further ranging import is one that is constantly evolving—perhaps converging to a world image in which key aspects are shared by most people—with his *creative participation*—then he is more likely to accept, internalize, and be guided by it. Leaders, people with superior or special insights and analytic

1. This is a situation in which everyone gains in the short run by ruining the common, shared resources, as for a number of herdsmen whose cattle graze on a common pasture (Hardin 1968).

skills, are contributors to this evolving image too. If their imput plays a greater role in shaping a world image, it is because it has proved itself more useful in steering wise courses.

The traditional criteria of science do not apply to world models. A model of the planets is judged by its power to explain observed planetary motions and to predict. It is absurd to talk about the planets choosing to change their orbits to forestall some disaster on the basis of their understanding of the planetary model. Yet that is precisely why we are interested in world models. After all, a key person (or a coalition of key persons) who understands a model such as Forrester's, even if it is refined to the point of taking into account *any* action that he "could" take, can always take at least one action not anticipated in the model or invalidate the model by his action.

A world model should, therefore, ride piggyback on information systems that help key decision makers, midelite representatives (e.g., opinion leaders) and the people who form mass opinions with what matters most to them. In a democratic society this may include how to get reelected. For mass opinion, it may effect or reflect a change in the climate of opinion by informing people of what others are doing, e.g., switching away from large cars. The information system must provide a campaigner with advice helpful in mapping an election campaign and in voting so as to represent his constituents, all in such a way that it registers or "clicks" with him, so that he believes it, acts on it, even depends on it. At the same time it must remind him when severe conflicts between "voting his conscience" and "voting the will of his constituents" begin to arise. Even more important than "voting his conscience" is "voting according to the longer-range interests of the community."

Computer conferencing, coupled with television, offers promise for such information systems. Suppose, for example, that an official in the U.S. Department of Agriculture, in response to his daily signing on his computer terminal, receives the message that a certain number of inhabitants of Calcutta are predicted to die of starvation at a specified future time. He probes the validity of the forecast in various ways, explores the range of possibilities, and examines his own reactions. He considers his job responsibilities, his powers, his authority, and the constraints on his action. What are his options for action? What will be the consequences of each option, and how will these matter to him? Here is where he first uses a model. If he is appointed, let us assume that he is motivated, at least in large part, by the desire to gain his superiors' approval, to reflect favorably upon his department, to maintain (obtain) reinforcement or support for his move. But he is also motivated, in part, by conscience and by views that others have expressed. If he is resourceful and imaginative, he may come up with options no one has anticipated or thought of before, at least in the context and at this time of decision.

Through his computer terminal, he can request that various scenarios be played out quickly via dramatized TV briefings. He does this by conversing with the system and with others in the system, though they be remote in space and time. The system is designed to help him ask incisive and wise questions. Above all, the system constantly evaluates how well it is performing, and utilizes such evaluation data to improve its own performance. Quite possibly, the best questions this user will ask will not have been anticipated. Thus, answers for these will not have been prerecorded. Often information will have been collected for purposes other than those it seems useful for, and that may lower its validity for such unanticipated uses.

A computer conference would permit those who have questions concerning previous papers, in a conference like this, that they were very eager to ask when they first occurred, to record them at just that time. They would simply enter them into the computer over a terminal. Later, someone would edit them and put the entire discussion into some (or several) structure(s). A face-to-face conference can easily drift off in many directions, and often there is possible loss of important aspects if the discussion is not channeled toward some kind of closure. Computer conferencing, in conjunction with other forms of communication, has a valuable potential for overcoming the constraints of cognitive time, space, and socioemotional barriers. But it would have to couple at least seven groups of people, as shown in Figure 22-1.

The purpose of such an on-line intellectual community is to jointly shape, use, and revise ideas, questions, and models, to begin to share some of the data that are available. It could begin with a simple directory of who is concerned with and about what. It could include detailed instructions about how to get an account number on the computer in question, what buttons to push, when, and how to participate.

A good information system must therefore not only be based on findings and facts reported prior to the time they are requested; it must also be able rapidly and reliably to provide for the acquisition of new information when needed or its valid inference from what is already recorded. This requirement imposes severe processing and storage requirements on the information technology. Moreover, it is to help the research community to mobilize investigators in acquiring needed data. If such investigations cannot be completed on time, even with technological aid, then the best judgments or estimates of selected experts need to be solicited. To control for possible estimation biases, variants of the Delphi Method would be set up.[2]

---

2. Delphi is a procedure for "structuring a group communication process so that the process is effective in allowing a group of individuals, as a whole, to deal with a complex problem" (Linstone and Turoff 1975, p. 3). In general, this involves several stages of discussion and revision of questions, and often individual biases are canceled out. Because some of the problems that would-be users of world models encounter do not lend themselves to precise analytical techniques but can benefit from subjective judgments on a collective basis, and because these problem solvers may have diverse backgrounds in experience and expertise, the Delphi Technique is an appropriate supplement to the use of world models.

Purpose of this sketch: To stimulate discussion, provide starting point for system development.

Goal of system: To enable world models to develop toward helping policy makers shape a better future by facilitating fruitful interactions among and between (1) modelers, (2) social scientists, (3) policy makers, (4) educators, (5) general public, (6) information scientists. Interacting includes informing, criticizing, intellectually influencing others in the network toward the emergence of shared or coherently interconnected world images that help their users improve their problem representations and act more wisely.

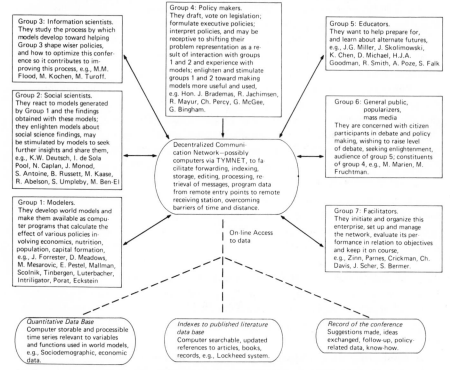

Group 3: Information scientists. They study the process by which models develop toward helping Group 3 shape wiser policies, and how to optimize this conference so it contributes to improving this process, e.g., M.M. Flood, M. Kochen, M. Turoff.

Group 4: Policy makers. They draft, vote on legislation; formulate executive policies; interpret policies, and may be receptive to shifting their problem representation as a result of interaction with groups 1 and 2 and experience with models; enlighten and stimulate groups 1 and 2 toward making models more useful and used, e.g. Hon. J. Brademas, R. Jachimsen, R. Mayur, Ch. Percy, G. McGee, G. Bingham.

Group 5: Educators. They want to help prepare for, and learn about alternate futures, e.g., J.G. Miller, J. Skolimowski, K. Chen, D. Michael, H.J.A. Goodman, R. Smith, A. Poze, S. Falk

Group 2: Social scientists. They react to models generated by Group 1 and the findings obtained with these models; they enlighten models about social science findings, may be stimulated by models to seek further insights and share them, e.g., K.W. Deutsch, I. de Sola Pool, N. Caplan, J. Monod, S. Antoine, B. Russett, M. Kaase, R. Abelson, S. Umpleby, M. Ben-El

Group 6: General public, popularizers, mass media They are concerned with citizen participants in debate and policy making, wishing to raise level of debate, seeking enlightenment, audience of group 5; constituents of group 4, e.g., M. Marien, M. Fruchtman.

Decentralized Communication Network—possibly computers via TYMNET, to facilitate forwarding, indexing, storage, editing, processing, retrieval of messages, program data from remote entry points to remote receiving station, overcoming barriers of time and distance.

Group 1: Modelers. They develop world models and make them available as computer programs that calculate the effect of various policies involving economics, nutrition, population, capital formation, e.g., J. Forrester, D. Meadows, M. Mesarovic, E. Pestel, Mallman, Scolnik, Tinbergen, Luterbacher, Intriligator, Porat, Eckstein

On-line Access to data

Group 7: Facilitators. They initiate and organize this enterprise, set up and manage the network, evaluate its performance in relation to objectives and keep it on course, e.g., Zinn, Parnes, Crickman, Ch. Davis, J. Scher, S. Bermer.

Quantitative Data Base Computer storable and processible time series relevant to variables and functions used in world models, e.g., Sociodemographic, economic data.

Indexes to published literature data base Computer searchable, updated references to articles, books, records, e.g., Lockheed system.

Record of the conference Suggestions made, ideas exchanged, follow-up, policy-related data, know-how.

Example of network use: The network could work in the following manner. A modeler from group 1 has just gained hands-on experience with a computer program which does population projections. The program was designed by another modeler in group 1. The experience gained is reported as an item in the conference. The item stimulates a social scientist to search the indexes to published literature data base and to report to the conference the literature which would be interesting to read. A second social scientist reads the item and the literature it suggests and begins to explore what material in the quantitative data base would be useful on the topic which the first item from the modeler presented. The findings on the quantitative data are entered as an item. Next, a policy maker notices the item and inserts a question to the conference participants as to the planning ramifications of the material reported to date. An educator notes the questions the policy maker is raising and points out to students now studying to become policy makers that they are probably going to have to learn to deal with such problems. One of the members of group 6 notices the discussion of the educator in group 5 and decides to write a newspaper article for the general public on the developments in population modeling. Finally, the information scientist in group 2 studies the record of the conference to see where this information exchange went smoothly and where it could have been improved. The findings of the information scientist are passed on to the facilitator in group 7 who uses the suggestions to improve the communication process for all members of the conference.

Key challenges: To foster attitudes of sharing and collaboration rather than competition by key members of participant groups. Requires creating and enhancing appropriate rewards, possibly selecting a narrower focus such as nutrition planning, bearing in mind that a total systems approach is required.

Possible support sources: UNEP, various national government planning agencies that may benefit, NSF, foreign currency programs, OECD, Toyota Foundation, Volkswagen Foundation.

Figure 22-1. A continuing multilogue to develop world models: sketch of a proposed pilot (computer conference).

If this kind of information system sounds ambitious and costly, then so is the task of developing workable world models. If there is merit to the belief, held by some, that better world models are necessary to improve human existence and that such information systems, in turn, are necessary for better world models, then the cost of not developing such systems could be vastly greater than that of creating them.

4. RETROSPECT AND PROSPECT

Some of what is required to create the information system suggested in section three is within reach, but some aspects demand the creation of new concepts and methods. Let us consider, in turn, the technological, conceptual, and organizational barriers and the prospects for identifying and overcoming them. Communication technologies developed for telemedicine may perhaps be adapted to meet the needs of both regional planners and developers of regional models. The Pacific Education and Communication Experiment by Sattelite, for example, is providing health consulting to Hawaii, Fiji, New Zealand, New Guinea, and American Samoa; and the Hospital Council of Southern California is the nucleus of an emergency communications network connecting 118 hospitals, police, public health, fire, and Red Cross facilities. A video journal servicing 81 medical schools has been in operation since 1972 and offers programs on videocassettes of interest to medical students, primarily on overcoming the dehumanizing effects of medical education.

The Volume two, Number four (November 1975) issue of *The Bulletin of the American Society for Information Science* is devoted entirely to "International Networks: Promises and Problems." It reports studies for the Policy Group of the Organization for Economic Cooperation and Development (OECD) as well as national policies with regard to networking. It is possible that networks can amplify and simplify what is now done through the grapevine, especially when it comes to keeping individuals aware of the activities of others.

The potential for collaboration among scientists over computer networks is evidenced by project SUMEX–AIM (Levinthal et al. 1975). This project aims to understand the principles underlying efficient acquisition and utilization of knowledge and representation of conceptual abstractions in reasoning and problem solving in the health sciences at distributed sites, to overcome geographical and operational barriers. It seems that "expertise" from scattered experts is being extracted for availability to a larger community. If medical clinicians and basic scientists succeed in evolving solutions to problems of common concern to them—possibly with the help of computers—what is learned can perhaps be transferred to real-world political decision makers and social scientists.

The most significant technological advance likely to bear on the development of world models is computer conferencing. There are about a million computer terminals now in use. It costs less than $1 per session to sign on, check for, send messages, and participate in the discussion. Several commercial computer and data communication networks exist. The potential of computer conferencing for Delphi experiments and the use of simulation models is still untapped and appears promising. It has been predicted that by 1980 computer conferencing will be in widespread use, with the home television receiver doubling as a terminal. Computer conferencing has been proposed as a bellweather technology within telecommunications as a whole (Price 1975).

To process information, a variety of newer capabilities can and should be brought to bear. Many more insights into the properties of an analytic model are possible from algebraic formulations of its implications than from numerical or even graphical outputs. Programming systems such as MACSYMA or REDUCE can help in this task, in that they can invert matrices or print out symbolic formulas representing solutions to systems of differential equations. For example, from the assumption that a quantity grows at a rate proportional to both how much of it has been depleted and how much is still left, it follows that the quantity grows as a logistic curve specified by several parameters, one of which is the maximum rate of growth. More important, it should be possible to use computers to help modelers derive the equations that define the model. Thus, it may be possible to instruct a computer how to derive an expression for the probability of an event that depends on many other events, where this expression involves far more variables than an individual could keep track of and combine without error.

As a more practical level of software advance, the availability of DYNAMO[3] in FORTRAN made it possible for students who were novices to computers to run a wide variety of simulations at $.50 per run. Only fourteen instructions were required to program a variant of Forrester's models. Such programming languages as SPEAKEASY make it possible for an English-speaking novice to express a new world model of his own within a few hours. The state of the art in both hardware (with large-scale integration still bringing computer costs down dramatically) and software has had an impressive growth, and the prospects for continued growth in the direction of useful applications to help develop world models appear to be good.

The prospects for overcoming conceputal barriers are fair. First, there is a considerable amount of mathematical work to be done, particularly along the path of inquiry opened up by S. Smale (1971) in the application of global analysis to investigate the systemic properties of complex systems, and possibly the line of inquiry initiated by Zadeh (1973).

Global properties of a surface or manifold that may represent the solution to a system of differential equations, such as closure, convexity, or bifurcation, lend themselves to topological analysis that may capture the essence of the mechanisms involved in world models at a more appropriate level of specificity

3. The simulation language in which Forrester's 1970 model was expressed.

than the more exact results of many current simulations. Learning curves, for example, are general logistic curves that are concave up during the early phase and convex up and asymptotic during later stages. Salk (1973) explored these global properties in his *Survival of the Wisest*. In the steepest middle part of the curve, the sign of the appropriate behavior reverses. Steering behavior should reverse *before* system behavior changes, to allow for the necessary lead time and slack.

Most learning can probably be described as such a growth curve, because the characteristic curve for a self-improving system could be estimated from its local properties in a small time-interval. That, however, is not the case for the kind of self-improvement that must take place if major changes in the present course of the world are to take place. That kind of self-improving system is characterized by the entire shape of the learning curve, by its global features. This may involve the kind of discontinuities called catastrophes (Thom 1975). Applications of catastrophe theory, though still very new and undeveloped, may provide help to an appropriate conceptualization underlying this kind of learning. This means that in revising the performance of a system on the basis of feedback, we must enable it to take leaps rather than small steps, but not randomly. Caution and small, timid steps do not necessarily, or always, go together, nor need leaps always be bold. It is the *general* direction, the qualitative, global nature of the learning curve that matters, not its exact course; and as long as a leap or big step preserves the global character, it is the "right" direction.

It is at this point that the notion of a linguistic variable may fruitfully apply. Air pollution level may be viewed as a linguistic variable, taking values in a range of words, such as life-threatening, health-threatening, uncomfortable, barely tolerable, harmless, or ideal. A calculus based on such variables (Zadeh 1973) including algorithms and a language for programming computers, is being developed and may provide the level of specificity that is appropriate for the global properties of the systems. We have yet to demonstrate that such a calculus can help us with global problems that cannot be dealt with, in principle, with methods that also work on local problems.

Current work on fuzzy set theory (Zadeh et al. 1975), global analysis (Smale 1971), and structural stability theory (Thom 1975), combined and extended so that they can apply to the analysis of social systems, may provide a fruitful direction for the further development of the theoretical underpinnings of world models. Such development may be a prerequisite to any major data collection efforts or attempts to better utilize existing data. At least they should proceed concurrently. The works cited above represent a significant start. The prospects for further advance are fair, and depend on highly gifted, motivated people to embark on high-risk avenues of research.

Finally, we come to organizational barriers that present the greatest challenge. Many early modelers became disillusioned when they realized that the creation and analysis of world models were respectable academic exercises but were not solving real social problems. Some felt that a deeper kind of stakeholder analysis was required, one that did not aggregate the expectations of individuals. Others, particularly those who worked in real environments of urban and regional planning, concluded with such principles for building simulation models as the following: "There is no such thing as a general regional model. One builds a model to supply answers to a class of questions defined a priori" (Chen 1972, p. 28).

The record of social science findings in solving social problems does not justify optimism. A recent survey (Caplan et al. 1975) in which 204 persons at upper levels of decision making in the executive branch of the U.S. government were interviewed for their utilization of social science knowledge showed that respondents were inclined to reject information when the results were counterintuitive, that they were willing to accept findings uncritically if they were intuitively satisfying, that political implications of findings appear to override any other consideration in determining utilization, and that respondents' feelings about the reliability of data—while an important factor in utilization—are less important than objectivity or political feasibility. There is a high degree of interest in noneconomic indicators of social well-being. Respondents tended to rely mainly on newspapers, government reports, and staff papers, rather than on scholarly publications, and at most 2 percent of the reported uses involved research produced outside the U.S.

Nor have the management games used to train company executives proved as effective in producing lasting improvement in decision making as had been expected. It is possible, however, that the next generation of decision makers may be more receptive to the newer techniques. But the newer techniques, developed in academia and occasionally even successfully tested in industry (under controlled conditions), occasionally fail in social systems. The "best and the brightest" brought analytic techniques into government, and the failure of these methods gave this line of social science inquiry a setback. Expectations were lowered, with a resulting loss of much of the early enthusiasm and excitement. More imaginative and innovative research is hampered by a credibility gap, despite the impact on practical operations that is now resulting from applications of earlier research.

The kind of information system suggested here and elsewhere (Kochen 1975) is likely to contribute significantly toward overcoming these severe organizational barriers because it will introduce new forms of communication, with the help of computer conferencing. This is necessary for realizing the potential now inherent in the various communities of inquiry for advances in learning how to plan, in fostering changes of viewpoint, in making decision makers more aware of the need to compromise and trade short-term self-interests and longer-term communal interests and to help meet these needs.

5. CONCLUSION

Information systems to help planners of world models are likely to grow together, each feeding on and nourishing the other. The world images that govern how we act—e.g., at what temperature to set the thermostat, what car to buy and when to use it, when to switch the light on—differ for each of us in specificity, precision, or scope. Creators of world models such as those of Forrester, Meadows–Meadows (1972) and Mesarovic-Pestel seem to believe that a master plan is desirable. They may also share the belief that computer models are superior to the less precise mental images now used for regional planning. They might agree, however, that such models should supplement—not replace—the insights of astute political observers with good intuition.

A model could, for instance, predict the effect on world copper prices resulting from collusion by all the Third World copper exporters. Unlike the situation in science, if this prediction varies grossly from what economists and political scientists with the best predictive record think is likely, then the prediction will not be believed or acted on. The model will have to help them check details, the effects of subtle assumptions, of widespread interlocking effects, while, on the whole, confirming their main intuitions. Gradually, however, even these intuitions may have to be reduced to deductions from explicit assumptions (Landsberg 1976).

The most important role of information in shaping useful images is to help validate and improve such world models by aiding in decisions about the choice of key concepts, variables, and assumptions on which they are based. Forrester is correct, in general, when he states that we are handicapped not so much by a shortage but by an excess of information about the real system from which to choose (1971, p. 17). The shortage is in good ideas on which to base models, and in information that helps to select planning goals and values. We have too many data that are low in quality and irrelevant to key problems, too few that help us to identify these key problems.

To Forrester's suggestion (p. 127) that the next frontier of human endeavor will be to pioneer a better understanding of our social systems, I would add that the *process* of reaching that understanding will be an emergent, systemic capability of any social system that survives. To the suggestion by Mesarovic and Pestel for a master plan or blueprint to bring about organic growth, I would add that the "master plan" will be a continuously changing product that reflects various world images. It will be the output of the evolving capabilities of social systems to understand, and to be conscious of, these capabilities. I would distrust any model or master plan advocated by any individual or elite group no matter how much he disavows self-interest. So would most politicians or others who have to translate plans into day-to-day action. Without consensus on the part of most of the key actors who must make a major enterprise work, such an enterprise is most unlikely to succeed.

For a world image to be effective in bringing out the changes needed to ensure human survival, it must be shared by key actors and it must interlink these images. The opposite is now the case. If such an image is to evolve, it is likely to do so by an organic social process that requires new kinds of information systems, new kinds of social scientists, and new conceptualizations of social dynamics. The kind of coherent regional outlook called for by Mesarovic and Pestel (p. 154) may perhaps be furthered by the kind of information system suggested in Figure 22-1.

Both information systems and world models evolve through use. While there are surely physical, and even social, limits to growth, we should not assume that there are limits to human ingenuity. It is not unreasonable to expect that, with the aid of technologies, such as computer conferencing, that exist now, we can interconnect the seven communities of inquiry sketched in Figure 22-1 into a learning system capable of utilizing knowledge and understanding to identify and cope with the most important problems facing us, fast enough to outpace the rate at which such traps and opportunities are being generated.

6. BIBLIOGRAPHY

Boulding, K. "Systems Analysis for the Classroom." Private communication, Feb. 18, 1976.

Bisco, R.L., ed. *Data Bases, Computers, and the Social Sciences.* New York: Wiley-Interscience, 1970.

Caplan, N., A. Morrison, and R.J. Stambaugh. *The Use of Social Science Knowledge in Policy Decisions at the National Level.* Ann Arbor: Institute for Social Research, University of Michigan, 1975.

Chen, K., ed. *Urban Dynamics: Expansions and Reflections.* San Francisco: San Francisco Press, Inc., 1971.

Dunn, E. *Economic and Social Development: A Process of Social Learning.* Baltimore: Johns Hopkins, 1971, pp. 254-255.

Forrester, J.W. *World Dynamics.* Cambridge: Wright-Allen Press, 1971.

Goguen, J.A. "Concept Representation in Natural and Artificial Languages: Axioms, Extensions and Applications for Fuzzy Sets." *Int'l Journal of Man-Machine Studies* 6, pp. 513-561, 1974.

Hardin, G. "The Tragedy of The Commons." *Science,* 162, pp. 1243-1248. 1968.

Hertz, D. "Has Management Science Reached a Dead End?" *Innovation* (now *Business Soc. Review*) 24:5 p. 14, 1971.

Kadanoff, L. "A Modified Forrester Model of the U.S. as a Group of Metropolitan Areas." In *Urban Dynamics: Extensions and Reflections,* ed. K. Chen San Francisco: San Francisco Press, p. 105, 1972.

Kochen, M. "Hypothesis Processing as a New Tool to Aid Managers of Mental

Health Agencies in Serving Long-Term Regional Interests." *International Journal of Biomedical Computing,* 6:4, pp. 299–313, 1975.

Kochen, M. "Cognitive Learning Processes: An Explanation." In *Artificial Intelligence and Heuristic Programming,* ed. N.V. Findler and B. Meltzer, Edinburgh: Edinburgh U. Press, 1971, pp. 261–317. (Revised German Edition, 1973.)

Landsberg, H.H. "Materials: Some Recent Trends and Issues." *Science,* 191, (1976), p. 637. (This entire issue of *Science* is devoted to Materials.), 1976.

Levinthal, E.C., Carhart, R.E., Johnson, S.M., Lederberg, J. "When Computers Talk to Computers." *Industrial Research,* Nov. 15, 1975, pp. 35–42, 1975.

Linstone, H.A., and Turoff, M., eds. *The Delphi Method: Techniques and Applications.* Reading: Addison-Wesley, p. 3, 1975.

Meadows, D.H., Meadows, D.L., Randers, J., and Behrens, III, W.W. *The Limits To Growth.* New York: McGraw Hill, 1972.

Mesarovic, M., and Pestel, E. *Mankind at the Turning Point.* New York: E.P. Dutton & Co./Readers Digest, 1974.

Michael, D.N. *On Learning to Plan and Planning to Learn.* San Francisco: Jossey-Bass Publishers, p. 54, 1973.

Platt, J.R. "Information Networks for Human Transformation," In *Information for Action,* ed. M. Kochen, New York: Academic Press, p. 49, 1975.

Price, C.R. "Computers and the Future of Delphi: Conferencing via Computer." In *The Delphi Method,* ed., H.A. Linstone and M. Turoff, Reading: Addison-Wesley, 1975.

Ralston, A., and Wilf, H. *Mathematical Methods for Digital Computers.* New York: Wiley, 1960.

Salk, J. *The Survival of the Wisest.* New York: Harper and Row, 1973.

Smale, S. "Global Analysis and Economics, I: Pareto Optimum and a Generalization of Morse Theory." Proceedings of the 1971 Brazil Dynamical Systems Symposium.

Thom. R. *Structural Stability and Morphogenesis.* Reading: W.A. Benjamin, 1975.

Westin, A. "Information Technology and Public Decision Making," in *Harvard University Prog. on Technology and Society, 1964-1972, A Final Review,* ed. Mesthene, Cambridge: Harvard University Press: p. 60, 1972.

White, C.M., and Associates. *Sources of Information in the Social Sciences.* Totowa, N.J.: The Bedminster Press, 1964.

Zadeh, L. "The Concept of a Linguistic Variable and its Application to Approximate Reasoning." Memo ERL-M411, October '73, Electronics Research Laboratory, University of California at Berkeley.

Zadeh, L., et al. eds. *Fuzzy Set Theory and Its Applications.* New York: Academic Press, 1975.

 *Conclusion*

Some Suggestions and Prospects

Chapter 23

World Order and the Problems of Values, Identities, and Community Formation

Saul Mendlovitz

Karl Deutsch, in asking me to participate in this conference, suggested that I make a few remarks about global modeling, especially as it might have been perceived from the perspective of the World Order Models Project. As most of you know, the individuals who are involved in that project have very independent and strong views. I therefore wish to emphasize that I do not speak for them. At the same time, the remarks I will make are informed by the work we have done together over these past half-dozen years.

There is one additional comment. My remarks, which certainly should be evaluated by traditional academic pretensions and standards, are more in the "grand manner" style. I hope, nevertheless, you will see the relationship to some of the more technical papers presented at this meeting.

It is still a truism of sociology that all societies either have a minimal consensus on fundamental values or else they do not function. To be sure, the primitive or, perhaps more accurately, comprehensive nature of the proposition becomes immediately clear as soon as we begin looking at the variety of elements and variables that provide the basis for the proposition. Class structure, forms of coercive authority and bureaucratic organization, kinds of legitimation, level of technology, to mention but a few notions, immediately begin to sophisticate and complicate the proposition. At the same time, the underlying notion, that human societies have cohesion and operate only when there is a sufficient core of agreed-upon values which are implemented and enforced, still remains one of the principles on which social science scholarship is based.

As someone who has been involved in soft modeling—and here I mean not only an absence of advanced mathematical techniques applied to data, but more important, an enterprise engaged in normative modeling—my point of entry into this subject matter is to argue that the study of values is the appropriate intellectual question for those scholars who wish to come to grips with the contemporary global political system. And, to relate more directly to the subject matter of this conference, my argument would be that in looking at public opinion and community formation, in concentrating on values within that context, we are focusing on the key dimension.

Permit me to carry the argument further. Most observers of the global political community now concur that human society is moving through some form of system change. In a few moments I will talk about the nature of that system change, but for now I wish merely to point out that system change invariably means change in fundamental values. Put in another way, during periods of system change consensus on fundamental values breaks down and either new values emerge as the basis for a new system, or old values are rearranged, reprioritized, and given new meaning. So, to focus on values is not merely to engage in an ethical, ideological, or idealistic enterprise, but is a way to focus on system change occurring now. Or, put more forcefully, appropriate projections and modeling for the contemporary world will be done only if we include—in fact initiate our investigation with—the study of attitudes, opinions, and values.

What then of the system change that is taking place? In reviewing the literature I find three views being expressed on the nature of this historical change throughout the globe. (For the purpose of brevity I shall have to oversimplify.)

There is one group of observers who believe we are going through what I will call a 200-year change. They believe there is a qualitative change within the nation state system itself. That is, the global political system has moved from a Eurocentric dominated globe to a globe in which wealth and power are now more widely distributed. The nature of this system change, is, of course, complicated by the growth of functional agencies of international, as well as some regional, organizations. However, in effect it is a 200-year change in the sense that we have moved away from a Eurocentric world to a global world of nation states which have organized themselves in a kind of accelerated and complicated version of the nineteenth-century balance-of-power system with some overlays. This represents one view, although I am sure I do an injustice to the level of sophistication of the people who espouse it.

There is a second view of systemic change, which I will call a 500-year change. This view states that we are going through a period of history equivalent in scope and depth to the breakdown of feudalism and the emergence of the modern nation state. (This may, in fact, be a very Eurocentric notion. Since the "Age of Discovery" and Western domination of the globe emerged with the state system in Europe, it does seem sensible, though, to look at the period between the fourteenth and sixteenth centuries as a major transformation of the global human community.) Those persons who hold this position believe the nation state system is undergoing radical change. World Wars I and II, the development of the League of Nations and the United Nations, the one-worldness of communication are all having a significant impact on the state system; and some new system— which I shall only lightly touch upon in this presentation—is likely to emerge by the twenty-first century. But the change, to reiterate, is the equivalent to the breakdown of the feudal world.

There is yet another view. It is held by very few scholars and thinkers, but I have become persuaded that it requires our serious consideration. It is rather an outrageous view. One way to look at the change is that we are going through what I will call a 10,000- to 15,000-year change. Now what do I mean by that pretentious notion? What I mean is that somewhere between 15,000 B.C. and 5,000 B.C. human society moved from hunting to agriculture. This change had a tremendous impact on the way we viewed the world. In fact, it is argued by many among those who bother to think about these things that two institutions, twin evils as it were, i.e., war and slavery, emerged at that time, concomitantly it might be pointed out, with the state and its bureaucratic organization. Prior to 10,000 B.C., we did not know of those three institutions in their routinized forms. I do not know enough about that period of history to assess the accuracy of these observations, but there seems to be a general consensus by those who study these matters that this was, in fact, the case.

If, in fact, in the change from hunting to agricultural societies what emerged was a new view of the world, then I would argue we had a breakdown of myths and the emergence of new myths. In relating this to what we are practically engaged in today, I think that what we are actually doing at this conference is to participate in the creation of the myth of the new world, the new system—the paradigm of the 10,000-year shift. (I use the term myth here to mean that set of images, attitudes, projections, feelings, emotions, and *Weltanschauungen* that provides meaning for human existence. It is what makes vivid and dramatizes for each human being his or her relationship to others, to society, to nature, and to the facts of mortality as well as the spiritual realm.)

Thus, if we want to do significant work relevant to attitudes, public opinion, and community formation, it will be necessary to dip into the process of new myth creation. What does it mean, for example, when you no longer reach for the moon but look down from the moon? What does it mean to move away from fertility rites based on scratching and eking out an existence, to break away from a class structure that needs slavery and war, and possesses a myth structure and world view that interact with the fixed agroindustrial territorial unit as the sociological product and foundation of that myth structure? It is precisely because that myth structure is breaking down that the sociological foundation— the agroindustrial territorial unit defined by boundaries—is also breaking down. We must ask ourselves the question: "What does it mean that suddenly all the old myths have been broken down and new myths are beginning to emerge at this particular historical juncture?"

This is a psychohistorical moment, when the human race knows it is part of itself. To be even more specific: take the years 1500 as a baseline. There are half a billion people on the face of the earth; one-tenth of 1 percent of them know that the world is round and that there are other people on the other side, and of these, 1 percent may have an identity with those people, i.e., a common sentiment. It is now 500 years later—thus in the history of humanity, a very short period of time: there are eight times as many people as there were on the face of the earth at that time; one-tenth of 1 percent do *not* know that there are people on the other side, and all of them understand that somehow, despite self-reliance—which I will come to—they are inexplicably interwoven—at least they are attentive—to one another. They have interpenetrated each other. And it is that new fact of *interpenetration*—not the atomic bomb, not the population explosion, not the space exploration—it is that new fact of interpenetration with which we are conjuring and from which we are creating new myths in the kinds of enterprises we are engaged in. (Not so incidentally, it is right and proper that certain people from the Third World, some of whom are not here at this meeting, are much upset. They are upset because they know we are in the process of creating the myth without them. They want to be part of that myth structure because it is going to set the paradigm for the next several thousand years. We are moving into that kind of a world, and everybody in the world should participate in this myth formation.)

It was John Dewey who said, "Society exists in and through communication"; and in that sense human society of the global community now exists. It is the interpenetrative, not *interdependent,* processes of the emerging global culture and global community to which we must respond. As I see it, there are four postural responses to the interpenetrative processes that work themselves out in attitudes, opinions, values, and myths.

The first, and the one best represented at this conference, is what I would call the *managerial* response. There are groups of us who are saying. "Yes, the globe is one: it is the spaceship Earth; we have seen the finite limits to it." There are people like ourselves looking at the whole globe and trying to find a managerial response. How do we manage this incredible thing that has occurred, from one-half billion to four billion to six and one-half billion by the end of the century, when we are suddenly discovering that there may be finiteness to what we can use?

The limits to growth response, the establishment of the OECD, the Trilateral Commission, and some aspects of the U.N. global conferences, as well as some aspects of U.S.-U.S.S.R. détente processes, tend to have this managerial response. Indeed, it is a kind of global modeling response. Within this, there is what I would call the intramural fight of growth versus no growth, but otherwise there is a kind of managerial response. The Soviets are joining this. We may persuade a few others along the way.

There is a second type of response. It has its own rhetoric and its own way of deciding what ought to be on the agenda of issues, what is the appropriate public opinion, what it is we should be communicating to one another. This is the *con-*

frontational response. This response is based on the belief of persons espousing it that never in the history of humanity have individuals, organizations, or bureaucratic structures willingly shared wealth, power and privilege; that it is only through confrontation and struggle that those who control the world are willing to share it with others. We know that this kind of response comes from NIEO (the New International Economic Order), the Third World solidarity in the face of the oil crisis. For the moment, I will call it a trade-union-government response, that is to say, people within the same trade union of governments operating with regard to one another. As I review the literature and the actual substance of the debates that took place, or at least the implementation machinery that took place at the NIEO special sessions, very little was done for the Fourth and Fifth Worlds. A good deal of talk about the Third World took place, and a lot of consideration was given to the Third World getting into the power structure, but I do not feel that the Fourth and Fifth Worlds were taken seriously. So we are seeing a redistribution in terms of power elites, of power and wealth to those territoral units throughout the globe that have some commodities that they can use for that redistribution, but it all occurs in terms of the governments of the world. (I am fully aware that many of my Third World friends and colleagues view the distinction between Third and Fourth Worlds as a tactic on the part of the developed world to fractionize the solidarity of the wretched of the earth. I share their concern but nevertheless would like to find a rhetoric that distinguishes those processes which will distribute wealth and power to other governing elites in various territorial units and those processes which are directed to alleviate misery and create participatory machinery for the lower third of humanity.)

There is a third response, which is the *self-reliance* response commonly associated with the People's Republic of China, Albania, and Tanzania. This response accepts the basic premise noted above as underlying the confrontational response to the transition period we are in. However, its adherents do not believe that it is possible to confront the structures of power and wealth that control the political and economic organization of the globe at this time. So it is that . . . this response tends to say, "We would prefer redistributive techniques on the globe, but since we don't think we are going to get it that way, we are going to develop some kind of minimal need structure, we are going to meet the minimal needs of our society, and then we will come back and join in to see how we do with regard to the rest of the globe." I should remind you in this connection that the self-reliance response is not confined to the developing world. After all, Nelson Rockefeller demanded "project independence." In many younger people from the upper middle class of the United States and Western societies there is a desire to "drop out" of existing organizational structures "to do their own thing" and be self-reliant. "Stop the world, I want to get off" is undoubtedly sensible emotionally, intellectually, and politically in a world in which myth, value, and social organization are all under attack and new ones are emerging. What portion of this response in what context is valid for the emergence of a humane global community are questions we shall have to address to the first two processes, i.e., the managerial and the confrontational as well.

There is then a fourth response, held by very few people, but I think held by most of the people in this room. That is what I will call the *populist–humanist* response, and the *globalist* response. There is a small group of people throughout the world which has come to recognize that the jurisdiction we are attending to is humanity. Regarding the kind of research that takes account of humanity, I prefer not to dissaggregate the information in terms of territories, although I am willing to disaggregate in terms of class structure, age, commodities, and other variables as well. But my effort would be directed to creating myth and vivid new ways of looking at the globe. It is the globe and its people that we are talking about, and the validity of nation states *within the present system* that is being questioned. Recognizing full well the passion and commitment of nationalism evidenced in the new developing states, as well as so-called secessionist movements within the older nation states, it is still essential to ask, "Is the nation state an antiquated myth?" Has it been worn out in terms of emerging global community?

Some of you may have noticed that I have said twice now that most of us in this room would hold a particular posture, first when I was discussing the managerial response, and now again when we are looking at the populist–humanist global response. This seeming contradiction actually stems from the fact that the four responses I have pointed out are held by various individuals, groups and societies at various times for various issues; and the particular mix is based on the political and social context. At the same time, I believe that these postures are beginning to develop an ideologically adherent constituency and are, therefore, likely to become more politicized in the decade ahead.

Thus, when it comes to public opinion, attitudes, and communications, I would like to know how we get the wit to find out whether or not the population at large knows that the king is naked. How do you ask the question that elicits the response that everybody really knows that the nation state system, as we have known it in its old form, is incapable of dealing with what I will call the four global problems: war, poverty, social injustice, and ecological instability? How do you create a communicative flow so that everybody is permitted to participate in the creation of myth? How can this be done in the new myth that has to do with global community?

We are concerned here with global modeling, and so let me, in conclusion, return to my original point. An analysis that starts with values will give you more predictive, causal, explanatory views than one that begins with population, commodity, and resource data, because it will tell you more about those authoritative structures that are likely to grow up, can grow up, or should grow up around the issues that are likely to emerge within the global political community.

Therefore, from my perspective, the kind of work that is being done in public opinion, mail flows, topics of that sort, provides us with data for more insight into the interpenetrative world we live in; and it provides us with more insight as to what kind of values are likely to emerge as the highest priorities throughout the globe—or more coherently—which of the integrated sets of values we can utilize to build a new and more viable global authority structure. (When I say "a new global authority structure," that does not necessarily mean a centralized authority; it could be decentralized if we had the wisdom and will to do so). I hope that these remarks will be helpful in identifying the concerns we should have as we continue our work in global modeling.

✳ *Chapter 24*

Four Major Areas of Concern

I will attempt to summarize the major areas of concern of the conference. In terms of our discussions, four main lines have emerged.

The first one, I would say, is that of methodological concerns; the second, implementation demands; the third, the problem of approaches; and the fourth, normative aspects of modeling.

Methodological concerns have given rise to a demand for a full view, an epistemological approach to this matter. The second theme within this topic reflects the possiblity of having holistic attempts to develop modeling projects. Heuristic considerations were evident in both of the above discussions. Attempts were made to build an agenda for future work. They represent a kind of formal approach to the evolution of world modeling endeavors.

Our discussions on the problems of implementation focused, to a large extent, on the use of political variables. Their incorporation into models raises a number of crucial methodological questions. Indeed, this topic led to a wider discussion and consideration of the kinds of variables, sectors, and dimensions that should and, at the present state of the art, could be utilized in modeling. In this context, consideration was given to intranational modeling, the problem of values, and the more general topic of causal modeling.

Formal approaches to modeling seem to have dominated our discussions. Four different approaches, however, were given serious consideration. First, we focused on the problem of holistic versus the interdisciplinary approach. To what extent can world models really be derived from an interdisciplinary context into a holistic approach? Second, we discussed specific developments in terms of which areas should be explored in world modeling. Third, the regional approach to modeling was also raised. The final approach suggested at the conference called for far-ranging disaggregation as a mode of world modeling.

The fourth theme of the conference centered on normative concerns. Some consideration was given to the question of targets for model building. Normative issues were also brought up in the context of methodological considerations and problems of implementation.

Index

About the Editors and Contributors

Hayward R. Alker, Jr. received his B.S. degree from MIT and his Ph.D. from Yale. He is currently Professor of Political Science at MIT.

James P. Bennett received his B.A. from Harvard and his Ph.D. from MIT. He is currently an assistant professor with the Peace Science Unit at the University of Pennsylvania.

Stuart A. Bremer holds a Ph.D. in Political Science from Michigan State University. He is presently a research scientist with the Institute of Comparative Social Research in Berlin.

Fernando Henrique Cardoso is the director of the Brazilian Center for Analysis and Planning and holds B.A., M.A. and Ph.D. degrees from the University of São Paulo.

Caleb M. Clark is assistant professor of Political Science at New Mexico State University. He received his B.A. from Beloit and his Ph.D. from the University of Illinois at Urbana-Champaign.

Karl W. Deutsch is the director of the Institute for Comparative Social Research in Berlin, as well as Stanfield Professor of International Peace with the Department of Government, Harvard University. He holds a Ph.D. from Harvard University and a JUDr. from Charles University, Prague, as well as honorary degrees from the universities of Geneva, Michigan and Illinois.

Otto Eckstein received his A.B. degree from Princeton, and his A.M. and Ph.D., in Economics, from Harvard. At present he is the Paul M. Warburg Professor of Economics at Harvard University, and is also president of Data Resources, Inc.

Bruno Fritsch holds the Dr. rer. pol. from the University of Basle and is currently affiliated with the Swiss Federal Institute of Technology in Zurich. He is the author of *Growth Limitation and Political Power,* also published by Ballinger (1976).

Walter Isard, chairman of both the Department of Peace Science and the Department of Regional Science at the University of Pennsylvania, received his A.B. from Temple University and his M.A. and Ph.D. from Harvard. He is also Provost of the World University of the World Academy of Art and Science.

Helio Jaguaribe holds the LLD degree from the Law School of the Pontifical Catholic University of Rio de Janeiro. He is currently professor of Political Science and Director of International Affairs at Candido Mendes University, Rio de Janeiro.

Nathan Keyfitz received his Ph.D. from the University of Chicago. He is currently Andelot Professor of Sociology and Demography at Harvard University.

Manfred Kochen is presently professor both of Information Science and of Urban/Regional Planning at the University of Michigan. He holds a B.S. degree from MIT and an M.A. and Ph.D. from Columbia University.

Celso Lafer, assistant professor of International Law and Organizations at the Law School of the University of São Paulo, received his Ph.D. from Cornell and his LLD from the University of São Paulo Law School.

Carlos A. Mallmann holds a Ph.D. in Physical and Mathematical Sciences from the National University of Buenos Aires. He is currently president of the board of directors and chairman of the future studies program for the Fundación Bariloche.

Andrei S. Markovits holds the B.A., M.B.A., M.A., M. Phil. and Pd.D. degrees from Columbia University. He is presently a postdoctoral research associate with the Center for European Studies at Harvard University, as well as assistant professor of Government at Wesleyan University.

Candido Mendes de Almeida is currently professor at the Instituto Universitario de Pesquisas do Rio de Janeiro. He is also the editor of *Dados,* a scholarly social science journal published in Brazil.

Saul Mendlovitz is president of the Institute for World Order and professor of Law at Rutgers University. He holds a B.A. degree from Syracuse, an M.A. in Sociology from the University of Chicago and a J.D. from the University of Chicago Law School.

Richard L. Merritt received his B.A. from University of Southern California, his M.A. from the University of Virginia and his Ph.D. from Yale. He is currently professor of Political Science at the University of Illinois at Urbana-Champaign.

Michael Mihalka holds a Ph.D. from the University of Michigan and is presently assistant professor of Government at the University of Texas at Austin.

William Nordhaus holds a B.A. degree from Yale University and a Ph.D. from MIT. Currently he is professor with the Department of Economics, Yale University, and a member of the Cowles Foundation and of the Council of Economic Advisors, Washington, D.C.

Anatol Rapoport, currently professor with the departments of Psychology and Mathematics of the University of Toronto, received his S.B., S.M. and Ph.D. degrees from the University of Chicago.

P.N. Rastogi holds M.A. and Ph.D. degrees from Agra University (India). He is currently associate professor of Sociology at the Indian Institute of Technology at Kanpur.

Bruce M. Russett is professor of Political Science at Yale University and editor of the *Journal of Conflict Resolution*. He received his B.A. from Williams College; the Diploma in Economics from King's College, Cambridge; and his M.A. and Ph.D. degrees from Yale.

Dieter Senghaas holds the Ph.D. degree from the University of Frankfurt/Main. He is presently professor at the Peace Research Institute at Frankfurt and professor of International Relations at the University of Frankfurt.

Erwin S. Solomon is the director of the Division for Socio-economic Analysis of UNESCO in Paris. He holds a B.A. degree from American University and an M.A. from New York University.

Richard Stone received his B.A., M.A. and Sc.D. degrees from the University of Cambridge (England), and has received honorary degrees from the universities of Oslo, Geneva and Warwick and from the Free University of Brussels. He is currently P.D. Leake Professor of Finance and Accounting at the University of Cambridge.

Charles L. Taylor holds a B.A. from Carson Newman College and M.A. and Ph.D. degrees from Yale University. He is presently professor at Virginia Polytechnic Institute and State University.

Ann Tickner received her B.A. from the University of London and her M.A. from Yale University. She is currently a Ph.D. candidate in Politics at Brandeis University.